NOVELL'S

Netware® 5 Administrator's Handbook

NOVELL'S

Netware® 5 Administrator's Handbook

KELLEY J. P. LINDBERG

Novell.
PRESS

Novell Press, San Jose

Novell's Netware® 5 Administrator's Handbook
Published by Novell Press
2180 Fortune Drive
San Jose, CA 95131

Library of Congress Catalog Card Number: 98-73339

ISBN: 0-7645-4546-9

Printed in the United States of America

10 9 8 7 6 5 4 3 2

1P/QW/QU/ZZ/IN

Distributed in the United States by IDG Books Worldwide, Inc.

Distributed by CDG Books Canada Inc. for Canada; by Transworld Publishers Limited in the United Kingdom; by IDG Norge Books for Norway; by IDG Sweden Books for Sweden; by Woodslane Pty. Ltd. for Australia; by Woodslane (NZ) Ltd. for New Zealand; by TransQuest Publishers Pte Ltd. for Singapore, Malaysia, Thailand, Indonesia, and Hong Kong; by ICG Muse, Inc. for Japan; by Norma Comunicaciones S.A. for Colombia; by Intersoft for South Africa; by Le Monde en Tique for France; by International Thomson Publishing for Germany, Austria and Switzerland; by Distribuidora Cuspide for Argentina; by Livraria Cultura for Brazil; by Ediciones ZETA S.C.R. Ltda. for Peru; by WS Computer Publishing Corporation, Inc., for the Philippines; by Contemporanea de Ediciones for Venezuela; by Express Computer Distributors for the Caribbean and West Indies; by Micronesia Media Distributor, Inc. for Micronesia; by Grupo Editorial Norma S.A. for Guatemala; by Chips Computadoras S.A. de C.V. for Mexico; by Editorial Norma de Panama S.A. for Panama; by American Bookshops for Finland. Authorized Sales Agent: Anthony Rudkin Associates for the Middle East and North Africa.

For general information on IDG Books WorldwideÒs books in the U.S., please call our Consumer Customer Service department at 800-762-2974. For reseller information, including discounts and premium sales, please call our Reseller Customer Service department at 800-434-3422.

For information on where to purchase IDG Books WorldwideÒs books outside the U.S., please contact our International Sales department at 317-596-5530 or fax 317-596-5692.

For consumer information on foreign language translations, please contact our Customer Service department at 1-800-434-3422, fax 317-596-5692, or e-mail rights@idgbooks.com.

For information on licensing foreign or domestic rights, please phone +1-650-655-3109.

For sales inquiries and special prices for bulk quantities, please contact our Sales department at 650-655-3200 or write to the address above.

For information on using IDG Books WorldwideÒs books in the classroom or for ordering examination copies, please contact our Educational Sales department at 800-434-2086 or fax 317-596-5499.

For press review copies, author interviews, or other publicity information, please contact our Public Relations department at 650-655-3000 or fax 650-655-3299.

For authorization to photocopy items for corporate, personal, or educational use, please contact Novell, Inc., Copyright Permission, 1555 North Technology Way, Mail Stop ORM-C-311, Orem, UT 84097-2395; or fax 801-228-7077

For general information on Novell Press books in the U.S., including information on discounts and premiums, contact IDG Books Worldwide at 800-434-3422 or 650-655-3200. For information on where to purchase Novell Press books outside the U.S., contact IDG Books International at 650-655-3021 or fax 650-655-3295.

John Kilcullen, *CEO, IDG Books Worldwide, Inc.*
Steven Berkowitz, *President, IDG Books Worldwide, Inc.*
Brenda McLaughlin, *Senior Vice President & Group Publisher, IDG Books Worldwide, Inc.*
The IDG Books Worldwide logo is a registered trademark or trademark under exclusive license to IDG Books Worldwide, Inc., from International Data Group, Inc. in the United States and/or other countries.

Marcy Shanti, *Publisher, Novell Press, Novell, Inc.*
Novell Press and the Novell Press logo are trademarks of Novell, Inc.

Welcome to Novell Press

Novell Press, the world's leading provider of networking books, is the premier source for the most timely and useful information in the networking industry. Novell Press books cover fundamental networking issues as they emerge — from today's Novell and third-party products to the concepts and strategies that will guide the industry's future. The result is a broad spectrum of titles for the benefit of those involved in networking at any level: end user, department administrator, developer, systems manager, or network architect.

Novell Press books are written by experts with the full participation of Novell's technical, managerial, and marketing staff. The books are exhaustively reviewed by Novell's own technicians and are published only on the basis of final released software, never on prereleased versions.

Novell Press at IDG Books Worldwide is an exciting partnership between two companies at the forefront of the knowledge and communications revolution. The Press is implementing an ambitious publishing program to develop new networking titles centered on the current versions of NetWare, GroupWise, BorderManager, ManageWise, and networking integration products.

Novell Press books are translated into several languages and sold throughout the world.

Marcy Shanti
Publisher
Novell Press, Novell, Inc.

Novell Press

Publisher
Marcy Shanti

Administrator
Diana Aviles

IDG Books Worldwide

Acquisitions Editor
Jim Sumser

Development Editor
Jennifer Rowe

Technical Editors
Mark Parratt
Tim Petru

Copy Editor
Larisa North

Project Coordinator
Valery Bourke

Graphics and Production Specialists
Lou Boudreau
Linda M. Boyer

J. Tyler Connor
Angela F. Hunckler
Anna Rohrer
Brent Savage
Kate Snell
Michael Sullivan

Proofreaders
Kelli Botta
Melissa D. Buddendeck
Jennifer Mahern
Rebecca Senninger
Ethel M. Winslow
Janet M. Withers

Indexer
York Graphics Services

About the Author

Award-winning author Kelley J. P. Lindberg worked at Novell for more than 11 years before leaving to become a full-time writer. While at Novell, she was the senior program manager for NetWare 3.12, NetWare 4.1, intraNetWare, and other Novell products. Ms. Lindberg, a CNE, has written numerous articles and many other Novell Press books about NetWare products, including all the books in the NetWare Administrator's Handbook series and *Novell's Introduction to intraNetWare*. She makes her home in Utah, and can be reached at lindberg@inconnect.com.

For my mom and dad, who continually show me that with a sense of humor and a sense of adventure, you can accomplish nearly anything.

Preface

As the administrator of a NetWare 5 network, you are responsible for ensuring that the network is installed correctly and runs smoothly. To do this, you may arm yourself with a variety of information sources: manuals, online documentation, magazines, books, and maybe even the phone numbers of a few knowledgeable friends. Because so much flexibility and functionality is built into NetWare 5, a tremendous amount of information is available to help you manage your network.

Sometimes, however, all you really want is a quick way to find just the information you need. You don't need a full-scale discussion of every aspect of managing the network. You don't want to wade through stacks of magazines, or hypertext your way through three dozen online manuals to find the information you know you saw once before. What you really want is a brief refresher, if necessary, and instant access to the command, utility, syntax, or parameter setting you want. This book was written with you in mind.

Filled with lists, tables, and installation procedures, this handbook is a vital tool in your administrator's bag of tricks. The Instant Access pages at the beginning of each chapter help you immediately identify the utilities or commands you use to complete a specific task. Like most other busy network administrators, if you don't have a lot of time to spend looking for information, keep this book handy.

What's New in NetWare 5?

If you're familiar with intraNetWare or NetWare 4.11, you will find a significant number of changes in NetWare 5. New features have been added, and enhancements have been made to almost every aspect of NetWare, and to nearly every utility. The following are just a few examples of the new features and enhancements you will find:

- ▶ The server installation has been replaced by a new graphical-based installation program, and INSTALL.NLM itself has been replaced by NWCONFIG.NLM — a utility that contains all the old INSTALL maintenance functionality, plus new features to manage your server.

- ▶ The old server migration utilities have been replaced by a new, easy-to-use utility called the Novell Upgrade Wizard.

▶ The server now includes a Java Virtual Machine (JVM), which allows Java applications and applets to run on the server. ConsoleOne, a network management utility, is an example of a graphical Java application that runs on the server.

▶ NetWare 5 now fully supports the IP protocol in native mode (not tunneled). In fact, IP is now the default protocol recommended by Novell. IPX is still available, of course. This means that with NetWare 5, you can run pure IP on your network, IP with IPX compatibility mode (which allows IPX-based applications to continue running on an IP network), pure IPX, or both IP and IPX in dual-stack mode on your network. The choice is yours.

▶ Novell Distributed Printing Services (NDPS) is a new printing service that provides advanced features, including automatic printer driver downloads and two-way communication. It is compatible with the older queue-based printing software that is still included in NetWare 5.

▶ The NetWare Application Launcher (NAL) has been replaced by a subset of Z.E.N.works, with powerful new application management, software distribution, and workstation management features.

▶ A new, optional file system, called Novell Storage Services (NSS), lets you mount huge volumes in seconds and supports trillions of files.

▶ The online documentation is now in HTML, and can be accessed using Netscape Navigator or Windows Internet Explorer.

▶ The Novell Web Server has been replaced by the new Netscape FastTrack Server for Novell.

▶ SBACKUP has been updated and replaced by Enhanced SBACKUP, which can run on either a server or a workstation.

▶ Novell Directory Services (NDS) has new utilities that help you manage NDS objects and NDS traffic more efficiently.

▶ NetWare 5 includes database services in the form of Btrieve and Oracle 8.

▶ NetWare 5 includes DNS/DHCP integration with NDS to help manage your IP addressing schemes more efficiently.

▶ Novell Internet Access Server (NIAS) 4.1 and ConnectView 2.0 are included to help you manage remote access and routing on your network.

You will also find that some of the older, outdated technologies you are familiar with have been removed or replaced, such as the following examples:

- ► SERVMAN.NLM functionality has been incorporated into MONITOR.NLM.

- ► PCONSOLE has been eliminated, with its functionality moved to the NetWare Administrator utility.

- ► Many of the seldom-used or obsolete DOS-based utilities have been removed.

- ► HCSS and file migration utilities have been removed.

- ► The DOS-based menu-creation program has been eliminated.

- ► Support for SFT III has been removed from the product.

- ► NetSync has been removed.

- ► VLM, OS/2, and Macintosh client software are no longer included in NetWare 5.

- ► The IPX/IP Gateway is no longer included, but can be purchased separately as part of the Novell BorderManager product.

What You Need to Know

This book is designed to provide quick-reference access to essential data and facts about setting up, reconfiguring, managing, and troubleshooting your NetWare 5 network. While the explanations provided throughout the book equip you with the basic concepts behind each NetWare feature, you should be somewhat familiar with how a NetWare network operates.

You should also have access to the online documentation that came with your NetWare 5 operating system, in case you need more detailed instructions or explanations of concepts that are unfamiliar to you.

Finally, you should be familiar with the operating systems that run on the workstations you'll be maintaining, such as DOS, Windows 3.1, Windows 95, Windows 98, or Windows NT.

What This Book Contains

Most of the major components of NetWare 5 are explained in the chapters and appendixes of this book.

- ► Chapter 1 describes the network topologies and network cabling architectures you can use when setting up a NetWare 5 network. It also introduces all the major software components that make up a NetWare network, including NDS and the protocols you can choose.

▶ Chapter 2 explains how to install a NetWare 5 server, and how to upgrade a server from a previous version of NetWare.

▶ Chapter 3 discusses the various ways you can manage, maintain, and monitor the performance of a NetWare 5 server and its storage devices.

▶ Chapter 4 describes how to install and upgrade network workstations running DOS, Windows 3.1, Windows 95 or 98, or Windows NT.

▶ Chapter 5 provides an overview of Novell Directory Services (NDS) and the tools you can use to manage it. It includes explanations of how to set up and manage NDS objects, bindery services, NDS partitions and replicas, WAN Traffic Manager, and NDS Catalog Services. It also explains how to merge NDS trees and how to troubleshoot your NDS setup.

▶ Chapter 6 includes instructions for creating and managing users and groups on the network. It describes how to create a user template to simplify the creation of users. It also explains how to set up login scripts and the Z.E.N.works Application Launcher to automatically set up your users' access to network directories and applications.

▶ Chapter 7 covers the various security tools provided in NetWare 5, which you can use to make sure your network is as secure as you need it to be.

▶ Chapter 8 discusses file management, covering the two different file systems available in NetWare 5: the traditional NetWare file system and the new NSS file system. This chapter includes tips on how to plan the directory structure, conserve the server's disk space, manage volumes, back up and restore files, and protect databases using NetWare's Transactional Tracking System (TTS).

▶ Chapter 9 covers both of NetWare 5's printing services — the new NDPS system and the older queue-based printing service. This chapter explains how to set up and manage both types of printing services.

▶ Chapter 10 explains how to set up and use the HTML-based online documentation that came with your NetWare 5 network operating system.

▶ Chapter 11 explains how to set up and use the Netscape FastTrack Server (the Web server included in NetWare 5).

- Chapter 12 provides tips on disaster planning and recovery.
- Appendix A lists all the available parameters that can be used in each workstation's NET.CFG file.
- Appendix B lists all the available SET parameters that can be used to modify your server's performance.
- Appendix C describes a variety of additional resources you can turn to for more help or information (such as user groups, Novell's Internet site, Novell publications, and so on).
- Appendix D supplies a variety of worksheets you may want to use to document information about your network, such as its hardware inventory, configuration settings, and backup schedules.
- Appendix E is an alphabetical reference to the utilities and NLMs (NetWare Loadable Modules) you can use in NetWare 5.

Acknowledgments

Once again, I find myself finishing up a book by thanking the people who helped make it happen. I can't think of a more appropriate sense of closure, because a book like this couldn't be published without the talents and hard work of a lot of dedicated people. This is one of those few times when an author can really sit down, take a deep breath, and genuinely thank the people who mean so much to her (instead of dashing off a quick e-mail and plunging back into the maelstrom of work).

First I want to thank the people at IDG Books Worldwide and Novell Press, who are always top-notch. As always, acquisitions editor Jim Sumser heads the list for his confidence in me, his encouragement, his unfailing dedication to doing the right thing, and (most important) his friendship. You're the greatest, Jim. Jennifer Rowe, my development editor, was always there with a word of encouragement and a good eye for organization — two things every writer needs. I also want to thank Larisa North, my copy editor, for her eagle-eyed attention to detail, and Marcy Shanti for taking care of the business issues that never seem to slow her down. And of course, many thanks go to all the other IDG Books and Novell Press people who made this book happen — the illustrators, indexer, graphics and production specialists, and all the other unsung heroes.

My technical reviewers for this book were great. I can't thank Mark Parratt and Tim Petru enough for going through the book so carefully, double-checking everything to make sure this book is as technically accurate as possible. Thanks so much, guys. And I am extremely grateful to Doug Isom for his help with the Netscape FastTrack Server product.

Of course, thanks go to all the wonderful people at Novell, who have always supported me any way they can to make sure that only the best information possible gets into my books. Novell people are some of the best you could ever hope to work with, and I really treasure my friendship with them.

I want to thank my family and friends, who supported me wholeheartedly when I decided to make the leap into full-time freelance writing. But above all, I thank my husband, Andy. Without him, none of this would be any fun at all.

Contents at a Glance

Preface   ix

Acknowledgments   xiv

Chapter 1   Introduction to NetWare 5   1

Chapter 2   Installing and Upgrading Servers   29

Chapter 3   Managing the Server   63

Chapter 4   Installing Workstations   113

Chapter 5   Managing Novell Directory Services   131

Chapter 6   Managing Users and Groups   171

Chapter 7   Network Security   223

Chapter 8   File Management   257

Chapter 9   Setting Up NetWare Print Services   311

Chapter 10 Installing and Using Online
            Documentation   353

Chapter 11 Netscape FastTrack Server
            for NetWare   365

Chapter 12 Disaster Planning and Recovery   399

Appendix A NET.CFG Parameters   411

Appendix B SET Parameters   435

Appendix C Sources of More Information
            and Help   461

Appendix D Worksheets   **469**

Appendix E NetWare Utilities and NLMs   **481**

Index   **569**

Contents

Preface   ix
Acknowledgments   xiv

Chapter 1   Introduction to NetWare 5   1

Components of a NetWare 5 Network 4
Network Topologies and Architectures 4
    Network Hardware — An Overview 7
    Ethernet Network Architecture 8
    Token Ring Network Architecture 14
    AppleTalk Network Architectures 17
    High-Speed Network Architectures 17
NetWare 5 Software Components 18
    The Server's Network Operating System 18
    The Workstation Software 19
    Novell Directory Services (NDS) 20
    Network Services 21
    NetWare Utilities 21
    Drivers 22
    Gateways and Routers 22
Network Protocols 24
    NetWare 5 and the Internet — A Tale of Two Protocols 25
    Choosing the Protocol for Your Network 26
Where to Go from Here 27

Chapter 2   Installing and Upgrading Servers   29

Preparing to Install or Upgrade a Server 31
    Preparing Existing Servers 31
    Planning the Server Information 32
    Planning the Volume Information 33
    Planning the Protocol Information 34
    Planning the NDS Information 36
    Planning the NDPS Broker Information 37
Installing a New Server 38
    Setting Up the Server Hardware and Volume SYS 38
    Setting Up the Server's Environment 41

Upgrading from Previous Versions of NetWare 46
    Upgrading from NetWare 4.1x 46
    Upgrading from NetWare 3.1x 46
    Upgrade Using INSTALL 47
    Upgrade Using the Novell Upgrade Wizard 55

Chapter 3   Managing the Server   63

Managing a NetWare Server 67
Server Tools 67
Using ConsoleOne 70
Stopping and Starting the Server 72
Using Remote Console to Control the Server from a Workstation 72
    Setting Up the DOS-Based Remote Console 73
    Setting Up the Java-Based Remote Console 79
Running Java Applications on the Server 84
Monitoring and Optimizing Server Performance 86
    Monitoring Cache Buffers 88
    Monitoring Packet Receive Buffers 88
    Monitoring Memory Usage 89
    Monitoring the Error Log Files 91
Protecting the Server 93
    Protecting the Server from Physical Damage 93
    Protecting the Server from Electrical Power Problems 93
    Protecting the Server from Viruses 95
    Protecting the Server from Hardware Failures 95
    Protecting the Server's Memory from Faulty NLMs 95
Performing Server Maintenance 96
    Displaying Information about the Server 97
    Installing Patches and Updated Modules 97
    Monitoring Workstation Connections 98
Adding Network Boards 99
Working with Hard Disks 99
    Using Hot Fix 99
    Using Disk Mirroring and Duplexing 100
    Adding a Hard Disk to a Server 102
    Replacing a Hard Disk in a Server 102
Using PCI Hot Plug Hardware 103
Working with CD-ROM Drives 104

Modifying Server Startup Activities 105
Charging Customers for Server Usage 107
Synchronizing the Servers' Time 109

Chapter 4   Installing Workstations   113

Novell Client Software 115
Windows 95/98 and Windows NT Workstations 116
    Installing the Client Software 116
    Configuring the Client Software 119
    Removing the Client Software 119
Windows 3.1x and DOS Workstations 120
    Installing the Client Software from Windows 3.1x 120
    Installing the Client Software from DOS 122
    Configuring the Client Software 124
    Removing the Client Software 126
Simplifying the Upgrade Process with ACU 128

Chapter 5   Managing Novell Directory Services   131

What Is NDS? 134
NDS Objects 135
    Categories of Object Classes 135
    The NDS Schema 137
    NDS Object Classes 138
    NDS Object Security 145
Planning the NDS Directory Tree 145
    Name Context — Your Location in the Tree 146
    NDS Replicas and Partitions 148
NDS Tools 149
    Using NetWare Administrator to Work with NDS Objects 149
    Using NDS Manager to Work with NDS Partitions and Replicas . . . 150
    Using Bindery Services to Make NDS Mimic a Bindery 155
    Using WAN Traffic Manager to Control NDS Traffic 156
    Using Catalog Services to Search the Tree 159
    Using DSMERGE to Merge Multiple NDS Trees 162
NDS Troubleshooting 164
    NDS TRACE 164
    DSREPAIR.NLM 166

Using Additional Services with NDS 167
 Using LDAP Services for NDS 167
 Using Novell DNS/DHCP Services 168
Keeping Up to Date 168

Chapter 6   Managing Users and Groups   171

What Do Users Need? 174
Creating Users and Groups 175
 Creating a User 176
 Assigning Identical Properties to Multiple Users 177
 Editing Information for Several Users at Once 177
 Creating Groups and Assigning Group Membership to a User 178
User Network Activities 178
 Logging In 179
 Logging Out 181
 Network Tasks from Windows 3.1 182
 Network Tasks from Windows 95/98 and Windows NT 183
 Managing Printers and Print Jobs 183
Making Applications Easy to Access 184
 Installing Z.E.N.works on the Server 185
 Running snAppShot 186
 Creating an Application Object 188
Login Scripts 191
 Creating a Login Script 193
 Assigning Profile Login Scripts to Users 194
 Login Script Commands 194
 Using Identifier Variables 211
 Login Script Example 218

Chapter 7   Network Security   223

The Keys to NetWare Security 225
Login Security 225
 Account Restrictions 226
 Passwords 227
NDS Security 228
 Inheriting NDS Rights 230
 NDS Security Equivalence 231
 Effective NDS Rights 232
 Seeing and Changing an Object's NDS Rights 232

File System Security 234
    File System Trustee Rights 235
    File and Directory Attributes 243
Intruder Detection 249
NCP Packet Signature 251
Server Protection 253
Additional NetWare 5 Security Features 255

Chapter 8   File Management   257

Understanding the NetWare File System 260
    NetWare Volumes 260
    Traditional NetWare Volumes 261
    NSS Volumes 262
Planning the File System 265
    Directories That Are Created Automatically 266
    Application Directories 267
Working with Traditional NetWare Volumes 269
    Creating and Mounting Traditional Volumes 269
    Dismounting and Deleting Traditional Volumes 270
    Increasing the Size of a Traditional Volume 271
    Repairing a Corrupted Traditional Volume with VREPAIR .. 272
Working with NSS Volumes 273
    Creating and Mounting NSS Volumes 273
    Dismounting and Deleting NSS Volumes 278
    Increasing the Size of an NSS Volume 280
    Repairing a Corrupted NSS Volume with REBUILD 282
Saving Disk Space 282
    File Compression 283
    Block Suballocation 286
    Restricting Users' Disk Space 287
    Purging and Salvaging Files 287
Adding a Name Space to a Volume 289
Backing Up and Restoring Files 290
    Planning a Backup Strategy 291
    Preparing to Use Enhanced SBACKUP 295
    Backing Up Files 301
    Restoring Files 305
Protecting Databases with TTS 307
Managing Files and Directories 308

Chapter 9   Setting Up NetWare Print Services   311

How NetWare Printing Works 314
NDPS Printing 315
  Understanding NDPS Printing 315
  Planning NDPS Printing 319
  Installing NDPS Printing 321
  Managing NDPS Printers 333
  Managing NDPS Print Jobs 333
Queue-Based Printing 334
  Understanding Queue-Based Printing 335
  Planning Queue-Based Printing 337
  Installing NetWare Queue-Based Printing 339
  Print Device Definitions 347
  Verifying Your Queue-Based Printing Setup 348
  Managing Queue-Based Print Jobs 349
  Unloading PSERVER.NLM 350

Chapter 10   Installing and Using Online
              Documentation   353

Novell's Online Documentation 355
Installing the Online Documentation Files 356
Setting Up the Browser on a Workstation 359
Launching the Netscape Communicator 361
Viewing the Novell Online Documentation 362

Chapter 11   Netscape FastTrack Server
              for NetWare   365

The FastTrack Server 367
Installing the FastTrack Server for NetWare 367
Connecting to the Administration Server 369
  General Administration Options 370
  Servers Supporting General Administration Options 378

Chapter 12   Disaster Planning and Recovery   399

Why Plan for Disasters? 401
Planning Ahead 401
Keeping Good Records of Your Network 403
Troubleshooting Tips 404
   Narrow Down the List of Suspects 405
   Check the Hardware 407
   Refer to the Documentation 407
   Look for Patches, Updates, or Workarounds 408
   Try Each Solution by Itself 408
   Call for Technical Support 408
   Document the Solution 409

Appendix A   NET.CFG Parameters   411

Appendix B   SET Parameters   435

Appendix C   Sources of More Information and Help   461

Appendix D   Worksheets   469

Appendix E   NetWare Utilities and NLMs   481

Index   569

CHAPTER 1

Introduction to NetWare 5

Instant Access

Planning the Network Architecture

▸ Ethernet, one of the most common network architectures, provides good performance at a reasonable cost, and it is relatively easy to install.

▸ Token Ring generally works well in situations that involve heavy data traffic because Token Ring is reliable. It is also fairly easy to install, but it is more expensive than Ethernet networks.

▸ AppleTalk networks can run on several different network architectures: LocalTalk, EtherTalk, and TokenTalk. AppleTalk, a networking protocol suite built into every Macintosh, provides peer-to-peer networking capabilities between all Macintoshes and Apple hardware.

▸ High-speed network architectures, the newest generation of architectures, are capable of supporting speeds from 100Mbps to 1Gbit/s. Many of these architectures use fiber-optic cabling.

Hardware and Software Components

▸ Networking hardware, such as cables, network boards, and connectors, depends on the type of network architecture you choose. Each architecture requires its own type of hardware.

▸ The NetWare 5 network operating system is installed on the server, replacing the machine's native operating system (such as DOS or Windows 95).

▸ NetWare 5 includes workstation software that must be installed on every workstation, to enable the workstations to communicate with the network.

▸ Novell Directory Services (NDS) is a database of information about all network entities. NDS provides the organizational structure for managing the entire network.

▸ Network services, such as print services, e-mail services, and security services, are software programs that are installed on the network and made available to network users or applications.

▸ Drivers are software programs that enable hardware components to communicate with the computer in which they're installed.

▸ Gateways and routers enable two networks to communicate with each other, even though they may be using different protocols.

Network Protocols

▸ The Internet uses the IP protocol suite to handle Internet communications.

▸ Historically, NetWare has always used the IPX/SPX protocol suite for NetWare network communications, and has supported IP protocols by tunneling IP packets through IPX communications.

▸ In NetWare 5, the IP protocol is the default protocol, enabling network administrators to move to a single protocol environment instead of having to maintain two protocol environments.

▶ · ◀

Components of a NetWare 5 Network

To understand a NetWare 5 network, it helps to begin with the components that make up the network. This chapter explores the three fundamental aspects of any network:

▶ The network's hardware, including the cabling, the connectors, and the network architectures those hardware elements create

▶ The network's software, including the software that must run on the server and the workstations to enable those machines to communicate, as well as the software that provides the network services that users need to use (such as printing services, mail services, file services, and so on)

▶ The communication protocols that regulate how all of the network's components communicate with each other

First, let's look at the network's hardware, and how that hardware works inside network topologies and network architectures.

▶ · ◀

Network Topologies and Architectures

The format in which a network's servers, workstations, printers, and other equipment are laid out is called the network's *topology*. For example, a network can be laid out in a bus format (see Figure 1.1), a ring format (see Figure 1.2), or a star format (see Figure 1.3). Variations or combinations of these topologies are also commonly used.

The cabling scheme that connects the servers, workstations, and other devices together into these topologies can be called the *network cabling architecture*, or just network architecture. The most common network architectures currently are Ethernet, Token Ring, and AppleTalk. (ARCnet is an older, slower architecture that is no longer supported in NetWare 5.) High-speed architectures such as Fast Ethernet are rapidly becoming the new standard for network connections. And now, Gigabit Ethernet (which transfers data a hundred times faster than regular Ethernet and ten times faster than Fast Ethernet) is also making inroads into the networking environment.

Because each of these network architectures handles data in a different way, each requires a unique type of network hardware.

FIGURE 1.1   *Bus topology*

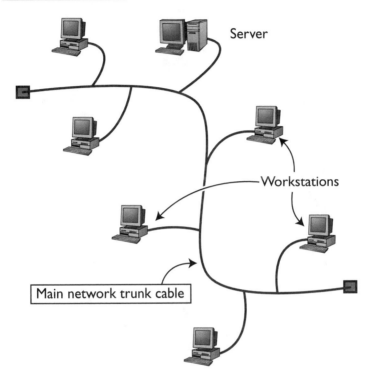

F I G U R E   1.2   *Ring topology*

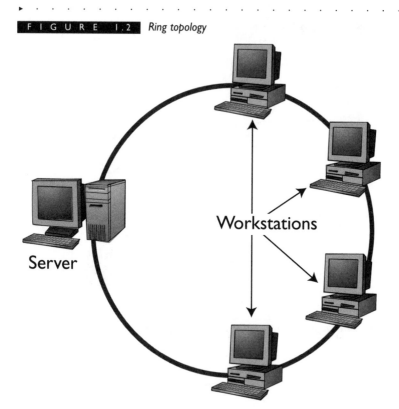

FIGURE 1.3
Star topology

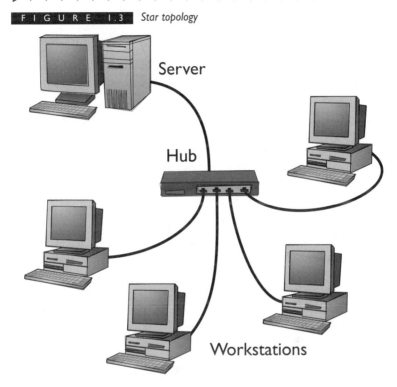

Server

Hub

Workstations

Network Hardware — An Overview

Networking hardware consists of the following components:

- *Network boards.* These special circuit boards, installed in each workstation or server, connect the computer to the network cables. (Some computers come with the network boards integrated into the rest of the computer system hardware. These boards are sometimes called built-in adapters.)

- *Cables.* Network cables connect each workstation and server to the network. These cables can be coaxial (also called coax), unshielded twisted-pair, shielded twisted-pair, or fiber-optic. The type of cable you use depends on the requirements of the topology you install.

- *Connectors and terminators.* Each type of cable requires different types of connectors to join cables together or connect them to other pieces of hardware (such as network boards). Some types of cable also require special connectors known as terminators to be attached to the open ends of any cables. Terminators keep electrical signals from reflecting back across the network, causing bad packets on the network.

- *Hubs.* Some network architectures require that the cables attached to workstations all feed into a separate piece of hardware before being connected to the main network cable. *Passive hubs* simply gather the signals and relay them. *Active hubs* actually boost the signals before sending them on their way. (The terms active hub and concentrator are often used interchangeably.)

Ethernet Network Architecture

Ethernet is currently the most commonly used network architecture. It is relatively easy to install at a moderate cost. Because Ethernet has been so widely used for many years, its technology has been well tested. Ethernet networks can use either bus or star topologies.

There are several variants of Ethernet, each of which package *data packets* (units of information packaged into a sort of electronic envelope and sent across the network) in different ways. These different types of Ethernet packet formats are called *frame types.* In some cases, a given network will support only one Ethernet frame type. However, NetWare allows a single network board to support more than one frame type by configuring the LAN driver for the server's network board to recognize two or more types.

Ethernet Frame Types

The four Ethernet frame types are shown in Table 1.1.

T A B L E 1.1	*Ethernet Frame Types*
FRAME TYPE	**DESCRIPTION**
Ethernet II	This is the original "official" Ethernet frame type. It is used on networks that use AppleTalk Phase 1 addressing or TCP/IP, and on networks that communicate with DEC minicomputers.

FRAME TYPE	DESCRIPTION
Ethernet 802.3	This is the default frame type supported by NetWare 3.11 and earlier versions of NetWare. This frame type can support either a bus or star topology. It is also called the *raw frame type*, because it uses only the defined 802.3 header and doesn't include the standard header extensions defined by the 802.2 and SNAP variants of Ethernet. Ethernet 802.3 is not a standard IEEE 802.2 frame type, and it was used primarily by Novell in earlier versions of NetWare. Don't use this frame type on networks that use protocols other than IPX.
Ethernet 802.2	This frame type can support either a bus or star topology. Because it is an IEEE standard, NetWare 3.12, NetWare 4.1x, and NetWare 5 use this frame type by default. If you are upgrading a NetWare 3.11 (or earlier) network to NetWare 5, or adding a NetWare 5 server to an existing 3.11 network, you have two choices. You can either make the LAN drivers in the NetWare 5 server recognize both frame types, or you need to change all LAN drivers in the older servers and workstations so they recognize 802.2 instead of 802.3. The latter solution is preferred because it allows for easier growth in the future, and it doesn't generate as much packet traffic on the network as supporting two frame types. Ethernet 802.2 packet frames have both the 802.3 header and the 802.2 header extension.
Ethernet SNAP	This is a variant of the 802.2 packet format. It is used on networks that have workstations using protocols such as AppleTalk Phase 2 addressing. Ethernet SNAP packet frames have both the 802.3 header and the SNAP header extension. SNAP stands for Sub-Network Access Protocol.

Ethernet Cable Options

In an Ethernet topology, the cables that connect the machines together are laid out in a specific fashion. The cables you use fall into three general types of functions. These are described in Table 1.2.

TABLE 1.2 *Categories of Cable Functions in an Ethernet Network*

CABLE'S FUNCTION	DESCRIPTION
Trunk cable	The trunk cable is the backbone of the network. All other nodes (workstations, servers, and so on) are connected to this trunk.
Drop cable	The drop cable can be used to connect a node to the trunk cable in a thick Ethernet network.
Patch cable	The patch cable can be used to connect two hubs.

How these types of cables are laid out depends on the cabling hardware (physical wiring) you select. Ethernet networks can be wired using any of the following types of physical cables:

- ▶ Thin coaxial cable (also called Thin Ethernet cable)
- ▶ Thick coaxial cable (also called Thick Ethernet cable)
- ▶ Twisted-pair cable

These types of cables are explained in the following sections.

Thin Ethernet Cable

Thin Ethernet cable is RG-58 (50-ohm) coaxial cable. It is ³⁄₁₆ inch in size. It is also called ThinNet, CheaperNet, and 10Base2. Thin Ethernet cabling is more popular than Thick Ethernet cable because it is less bulky, more flexible, and relatively easy to handle.

Thin Ethernet, like most coaxial cable, is covered with PVC so it can be run through air-conditioning and heating ducts. However, PVC-covered cable cannot be used in the space between a false ceiling and the next floor (called the *plenum space*) because PVC is quite toxic if it burns. Another type of cable, called *plenum cable,* must be used in those areas. If you use thin Ethernet, you will need the following types of hardware components:

- ▶ Ethernet network boards are necessary for each workstation and server.
- ▶ BNC barrel connectors are used to connect lengths of the trunk cable together into one trunk segment.
- ▶ BNC T-connectors are used to connect each node to the network cable.
- ▶ BNC terminators are used to terminate one end of each trunk segment.

▶ BNC grounded terminators are used to terminate and ground the other end of each trunk segment.

▶ Repeaters, if needed, regenerate the signal and pass it on to another trunk segment, thereby extending the normal limits of the network. (Be sure to follow cabling guidelines, however.)

Thin Ethernet cable, like all cable, has limits and restrictions (described in Table 1.3) that will affect how you can set up the network.

T A B L E 1 . 3	Limits and Restrictions of Thin Ethernet Cable
NETWORK ITEM	**LIMITS AND RESTRICTIONS**
Trunk segments	Maximum segment length (segments can consist of several shorter cables linked with BNC barrel connectors) is 607 feet (185 meters).
	Maximum number of segments per network (linked by repeaters) is five, for a total of 3,035 feet (925 meters). Only three of the segments can be populated with nodes, however.
	All trunk segments must be terminated at one end and terminated and grounded at the other end.
Nodes	Maximum number of nodes per trunk segment (including repeaters, which count as nodes) is 30.
	Maximum number of nodes (including repeaters) on the entire network is 90.
	Minimum cable distance between nodes is 1.6 feet (0.5 meters).

Thick Ethernet Cable

Thick Ethernet cable is RG-8 (50-ohm) coaxial cable. It is ⅜ inch in size. It is also called ThickNet, Standard Ethernet, or 10Base5. Because Thick Ethernet cable is bulkier, stiffer, and more difficult to handle than Thin Ethernet cable, it is usually used as the trunk cable, with twisted-pair drop cables used to connect the nodes to the thick Ethernet trunk.

Thick Ethernet, like most coaxial cable, is covered with PVC so it can be run through air-conditioning and heating ducts. As previously mentioned, however, PVC-covered cable cannot be used in the space between a false ceiling and the next floor because PVC is toxic if it burns. Another type of cable, called plenum cable, must be used in those areas.

If you use thick Ethernet, you will need the following types of hardware components:

▶ Ethernet network boards are necessary for each workstation and server.

▶ N-series barrel connectors are used to connect lengths of the trunk cable together into one trunk segment.

▶ Transceivers (one for every node) connect the nodes' drop cables to the trunk segment.

▶ N-series T-connectors or vampire taps attach the transceivers to the trunk cable.

▶ Drop cables (also called transceiver cables) connect the network board in the node to the transceiver. The drop cable must have DIX connectors on each end.

▶ N-series terminators are used to terminate one end of each trunk segment.

▶ N-series grounded terminators are used to terminate and ground the other end of each trunk segment.

▶ Repeaters, if needed, regenerate the signal and pass it on to another trunk segment, thereby extending the normal limits of the network.

Thick Ethernet cable, like all cable, has limits and restrictions (described in Table 1.4) that will affect how you can set up the network.

TABLE 1.4	Limits and Restrictions of Thick Ethernet Cable
NETWORK ITEM	**LIMITS AND RESTRICTIONS**
Trunk segments	Maximum segment length (segments can consist of several shorter cables linked with N-series barrel connectors) is 1,640 feet (500 meters).
	Maximum number of segments per network (linked by repeaters) is five, for a total of 8,200 feet (2,500 meters). Only three of the segments can be populated with nodes, however.
	All trunk segments must be terminated at one end and terminated and grounded at the other end.

NETWORK ITEM	LIMITS AND RESTRICTIONS
Nodes	Maximum number of nodes per trunk segment (including repeaters, which count as nodes) is 100.
	Maximum number of nodes (including repeaters) on the entire network is 300.
	Every node must have its own drop cable connected to its own transceiver to connect to the trunk.
	Minimum cable distance between transceivers is 8 feet (2.5 meters).
	Maximum drop cable length between node and transceiver is 165 feet (50 meters).

Twisted-Pair Cable

There are two types of twisted-pair cabling: unshielded and shielded. *Unshielded twisted-pair* cable is commonly used as telephone wire. *Shielded twisted-pair* cable uses heavier-gauge wire and is protected with insulation and foil shielding.

Unshielded twisted-pair cable, although commonly found in abundance in buildings, is a poorer choice for network cabling because it can be very susceptible to electromagnetic interference from sources such as fluorescent lights, elevators, and telephone ring signals. This type of cable is also called UTP Ethernet or 10BaseT.

Shielded twisted-pair cable is a better choice for networks because of its extra insulation and foil shielding.

If you use twisted-pair cabling, you will need the following types of hardware components:

▶ Ethernet network boards are necessary for each workstation and server.

▶ Wiring hubs can be used to connect nodes to the network. *Standalone hubs* are devices with their own power supply. *Peer hubs* are boards that can be installed in one of the computers on the network and physically connected to that computer's network board.

▶ Twisted-pair cables connect the nodes to wiring hubs.

▶ An external concentrator, if needed, connects nodes that use coaxial or fiber-optic cable to the network.

▸ Punch-down blocks, if desired, make cable termination easier to change.

▸ RJ-45 connectors are used to connect the cables to wall plates, network boards, and wiring hubs.

Twisted-pair cable, like all cable, has limits and restrictions (described in Table 1.5) that will affect how you can set up the network.

TABLE 1.5	Limits and Restrictions of Twisted-Pair Cable
NETWORK ITEM	**LIMITS AND RESTRICTIONS**
Hubs	The maximum distance between a node and a wiring hub is 330 feet (100 meters).
	A twisted-pair network can have up to four linked wiring hubs.
Nodes	All nodes must be connected to a wiring hub, either directly (through a cable) or through a wall plate or concentrator.

Token Ring Network Architecture

A Token Ring network is cabled like a star, but it acts like a ring. Data flows from workstation to workstation around the ring. Because the network is cabled like a star, however, the data ends up going through the central point between each workstation on the trip around the ring.

Token Ring networks can run on twisted-pair (either shielded or un-shielded) or fiber-optic cables. They generally work well in situations that involve heavy data traffic because Token Ring is reliable. It is also fairly easy to install, but it is more expensive than Ethernet networks.

Unshielded twisted-pair cabling is a poorer choice for network cabling because it can be very susceptible to electromagnetic interference from sources such as fluorescent lights, elevators, and telephone ring signals.

Shielded twisted-pair is a better choice for networks because of its extra insulation and foil shielding.

There are two different versions of Token Ring—one that supports a 4Mbps transmission speed and one that supports 16Mbps. A single network can run only one or the other, but networks of differing speeds can be connected through a bridge or router.

If you use Token Ring, you will need the following types of hardware components:

▶ Token Ring network boards are necessary for each workstation and server.

▶ *Multistation Access Units* (MAUs) are wiring concentrators. Nodes connect to these MAUs, which in turn are connected to other MAUs to form the ring. The wiring inside a MAU forms a ring of the attached nodes.

▶ Cabling is necessary to connect the MAUs in the main ring.

▶ Patch cables are used to connect the nodes to the MAUs.

▶ Repeaters, if needed, regenerate the signal and pass it on, thereby extending the normal limits of the network.

IBM defined different types of cabling for use in Token Ring networks. These cabling types are as follows:

▶ Type 1 cable is shielded twisted-pair cable. It has two pairs of 22-gauge solid wire and can supply data-quality transmission. It can be used for the main ring (similar to a trunk cable in an Ethernet network) or to connect nodes to MAUs.

▶ Type 2 cable is a hybrid cable, containing four pairs of unshielded 22-gauge solid wire for voice transmission, and two pairs of shielded 22-gauge solid wire for data transmission.

▶ Type 3 cable is unshielded twisted-pair cable, which is only required to support voice-quality transmission. It can have two, three, or four pairs of 22-gauge or 24-gauge solid wire, with each pair having at least two twists per foot. This cable is not recommended for Token Ring networks.

▶ Type 4 cable is undefined.

▶ Type 5 cable is fiber-optic cable, with two glass fiber cores. Type 5 cables are used to cable the main ring in a Token Ring network and can also be used to extend the distance between MAUs or to connect network segments between buildings.

▶ Type 6 cable is shielded twisted-pair cable, with two pairs of 26-gauge stranded wire. Type 6 cable is commonly used as an adapter cable to connect a node to an MAU.

▶ Type 7 cable is undefined.

▸ Type 8 cable is shielded twisted-pair cable, with two pairs of flat, 26-gauge solid wire. It is designed to run underneath carpeting.

▸ Type 9 cable is shielded twisted-pair cable, with two pairs of 26-gauge solid or stranded wire. It is covered with a plenum jacket and is used to go between floors.

Token Ring cable, like all cable, has limits and restrictions (described in Table 1.6) that will affect how you can set up the network.

T A B L E 1 . 6	*Limits and Restrictions of Token Ring Cable*
NETWORK ITEM	**LIMITS AND RESTRICTIONS**
MAUs	Maximum number of MAUs on a network that uses Type 1 or 2 cabling is 33.
	Maximum number of MAUs on a network that uses Type 6 or 9 cabling is 12.
Cabling	Maximum distance between a node and an MAU is as follows: For Type 1 and 2 cable: 330 feet (100 meters) For Type 6 and 9 cable: 220 feet (66 meters) For unshielded twisted-pair: 150 feet (45 meters)
	Maximum distance between MAUs is as follows: For Type 1 and 2 cable: 660 feet (200 meters) For Type 6 cable: 140 feet (45 meters) For unshielded twisted-pair: 400 feet (120 meters) For fiber-optic cable: 0.6 miles (1 km)
	Maximum number of cable segments (separated by repeaters) in a series is three.
	All cable segments must be terminated at one end and terminated and grounded at the other.
Nodes	Maximum number of nodes is as follows: For networks using Type 1 and 2 cable: 260 For networks using Type 6 and 9 cable: 96 For networks using unshielded twisted-pair: 72
	Minimum cable distance between a node and an MAU is 8 feet (2.5 meters).

AppleTalk Network Architectures

AppleTalk is the networking protocol suite developed by Apple Computers. It provides peer-to-peer networking capabilities between all Macintoshes and Apple hardware. AppleTalk capability is automatically built into every Macintosh.

AppleTalk can run with several types of architectures:

▶ LocalTalk was Apple's built-in architecture in most older Macintoshes. A Macintosh doesn't need a separate network board to communicate over LocalTalk cables, but it does need a separate network board to use other topologies.

▶ EtherTalk is Apple's implementation of Ethernet. EtherTalk Phase 1 was based on the Ethernet II version of Ethernet. EtherTalk Phase 2 is based on the Ethernet 802.3 version. EtherTalk Phase 2 has replaced LocalTalk as the built-in networking architecture in most newer Macintoshes.

▶ TokenTalk is Apple's Token Ring implementation.

▶ FDDITalk is Apple's implementation of the 100Mbps FDDI architecture.

For more information about using AppleTalk with NetWare 5, see Novell's online documentation.

High-Speed Network Architectures

Several new types of high-speed network architectures currently are being developed. Fast Ethernet is already fairly well established, and is designed to transmit 100Mbps over unshielded twisted-pair cable. Gigabit Ethernet will be well established soon, no doubt. Gigabit Ethernet and other new architectures under development use fiber-optic cabling. Because these technologies are rapidly evolving, a book like this probably can't keep up and do justice to them. Therefore, the best recommendation is to hire a qualified, experienced vendor to take care of the network hardware installation. It's also important to get your vendor to guarantee that the components it installs will work together, especially when using the latest technology.

NetWare 5 Software Components

After all the network's hardware components are connected, it's time to focus on the software elements of a network. The NetWare 5 networking software enables all the hardware components to communicate with each other and keep the network running smoothly. The next few sections examine the following types of networking software:

- The network operating system, which runs on the server
- The client software, which runs on every workstation
- Novell Directory Services (NDS), which keep track of every network entity and resource, enabling network administrators to manage the network efficiently
- Service software, which provides services to the network (such as print services, file services, e-mail services, and so on)
- NetWare utilities, which enable network administrators and users to work with different aspects of the network
- Drivers, which enable individual pieces of hardware to function within a computer
- Routers and gateways, which connect networks together

The Server's Network Operating System

The NetWare server is a computer with the NetWare network operating system installed on it. The network operating system (sometimes called the NOS) replaces the computer's regular operating system (such as DOS or Windows 95). The network operating system manages all communication that takes place over the network.

On an ordinary computer, the OS (such as Windows 95) controls how data is transferred and how files are stored within the computer. It also dictates how attached pieces of hardware (such as disk drives or printers) communicate with the computer.

When NetWare takes over the server computer, it does the same tasks but on a larger (network-wide) scale. It controls data transfer over the network, the way users' files are stored on the server, and all communication between the network and attached hardware (such as network printers). In addition, NetWare manages network security (providing access to authorized users only), handles communication between multiple networks, and regulates other network activities.

When you install NetWare on your server computer, you typically divide the server's hard disk into two partitions. (A disk partition is just a portion of the hard disk that is formatted in such a way that it can store and handle files.) One partition — a small one — will be formatted with DOS so that the computer can boot up normally and run any DOS programs that the server needs. The other partition — which is the bulk of the hard disk — will be formatted with the NetWare operating system.

Although the NetWare format is a different format than DOS, it performs many of the same functions. It enables all network files and directories (or folders) to be created and stored on the server's hard disk, just as they would be stored on a DOS disk. The main difference is simply that NetWare requires some specific formatting characteristics to handle all of its security and management features.

NOTE You create the DOS partition by using the DOS commands FDISK and FORMAT, as described in Chapter 2. The remaining NetWare partition will be created by the NetWare 5 installation program.

The Workstation Software

To enable workstations to communicate with the network, you must install special NetWare software on each one. This workstation software is called *client software*, because it acts like a client, requesting services from the network server.

In simple terms, NetWare's client software on the workstation forms a connection with the network. This enables users to log in, transfer data across the network, and find and use network resources (such as printers).

Novell's NetWare client software doesn't replace the workstation's regular OS, such as Windows 95. Instead, the client software allows the workstation's own OS to handle normal processing tasks, and then steps in whenever a task requests a network service. When a network request occurs, the client software manages the request and data transfer across the network.

TIP Other companies — most notably Microsoft — also produce client software that can be used with networks. If you're using NetWare, you should replace Microsoft's client with the NetWare client, because the NetWare client is optimized to run with NetWare.

Novell Directory Services (NDS)

Once the network is connected and the software is communicating, you need a powerful system to manage all the elements of the network. The first key to managing a complex system is to impose a structure on it that will organize and simplify all of the components. Novell Directory Services (NDS) is NetWare's foundation for organizing the network.

NDS is simply a database that contains information about every object in the network. Using this database, NetWare can identify each object and know where it's supposed to be in the network, who's permitted to use it, and to what it's supposed to be connected. This makes it possible for the network administrator to manage all the entities on a network from a single location.

Physical components on the network, such as servers and printers, have their own unique NDS objects defined in the NDS database. Software entities, such as print queues (directories that contain pending print jobs) and volumes, also have their own NDS objects. In fact, all users and organizations (departments, companies, or even project teams, if you like) have their own objects defined in the NDS database. If a user, server, or other type of entity doesn't have an NDS object defined for it in the database, that user or device can't access network services.

If your network is small and contains only one server, the NDS database is stored on that server. If you have more than one server on your network, all of them share a single, distributed NDS database. That way, any object defined anywhere in the network will be recognized by all the servers in that network.

Having a distributed database makes the database itself more flexible and easier for the network administrator to use. For example, instead of being limited to a single server, an administrator can make changes to the database from any number of servers, and all of those servers will receive the same updates.

In addition, a distributed database means that a single server can't make the entire network fail. If one server goes down, the whole database still exists on other servers, so users can still log in, most services will still be available, and so on. NDS makes it easy for network administrators to keep track of their networks and update new information as users or network resources come and go. By defining objects once for an entire network, administrators cut out a lot of the repetitive work they once had to do with some earlier versions of NetWare and other network products. Chapter 5 goes into more explanation about NDS objects and trees.

Network Services

The value of a network lies not in connecting the machines together physically, but in allowing those machines to access various types of services that reside on the network. For example, network users have access to print services, which enable them to send documents to any printer on the network. E-mail services handle users' e-mail needs, such as storing messages, sending them to correct addresses, and so on.

Often, a network service is managed by a main software program called a *server*. These servers are software programs that manage the communication traffic associated with that type of product. For example, a fax server manages the communication necessary for network users to send faxes through the network. A Web server is basically software that is used to post and control information on the World Wide Web (WWW).

Some of these specialty servers may be programs installed and running on the NetWare server itself. Other specialty servers may be running on separate computers connected to the network. For example, if you have a smaller network, you could have a mail server running within your NetWare server. On a larger network, you may decide to dedicate a separate machine for the mail server.

NOTE The term *server* is often used to describe any software program that provides a service to network clients. Technically, the term *server* seldom refers to a physical computer. In common usage, however, people often use the word *server* when referring to both the program and the machine it's running on (such as the NetWare server or an e-mail server). This is especially true when a single computer houses a single server program for the sake of efficiency.

NetWare Utilities

NetWare 5 includes a large set of utilities (software programs or applications) that the network administrator and users can use to work on the network. Some NetWare utilities run on the server, and others can be executed from a workstation.

NetWare utilities provide a wide variety of functions. Some are used to configure the server or workstation, some add services to the network, and others let you manage those services and modify how they work. All of the NetWare 5 utilities are listed in alphabetical order in Appendix E; however, the main utilities you will need to use are described throughout this book within each pertinent chapter.

Drivers

Drivers are small software programs associated with a piece of hardware. A driver enables the hardware device to communicate with the computer in which it's installed.

On a network, you will install a LAN driver on each server and workstation. A LAN driver enables a network board to communicate with the computer in which it's installed, as well as with other devices on the network. Most network boards require their own matched brand of driver.

Disk drivers are another important type of driver. They make it possible for the computer to communicate with its hard disk (actually, with the hard disk's controller board). CD-ROM drives and tape drives also have their own corresponding drivers. The term *device drivers* is sometimes used as a generic name for all the hardware-related drivers your computer may require.

When you install NetWare, the installation program looks at your hardware and attempts to find a matching LAN driver and disk driver. It then attempts to install them automatically from the set of drivers shipped on the NetWare CD-ROM. If it can't find a driver it needs, the installation program will ask you to insert a diskette with the necessary driver on it. (When you buy a network board, the package usually includes a diskette with the board's associated LAN driver on it.)

TIP   Novell's NetWare includes a large selection of the most common types of LAN drivers. However, board manufacturers frequently update their drivers, so if you're installing a network board, check with the manufacturer for an updated driver (Web sites are a good place to check for updated drivers).

Gateways and Routers

Routers are software programs that enable network communication to travel across networks of mixed topologies, architectures, or protocols. Many people think of routers as hardware components, too, because the router programs are sometimes housed in their own hardware devices. The actual routing of packets from one network to the other is controlled by the software. The router's hardware forms the necessary physical connection by linking the cabling systems together. Routers take packets of data from one network and reformat them (if necessary) to conform to the next network's requirements. The routers then send the packets along to their destination. Routers can also track routes between servers or networks. They keep track of which servers are up and running, which route between two servers is shortest, and so on. This ensures that network communication isn't interrupted or slowed down unnecessarily.

Routing software is built into the server in NetWare. The server machine itself forms the physical connection between two networks. For example, the server may have both an Ethernet network board and a Token Ring network board installed in it. The router software then manages the flow of data packets between the two networks via their respective network boards.

Other companies also create extremely good routers that can work with NetWare. These third-party routers are usually contained within their own specialized hardware to make routing work more efficiently with their routing software.

Gateways are another product that can translate one protocol's format into another, and back again. The difference between routers and gateways is a little confusing, and with advancements in technology, the line between them is getting somewhat blurred.

One way to look at the difference, although it's not necessarily a precise definition, is that a router links multiple networks so they appear to be one seamless network. If your company has hundreds of servers scattered all over the globe, you're using a large number of routers every time you communicate with someone. The routers work together to scatter information across a spiderweb of connections to get the data to its destination. A piece of data, traveling across the network, may go through a variety of paths. If one router is down, the data can travel through another router on a different path, but still wind up at the same destination.

A gateway generally connects your network to a completely different type of network or computer system, through a single point. If, for example, you're using a workstation on a network and you want to connect to a mainframe computer, your communications can go through a gateway installed somewhere on the network. The gateway takes your data and transfers it to the mainframe, reversing the process when the mainframe replies to you. If the gateway is down, you won't be able to communicate with the mainframe. There may not be another gateway that is set up to automatically retrieve your data and send it on an alternate route to the mainframe.

Network Protocols

A protocol is a set of defined rules that control how processes or machines communicate. For example, a protocol regulates how two computers establish a connection for communication, and the way they terminate the connection when finished.

In addition, protocols control how data is transferred over a network. When data is sent across the network, it (the data) is packaged in small units, called *packets*. Each packet includes a small amount of data, plus addressing information to ensure the data gets to the right destination. A protocol dictates exactly how these packets should be formed, so that every device on the network can understand the packets it receives. Each protocol forms packets in a unique way.

Several different types of protocols have been developed by various organizations to control how information is exchanged across a network. Many of these protocols are supported by NetWare.

Discussions about protocols can be very confusing because there are so many different types of protocols, as well as protocols that layer on top of each other. Protocols are associated with several types of characteristics, such as:

- The network architecture they support, such as a bus- or ring-oriented architecture. Protocols designed for a bus architecture behave differently than protocols designed for a ring architecture.

- The way they transmit data

- How they determine where data should go

- The types of communication they're facilitating

When you configure your NetWare network, you will configure primarily two types of protocols:

- *Data link protocols (Ethernet, Token Ring, AppleTalk, or FDDI)*. These protocols create, transmit, and receive data packets in a form that is appropriate for the particular network architecture you're using.

- *Network protocols (IPX, IP, or AppleTalk)*. These protocols are responsible for tracking hardware and network addresses. Once those addresses are determined, these protocols find and establish routes between sources and destinations, so that data can be safely transferred. Network protocols allow applications to communicate over different network links, regardless of differences in data link protocols, packet formats, or hardware specifications.

You decide on the data link protocol you want to use when you select your network architecture. Configuring these protocols essentially means that you load a LAN driver for a network board and specify a few parameters for that board. This is accomplished during the server installation.

Choosing a network protocol may be a little more complicated. Fortunately, NetWare 5 supports both of the major network protocols: IPX, which is Novell's own protocol, and IP, which is used by the Internet. The next sections discuss the needs for the different protocols, and they describe how NetWare 5 supports both.

NOTE NetWare 5 also supports the AppleTalk protocol. If you want your network to support AppleTalk, you can add the AppleTalk protocol to the server so that the network supports both IPX or IP and AppleTalk. See the NetWare documentation for more information about using AppleTalk on your NetWare network.

NetWare 5 and the Internet — A Tale of Two Protocols

Although the Internet has been around for many years, its popularity with the general population and businesses didn't really begin to explode until the last few years. Before that time, businesses concentrated primarily on their own internal networks. For the large majority of businesses, that meant NetWare.

During NetWare's development, Novell created a protocol suite, called IPX/SPX, to handle network communication. IPX/SPX was designed to be incredibly reliable and easy to manage, in contrast to some of the other protocols available. Thousands of network applications have been developed using this protocol suite.

Meanwhile, the Internet was growing, based on another protocol suite called TCP/IP. The TCP/IP protocol suite was more cumbersome to manage, with its IP addresses and domains, but the Internet had enough appeal that network administrators were willing to learn the intricacies of IP addressing if they had to.

As the need for communicating with the IP-based Internet grew, Novell began supporting the TCP/IP protocols within NetWare. For years, Novell has offered TCP/IP solutions that allowed TCP/IP packets to be encapsulated within an IPX packet (called *tunneling*), which enabled TCP/IP support while still taking advantage of IPX/SPX speed, reliability, and ease of management.

As the Internet continues to grow, and as new applications are being developed that use the IP protocol, many network administrators are now asking for a single protocol that they can use on their entire network, so that they no longer need to worry about two protocols. In addition, Novell has begun aggressively pursuing a goal of supporting "open standards" (as opposed to proprietary ones) so application developers can more readily create applications for use in any networked environment.

In response to these growing needs, NetWare 5 is the first version of NetWare to provide pure (nontunneled) support of IP on the network. In fact, NetWare 5 has been changed to use the IP protocol as its default protocol instead of IPX.

Choosing the Protocol for Your Network

Just because NetWare 5 has IP as its default protocol doesn't mean, however, that you must use IP if you don't want to. In fact, as is typical with NetWare throughout its history, the choice is up to the network administrator. You can choose to set up your network to use pure IP, both IP and IPX, or pure IPX.

Choosing Pure IP with the Compatibility Mode

You can choose to run your network in a pure IP environment, with no IPX packets anywhere on the network. This requires that all your applications use only IP and not IPX/SPX.

In reality, chances are good that you have IPX dependencies right now in your network. IPX/SPX uses a protocol called SAP (Service Advertising Protocol) to locate resources on the network. Many network applications, including most current virus detectors and backup programs, use SAP or other parts of SPX to operate on the network.

Therefore, if your goal is to become a pure IP environment, you probably need to plan to go through a gradual migration, systematically eliminating IPX dependencies from your applications over time.

Fortunately, you can set up your network to run pure IP, but still support IPX-based applications through NetWare 5's IPX Compatibility Mode feature. Compatibility Mode enables you to gradually phase IPX traffic out of your network while you transition to a pure IP environment.

Compatibility Mode handles IPX packets by encapsulating them into IP format. In addition, it makes the entire IP segment of the network look like a single IPX segment with a single IPX internal network number. This enables IPX-based applications to understand and work with the IP portion of the network.

Compatibility Mode is automatically installed as part of NetWare 5; you don't need to do anything to turn it on — it automatically works. In addition, Compatibility Mode doesn't take any overhead if there are no IPX packets to deal with. Therefore, running Compatibility Mode is the best way to transition your network to pure IP.

Choosing a Dual Stack Network

Instead of running pure IP, you can choose to load both the IP protocol and the IPX protocol on your server. This is called a *dual stack* environment. (A protocol suite is sometimes referred to as a protocol *stack* when it is loaded on the server.)

In a dual stack situation, IP packets are handled by the IP protocol stack, and IPX packets are handled by the IPX protocol stack. This is the same way previous versions of NetWare supported multiple protocols on the network. The only drawback to this solution is that you must manage two different protocols instead of one — which may not be all that disagreeable in some situations.

If you select a dual stack network, you won't have the Compatibility Mode. The two protocols will work independently of each other.

If you're familiar with both protocols, have a mixed protocol environment, and expect to continue to support both protocols, you may want to choose this solution.

Choosing Pure IPX

Of course, if you are currently running pure IPX and don't anticipate needing to support IP in the future, you can continue to run an all-IPX network. If you choose, you can connect an IPX-based network to the Internet by using a product such as Novell's BorderManager, which includes an IPX/IP Gateway that workstations can use. Workstations can also connect to the Internet directly through modems.

Where to Go from Here

If you're ready to install or upgrade the network server, continue on with Chapter 2. That chapter also explains more details about installing the IP protocol and its Compatibility Mode. If you are new to Novell Directory Services (NDS), you may want to read Chapter 5, "Managing Novell Directory Services," before installing the server.

CHAPTER 2

Installing and Upgrading Servers

Instant Access

Installing

▸ To install a new server, run INSTALL from the *NetWare 5 Operating System* CD-ROM.

Upgrading from NetWare 4.1x

▸ To upgrade a NetWare 4.1x server, use INSTALL and choose the Upgrade from 3.1x or 4.1x option.

Upgrading from NetWare 3.1x

▸ To upgrade an existing NetWare 3.1x server, use INSTALL and choose the Upgrade from 3.1x or 4.1x option. (This is the simplest upgrade option.) The NetWare 3.1x server must meet all of the hardware requirements for a NetWare 5 server.

▸ To transfer all the NetWare 3.1x server's data to a new machine on which NetWare 5 has already been installed, use the Novell Upgrade Wizard.

Preparing to Install or Upgrade a Server

How you install your NetWare 5 server depends on whether you are installing a new server or upgrading one from an earlier version of NetWare. This chapter discusses three different scenarios:

- ▶ Installing a new server
- ▶ Using the installation program to upgrade an existing NetWare 4.1x or 3.1x server to NetWare 5
- ▶ Using the Novell Upgrade Wizard to migrate the bindery and data from a NetWare 3.1x server to a NetWare 5 server

Regardless of whether you are upgrading or installing a new server, there are several decisions you have to make about your server. You may want to refer to the "Server Installation and Configuration" and "Volumes" worksheets in Appendix D to help you plan your server's installation. If you answer all the questions on these worksheets before you tackle the actual installation procedure, the process should go more smoothly.

You may also need to read other chapters in this book if you are not familiar with some of the issues discussed during installation, such as planning the NDS tree and setting up time synchronization.

NOTE

The following sections itemize most of the preparatory steps and list the information you'll need to have on hand before starting the installation or upgrade.

Preparing Existing Servers

If you will be installing a NetWare 5 server into a network that already has NetWare 4.1x servers running on it, you must first make sure all of the NetWare 4.1x servers are running DS.NLM (the main NDS module) version 5.99 or higher. To see the DS.NLM version, run the MODULES console utility (type **MODULES DS.NLM** at the server console). If you are not running version 5.99 or higher, you must update the existing DS.NLM on all of the NetWare 4.1x servers before you can install a NetWare 5 server into the network. The 5.99 version of DS.NLM is included on the NetWare 5 CD-ROM.

Instructions for upgrading DS.NLM are in the readme file on the *NetWare 5 Operating System* CD-ROM. The readme file is called 411_UPG.TXT, and it is located in the PRODUCTS\411_UPG folder.

Planning the Server Information

You will need to plan the following information about the server:

▸ *The server's processor speed.* The server must be running a Pentium processor or higher.

▸ *The server's CD-ROM drive.* The server must have a CD-ROM drive that can read ISO 9660 CD-ROMs. (Most CD-ROM drives installed in PCs can read this type of CD-ROM.) CD-ROM drives that are fully compatible with El Torito specifications will be able to boot from the CD-ROM, as well.

▸ *The server's name.* The name can be between 2 and 47 characters long, using letters, numbers, hyphens, or underscores.

▸ *The server's memory.* A NetWare 5 server should have a minimum of 64MB of RAM. (128MB is recommended if you intend to run Java-based applications on the server.) Depending on the size of the network (the number of servers, number of users on the server, total disk space on the server, and so on), you may want even more memory.

▸ *The amount of hard disk space you will allocate for a DOS disk partition.* The DOS partition is the portion of the hard disk that is reserved for DOS system files and other DOS files that you want to store on the server. The rest of the disk becomes a NetWare partition, which stores the NetWare files and network data. Plan for at least a 50MB DOS partition, but a rule of thumb is to add 1MB to the DOS partition for every MB of server RAM installed. You should create the DOS disk partition before running the installation program. (The installation process will create the partition for you if you want, but it's generally easier to do it yourself so you can avoid having to reinstall the CD-ROM drive's drivers and other configuration information.)

▸ *The server's hardware configuration.* Does the server support multiple processors or PCI Hot Plug technology? If so, NetWare 5 can take advantage of those features. You will need to know the name of the appropriate drivers.

▶ *The server's storage adapters and devices.* Know the name of the server's storage adapters (boards), and the types of devices (CD-ROM drives, hard disk drives, tape drives, and so on) that are attached to those adapters.

▶ *The server's network boards.* Know the name of the server's network boards and their associated LAN drivers. You will also need to know each board's settings and the frame type you will use (such as Ethernet 802.2, Ethernet 802.3, Ethernet SNAP, Ethernet II, Token Ring, or Token Ring SNAP). Be sure to record this information for later reference. NetWare 5's default Ethernet frame type is Ethernet 802.2 for IPX, and Ethernet_2 for IP.

Planning the Volume Information

You will need to plan the following information about the volumes you intend to create on your server:

▶ *The size of NetWare volume SYS.* A volume named SYS is mandatory for NetWare system and utility files. The server must have a minimum of 500MB of disk space available for volume SYS. However, planning for a larger SYS volume gives you more room to install additional products. Therefore, you may want to plan for 1000MB of disk space for SYS.

▶ *The size and names of any additional NetWare volumes.* It's often a good idea to reserve SYS for NetWare files only, and create one or more separate volumes for regular applications and data files. In addition, if you will be supporting Macintosh files, you may want to create a volume just for those files. Because Macintosh systems support different file formats, you must load a special type of program, called a *name space module,* on the server to support Macintosh files. Then you must assign that name space to the volume that you want to store those files. The name space for Mac OS files is called MAC.NAM. See Chapter 8 for more information about adding the Macintosh name space to a volume.

▶ *The type of volumes you want to create.* NetWare 5 lets you create traditional NetWare volumes, as well as a new type of volume to support the new NetWare Storage Services (NSS) file system. Traditional NetWare volumes support all the features found in previous versions of NetWare, such as file compression and block suballocation. NSS volumes don't support all of those volume features in this first release; however, they support much larger files, larger numbers of files, and much faster mounting times. See Chapter 8 for more information about the difference between traditional NetWare volumes and NSS volumes.

▶ *Whether you want to use file compression on any traditional NetWare volumes.* File compression typically can save more than 60 percent of your hard disk space by compressing unused files. By default, all NetWare volumes are enabled for file compression. However, just because a volume is enabled for compression doesn't mean the files will be compressed — you must turn on file compression for specific directories. For more information about file compression, see Chapter 8.

▶ *Each traditional NetWare volume's block size and whether you want the volume to use block suballocation.* A block is a unit of disk space that is allocated to store a file. Block suballocation divides a block into 512-byte suballocation blocks, so that several smaller files can share a single block. By default, block suballocation is turned on automatically. (For more information about block suballocation, see Chapter 8.) The default block size depends on the volume's size, as shown in the following list.

Volume Size	Block Size
0 to 31MB	4K
32 to 149MB	8K
150 to 499MB	16K
500MB to 1999MB	32K
2000MB or more	64K

Planning the Protocol Information

You will need to plan the following information about the protocols you want to use on your server:

▶ *The protocol you will use on the network.* You can install IP with Compatibility Mode turned on, IP with Compatibility Mode turned off, IPX, or both IP and IPX:

  • If you want to use the IP protocol, you will most likely choose to install IP with Compatibility Mode turned on. This allows all

INSTALLING AND UPGRADING SERVERS

existing IPX-based applications and services to continue to work on your IP-based network.

- If you have no need for the IP protocol on your network, using IPX alone is probably the simplest option, because you don't need to understand or plan for things like IP addresses, subnet masks, and so on.

- Choosing to install both IP and IPX protocols on the same network means you must manage both types of protocols. You will need to install a Migration agent on the server to make sure that both halves of the network (the IP segment and the IPX segment) can communicate with each other.

- If you are sure you have a pure IP environment, with no dependencies on IPX anywhere in any of your applications or services, you can install IP and then turn off the IPX Compatibility Mode option. However, because the Compatibility Mode option is dormant and requires no overhead if there are no IPX packets to deal with, leaving it turned on is generally a safer option.

▶ *(For IPX servers) The server's internal IPX network number.* A number will be generated randomly for you, or you can specify your own. Each IPX server on the network must have a unique internal IPX network number.

▶ *(For IP servers) The server's IP address.* Each IP server must have a unique IP address. If you plan to connect your network to the Internet, you will have to register with the Internet Network Information Center (InterNIC) and obtain a unique IP address from them. For more information about getting a registered IP address, contact InterNIC at hostmaster@internic.net, or call your Internet Service Provider (ISP).

▶ *(For IP servers) The server's subnet mask.* The subnet mask is a number designating a portion of the network. Subnet masks enable you to divide a large network into smaller, more manageable units.

▶ *(For IP servers) The router/gateway address.* You can either specify a router (or gateway) address, or you can allow the server to locate the nearest one automatically. If you do not want to specify a particular address, leave that option blank in the installation procedure.

▶ *(For IP servers) Whether you want to install a Migration Agent on this server.* A Migration Agent can be enabled as part of the IPX

Compatibility Mode. A Migration Agent acts as a gateway between an IP segment of the network and an IPX segment. The Migration Agent takes packets from each side of the network and repackages them in the other protocol's format for transmission across the network to other destinations.

▸ *(For IP servers) DNS information.* If you want to use Domain Name Services on your network, you need to know your network's domain name, as well as the addresses of name servers you want to use. For more information about DNS and name servers, see the Novell online documentation. (Search for the DNS/DHCP Administrator's Guide, which is included in the online documentation.)

▸ *SNMP information.* If you intend to use SNMP-based network management utilities, you can configure some SNMP event information during installation. (SNMP stands for Simple Network Management Protocol.) Know the type of information about this server that you want to be sent whenever an event occurs (such as the server's hardware description, its location, and the name of the responsible administrator). Also know the IPX or IP address of the node (workstation or server) that you want to be notified when the event occurs.

Planning the NDS Information

You will need to plan the following information about the server's NDS tree and environment:

▸ *The server's time zone.* You need to know the name of the server's time zone and whether that time zone supports Daylight Saving Time.

▸ *The server's Directory tree.* You must know the name of the NDS tree into which the server will be installed. For more information about Novell Directory Services, see Chapter 5.

▸ *The server's location (name context) in the Directory tree.* Before you install the server, be sure you are familiar with Novell Directory Services and how you want your network to be laid out in the Directory tree. You'll need to specify to which Organization object or Organizational Unit object this server belongs. For more information about Novell Directory Services, see Chapter 5.

▸ *The Admin user's name, context, and password.* If you are installing the first server in a new tree, you can specify any password you choose, and you can select the context where the Admin user will reside. If you are installing a server in a tree that already exists, you will need to know the context, name, and password of the existing Admin user.

▶ *The server's type of time synchronization.* You may have Single Reference, Reference, Primary, or Secondary time servers. By default, the installation program will make the first server in the tree into a Single Reference time server, and all others will be Secondary time servers. This should be adequate for networks of fewer than 30 servers that are all located in the same geographical area (with no WAN links between them). For more information about time synchronization services, see Chapter 3.

Planning the NDPS Broker Information

NDPS is the new printing service of NetWare 5. Although you can still use the older queue-based printing service that was used in previous versions of NetWare, NDPS support is recommended because of its new features and capabilities. See Chapter 9 for more information about both NDPS and queue-based printing in NetWare 5.

You will need to plan the following decisions about NDPS on this server:

▶ *Whether to install NDPS on this server.* NDPS support is one of the additional products you can specify at the end of the installation procedure.

▶ *Whether to install an NDPS Broker on this server.* When NDPS is installed, the installation program surveys the network to see if any other servers have been installed with an NDPS Broker. By default, the installation program will only install an NDPS Broker on a server if the server is more than three servers away from an existing Broker. You can override this default setting, however, and specify whether or not you want the Broker installed on this server.

▶ *Whether you want to disable any of the three available Broker services on this server.* By default, all three of the Broker's services are enabled: Event Notification Service, Resource Management Service, and Service Registry Service. However, you can disable any of them if you prefer.

Installing a New Server

After you've gathered all the information you need, you can install the server. The following sections explain how to install a new server. If you are upgrading a server, skip to "Upgrading from Previous Versions of NetWare" later in this chapter.

There are two halves of the installation program. The first half, which takes you through the hardware setup and creates volume SYS, is text-based and runs in DOS on the server. Throughout the text-based installation program, you usually have to choose between Modify and Continue at each screen. Choose Modify to make changes to the default values that the installation program offers. Choose Continue to accept the values and continue with the installation. In some screens, when you make changes to the values, you have to press F10 to save your changes and continue.

The second half of the installation program, which sets up the server's environment, switches to a graphical format, called the NetWare 5 Installation Wizard. During this portion of the installation (which is running in Java), you can use a mouse.

The following sections explain how to install a new server.

Setting Up the Server Hardware and Volume SYS

Complete the following steps to set up the server hardware and create the volume SYS:

1. Set up the server hardware.

   a. Any existing data on this computer will be erased during the installation, so back up any data you want to save onto another medium. In addition, you may want to make backup copies of the computer's AUTOEXEC.BAT and CONFIG.SYS files, as well as any device drivers (such as CD-ROM drivers).

   b. Install and configure network boards in the server. Refer to the network board manufacturer's documentation for configuration instructions.

   c. Using the DOS FDISK and FORMAT commands, create a DOS disk partition of at least 50MB. Leave the rest of the disk space free. (If the computer you're using doesn't have DOS installed, you can boot from the license diskette that came with NetWare 5.

The necessary DOS commands to reformat the server's hard disk are contained on that diskette. Do not use the version of DOS that comes on Windows 95, 98, or NT computers.)

d. Install the CD-ROM drive as a DOS device on the server, following the manufacturer's instructions.

e. Using the DOS DATE and TIME commands, verify that the computer's date and time are set correctly, and change them if necessary.

f. Edit the CONFIG.SYS file to make sure it contains the following commands. (You will have to reboot the computer to make these commands take effect.)

```
FILES=40
BUFFERS=30
```

2. Insert the *NetWare 5 Operating System* CD-ROM into the computer's CD-ROM drive.

3. From the DOS command prompt, change to the CD-ROM drive's letter (usually D), and enter the following command:

```
INSTALL
```

(If you boot the server from the *NetWare 5 Operating System* CD-ROM, the installation program will automatically launch.)

4. If prompted, choose the language you want to use.

5. Read the Terms and Conditions that outline the license agreement for using NetWare 5, and then press F10 (or select Accept the Agreement) to accept the agreement.

6. From the screen that appears, choose the New Server type of installation, and then select a startup directory. The default startup directory (where the server's startup files will be located) is C:\NWSERVER.

7. (Optional) From the same screen, press F2 to specify advanced settings. From the Advanced Settings screen, you can make the following changes:

a. If necessary, choose whether you want the installation program to access the CD-ROM drive through a NetWare driver or a DOS device. If possible, choose NetWare. However, if a NetWare driver doesn't exist for your CD-ROM drive, you can choose DOS.

b. If necessary, specify a server ID number (only necessary if you don't want to use the one that will be assigned automatically). This number is similar to an IPX internal network number.

c. If necessary, specify that you do not want the AUTOEXEC.BAT file to automatically load the server (SERVER.EXE). If you do not allow AUTOEXEC.BAT to automatically load the server, you will have to load the server by typing **SERVER** at the DOS prompt any time the server is rebooted.

d. If necessary, specify any particular SET parameters that may be required by your device drivers.

8. Choose the country, code page, and keyboard mapping for your server. (To select these, choose Modify, and then press Enter on the field you want to change and choose the correct selections from the lists that appear.)

9. Select your computer's mouse type and video type. At this point, the installation program copies files, including device drivers, to the DOS partition.

10. Select your computer's device drivers. At this point, you can select Platform Support Modules (if your computer supports more than one processor), Hot Plug Support Modules (if your computer supports PCI Hot Plug technology), and Storage Adapters. If the installation program detects any of these drivers or a storage adapter (board), it will display them for you. If the information is correct, choose Continue. If not, choose Modify and specify the drivers you need. You can also configure the drivers at this point. (If the installation program does not detect any PSM or Hot Plug drivers, your computer probably does not support these technologies.)

11. Select your computer's storage devices (which are controlled by the adapters you chose in Step 10) and network boards. If the installation program detects any of these devices or network boards, it will display them for you. If the information is correct, choose Continue. If not, choose Modify and specify the drivers you need. You can also configure the drivers at this point. (This screen also enables you to specify any optional NLMs that are required for the installation program to continue. For example, you can load ROUTE.NLM if you are installing the server into a Token Ring network.)

12. (Optional) If you are installing NetWare 5 on a computer that was previously used as a server, the installation program will detect existing NetWare partitions and the SYS volume. Choose either "Replace volume SYS and its NetWare Partition" or "Remove all NetWare volumes and NetWare/NSS Partitions." The first option will erase volume SYS only, leaving any other volumes intact. You will then see a screen displaying Available Free Spaces, from which you can select the free space you want to use for SYS. The second option will remove all volumes, allowing you to create new volumes from scratch.

13. A screen appears, showing the proposed size for the NetWare partition that will contain the SYS volume. You can change the size of this partition (and therefore, of volume SYS) by choosing Modify. Highlight the NetWare Partition Size field and enter the size you want to use. Remember that volume SYS should be a minimum of 500MB. If you want to include the online Novell documentation on SYS, choose a minimum size of 1000MB. When you specify a size for the partition, the SYS size will change automatically to match it. The Hot Fix size will be determined by default. Accept the default Hot Fix size. Any disk space left over after you've specified the NetWare partition and volume SYS can be used later to specify additional traditional or NSS volumes.

14. (Optional) Press F3 to see additional properties for volume SYS. From this screen, you can turn off file compression or block suballocation, if you want. However, in most cases, it is better to leave these options turned on.

15. Press F10 to save the information for volume SYS.

At this point, the installation program mounts volume SYS and begins copying files to it. Then the installation program launches the NetWare 5 Installation Wizard, a graphical program that will take you through the rest of the server installation, as explained in the following section.

Setting Up the Server's Environment

Continue with the following steps to set up the server's environment:

1. Enter a name for this server, and then click Next.

2. (Optional) If you left disk space free for additional volumes, you can configure new volumes now. If you used all the available disk space for volume SYS, skip to Step 3. If you do not want to create new volumes now, click Next and skip to Step 3. If you do want to create new volumes, complete the following steps:

a. Click the Free Space in the list of volumes, and then click Create.

b. Enter a volume name.

c. Select whether you want the volume to be a Traditional volume or an NSS volume. (See Chapter 8 for more information about the difference.)

d. Enter the size of the volume in the Space to Use field, and then click Apply to Volume.

e. Click OK to return to the list of volumes, and then click Next to continue.

3. Specify whether you want to mount volumes now or when the server reboots after the installation is complete. If you want to install some Novell products during this installation procedure to volumes other than SYS, choose to mount the volumes now. Otherwise, if you intend only to install products into SYS, you can choose to mount the volumes later.

4. When the Protocols screen appears, click the server in the diagram to display the network boards installed in it.

5. Click a network board, and choose the protocol you want to use for that board. You can choose IP, IPX, or both. If you choose IP, you must also specify the server's IP address and subnet mask. You can also specify a router address if you need to (or leave that field blank to allow the network to find the nearest router automatically). Choosing IP alone will automatically install the IPX Compatibility Mode.

6. Select the time zone in which this server will exist. If your location uses Daylight Saving Time, make sure the box is checked to allow for that adjustment.

7. Choose whether you want to create a new NDS tree or install this server into an existing NDS tree. Then click Next.

8. If you are installing this server into an existing NetWare Directory tree, select the correct tree. If this is a new tree, give the tree a name.

9. Create a context for the server. By entering the name of the organization (such as your company) and the names of descending levels of Organizational Units (such as a division and a department), you actually create the branch of the NDS tree that will contain this server if the branch doesn't already exist. If a branch already exists,

click the Browse button and select the Organizational Unit objects you want.

10. Enter a name, context, and password for the Admin user. If this is the first server in the tree, enter any password you want. If this server is being installed into an existing tree, type in the Admin name and password that have already been assigned, or enter the name and password of another User object already in the NDS tree. This User object must have enough NDS trustee rights to add the server to the context specified. See Chapter 7 for more information about NDS trustee rights.

11. At the summary screen that appears, review the information. Record the Admin's name and context for future reference. Then click Next to continue.

12. When prompted, insert the license diskette and specify the location of the license file (usually A:\LICENSE\). Then click Next to continue.

13. After the remaining files are copied to the server, the Additional Products and Services screen appears. Choose any additional products you want to install, such as NDPS, NDS Catalog Services, or Novell PKI Services. It is strongly recommended that you choose NDPS, as well as any others that are checked by default. You can click each service to see a description of that service at the bottom of the screen. When finished selecting the products you want, click Next to continue.

14. Depending on the products you selected, you may receive additional screens to specify information for those products. Follow the prompts on the screen.

15. When the Summary screen appears, review the list of products to be installed. At this point, you can either click Finish to complete the installation, or you can customize the properties of some of the products you've selected, as explained in the following steps. To finish the installation, skip to Step 22. To customize products you've selected, continue with Step 16.

16. Click the Customize button.

17. (Optional) If you want to customize the protocols you've chosen to use, select Protocols, and then click the Properties button. (You may have to open the NetWare Operating System in the diagram to display Protocols.) This option lets you disable IPX Compatibility Mode, install a Migration Agent, specify a domain name and name servers, and set up SNMP notification information.

a. On the Protocols tab, you can change the protocol choices you made earlier in the installation program. You can also specify a particular IPX frame type, if necessary.

b. On the IPX Compatibility tab, you can choose to disable the IPX Compatibility Mode for this server, if your network uses only IP and you don't need any compatibility with IPX applications. You can also choose to load the Migration Agent on this server by checking the appropriate box. A Migration Agent functions like a gateway between IP and IPX network segments.

c. On the Domain Name Service tab, you can specify the domain name your company uses, such as blue.com. You can also enter the IP addresses of any domain name servers you want NetWare 5 to use. The name server is a computer that translates names into IP addresses.

d. On the SNMP tab, you can specify the type of information about this server that you want to be sent whenever an event occurs (such as the server's hardware description, its location, and the name of the responsible administrator). You can also specify which node (workstation or server) is notified when the event occurs by entering either the node's IPX or IP address.

e. When finished customizing the network protocol information, click OK to return to the Product Customization screen.

18. (Optional) If you want to customize NDS, select NDS from the Product Customization screen, and then click the Properties button. This option enables you to modify the NDS tree and time zone information you entered earlier in the installation program. It also lets you modify the default time synchronization information.

a. On the NDS Summary tab, make any modifications to the NDS tree name, the server's context, or the administrator's name and context.

b. On the Time Zone tab, you can change the time zone information you selected earlier. You can also specify when your location begins and ends Daylight Saving Time.

c. On the Time Synchronization tab, you can change this server's time server designation. If you have fewer than 30 servers on your network, all located in the same geographical area, you will probably want to retain the default designation (the first server installed is a Single Reference server, and all subsequent servers in the tree are Secondary servers). If you have more than 30 servers in the tree, or if your network contains WAN links, see Chapter 3 for information on how to best plan your time server setup.

d. When finished customizing the NDS information, click OK to return to the Product Customization screen.

19. (Optional) If you want to customize NDPS printing information, select Novell Distributed Print Service (NDPS) from the Product Customization screen, and then click the Properties button. This option enables you to specify whether or not to create an NDPS Broker on this server. It also lets you disable any of the three services that the NDPS Broker handles: Service Registry Service, Event Notification Service, and Resource Management Service. (See Chapter 9 for more information about planning your NDPS printing setup.) When finished customizing the NDPS information, click OK to return to the Product Customization screen.

20. (Optional) If you want to customize other products you've selected to install, repeat the same process. Select the product, click the Properties button, and then open any configuration tabs and specify the information you want to change. When finished, click OK to return to the Product Customization screen.

21. When you've finished customizing products, click Close from the Product Customization screen.

22. From the Summary screen, click Finish. The installation program will finish installing all the products you've selected.

23. When asked if you want to reboot the server, click Yes. (You can also choose to view the readme file before rebooting the server.) Remove the installation CD before you reboot the server.

When the computer reboots, it will automatically load the server. When the server is running, you will see the server desktop — a graphical screen that can display utilities. To bring up the ConsoleOne utility, click the Novell button at the bottom of the screen and select ConsoleOne. To toggle the screen to a text-based server screen (the more familiar server prompt for users who have worked with previous versions of NetWare), press Alt+Esc.

NOTE

If you specified during the installation program that you did not want the SERVER.EXE file executed from within AUTOEXEC.BAT, the server will not automatically load when the computer is rebooted. You will have to load the server manually from DOS. To do this, type CD NWSERVER to change to the correct directory, and then type SERVER.

Upgrading from Previous Versions of NetWare

There are two methods for upgrading servers from previous versions of NetWare to NetWare 5. The method you use depends on the version of NetWare you're currently running and the type of data transfer method you prefer. Depending on the version of NetWare you have, you will use either INSTALL or the Novell Upgrade Wizard to upgrade your server.

Upgrading from NetWare 4.1x

To upgrade an existing NetWare 4.1x (or intraNetWare) server to NetWare 5, you can use the regular server installation program (INSTALL) and choose the Upgrade From 3.1x or 4.x option. This is the simplest way to upgrade a server. With this option, the installation program copies new NetWare files and the new NetWare 5 operating system onto the existing server. It also upgrades Novell Directory Services.

Make sure the server you are upgrading meets the minimum qualifications for a NetWare 5 server. If the boot partition size is too small (minimum 50MB), you need to create a new boot partition and install the server using the New Server steps instead of using the Upgrade steps.

For instructions on upgrading a NetWare 4.1x server, see the section "Upgrade Using INSTALL."

Upgrading from NetWare 3.1x

There are two options for upgrading a NetWare 3.1x server to NetWare 5:

▶ Upgrade an existing NetWare 3.1x server to NetWare 5. You use INSTALL to upgrade an existing NetWare 3.1x server, just as you do if you are upgrading from NetWare 4.1x. You just need to make sure that the computer being used as the server meets all the hardware requirements for a NetWare 5 server. See the section "Upgrade Using INSTALL" for upgrade instructions.

► Transfer all of the NetWare 3.1x server's data to a new machine on which NetWare 5 has already been installed. This is called an across-the-wire migration or upgrade (because the data is transferred to another machine across the network cabling) and it requires the Novell Upgrade Wizard utility. This method of upgrading a server enables you to see and modify a model of how your Directory tree will look before you actually finish the migration. See the section "Upgrade Using the Novell Upgrade Wizard" for instructions.

When upgrading a NetWare 3.11 or 3.12 server, the server's existing bindery data is upgraded into a Novell Directory Services (NDS) database. All of the server's bindery objects become NDS objects, and they are all placed in the same location (name context) in the Directory tree as the server. In fact, the server itself will appear as a Server object in the Directory tree.

Binderies are specific to particular servers. This means that if you want user John to access three different NetWare 3.1x servers, you have to create John as a separate user on all three servers. With NDS, a single NDS database is common to all servers in the network. Therefore, you only need to create John once, and then just give him trustee rights to files on those three servers.

Keep this in mind if you are upgrading several NetWare 3.1x servers into a NetWare 5 Directory tree. If you have multiple instances of user John on different NetWare 3.1x servers, and you install the servers into the same location (name context), the installation program will ask you if you want to delete, rename, or merge the user with the one that already exists. If one of the NetWare 3.1x users named John is actually a different person than the other two Johns, you should rename one of them before starting the upgrade to ensure that they don't merge.

Upgrade Using INSTALL

INSTALL can be used to upgrade NetWare 3.1x and 4.1x servers to NetWare 5. With this utility, new files are copied from the CD-ROM to the existing server to upgrade it.

There are two halves of the installation program. The first half, which takes you through the hardware setup and creates volume SYS, is text-based and runs in DOS on the server. Throughout the text-based installation program, you usually have to choose between Modify and Continue at each screen. Choose Modify to make changes to the default values that the installation program offers. Choose Continue to accept the values and continue with the installation. In some screens, when you make changes to the values, you need to press F10 to save your changes and continue.

The second half of the installation program, which sets up the server's environment, switches to a graphical format, called the NetWare 5 Installation Wizard. During this portion of the installation (which is running in Java), you can use a mouse.

The following sections explain how to upgrade a server.

Setting Up the Server Hardware and Volume SYS

Complete the following steps to set up the server hardware and create the volume SYS:

1. Because deleted files in NetWare 3.1x and 4.1x remain on the server in a salvageable state, you may want to see whether there are any deleted files you want to salvage before you upgrade the server. The upgrade process will purge any deleted files still on the server.

2. Make two backups of all network files.

3. Copy the server's LAN drivers and AUTOEXEC.NCF files from the SYS: volume onto a diskette, so you can have backups of these files if necessary.

4. If necessary, edit the existing AUTOEXEC.NCF file to specify the Ethernet frame type you want. NetWare 3.12, 4.11, and 5 use Ethernet 802.2 by default. (NetWare 3.11 used Ethernet 802.3 by default.)

5. Bring down the existing server by entering the following console command:

   DOWN

6. If you are upgrading from NetWare 3.1x, rename the SERVER.31x directory to NWSERVER.

7. If necessary, set up the server hardware.

   a. Install and configure network boards in the server. Refer to the network board manufacturer's documentation for configuration instructions.

b. Install the CD-ROM drive as a DOS device on the server, following the manufacturer's instructions.

c. Using the DOS DATE and TIME commands, verify that the computer's date and time are set correctly, and change them if necessary.

d. Edit the CONFIG.SYS file to make sure it contains the following commands. (You will have to reboot the computer to make these commands take effect.)

```
FILES=40
BUFFERS=30
```

8. Insert the *NetWare 5 Operating System* CD-ROM into the computer's CD-ROM drive.

9. From the DOS command prompt, change to the CD-ROM drive's letter (usually D), and enter the following command:

```
INSTALL
```

(If you boot the server from the *NetWare 5 Operating System* CD-ROM, the installation program will automatically launch.)

10. If prompted, choose the language you want to use.

11. Read the Terms and Conditions that outline the license agreement for using NetWare 5, and then press F10 (or select Accept the Agreement) to accept the agreement.

12. From the screen that appears, choose Upgrade From 3.1x or 4.1x, and then select a startup directory. The default startup directory (where the server's startup files will be located) is C:\NWSERVER.

13. (Optional) From the same screen, press F2 to specify advanced settings. From the Advanced Settings screen, you can make the following changes:

a. If necessary, choose whether you want the installation program to access the CD-ROM drive through a NetWare driver or a DOS device. If possible, choose NetWare. However, if a NetWare driver doesn't exist for your CD-ROM drive, you can choose DOS.

b. If necessary, specify that you do not want the AUTOEXEC.BAT file to automatically load the server (SERVER.EXE). If you do not allow AUTOEXEC.BAT to automatically load the server, you will have to load the server by typing **SERVER** at the DOS prompt anytime the server is rebooted.

c. If necessary, specify any particular SET parameters that may be required by your device drivers.

14. Select your computer's mouse type and video type.

At this point, the installation program copies files, including device drivers, to the DOS partition.

15. Select your computer's device drivers. At this point, you can select Platform Support Modules (if your computer supports more than one processor), Hot Plug Support Modules (if your computer supports PCI Hot Plug technology), and Storage Adapters. If the installation program detects any of these drivers or a storage adapter (board), it will display them for you. If the information is correct, choose Continue. If not, choose Modify and specify the drivers you need. You can also configure the drivers at this point. (If the installation program does not detect any PSM or Hot Plug drivers, your computer probably does not support these technologies.)

16. Select your computer's storage devices (which are controlled by the adapters you chose in Step 15) and network boards. If the installation program detects any of these devices or network boards, it will display them for you. If the information is correct, choose Continue. If not, choose Modify and specify the drivers you need. You can also configure the drivers at this point. (This screen also lets you specify any optional NLMs that are required for the installation program to continue. For example, you can load ROUTE.NLM if you are installing the server into a Token Ring network.)

At this point, the installation program mounts volume SYS and begins copying files to it. Then the installation program launches the NetWare 5 Installation Wizard, a graphical program that takes you through the rest of the server installation, as explained in the following sections.

Setting Up the Server's Environment

Continue with the following steps to set up the server's environment:

1. (Optional) If your server has available disk space that has not been converted into a volume yet, you can configure new volumes now. If all the available disk space has already been taken up by volumes, skip to Step 2. If you are prompted to create new volumes, but you do not want to create new volumes now, click Next and skip to Step 2. If you do want to create new volumes, complete the following steps:

a. Click the Free Space in the list of volumes, and then click Create.

b. Enter a volume name.

c. Select whether you want the volume to be a Traditional volume or an NSS volume. (See Chapter 8 for more information about the difference.)

d. Enter the size of the volume in the Space to Use field, and then click Apply to Volume.

e. Click OK to return to the list of volumes, and then click Next to continue.

2. Specify whether you want to mount volumes now or when the server reboots after the installation is complete. If you want to install some Novell products during this installation procedure to volumes other than SYS, choose to mount the volumes now. Otherwise, if you intend only to install products into SYS, you can choose to mount the volumes later.

3. When the Protocols screen appears, click the server in the diagram to display the network boards installed in it. Because previous versions of NetWare used the IPX protocol, this server already has IPX installed. You cannot remove IPX during an upgrade. However, you can add IP to the server, or you can specify that you want to retain only IPX.

4. Click a network board, and choose the protocol you want to use for that board. You can click IP to add it, or you can leave only IPX checked. If you choose IP, you must also specify the server's IP address and subnet mask. You can also specify a router address if you need to (or leave that field blank to allow the network to find the nearest router automatically).

5. If you are upgrading from NetWare 3.1x, select the time zone in which this server will exist. (NetWare 4.1x servers already have this information stored.) If your location uses Daylight Saving Time, make sure the box is checked to allow for that adjustment.

6. Choose whether you want to create a new NDS tree or install this server into an existing NDS tree. Then click Next.

7. If you are upgrading a NetWare 4.1x server that already has NDS installed, enter the Admin user's name and password. Then skip to Step 9.

8. If you are upgrading a server that does not have NDS already installed (such as a bindery-based NetWare 3.1x server), you have to set up NDS information now.

    a. If you are upgrading this server into an existing tree, enter the tree name. If you are upgrading this server and creating a new tree, enter a name for the new tree.

    b. Create a context for the server. By entering the name of the organization (such as your company) and the names of descending levels of Organizational Units (such as a division and a department), you actually create the branch of the NDS tree that will contain this server if the branch doesn't already exist. If a branch already exists, click the Browse button and select the Organizational Unit objects you want.

    c. Enter a name, context, and password for the Admin user. If this is the first server in the tree, enter any password you want. If this server is being installed into an existing tree, type in the Admin name and password that has already been assigned or enter the name and password of another User object already in the NDS tree. This User object must have enough NDS trustee rights to add the server to the context specified. See Chapter 7 for more information about NDS trustee rights.

9. At the summary screen that appears, review the information. Record the Admin's name and context for future reference. Then click Next to continue.

10. When prompted, insert the license diskette and specify the location of the license file (usually A:\LICENSE\). Then click Next to continue.

11. After the remaining files are copied to the server, the Additional Products and Services screen appears. Choose any additional products you want to install, such as NDPS, NDS Catalog Services, or Novell PKI Services. It is strongly recommended that you choose NDPS, as well as any others that are checked by default. You can click each service to see a description of that service at the bottom of the screen. When finished selecting the products you want, click Next to continue.

12. Depending on the products you selected, you may receive additional screens to specify information for those products. Follow the prompts on the screen.

13. When the Summary screen appears, review the list of products to be installed. At this point, you can either click Finish to complete the installation, or you can customize the properties of some of the products you've selected, as explained in the following steps. To finish the installation, skip to Step 20. To customize products you've selected, continue with Step 14.

14. Click the Customize button.

15. (Optional) If you want to customize the protocols you've chosen to use, select Protocols, and then click the Properties button. (You may have to open the NetWare Operating System in the diagram to display Protocols.) This option lets you install a Migration Agent, specify a domain name and name servers, and set up SNMP notification information.

   a. On the Protocols tab, you can change the protocol choices you made earlier in the installation program. You can also specify a particular IPX frame type, if necessary.

   b. On the IPX Compatibility tab, you can choose to load the Migration Agent on this server by checking the appropriate box. A Migration Agent functions like a gateway between IP and IPX network segments.

   c. On the Domain Name Service tab, you can specify the domain name your company uses, such as blue.com. You can also enter the IP addresses of any domain name servers you want NetWare 5 to use. The name server is a computer that translates names into IP addresses.

   d. On the SNMP tab, you can specify the type of information about this server that you want to be sent whenever an event occurs (such as the server's hardware description, its location, and the name of the responsible administrator). You can also specify which node (workstation or server) is notified when the event occurs by entering either the node's IPX or IP address.

   e. When finished customizing the network protocol information, click OK to return to the Product Customization screen.

16. (Optional) If you want to customize NDS, select NDS from the Product Customization screen, and then click the Properties button. This option enables you to modify the NDS tree and time zone information you entered earlier in the installation program. It also lets you modify the default time synchronization information.

   a. On the NDS Summary tab, make any modifications to the NDS tree name, the server's context, or the administrator's name and context.

   b. On the Time Zone tab, you can change the time zone information you selected earlier. You can also specify when your location begins and ends Daylight Saving Time.

   c. On the Time Synchronization tab, you can change this server's time server designation. If you have fewer than 30 servers on your network, and they are all in the same geographical area, you will probably want to retain the default designation (the first server installed is a Single Reference server, and all subsequent servers in the tree are Secondary servers). If you have more than 30 servers in the tree, or if your network contains WAN links, see Chapter 3 for information on how best to plan your time server setup.

   d. When finished customizing the NDS information, click OK to return to the Product Customization screen.

17. (Optional) If you want to customize NDPS printing information, select Novell Distributed Print Service (NDPS) from the Product Customization screen, and then click the Properties button. This option enables you to specify whether or not to create an NDPS Broker on this server. It also lets you disable any of the three services that the NDPS Broker handles: Service Registry Service, Event Notification Service, and Resource Management Service. (See Chapter 9 for more information about planning your NDPS printing setup.) When finished customizing the NDPS information, click OK to return to the Product Customization screen.

18. (Optional) If you want to customize other products you've selected to install, repeat the same process. Select the product, click the Properties button, and then open any configuration tabs and specify the information you want to change. When finished, click OK to return to the Product Customization screen.

19. When you've finished customizing products, click Close from the Product Customization screen.

20. From the Summary screen, click Finish. The installation program will finish installing all the products you've selected.

21. When asked if you want to reboot the server, click Yes. (You can also choose to view the readme file before rebooting the server.) Remove the installation CD before you reboot the server.

22. (NetWare 3.1x upgrades only) If you have upgraded a NetWare 3.1x server, you should run DSREPAIR.NLM on the server to verify the integrity of all new NDS information. After the server reboots and brings up the graphical server desktop, press Alt+Esc to go to the server's text-based screen. At the prompt, type **DSREPAIR**. Then select Unattended Full Repair.

When the computer reboots, it will automatically load the server. When the server is running, you will see the server desktop — a graphical screen that can display utilities. To bring up the ConsoleOne utility, click the Novell button at the bottom of the screen and select ConsoleOne. To toggle the screen to a text-based server screen (the more familiar server prompt for users who have worked with previous versions of NetWare), press Alt+Esc.

NOTE If you specified during the installation program that you did not want the SERVER.EXE file executed from within AUTOEXEC.BAT, the server will not automatically load when the computer is rebooted. You will have to load the server manually from DOS. To do this, type CD NWSERVER to change to the correct directory, and then type SERVER.

Upgrade Using the Novell Upgrade Wizard

The Novell Upgrade Wizard can be used to upgrade NetWare 3.1x servers to NetWare 5. Use this upgrade method if you want to replace your old server computer with a new computer.

To upgrade a server this way, you actually install a new NetWare 5 server elsewhere on the network (using the procedure described in the section "Installing a New Server"). Then you log in to both the NetWare 3.1x network and the NetWare 5 network from a workstation that's running the Novell Upgrade Wizard utility.

The first step in using the Wizard utility is to create a "project" — a model that lets you place the NetWare 3.1x bindery objects into the NDS tree. With this project, you can safely model the proposed NDS information so that it will be converted into the NDS tree the way you want it. From the main project window, you can simply "drag and drop" the NetWare 3.1x server's bindery and volume objects to desired locations in the NDS tree. You can add or delete objects, move them around, assign trustee rights, and so on, without actually affecting the tree. When you have created the project the way you want, you can then migrate the bindery objects and the file system into the NDS tree.

The bindery information that gets migrated includes all user accounts and their properties, printing objects, the system login script (which gets added to the NDS container's login script), print job configurations, and trustee assignments.

When the NetWare 3.1x server's printing information is migrated to the NDS tree, it is set up in a queue-based printing system. It is not migrated to the NDPS printing system. For more information about the difference between the two printing systems available in NetWare 5, see Chapter 9.

After the bindery information is migrated, the old server's volumes are migrated. The files in those volumes are copied to folders you specify under volumes in the NDS tree.

Preparing the NetWare 3.1x Server

Before you can run the Novell Upgrade Wizard, you must prepare the NetWare 3.1x server for the upgrade. To prepare the server, you must install the Wizard utility on your workstation. (The Wizard is not installed automatically during the NetWare 5 installation.) Then you must also back up (or salvage) any files you want to keep from the old server, run BINDFIX to delete any unnecessary mail directories, copy new NLMs to the NetWare 3.1x server, and so on, as explained in the following procedure.

The Wizard utility is located on the *NetWare 5 Operating System* CD-ROM. You must install it on a Windows 95/98 or Windows NT workstation before you can use it to upgrade a server. (The workstation must be running the Novell Client software that came with NetWare 5, or a later version.) To install the Wizard and prepare to run the upgrade procedure, complete the following steps:

1. Insert the *NetWare 5 Operating System* CD-ROM into a drive on the workstation you will be using to run the utility.

2. From the CD-ROM, run the file called UPGRDWZD.EXE, located in the PRODUCTS\UPGRDWZD folder. This is a self-extracting file, which will install the necessary files on the workstation.

3. At the Welcome screen, click Next.

4. At the License screen, read the agreement and click Accept.

5. Accept the default location on the workstation for the Upgrade Wizard, and then click Finish. The Wizard and its related files are installed on the workstation.

6. When the Wizard installation is finished, click OK.

7. Ask all users to log out of the NetWare 3.1x server.

8. Because deleted files in NetWare 3.1x remain on the server in a salvageable state, you may want to see whether there are any deleted files you want to salvage before you upgrade the server. The upgrade process will purge any deleted files still on the server.

9. Run BINDFIX on the old server to delete any MAIL directories for users who no longer exist.

10. Make two backups of all network files.

11. If you haven't already, install the NetWare 5 server on a new machine. See "Installing a New Server" earlier in this chapter.

12. Copy the following files from the workstation (in the folder C:\Program Files\Novell\Upgrade\products\nw3x) to the SYS:SYSTEM directory on the old NetWare 3.1x server. These are new versions of these NLMs, which are necessary for the Wizard to run.

- TSA311.NLM or TSA312.NLM (use the version that matches your server's version number)
- SMDR.NLM
- SPXS.NLM
- TLI.NLM
- AFTER311.NLM
- CLIB.NLM
- A3112.NLM
- STREAMS.NLM
- MAC.NAM (if the NetWare 3.1x server stores Macintosh files)

13. Reboot the NetWare 3.1x server, so that the new NLMs take effect.

14. Load the new TSA311.NLM (or TSA312.NLM) by typing the following command (substitute TSA312 if your server is running NetWare 3.12):

```
LOAD TSA311
```

15. If the NetWare 3.1x server contains Macintosh files, add the Macintosh name space to the NetWare 5 volumes that will contain the files after the upgrade. To do this, load the MAC.NAM name space module by typing the following commands at the NetWare 5 server console. Substitute the name of the volume that will store the Macintosh files for *volume*.

```
LOAD MAC
ADD NAME SPACE MAC TO volume
```
Now you are ready to run the Wizard.

Starting the Novell Upgrade Wizard

To begin upgrading a NetWare 3.1x server to a new NetWare 5 server, complete the following steps:

1. From the workstation that has the Upgrade Wizard installed, launch the Wizard. To do this, open the Windows 95/98 or Windows NT Start menu. Then select Programs, then Novell, and then Novell Upgrade Wizard. Choose Novell Upgrade Wizard.

2. Select Create a New Upgrade Wizard Project and click OK.

3. Enter a name for this project, and select the location where you want the project to be saved. Then click Next.

4. Select the NetWare 3.1x server you want to migrate (the "source").

5. Select the destination NDS tree into which you want the bindery information and file system to be migrated.

6. Click Next to continue.

7. When a screen appears showing information about the Wizard's database, click Create. The project window appears, showing the source server's bindery and volumes in the left-hand panel and the destination NDS tree in the right-hand panel.

8. (Optional) If you want to create a new container in the NDS tree for the bindery, or a new folder in the tree to contain the NetWare 3.1x server's volumes, do this now. Right-click a container object or folder to create a new container object or folder beneath it.

9. Click and drag the NetWare 3.1x server's bindery to the desired container object in the NDS tree.

10. Click and drag each of the NetWare 3.1x server's volumes to a volume or folder in the NDS tree.

Next, you will verify that the project you've created will run without problems, as described in the next section.

Verifying the Project

Complete the following steps to verify the project you've created:

1. From the Project menu, choose Verify Project, and then click Next at the overview screen. The verification process looks for any potential problems with the migration, such as object conflicts, disk space limitations, sufficient trustee rights, and so on.

2. When prompted to decide if you want to migrate the NetWare 3.1x server's print information, leave the checkbox marked. (If you do not want to migrate print information, clear the box.) Then select the volume where you want the print information to reside, and click Next.

3. If you want to create a Template object to apply to all the users you will be migrating, leave the appropriate checkbox marked.

- To use an existing Template object, locate and select the object, and then click Next.

- To create a new Template object to use, click Create a Template Object. Then enter a name for the Template object and click Next. This Template object will include the default account balance and restrictions (such as password requirements and other login restrictions) from the NetWare 3.1x Supervisor user. (Use the SYSCON utility on the NetWare 3.1x server to see the Supervisor's restrictions.)

4. Select how you want to handle occurrences of duplicate file names while the NetWare 3.1x files are being migrated, and then click Next.

5. Enter passwords for the source server and for the destination tree, and then click Next.

6. Choose the categories that you want to be verified by marking the appropriate checkboxes, and then click Next. The verification process will run.

7. If any naming conflicts are found between objects of the same type, they will be displayed. Select each object and then choose how you want to resolve the conflict. (If you do not choose a conflict resolution option, the object will be renamed.)

8. If any naming conflicts are found between objects of different types or objects that cannot be merged together (such as print forms, print devices, and print configurations), select each object and then choose how you want to resolve the conflict. (If you do not choose a conflict resolution option, the object will be renamed.)

9. If any errors or warnings occurred during the verification process, they will be displayed. Resolve each error before clicking Next to continue.

10. When the verification summary page appears, review it and then click Finish.

Now you are ready to run the upgrade itself, as explained in the next section.

Running the Upgrade Program

Complete the following steps to upgrade the server according to the project you've defined. You will go through many of the same steps you completed during the verification phase — any issues that were not resolved during the verification phase will reappear during the upgrade phase, so you can try again to resolve them.

1. From the Project menu, select Start Migration.

2. At the overview screen, click Next.

3. When prompted to decide if you want to migrate the NetWare 3.1x server's print information, leave the checkbox marked. (If you do not want to migrate print information, clear the box.) Then select the volume where you want the print information to reside, and click Next.

4. If you want to create a Template object to apply to all the users you will be migrating, leave the appropriate checkbox marked. Then locate and select the Template object, and click Next.

5. Select how you want to handle occurrences of duplicate file names while the NetWare 3.1x files are being migrated, and then click Next.

6. Enter passwords for the source server and for the destination tree, and then click Next.

7. Choose the categories that you want to be verified by marking the appropriate checkboxes, and then click Next. The verification process will run again.

8. If any conflicts or errors are found, they will be displayed. Any conflicts that were displayed during verification but were not corrected

are indicated by a checked icon, showing that you have already seen the conflict. Select each object and then choose how you want to resolve the conflict.

9. When the summary page appears, review it, and then click Proceed to continue. The Upgrade Wizard now converts and transfers the bindery objects into the NDS tree. Then it will migrate all of the files in the NetWare 3.1x volumes to their new locations in the NetWare 5 volumes.

10. When the migration is complete, you can choose to read the Success Log or the Error Log, or you can click Close.

After the migration is complete, you may need to perform some or all of the following additional tasks to complete the upgrade:

▶ Use the NetWare Administrator to view the tree and verify that all of the users, groups, print objects, and files all migrated successfully and ended up where you expected. Also verify and make modifications, if necessary, to trustee rights and other associated properties.

▶ Review all system and user login scripts and make any necessary changes to remove references to old servers, outdated print queues, and so on. The server's system login script was attached to the container object.

▶ Move any printers that were connected directly to the NetWare 3.1x server. You may need to install printer software on the new server. See Chapter 9 for more information about printing.

▶ If the NetWare 3.1x server had a printer server running on it (PSERVER.NLM), unload it. Then load PSERVER.NLM on the NetWare 5 server. (You must unload the NetWare 3.1x print server before loading the NetWare 5 print server to avoid any name conflicts on the network.)

▶ When you've evaluated the migrated data's final state, you can erase all the information from the old server and convert it into a workstation.

CHAPTER 3

Managing the Server

Instant Access

Optimizing Performance

- ▶ To monitor performance, use MONITOR.NLM.

- ▶ To optimize performance, use MONITOR.NLM to change server parameters (or change the same server parameters from the console using SET commands).

- ▶ To manage server memory, use MONITOR.NLM and the MEMORY, MEMORY MAP, and REGISTER MEMORY console utilities.

- ▶ Manage a virtual memory swap file using the SWAP console utility.

- ▶ To see a history of errors that have occurred with the server, the volume, or TTS, use a text editor or EDIT.NLM to read the error log files: SYS$LOG.ERR, VOL$LOG.ERR, TTS$LOG.ERR, BOOT$LOG.ERR, and ABEND.LOG.

- ▶ To capture server messages to a screen so you can read them for diagnostic purposes, use CONLOG.NLM.

Running Java Applications

- ▶ To run Java applications or applets on a server, specify a Just In Time (JIT) compiler and load JAVA.NLM on the server.

Protecting the Server

- ▶ To use an uninterruptible power supply (UPS) to protect the server from power outages, use UPS_AIO.NLM or third-party UPS-management software.

- ▶ To protect the server and network from virus infections, use a virus detector, assign executable files the Execute Only file or Read-Only attributes, and warn users against loading files from external sources.

- ▶ To keep faulty NLMs from corrupting server memory, load them in protected address spaces using the PROTECTED load command.

Maintaining the Server

- ▶ To display a server name, use the NAME console utility.

- ▶ To display the server's hardware information, use the CONFIG, CPUCHECK, and LIST DEVICES console utilities.

- To display the server's version information, use the VERSION console utility.

- To display a list of the server's volumes and the name spaces they support, use the VOLUMES console utility.

- To bring down the server, use the DOWN console utility.

- To reboot the server, use the RESTART SERVER console utility.

- To obtain patches and updated modules, download them from Novell's Web site (www.novell.com).

- To control the server from a workstation, use the Remote Console feature.

- To control server startup activities, use the server startup files: AUTOEXEC.NCF and STARTUP.NCF. (Edit these files by using EDIT.NLM.)

- To manage workstation connections, use MONITOR.NLM and the ENABLE LOGIN and DISABLE LOGIN console utilities.

- To charge for server usage, use the accounting services in the NetWare Administrator utility and ATOTAL.

- To monitor or modify a server's time, use the SYSTIME workstation utility and the TIME, SET TIME, and SET TIME ZONE console utilities.

- Use TIMESYNC.NLM to manage time synchronization between servers on a tree.

- To unload or display currently loaded NLMs, use the UNLOAD and MODULES console utilities.

Managing Storage Devices

- To add a new hard disk or replace an existing one, use NWCONFIG.NLM.

- To add or remove a PCI Hot Plug adapter, use NCMCON.NLM.

- To protect network data by mirroring hard disks, use NWCONFIG.NLM and the MIRROR STATUS, REMIRROR PARTITION, and ABORT REMIRROR console utilities.

▶ To protect network data from bad blocks on the hard disk, use the Hot Fix feature. Set up Hot Fix during installation or when creating a new partition. Monitor the number of bad blocks found with NWCONFIG.NLM.

▶ To mount CD-ROMs as network volumes, use CDROM.NLM.

Managing Routing Between Servers

▶ To list networks, use the DISPLAY NETWORKS console utility.

▶ To list servers, use the DISPLAY SERVERS console utility.

▶ To execute protocol configuration commands made using INETCFG.NLM, use the INITIALIZE SYSTEM and REINITIALIZE SYSTEM console utilities.

▶ To configure protocols, use INETCFG.NLM.

▶ To configure IPX, AppleTalk, and TCP/IP protocols, use INETCFG.NLM.

▶ To configure RIP/SAP packet filtering, use FILTCFG.NLM.

▶ To display routing information, use the TRACK ON and TRACK OFF console utilities.

Managing a NetWare Server

Managing a NetWare server involves many different types of tasks, from monitoring performance to adding new hard disks to charging customers for their usage. This chapter will start by explaining some of the tools and utilities you will use to manage the server. Then we will look at the different types of server management tasks you will need to perform as you manage a NetWare 5 network, such as:

- ▸ Monitoring and optimizing server performance
- ▸ Protecting the server
- ▸ Performing typical server maintenance tasks
- ▸ Installing and replacing server hardware, such as hard disks and network boards
- ▸ Working with CD-ROMs as network volumes
- ▸ Changing server startup files
- ▸ Setting up server-based accounting
- ▸ Synchronizing time between all the network servers

Server Tools

There are three types of tools you can use when you work with the NetWare server: console utilities, the ConsoleOne management utility, and NetWare Loadable Modules.

Console utilities are commands you type at the server's console (keyboard and monitor) to change some aspect of the server or view information about it. These console utilities are built into the operating system, just as internal DOS commands are built into DOS. To read online help for console utilities, type the following command at the server's console, replacing *utility* with the name of the utility whose help you want to read:

```
HELP utility
```

For example, to read help about the SCAN FOR NEW DEVICES console utility, type:

```
HELP SCAN FOR NEW DEVICES
```

To see a list of all the available console utilities, just type **HELP**.

The ConsoleOne management utility is a Java-based utility that runs either on the server or on a workstation, provided the server or workstation is running a Java engine. The ConsoleOne utility combines many of the management tasks available in other console utilities or NLMs, so you can execute server management tasks from a single utility. ConsoleOne gives the server a graphical interface, much like using an application in Windows instead of in DOS. ConsoleOne is explained later in this chapter.

NetWare Loadable Modules (NLMs) are software modules that you load into the server's operating system to add or change functionality. Many NLMs are automatically installed with the NetWare operating system. Others are optional; you can load them if your particular situation requires them. There are four common types of NetWare Loadable Modules you can use to add different types of functionality to your server: NLMs, name space modules, LAN drivers, and storage drivers (also called disk drivers). These NLMs are described in Table 3.1. Many third-party software manufacturers create different types of NLMs to work on NetWare 5. Additional types of NLMs, such as PSMs (Platform Support Modules, which support multiprocessor computer devices) also exist. Table 3.1 lists only the four most common types of NLMs.

T A B L E 3.1	*Different Types of NLMs*	
TYPE OF NLM	**FILENAME EXTENSION**	**DESCRIPTION**
NLM	.NLM	Changes or adds to the server's functionality. Such an NLM might allow you to back up network files, add support for another protocol, or add support for devices such as a CD-ROM drive or a UPS (uninterruptible power supply).
Name space module	.NAM	Allows the operating system to store Macintosh, OS/2, Windows NT, Windows 95/98, or NFS files, along with their unique file formats, long filenames, and other characteristics.

TYPE OF NLM	FILENAME EXTENSION	DESCRIPTION
LAN driver	.LAN	Enables the operating system to communicate with a network board installed in the server.
Storage driver	.CDM and .HAM	Enables the operating system to communicate with a storage device (such as a hard disk) and its controller board (also called adapter) installed in the server. The .CDM driver (custom device module) drives the storage device. Its accompanying .HAM driver (host adapter module) drives the storage device's adapter. You need both drivers for a single storage device. The .CDM and .HAM drivers replace the older .DSK drivers used in previous versions of NetWare.

You can load and unload NLMs while the server is running. Many NLMs have their own status screen that displays on the server. To move between NLM screens on the server's console, use Alt+Esc to cycle through the available NLM screens and use Ctrl+Esc to bring up a list of available screens, from which you can select one.

To load an NLM, simply type the NLM's name at the server console. You do not need to include the NLM's filename extension. For example, to load MONITOR.NLM, type:

```
MONITOR
```

NOTE

In previous versions of NetWare, to load an NLM you had to type the command LOAD, followed by the NLM's name. In NetWare 5, however, you no longer need to type the command LOAD. Simply typing the NLM's name will load it.

To unload an NLM, type the following command, substituting the name of the module for *module*:

UNLOAD *module*

To see a list of all the NLMs currently loaded on the server, type:

MODULES

Using ConsoleOne

A new feature of NetWare 5 is the GUI server desktop. (GUI stands for graphical user interface.) The GUI server desktop provides a graphical mouse-oriented screen on the server, as opposed to the traditional text-based server screens. The main application that runs on the server desktop at this release is ConsoleOne, a management utility. The server desktop and ConsoleOne are Java-based, and run on top of the Java Virtual Machine running in the server.

The first release of ConsoleOne contained in NetWare 5 is a relatively simple administrative application, encompassing some of the features of other familiar NetWare utilities, such as MONITOR and NetWare Administrator. ConsoleOne is built in a modular fashion so that future modules, called *snapins*, can be added to it as they are developed.

At this point, you can use ConsoleOne to do the following types of tasks:

► List volumes, folders, and files on the server

► Create and delete folders

► Edit the server's configuration (NCF) files

► Use the Java-based Remote Console to access another server's console

► Show NDS objects in the NDS tree, and display their properties (like the information displayed in NetWare Administrator)

► Create Organization, Organizational Unit, User, and Group objects in the tree

► Execute Java applets (small Java-based applications)

NOTE   Being a Java-based application, ConsoleOne can also run on workstations, but with more limited functionality. See the Novell documentation for more information about running ConsoleOne on the workstation.

By default, the blank server desktop automatically loads whenever the server is booted, but ConsoleOne does not. You can switch from the desktop screen to other NLM screens active on the server by pressing Alt+Esc, as normal.

When the server desktop is active, you can change the server desktop's keyboard properties, display properties, or background. To do this, click the Novell button in the bottom corner (or click anywhere on the screen, for that matter) and select Tools from the menu that appears. Then choose the option you want to change and follow the prompts that appear.

To unload the server desktop, click the Novell button and choose Exit GUI. Then, to restart the desktop, type the following command at the server prompt:

STARTX

To load ConsoleOne from the server desktop, click the Novell button and select ConsoleOne from the menu that appears. When ConsoleOne loads, you must log in to NDS by typing in the tree name, your context, your user name, and your password.

If the desktop has been unloaded, you can start the desktop and ConsoleOne at the same time by typing the following command at the server prompt:

C1START

Because of the capabilities of Java at this time, you'll probably find that ConsoleOne is much slower, and uses much more memory than comparable Windows-based applications. (ConsoleOne requires 64MB minimum on the server and 64MB on the workstation, plus a virtual memory swap file of equal size.) However, with technology advancing the way it is, future versions will probably be much more appealing. At this point, ConsoleOne is more a useful demonstration of things to come than a viable management tool. Because of this, this book will concentrate on using the administrative utilities that are faster and more convenient, such as NetWare Administrator. However, feel free to explore and use ConsoleOne. For more information about ConsoleOne, see the Novell online documentation or the online help inside ConsoleOne itself.

Stopping and Starting the Server

If you need to shut down or reboot the server, try to make sure users have been notified and have been given time to close any files on that server that they were using. Then, shut down the server by typing:

DOWN

This will stop the NetWare server operating system from running on this computer, and will return the computer to DOS. From the DOS prompt, you can turn off the computer, reboot it, or restart the server.

If you want, you can reboot the server without first bringing the computer back to DOS. To simply reboot the server, instead of typing DOWN, type the following command at the server's prompt:

RESTART SERVER

To start the server from the DOS prompt, go to the NWSERVER directory and type the following command:

SERVER

Typing SERVER executes SERVER.EXE, which loads the NetWare operating system on the computer, turning it back into a server.

By default, the following commands are added to the computer's AUTOEXEC.BAT file during server installation so that the server automatically starts up whenever the computer is rebooted:

CD NWSERVER

SERVER

If you do not want the server to automatically start when the computer is rebooted, you can edit the AUTOEXEC.BAT file to remove these commands. Then you will have to execute these commands manually to restart the server.

Using Remote Console to Control the Server from a Workstation

To control the server from a workstation, you can temporarily transform your workstation into a "remote console." With the Remote Console feature running, you can enter console utilities and load NLMs, and the commands you execute will work just as if you were using the server's real keyboard and monitor. Using Remote Console enables you to access the server from any workstation on the network, which gives you greater freedom when administering your network.

NetWare 5 contains two different versions of Remote Console: a Java version and a DOS version. The Java version can run on any workstation or server that is running a Java engine, whereas the DOS version can run on DOS workstations, or in a DOS box on a Windows workstation. In NetWare 5, the Java-based version of Remote Console and the DOS-based Remote Console can perform most of the same tasks, with the following exceptions:

▶ The Java-based version cannot be used to transfer files to a server, whereas the DOS-based version can.

▶ The Java-based version cannot be used to remotely install or upgrade a server, whereas the DOS-based version can.

▶ The DOS-based version requires an IPX connection, and the Java-based version requires an IP connection (but can access IPX servers through a proxy server).

▶ Only the Java-based version can control one server from another server. The DOS-based version cannot run on a server, so you can't control one server from another's console using the DOS-based version.

The following sections explain how to run both versions of Remote Console.

Setting Up the DOS-Based Remote Console

The DOS-based version of Remote Console can run on DOS workstations, or in a DOS box on a Windows workstation. The following sections explain how to establish a connection for DOS-based Remote Console, and how to use it.

You can use the DOS-based Remote Console over a direct connection to the network or via asynchronous lines through a modem. The DOS-based Remote Console requires an IPX connection. You cannot use it on an IP-only network. (For IP-only networks, see "Setting Up the Java-Based Remote Console" later in this chapter.)

To establish a Remote Console session, you first activate Remote Console functionality on the server, and then you load RCONSOLE on the workstation. The following sections explain how to perform these tasks over a direct connection and over a modem.

NOTE

In general, Remote Console should work when running inside a DOS box in Windows. However, Windows can exhibit some peculiarities when running programs in DOS boxes, so if Remote Console has problems running in a DOS box, run it in native DOS instead.

Establishing a Direct Network Connection

To run Remote Console over a direct network connection, complete the following steps:

1. Load RSPX.NLM (which automatically loads REMOTE.NLM) on the server by typing the following command at the server's console:

`RSPX`

2. When you load RSPX.NLM, you are asked for a password. Enter any password you choose. (You will have to supply this same password when you use Remote Console from the workstation.)

3. From the workstation, make sure a search drive is mapped to SYS:PUBLIC to give the workstation access to the Remote Console files.

4. Launch the Remote Console software from the workstation by using one of the following methods:

- From the NetWare Administrator utility, open the Tools menu, and then choose Remote Console.

- From the Windows Start or Run option, locate and execute the RCONSOLE.EXE file in the SYS:PUBLIC folder.

- From the workstation's DOS prompt (or from a DOS box inside Windows), type:

`RCONSOLE`

5. From the Connection Type menu, choose LAN.

6. Select the server to which you want to connect.

7. Enter the Remote Console password you assigned when you loaded RSPX.NLM.

8. When the console prompt appears on the workstation's screen, you can begin your Remote Console work.

Establishing a Modem Connection

The Remote Console feature enables you to connect to the server over a modem line. You can choose to increase security by creating a *callback* list of authorized phone numbers for the server to check. When you use the Callback option, the server accepts the incoming call long enough to identify the phone number, and then disconnects. The server then verifies the incoming phone number with its callback list. If the number is listed, the server calls back the workstation and establishes a remote console connection. If the number isn't listed, the server does not call back the workstation.

If you don't use the Callback option, the server accepts the incoming call as long as the Remote Console user enters the correct Remote Console password. The server doesn't disconnect or call back the workstation.

To create a callback list on a server, use a text editor to create a text file called CALLBACK.LST in the server's SYS:SYSTEM directory. In the file, type a list of each phone number that is authorized to access the server. The phone numbers can include area codes if necessary, or they can be local numbers or even internal extensions. Use the exact number that the server must dial to access the workstation's modem. Remember to include any numbers required to obtain an outside line, if necessary (such as 9). For example, the following numbers could all be included in the same CALLBACK.LST file:

```
912125556197
312
95558312
```

The first number is a long-distance number, preceded by a 9 to obtain an outside line. The second number is an internal extension. The third number is a local number, again preceded by a 9 to obtain an outside line.

To run Remote Console over a modem (with or without the Callback option), complete the following steps:

1. Load REMOTE.NLM on the server by typing the following command at the server's console:

```
REMOTE
```

2. When you load REMOTE.NLM, you are asked for a password. Enter any password you choose. (You will have to supply this same password when you use Remote Console from the workstation.)

3. Load RS232.NLM on the server and, when prompted, enter the COM port and baud rate that the modem will use.

- If you don't want to use the callback option, just load RS232 by typing the following command:

  RS232

- If you do want to use the callback option, load RS232 with the "C" parameter:

  RS232 C

4. Load a communications port driver on the server. You may have a driver from the modem's manufacturer, or you can use the driver supplied with NetWare 5 (AIOCOMX.NLM). For example, to load AIOCOMX.NLM on the server, type:

  AIOCOMX

5. Create a directory on the workstation, and copy the following files from their network directories to the new workstation directory to give the workstation access to Remote Console files:

- RCONSOLE.EXE (located in SYS:PUBLIC)
- IBM_RUN.OVL (located in SYS:PUBLIC)
- _RUN.OVL (located in SYS:PUBLIC)
- IBM_AIO.OVL (located in SYS:PUBLIC)
- TEXTUTIL.IDX (located in SYS:PUBLIC)
- RCONSOLE.HEP (located in SYS:PUBLIC\NLS\ENGLISH)
- RCONSOLE.MSG (located in SYS:PUBLIC\NLS\ENGLISH)
- TEXTUTIL.HEP (located in SYS:PUBLIC\NLS\ENGLISH)
- TEXTUTIL.MSG (located in SYS:PUBLIC\NLS\ENGLISH)

6. Launch the Remote Console software from the workstation using one of the following methods:

- From the NetWare Administrator utility, open the Tools menu, and then choose Remote Console.
- From the Windows Start or Run option, locate and execute the RCONSOLE.EXE file in the SYS:PUBLIC folder.
- From the workstation's DOS prompt (or from a DOS box inside Windows), type:

  RCONSOLE

7. From the Connection Type menu, choose Asynchronous.

8. (Optional) If this is the first time you have run Remote Console from this workstation, choose Configuration. Enter the information about your modem. You also must enter a user ID (which can be any identifier you want to use, such as a name or phone number) and the Callback number (the modem's telephone number from which you are calling). When finished entering information, press Esc to exit the window, and answer Yes to save your data.

9. From the Asynchronous Options menu, choose Connect to Remote Location.

10. Select the server to which you want to connect and enter the remote console password you assigned when you loaded REMOTE.NLM.

If you used the Callback option, the server will disconnect the call at this point and call your workstation back if the modem number appears in the server's callback list.

11. When the console prompt appears on the workstation's screen, you can begin your Remote Console work.

Activating Remote Console on the Server from AUTOEXEC.NCF

When you establish a Remote Console session, the first step, as explained in the previous sections, is to activate Remote Console functionality on the server. The previous instructions showed how to activate this functionality manually. If you prefer, you can add commands to the server's AUTOEXEC.NCF file to ensure that every time the server is rebooted, the Remote Console feature is activated.

It is important to encrypt the Remote Console password in a special file in order to make the Remote Console feature more secure. The following steps explain how to add the Remote Console commands to the AUTOEXEC.NCF file and how to encrypt the password so that the server remains secure.

1. Load REMOTE.NLM by typing the following command at the server's console:

```
REMOTE
```

2. To encrypt the Remote Console password, type the following command:

```
REMOTE ENCRYPT
```

3. When prompted, enter the password you want to encrypt.

4. The server displays the command you will have to type in the future if you want to load REMOTE manually on the server and use this password. It also asks you if you want to write the command, including this encrypted password, to a file called LDREMOTE.NCF in the SYS:SYSTEM directory. To simplify your life, type *Y* to answer Yes. This stores the encrypted password in the LDREMOTE.NCF file. Then you won't have to remember the encrypted password.

5. Open the AUTOEXEC.NCF file to edit it. (To edit this file, you can load NWCONFIG.NLM, choose NCF Files Options, and then choose Edit AUTOEXEC.NCF File.)

6. At the end of the AUTOEXEC.NCF file, type the following command:

```
LDREMOTE
```

7. After the LDREMOTE command, add the additional command(s) to load the remaining Remote Console modules, as indicated:

- (LAN connections only) If you are connecting to the server via a direct network connection, add the following command:

```
LOAD RSPX
```

- (Modem connections only) If you are connecting to the server via modem, add the following commands. (In the LOAD RS232 command, substitute your modem's COM port for *port*, substitute your modem's baud rate for *baud*, and only use the "C" option if you want the server to use the Callback option.)

```
LOAD AIOCOMX
LOAD RS232 port baud C
```

8. Save the AUTOEXEC.NCF file and exit the text editor you were using.

Now, whenever the server is rebooted, Remote Console will automatically be loaded with the encrypted password.

Using the DOS-based Remote Console

When you execute a Remote Console session from a workstation, you can enter any commands and see any screens on the workstation just as they would be displayed on the server's own monitor. The only exception is the graphical interface used by ConsoleOne. Remote Console cannot display any graphical server screens. It can, however, display all text-based screens, such as those for MONITOR.NLM, the NDPS Broker, and so on.

When using Remote Console, you cannot load NLMs directly from your workstation's local drive. You can, however, load NLMs from the SYS:SYSTEM network directory. Therefore, when you are running Remote Console, press Alt+F1 and select the Transfer Files to Server option. With this option, you can copy files from your local drive to SYS:SYSTEM. Once they are in SYS:SYSTEM, you can load the NLMs with Remote Console as usual.

The keystrokes shown in Table 3.2 let you navigate through the Remote Console screen after you've executed RCONSOLE.

TABLE 3.2 *Remote Console Keystrokes*

KEYSTROKE	DESCRIPTION
F1	Displays help (may not work if using Remote Console from a DOS box inside Windows)
Alt+F1	Displays the Available Options menu
Alt+F2	Quits the Remote Console session
Alt+F3	Moves you forward through the current server screens
Alt+F4	Moves you backward through the current server screens
Alt+F5	Shows this workstation's address

Setting Up the Java-Based Remote Console

If your network is using IP, you must use the Java-based version of Remote Console, called RConsoleJ. The Java-based Remote Console enables you to connect to a server through an IP connection.

In addition, if you want to use the Java-based Remote Console to connect to an IPX server, you can. To do this, you have to install additional software on another IP server on the network, called a proxy server. Then, you can go through the proxy server to communicate with the IPX server.

You can run a Remote Console session from a Windows 95/98 or Windows NT workstation. In addition, you can use the Java-based Remote Console to run a Remote Console session from another server. This feature is new, and is not available in the DOS-based version of Remote Console.

NOVELL'S NETWARE 5 ADMINISTRATOR'S HANDBOOK

To set up a Java-based Remote Console, you will run the following software:

▶ Remote Console agent software on the target server (this is the server whose console you want to access remotely)

▶ RConsoleJ software on the workstation or server from which you want to run the Remote Console session

▶ If necessary, proxy software on another server if the target server you're accessing runs IPX

The following sections explain how to set up, run, and start the Java-based Remote Console.

Setting Up an IP Target Server

The target server is the server whose console you want to access during the Remote Console session. The target server can run on either IP or IPX.

To prepare a target server that runs on IP, complete the following steps.

1. At the target server's console prompt, type the following command:

RCONAG6

2. When you load RCONAG6.NLM, you are asked for a password. Enter any password you choose. (You will have to supply this same password when you use Remote Console from the workstation.)

3. When prompted, enter the TCP port number through which the server will receive messages for a Remote Console session. The default is 2034. To allow the server to receive messages over a dynamically assigned port, enter **0**.

4. When prompted for an SPX port number, enter **-1** to indicate that the server communicates using IP only. This prevents the server from listening for SPX communications from a proxy server.

Now the IP target server is ready to accept Remote Console sessions running on a workstation or another server, as explained in the sections "Running Remote Console from a Workstation" and "Running Remote Console from a Server."

Activating an IP Target Server from AUTOEXEC.NCF

The previous instructions showed how to activate Remote Console functionality manually on an IP target server. If you prefer, you can add commands to the server's AUTOEXEC.NCF file to ensure that every time the IP server is rebooted, the Java-based Remote Console feature is activated. It is important to encrypt the Remote Console password in a special file in order to make the Remote Console feature more secure.

The following steps explain how to add the Remote Console commands to the AUTOEXEC.NCF file and how to encrypt the password so that the server remains secure.

1. To encrypt the Remote Console password, type the following command:

```
RCONAG6 ENCRYPT
```

2. When prompted, enter the password you want to encrypt.

3. When prompted, enter the TCP and SPX port numbers you want this server to use. See the previous sections on setting up target servers for information on how to handle these port numbers.

4. The server displays the command you will have to type in the future if you want to load RCONAG6 manually on the server and use this password. It also asks you if you want to write the command, including this encrypted password, to a file called LDRCONAG.NCF in the SYS:SYSTEM directory. To simplify your life, type **Y** to answer Yes. This stores the encrypted password in the LDRCONAG.NCF file. Then you won't have to remember the encrypted password.

5. Open the AUTOEXEC.NCF file to edit it. (To edit this file, you can load NWCONFIG.NLM, choose NCF Files Options, and then choose Edit AUTOEXEC.NCF File.)

6. At the end of the AUTOEXEC.NCF file, type the following command:

```
LDRCONAG
```

7. Save the AUTOEXEC.NCF file and exit the text editor you were using. Now, whenever the server is rebooted, Remote Console will automatically be loaded with the encrypted password.

Setting Up an IPX Target Server

If the server you want to access remotely communicates over IPX, you need to set up Remote Console software on two different servers:

- ▶ The target IPX server itself
- ▶ An IP-based proxy server, which will be the "middleman" between the IPX target server and the workstation or server running the Remote Console session

To set up both the IPX target server and the proxy server, complete the following steps:

1. At the target server's console prompt, type the following command:

   RCONAG6

2. When you load RCONAG6.NLM, you are asked for a password. Enter any password you choose. (You will have to supply this same password when you use Remote Console from the workstation.)

3. When prompted for a TCP port number, enter -1 to indicate that server communicates using IPX only. This prevents the server from listening for TCP communications.

4. When prompted, enter an SPX port number through which the server will listen for a proxy server. The default port number is 16800. To enable listening over a dynamically assigned port, you would enter **0**.

5. Now move to the proxy server, and type the following command at the proxy server's prompt:

   RCONPRXY

6. When prompted, enter the SPX port number you assigned to the target server in Step 4.

Now the IPX target server is ready to accept Remote Console sessions, via a proxy server, from a workstation or another server, as explained in the following sections.

Running Remote Console from a Workstation

To run a Remote Console session from a Windows 95/98 or Windows NT workstation, the workstation must meet the following requirements:

- ▶ The workstation must have at least 24MB of RAM and an equal size virtual memory swap file.

- ▶ The workstation must have the Novell client software installed. (The client software must be the version that came with NetWare 5, or more recent.)

- ▶ The workstation must have a drive mapped to SYS:PUBLIC on a NetWare 5 server. (For more information on mapping drives, see Chapter 6.)

- ▶ The workstation must have an IP connection to the network.

Complete the following steps to run a Remote Console session from a workstation:

1. Launch the Remote Console software (called RConsoleJ) from the workstation using either of the following methods:

   - From the NetWare Administrator utility, open the Tools menu, and then choose Pure IP Remote Console.

   - From the Windows Start or Run option, locate and execute the RCONJ.EXE file in the following path: SYS:PUBLIC\MGMT.

2. Click Remote Servers.

3. If the target server you want to access is displayed in the list, select the server, enter the Remote Console password you gave when you set up the target server, and continue with Step 4. If the target server you want is not displayed in the list, click Cancel and enter the following information to locate the target server:

   a. In the Server Address field, enter the IP address of the target server or case-sensitive name entered in DNS. If the target server is an IPX server, enter the case-sensitive name or the IPX address and IPX number separated by a colon.

   b. In the Password field, enter the Remote Console password you gave when you set up the target server.

   c. Click Advanced.

   d. In the Remote Server Port field, enter the TCP port number you gave when you set up the target server. (You don't have to enter a port number if you are using the default port.)

   e. If the target server is running IPX and you are using a proxy server, mark the checkbox next to Connect through Proxy. Then enter the address and port number for the proxy server.

4. Click Connect to start the Remote Console session.

5. When the console prompt appears on the workstation's screen, you can begin your remote console work.

Running Remote Console from a Server

Complete the following steps to run a Remote Console session from a server that is connected to the network via IP:

1. Launch the Remote Console software (called RConsoleJ) from the server using one of the following methods:

   • From the server console prompt, type RCONJ.

   • From the server's ConsoleOne screen, open My Server, then open Tools, and then click RConsoleJ.

2. Click Remote Servers.

3. If the target server you want to access is displayed in the list, select the server, enter the Remote Console password you gave when you set up the target server, and continue with Step 4. If the target server you want is not displayed in the list, click Cancel and enter the following information to locate the target server:

   a. In the Server Address field, enter the IP address of the target server or case-sensitive name entered in DNS. If the target server is an IPX server, enter the case-sensitive name or the IPX address and IPX number separated by a colon.

   b. In the Password field, enter the Remote Console password you gave when you set up the target server.

   c. Click Advanced.

   d. In the Remote Server Port field, enter the TCP port number you gave when you set up the target server. (You don't have to enter this number if you are using the default port number.)

   e. If the target server is running IPX and you are using a proxy server, mark the checkbox next to Connect through Proxy. Then enter the address and port number for the proxy server.

4. Click Connect to start the Remote Console session.

5. When the console prompt appears on the server's screen, you can begin your remote console work.

Running Java Applications on the Server

NetWare 5 includes a Java Virtual Machine (JVM), which is software that allows Java-based applications and applets to run on the server. Complete the following steps to load the JVM on the server and to install and run an application or applet on the server:

1. Copy the application or applet files to the default Java directory on the server. The default directory is SYS:JAVA\CLASSES. This directory is included in the CLASSPATH environment variable, so the server will be able to find the application or applet without users having to specify the path.

2. Specify a Just In Time (JIT) compiler for the server to use. This will improve the performance of Java-based applications. You can use the Symantec JIT compiler that comes with NetWare 5, or you can install another manufacturer's JIT compiler. To use the Symantec JIT compiler, type the following command at the server prompt:

   ```
   ENVSET JAVA_COMPILER=SYMCJIT
   ```

3. Load Java on the server by typing the following command:

   ```
   JAVA
   ```

4. To execute a Java-based applet, type the following command at the server prompt, substituting the applet's filename for *html_file*:

   ```
   APPLET html_file
   ```

5. To execute a Java-based application, the command you type depends on how you want the application to run. Type one of the following commands at the server prompt, substituting the application's name for *class*:

   - If the application doesn't require user input, or if it runs in a graphical user interface, type the following command:

     ```
     JAVA class
     ```

   - If the application is text-based and requires user input, use the following command, which will bring up a separate console screen for the application:

     ```
     JAVA -NS class
     ```

   - If you want to designate a specific amount of virtual memory for the application to use, type the following command, substituting the amount of memory (in megabytes) for *size*. The default size is 32MB.

     ```
     JAVA -VMsize class
     ```

If you need to shut down a Java process because it is hung or there is no other way to stop it, complete the following steps:

1. Display a list of all processes that are currently running on the server by typing the following command at the server prompt:

    JAVA -SHOW

2. The list displays an ID number for each process. Note the ID number for the process you want to shut down.

3. Type the following command at the server prompt, substituting the ID number for *id*. To kill all the processes, substitute the word ALL for *id*. (Do not put a space between -KILL and the ID number):

    JAVA -KILL*id*

Monitoring and Optimizing Server Performance

When you monitor the server's performance, you look for key indicators that the server is functioning at an optimal level. Some of the things you should monitor include the utilization percentage of the server's processor, the number of cache buffers and packet receive buffers being regularly used, and the server's memory allocation.

Every network has different needs and usage patterns. By default, server parameters are set so that the server will perform well on most networks. In addition, the server is self-tuning, meaning that it will gradually adjust itself over time to accommodate changing usage patterns. However, it's a good idea to monitor the server's performance periodically anyway. By doing so, you can track how your server performs under different conditions, discover potential problems, and make improvements.

Server parameters, also called SET parameters, control things such as how buffers are allocated and used, how memory is used, and so on. You can change these parameters by loading MONITOR.NLM, or by typing the full SET command at the server's console prompt. Using MONITOR.NLM is much easier, because you can select the server parameters you want from menus, without having to type a long command. For more information about server parameters, see Appendix B.

NOTE In NetWare 5, any changes to server parameters are automatically remembered and stored by the server. You no longer have to add a SET command to the AUTOEXEC.NCF or STARTUP.NCF command to make it permanent, as you did in previous versions of NetWare.

The server optimizes itself over a period of time by leveling adjustments for low-usage times with peak-usage bursts. Over a week or two, the server allocates an optimal number of buffers for each parameter, such as packet receive buffers. You can also set these parameters manually if you are not satisfied with the server's self-tuned settings.

The primary utility for monitoring and managing your server's performance is MONITOR.NLM. This utility displays a tremendous amount of information about the server, as well as its disk information, processor utilization, memory utilization, file activity, workstation connections, and the like.

To load MONITOR.NLM on the server, simply type **MONITOR** at the server's console. Figure 3.1 shows MONITOR.NLM's main menu, along with its General Information screen (viewed through a Remote Console session). To expand the General Information screen, press Tab.

F I G U R E   3.1   *MONITOR.NLM's main menu*

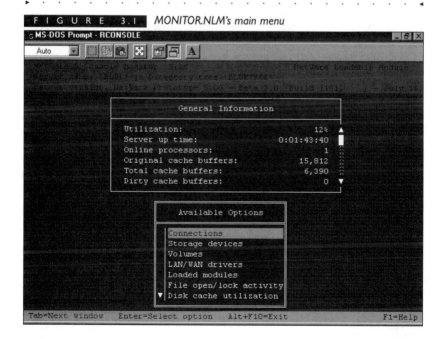

The following sections describe some of the ways to monitor and optimize your server's performance.

Monitoring Cache Buffers

If directory searches are slow, you may need to change some server parameters (also called SET parameters) to increase the allocation and use of directory cache buffers. (Directory cache buffers are only used in traditional NetWare volumes. They are not used in NSS volumes. See Chapter 8 for more information about volumes.)

Use MONITOR.NLM to change some or all of the following server parameters that relate to directory cache buffers (located under MONITOR's Server Parameters option, in the Directory Cache category):

- ▶ Directory Cache Allocation Wait Time
- ▶ Maximum Directory Cache Buffers
- ▶ Minimum Directory Cache Buffers

If disk writes are slow, use MONITOR's General Information screen to see if more than 70 percent of the cache buffers are "dirty" cache buffers. Dirty cache buffers are the file blocks in the server's memory that contain information that has not yet been written to disk, but needs to be. Then use MONITOR.NLM and choose the Server Parameters option to increase some or all of the following server parameters:

- ▶ Maximum Concurrent Directory Cache Writes (listed under the Directory Caching category)
- ▶ Dirty Directory Cache Delay Time (listed under the Directory Caching category)
- ▶ Maximum Concurrent Disk Cache Writes (listed under the File Caching category)
- ▶ Dirty Disk Cache Delay Time parameters (listed under the File Caching category)

See Appendix B for more information about these server parameters.

Monitoring Packet Receive Buffers

If the server seems to be slowing down or losing workstation connections, use MONITOR's General Information screen to see how many packet receive buffers are allocated and how many are being used. If the allocated number is higher than ten but the server doesn't respond immediately when rebooted, you may need to increase the minimum number of packet receive buffers. To do this, use MONITOR.NLM to increase the server parameter Minimum Packet Receive Buffers (under the Communications category) so that each board in the server can have at least five buffers.

You can also increase the Maximum Packet Receive Buffers parameter (under the Communications category) in increments of ten until you have one buffer per workstation.

After a couple of days of average network usage, use MONITOR to see how many packet receive buffers are being allocated, and compare that with the maximum number. If the two numbers are the same, increase the maximum value by 50 buffers. Continue to monitor the buffers periodically and increase the maximum value until the allocated number no longer matches the maximum.

When you've determined the optimal maximum number of packet receive buffers for your system, use MONITOR to set both the maximum and minimum values, so the server can quickly optimize these values if it is rebooted.

See Appendix B for more information about these server parameters.

Monitoring Memory Usage

One of the most common causes of server performance problems is a lack of adequate memory in the server. If the network seems to be operating slowly, or if you don't have enough memory to load NLMs, you may need to add more RAM to the server.

Use MONITOR's General Information screen to track the percentage of Long Term Cache Hits. This parameter indicates the percentage of requests for disk blocks that were already being held in memory. Because holding data in memory makes access to that data faster than if the request has to read the data from the disk, this number should be high. If Long Term Cache Hits shows less than 90 percent consistently, add more RAM to the server to improve its performance. You can use the MEMORY and MEMORY MAP console utilities to see how much memory the server is using.

NetWare 5 includes a new feature to help utilize memory more efficiently: virtual memory. Although the NetWare operating system itself does not use this virtual memory, some processes running on the server can. The Java Virtual Machine and any modules that are loaded into protected memory address spaces can use this virtual memory. (Running processes in protected address space is described later in this chapter.)

With virtual memory, data that hasn't been accessed recently can be moved from memory to the disk, where it is temporarily stored in a *swap file*. When the data is accessed again, it is quickly restored back into memory. By storing the data in this swap file, it can still be accessed more quickly than if it were being accessed strictly from its permanent location on the disk. In addition, this allows for existing RAM to be used more efficiently, helping reduce the possibility of encountering low memory conditions.

A swap file is created automatically for the SYS volume. You can create additional swap files for each volume if you wish. The swap files don't necessarily need to reside on the volume for which they're designated, but it's a good idea to have one swap file per volume.

To view, create, and delete swap files, use the SWAP console utility. For example, to see information about a server's swap files, type the following command at the server's console:

SWAP

To create a new swap file, type the following command; substitute the name of the volume for *volume*:

SWAP ADD *volume*

By default, this command will create a swap file with a minimum size of 2MB, a maximum size of 5MB, and will leave a minimum of 5MB of free space on the volume. To change any of these parameters (all of which are optional), type the following command instead (substituting the number of megabytes for *size*). You can use any (or all) of these optional parameters:

SWAP ADD *volume* MIN=*size* MAX=*size* MIN FREE=*size*

To delete a swap file from a volume, type:

SWAP DEL *volume*

For more information about the SWAP console utility, type:

HELP SWAP

To provide more memory to NLMs without adding RAM, use MONITOR.NLM to change the Minimum File Cache Buffers (under the File Caching category) and Maximum Directory Cache Buffers (under the Directory Caching category) parameters, which limit the memory for file and directory caching. Then reboot the server. However, you should only use this as a temporary solution until you can add more RAM to the server.

If you're using an ISA bus or PCI bus in the server, remember to use the REGISTER MEMORY console utility to register any memory above 16MB for an ISA bus or 64MB for a PCI bus.

Monitoring the Error Log Files

You can monitor several different error log files to see if your network has generated any error messages. You should make a practice of reviewing these files on a regular basis to ensure that nothing out of the ordinary is happening to your network.

The error log files you should monitor include the following:

▸ SYS$LOG.ERR logs error messages for the server. It is stored in the server's SYS:SYSTEM directory. All of the messages or errors that appear on the server's console are stored in this file.

▸ VOL$LOG.ERR logs error messages for a volume. Each volume has its own log file, which is stored at the root of the volume. Any errors or messages that pertain to the volume are stored in this file.

▸ ABEND.LOG tracks any abends that may have happened on the server. (An abend, which is short for "abnormal end," is a serious error that stops the server from operating.) NetWare 5 has a feature that enables the server to suspend the offending process and continue running. If the abend is more serious, the server can shut itself down and restart automatically. Because of this abend recovery feature, you may not be aware that the server has abended unless you view this file. This file is created on the server's boot partition but gets copied to SYS:SYSTEM when the server restarts.

▸ TTS$LOG.ERR logs all data that is backed out by the NetWare Transaction Tracking System (TTS). This file is stored in the SYS volume. To allow this file to be created, use MONITOR.NLM to turn the TTS Abort Dump Flag parameter to On.

▸ BOOT$LOG.ERR logs all the errors that occur during server startup. This file is stored in the SYS:SYSTEM directory.

▸ CONSOLE.LOG is a file that can capture all console messages during system initialization. To capture messages in this file, load CONLOG.NLM in the AUTOEXEC.NCF file. CONSOLE.LOG is stored in the SYS:ETC directory. To stop capturing messages in this file, enter the following command at the server console:

```
UNLOAD CONLOG
```

To view any of these error log files, you can use a text editor from a workstation, or you can use EDIT.NLM from the server. To use EDIT.NLM, enter the command

```
LOAD EDIT
```

and then specify the path and name of the desired log file.

To limit the size of the CONSOLE.LOG file, you can specify its maximum size in the command that loads CONLOG.NLM. In addition, you can specify that the previous CONSOLE.LOG file be saved under a different name. For example, to specify that the previous file be saved and named LOG.SAV, and to limit the new CONSOLE.LOG file to be no more than 100K in size, you would use the following command:

```
LOAD CONLOG SAVE=LOG.SAV MAXIMUM=100
```

To limit the size of SYS$LOG.ERR, VOL$LOG.ERR, TTS$LOG.ERR, and BOOT$LOG.ERR, use MONITOR.NLM to change the appropriate server parameters. To get to these server parameters, choose MONITOR's Server Parameters option, and then select Error Handling.

▶ Server Log File Overflow Size=*number* lets you specify the maximum size (in K) that the SYS$LOG.ERR file can become.

▶ Volume Log File Overflow Size=*number* sets the maximum size for VOL$LOG.ERR

▶ Volume TTS Log File Overflow Size=*number* sets the maximum size for TTS$LOG.ERR.

▶ Boot Error Log File Overflow Size=*number* sets the maximum size for BOOT$LOG.ERR.

To specify what happens to a log file when it reaches the maximum size, use MONITOR.NLM to change the following Error Handling parameters:

▶ Server Log File State=*number*

▶ Volume Log File State=*number*

▶ Volume TTS Log File State=*number*

▶ Boot Error Log File State=*number*

With these parameters, replace *number* with 0 (leaves the log file in its current state), 1 (deletes the log file), or 2 (renames the log file and starts a new one). (The BOOT$LOG.ERR file has one more option: 3, which causes a new log file to be created every time the server is rebooted.) The default is 1.

Protecting the Server

Protecting the server is a very important safeguard that cannot be overlooked. Damage to the server can affect the entire network. The following types of activities can help you protect your server. In addition, see Chapter 7 for information about preventing other types of problems, such as unauthorized access of files.

Protecting the Server from Physical Damage

If the server is in an exposed public area where anyone can have access to it, accidents may happen. For example, someone may unplug the power cord or turn off the server, thinking it had been left on accidentally.

Be sure to store the server in a locked room. In fact, you may also want to remove its keyboard and monitor, and access it only with the Remote Console feature when necessary.

Secure the server to a desk or counter if you are in an earthquake-prone area. Even a small shake can knock a computer to the floor.

Protecting the Server from Electrical Power Problems

Because electrical power is not always consistent, you need to ensure that your server will not be damaged and files won't be corrupted if a brownout, surge, spike, or outage occurs.

Use a UPS for the server. This provides the server with a backup battery in case of a power outage, which allows enough time for the UPS to shut down the server cleanly, leaving no open files exposed to corruption.

If possible, attach each workstation to a UPS, too. If a UPS isn't feasible, at least use surge suppressors on the workstations and peripherals (such as printers) to prevent electrical surges from damaging the equipment.

Typically, UPS manufacturers provide software to manage their UPS products. You should use the manufacturer's software to manage your UPS whenever possible. However, if you don't have software from the UPS manufacturer, you can use NetWare's UPS_AIO.NLM to support the UPS attached to a serial port on the server.

Use the following steps to install a UPS on a server using Novell's UPS_AIO.NLM. Use this module if your UPS is connected through a serial port.

I. Attach the UPS to the server using the manufacturer's instructions.

2. Load the UPS hardware driver on the server.

3. Load an AIO device driver on the server. AIOCOMX.NLM is the default driver that comes with NetWare.

4. Load UPS_AIO.NLM on the server, specifying the correct options in the following format (the options are explained in Table 3.3):

```
UPS_AIO options
```

If you want the UPS to be configured the same way every time the server is rebooted, put this same command in the server's AUTOEXEC.NCF file.

T A B L E 3.3 *UPS_AIO Options*

OPTION	DESCRIPTION
Downtime = *value*	The time, in seconds, that the server will run on battery power before shutting down. Default: 300. Values: Minimum 30 seconds (no maximum).
MSGDelay = *value*	The time, in seconds, before the system sends a message to users about the approaching shutdown. Default: 5. Values: Minimum 0 (no maximum).
MSGInterval = *value*	The time, in seconds, between broadcasts. Default: 30. Values: Minimum 20 (no maximum).
DriverType = *value*	The AIO device driver type. See the manufacturer's documentation for the type. Default: 1 (AIOCOMX). Values: 1, 2, or 3.
Board = *value*	The AIO board number. If you use AIOCOMX, the board number is displayed when you load AIOCOMX. If you use another driver, see the manufacturer's documentation for the number. Default: 0.
Port = *value*	AIO port number. If you use AIOCOMX, the port number is displayed when you load AIOCOMX. If you use another driver, see the manufacturer's documentation for the number. Default: 0.
Signal_High	Sets normal RS232 signaling state to "high." Use the high setting only if your system uses high values instead of low values to determine if the power is low. See the manufacturer's documentation for more information. Default: none.

Protecting the Server from Viruses

Unfortunately, software viruses are a fact of life. Use a third-party product to check for viruses and to disinfect your network if one is found. Several companies are manufacturing virus detectors for NetWare networks.

Because new viruses are being created continually, keep your virus detection software up to date (get all available updates of the software, follow manufacturer's procedures for updating, and so on).

If necessary, establish policies against users loading their own software on the network or downloading software from outside online sources or e-mail messages, or provide diskless workstations to the users.

To prevent viruses from infecting executable files, you can assign those files the Execute Only file attribute, or you can remove users' Modify right from the directory that contains the executable files and assign the Read-Only attribute to the executables. If a user still has the Modify right to a file, the virus can change the Read-Only attribute to Read-Write, infect the file, and then change the attribute back. Therefore, it's important to remove the Modify right from the user if you are going to use the Read-Only attribute for virus protection.

Protecting the Server from Hardware Failures

To protect your server from hard disk problems, the NetWare feature called Hot Fix monitors any bad blocks that develop on the hard disk. (Hot Fix is explained in the section "Using Hot Fix," later in this chapter.) For more protection, you can use disk mirroring and disk duplexing to store identical copies of all network files on two disks, so if one disk goes bad, the data is still available from the other. This protection feature is explained in the section "Using Disk Mirroring and Duplexing," later in this chapter.

Protecting the Server's Memory from Faulty NLMs

Occasionally, an NLM may exhibit problems using the server's memory. It may corrupt the server's memory or overwrite memory being used by another process, causing the server to *abend*. (An abend is an "abnormal end" — a serious error that causes the process to hang, and can hang the server as well.)

Usually, this sort of problem is limited to third-party NLMs that have not been fully tested, or perhaps an NLM being developed and tested. If you have an NLM that you suspect is being troublesome, or if you are developing an NLM and want to test it in a safe environment, you can use a feature of NetWare 5 called *protected address spaces*.

NOTE All NLMs from Novell have been thoroughly tested and should never require that you load them in protected address spaces. This feature is used primarily when testing new NLMs you may be developing in-house.

With this feature, you can load the suspect NLM in a protected address space (sometimes called "Ring 3"), where it is insulated from the operating system. NLMs running in a protected address space use virtual memory.

Some types of programs cannot run in protected address spaces, such as:

- ▸ SERVER.EXE (the NetWare operating system)
- ▸ LAN drivers and storage (disk) drivers
- ▸ MONITOR.NLM
- ▸ The NSS file system

Whether an NLM can run in protected address space depends on the types of calls it makes to the operating system.

To load an NLM into a protected address space, type the following command when you load the NLM, substituting the module's name for *module*:

PROTECTED *module*

This creates a new protected address space, called ADDRESS_SPACE*n*, and loads the NLM into it. To unload the NLM, simply use the normal UNLOAD command:

UNLOAD *module*

To list and see information about the protected address spaces currently being used on the server, type the following console command:

PROTECTION

You can use the MODULES console command to list all the NLMs currently running on the server and show which address space each NLM is occupying.

For more information about using protected address spaces when loading NLMs, see the Novell online documentation.

Performing Server Maintenance

From time to time, you may find you need to perform some type of maintenance on your server. For example, you may need to add a new hard disk, load the latest patches (bug fixes or enhancements) on the server, or clear a workstation connection. The following sections explain how to do some of these common maintenance tasks.

Displaying Information about the Server

You can see information about the server by executing various console utilities at the server's console. Table 3.4 lists the types of information about the server that you can see and the console utilities you use to display that information.

TABLE 3.4 *Console Utilities Used to Display Server Information*

TYPE OF INFORMATION	CONSOLE UTILITIES TO USE
The server's name	NAME, CONFIG
The server's IPX internal network number	CONFIG
The server's directory tree	CONFIG
The server's bindery context	CONFIG
The server's network board information	CONFIG
The server's storage device information	LIST DEVICES, LIST STORAGE ADAPTERS
All currently loaded NLMs	MODULES
The server's processor speed	SPEED, CPUCHECK
The status of the server's processors	DISPLAY PROCESSORS
The server's version number and license information	VERSION
The server's current server parameter settings	DISPLAY ENVIRONMENT
Server parameters that are different from default values	DISPLAY MODIFIED ENVIRONMENT
A list of all volumes mounted on the server	VOLUMES

Installing Patches and Updated Modules

As with almost all software products, no matter how thoroughly the product is tested, there is always some flaw or unexpected behavior that crops up after the product has shipped. Usually, these types of flaws show up when the product is used in a customer configuration that varies from the testing configurations used within the manufacturer's labs.

To fix these problems, Novell releases software patches and updated modules that can be installed on your NetWare server. Not all patches or updates are needed in most customers' configurations, but it's a good idea to regularly review the patches and updates to make sure you install any that may apply to your situation.

Novell releases these patches and updates in a variety of ways. The patches are available via the Internet at Novell's Web site (`www.novell.com`). All patches and updates are also included on the *Novell Support Connection*, a collection of CDs that is produced regularly by Novell's technical support division and sent to subscribers.

For more information about all of these sources, see Appendix C.

Monitoring Workstation Connections

Some types of server maintenance require that you break a workstation's connection to the server or that you prevent users from logging in while you're completing the maintenance task. Use the utilities listed in Table 3.5 to perform these tasks.

T A B L E 3.5	Utilities Used to Monitor Workstation Connections
TASK	**UTILITY TO USE**
See which workstations are connected and which files they have open.	MONITOR.NLM's Connections screen
Clear the workstation connection if the workstation has crashed and left files open on the server.	MONITOR.NLM's Connections screen (select the connection and press the Delete key)
Prevent users from logging in.	DISABLE LOGIN console utility
Allow users to log in again after you've disabled login.	ENABLE LOGIN console utility

Adding Network Boards

Whenever you add a new network board to the server, you can use NWCON-FIG.NLM to configure and load the appropriate LAN driver (also called a network driver) for the board. NWCONFIG will automatically detect and load most network drivers, but you can also manually load the driver you want.

To add a network board to a server, first install the board according to the manufacturer's instructions. Then, load NWCONFIG.NLM by typing the following command at the server's console:

```
NWCONFIG
```

From NWCONFIG's main menu, select Driver Options, and then choose Configure Network Drivers. From there, you can tell NWCONFIG whether you want it to discover and load the appropriate driver, or whether you want to load it manually. You can also use these options to configure the driver to the options you prefer.

Working with Hard Disks

One of the most annoying problems that can happen to a server is a hard disk failure. There are several NetWare features, explained in the following sections, that can help you monitor and work with your server's hard disks. (For information about creating and managing volumes on hard disks, see Chapter 8.)

Using Hot Fix

NetWare provides a feature called Hot Fix, which monitors the blocks that are being written to a traditional NetWare volume on a disk. When NetWare writes data to the server's hard disk, NetWare writes the data, and then verifies that the data was written correctly by reading it again (called read-after-write verification). When a bad block is encountered, the data that was being written to that block is redirected to a separate area on the disk, called the *disk redirection area,* and the bad block is listed in a bad block table.

Some manufacturers' hard disks maintain their own version of data redirection and do not need to use NetWare's Hot Fix feature. (In addition, Novell's NSS volumes do not use Hot Fix.) If your disk does use Hot Fix, the size of the redirection area is set up by default when you first create a volume on the disk.

You should monitor the NetWare Hot Fix statistics periodically to see if a disk is showing a high number of bad blocks and is filling up the allocated redirection area. To see the number of redirection blocks being used, use MONITOR.NLM. Choose Storage Devices from the main menu, and then select a "hotfixed" partition from the list of partitions that is displayed. Press Tab to see the entire information screen for this partition.

Track the number of bad blocks being found (Used Hot Fix Blocks) over time so you can see if the disk suddenly starts to generate bad blocks at an undesirable frequency. (You may want to use a worksheet such as the Hot Fix Bad Block Tracking worksheet in Appendix D.) If more than half of the total Hot Fix blocks have been used for redirected data, or if the number of redirected blocks has increased significantly since the last time you checked it, the disk may be going bad. Use the manufacturer's documentation to try to diagnose the disk problem.

Using Disk Mirroring and Duplexing

Another way to protect your network data from possible disk corruption is to implement disk mirroring, which ensures that data is safe and accessible even if one disk goes down. When you mirror disks, both disks are updated simultaneously with network data so that both disks contain identical copies of all network files. If one disk fails, the other takes over so that the network operates normally. Users don't typically see any difference in services.

If the mirrored disks are using the same disk controller board, it's simply called *disk mirroring*. If the mirrored disks are using separate disk controller boards, it's called *disk duplexing*. Disk duplexing provides more security than disk mirroring because it duplicates not only the disk, but also the controller channel. Disk duplexing also increases the performance of data reads because the server sends the reads to both controllers. Whichever controller is least busy services the requests.

With mirrored or duplexed disks, if a disk problem causes the server to stop, you should turn off the server, remove the bad disk, and restart the server. Then replace the bad disk as soon as possible. When you install the new disk, the server will remirror the new drive with the existing one, which also means the server will copy all the data onto the new disk automatically.

Having disk mirroring or duplexing does not eliminate the need for keeping regular backups of your network. Be sure you always have a current backup of your network data before you change disks or change the server's hardware configuration.

Managing Mirrored or Duplexed Disks

You can use the utilities shown in Table 3.6 to work with mirrored disks.

T A B L E 3 . 6	*Utilities Used to Manage Mirrored Disks*
TASK	**UTILITY TO USE**
Set up, monitor, and change disk mirroring or disk duplexing.	NWCONFIG.NLM
Show the status of mirrored disk partitions.	MIRROR STATUS console utility
Stop the server from remirroring a disk partition.	ABORT REMIRROR console utility
Restart the remirroring process if something halted the server's remirroring task.	REMIRROR PARTITION console utility

Recovering Files from an Out-of-Sync Disk

Usually, when a mirrored disk partition becomes unmirrored, its status in NWCONFIG (under Standard Disk Options) is listed as Not Mirrored.

If the disk is listed as Out of Sync, NetWare does not recognize any volume information on the disk. To salvage the data from this partition, you must rename the partition so it can be mounted as a separate volume. To do this, complete the following steps:

1. At the server's console, load NWCONFIG.NLM.

2. Choose Standard Disk Options, and then choose Mirror/Unmirror Disk Partitions.

3. Select the out-of-sync partition and press F3.

4. If another volume of the same name exists on another disk, you'll receive a warning that the partition you selected contains the name of a volume that is already defined. Press Esc to continue.

5. When asked if you want to rename the volume segment, answer Yes.

6. Enter a new, unique name for this volume segment.

7. Answer Yes when asked if you want to salvage the volume segment.

8. Mount the segment as an independent volume.

Adding a Hard Disk to a Server

Complete the following steps to install a new hard disk in a server:

1. Bring down the server and turn off its power (or the power to the disk's subsystem).

2. If necessary, install a new disk controller board.

3. Install the hard disk and cable it to the server as necessary, according to the manufacturer's instructions.

4. If necessary, configure the computer to recognize the new disk.

5. Reboot the server.

6. To load the disk driver, load NWCONFIG.NLM. Choose Driver Options, and then choose Configure Disk and Storage Device Drivers. Then select either Discover and Load an Additional Driver, or Load an Additional Driver, and follow the prompts to load the driver.

7. To create the new NetWare partition, choose Standard Disk Options, and then choose Modify Disk Partitions and Hot Fix. Then choose Create NetWare Disk Partition.

8. Continue using NWCONFIG.NLM to either mirror the disk to another existing disk, create a new volume on it, or add its partition to an existing volume.

For more information about creating volumes (and for information about using traditional NetWare volumes and NSS volumes), see Chapter 8.

Replacing a Hard Disk in a Server

Complete the following steps to replace an existing hard disk in a server.

1. Back up the files on the existing hard disk.

2. If the disk is mirrored, use NWCONFIG.NLM to dismount all of the disk's volumes and to unmirror the disk.

3. Bring down the server and turn off its power (or the power to the disk's subsystem).

4. Remove the original disk.

5. Install the new disk and cable it to the server as necessary, according the manufacturer's instructions.

6. If necessary, configure the computer to recognize the new disk.

7. Reboot the server.

8. To load the disk driver, load NWCONFIG.NLM. Choose Driver Options, and then choose Configure Disk and Storage Device Drivers. Then select either Discover and Load an Additional Driver, or Load an Additional Driver, and follow the prompts to load the driver.

9. Choose Standard Disk Options to delete any existing partitions on the new disk and to create a new NetWare partition on it.

10. Continue using NWCONFIG.NLM to either remirror the disk to the original disk's partner or re-create the volumes that were on the old disk (and then restore the files from a backup).

11. Restore data to the new hard drive. For more information about deleting and creating volumes (and for information about using traditional NetWare volumes and NSS volumes), see Chapter 8.

Using PCI Hot Plug Hardware

If your server uses PCI Hot Plug technology, you can add and remove PCI disk and network adapters without having to turn off the server. When you install NetWare 5 on the server, the installation program detects whether your server supports Hot Plug and has the appropriate driver. If it does, it automatically installs the necessary modules. It also adds commands to the AUTOEXEC.NCF file to load the PCI bus driver and load NCMCON.NLM.

NCMCON is the management utility that enables you to monitor, install, and remove PCI adapters. When it is loaded on the server, it constantly monitors the status of PCI slots and the adapters in them, and displays any change of status.

NOTE

When the installation program edits AUTOEXEC.NCF to add a command to load NCMCON, the line is commented out. If you want NCMCON to automatically load every time the server is rebooted, you need to edit the AUTOEXEC.NCF file to remove the # character from the beginning of the LOAD NCMCON command, so it will execute.

To remove a PCI Hot Plug disk or LAN adapter, complete the following steps:

1. Load NCMCON.NLM by typing the following command at the server prompt:

```
NCMCON
```

2. Choose the slot into which you want to install the PCI adapter.

3. Choose Remove Adapter.

4. When the slot's status changes to Powered Off and the slot's green LED goes out, you can safely remove the adapter.

To install a PCI Hot Plug disk or LAN adapter, complete the following steps:

1. Load NCMCON.NLM by typing the following command at the server prompt:

```
NCMCON
```

2. Install the PCI adapter into the Hot Plug slot.

3. When prompted to decide if you want to supply power, answer Yes. The green LED will light up, and NCMCON will try to automatically detect and load the adapter's drivers.

4. If you choose No, select the slot and adapter from the main menu. Then choose Add Adapter or Power On Slot (whichever option appears). NCMCON will then try to automatically detect and load the driver.

Working with CD-ROM Drives

With NetWare, a CD-ROM mounted in a drive that is attached to the server can appear as a NetWare NSS volume. Users on the network can access the CD-ROM just like any other volume, except that it is read-only. (For more information on NSS volumes, see Chapter 8.)

Because a CD-ROM is read-only, do not enable file compression or block suballocation on the CD-ROM volume, or you will corrupt the CD-ROM's volume index data.

To mount a CD-ROM as a NetWare volume, use CDROM.NLM. This NLM supports the High Sierra and ISO 9660 formats, along with HFS (Apple) extensions. (This means you can access Mac files on the CD from a Mac workstation.)

Complete the following steps to install a CD-ROM and mount it as a NetWare volume:

1. Bring down the server and turn off its power.

2. If necessary, install a new disk controller board for the CD-ROM drive.

3. Install the CD-ROM drive and cable it to the server as necessary, according to the manufacturer's instructions.

4. If necessary, configure the computer to recognize the new drive.

5. Reboot the server.

6. To load the disk driver for the CD-ROM, load NWCONFIG.NLM. Then choose Driver Options, and then choose Configure Disk and Storage Device Drivers. Then select either Discover and Load an Additional Driver, or Load an Additional Driver, and follow the prompts to load the driver.

7. In the CD-ROM drive, insert the CD-ROM that you want to be mounted as a volume.

8. Load CDROM.NLM on the server by typing the following command at the server's prompt:

```
CDROM
```

9. If you want the CD-ROM to be mounted as a volume every time the server is rebooted, put the following command in the AUTOEXEC.NCF file:

```
LOAD CDROM
```

Loading CDROM.NLM on the server automatically loads two separate modules: CD9660.NSS (which supports ISO 9660-standard CD-ROMs), and CDHFS (which supports HFS CD-ROMs, used in Macintosh systems).

Loading CDROM.NLM also automatically mounts the CD-ROM that is in the CD-ROM drive. Now you can type **VOLUMES** to see the CD-ROM volume listed as an active volume on the server. You can dismount and mount the CD-ROM just like any other volume on the server.

Modifying Server Startup Activities

When you start up or reboot the NetWare server, its boot files execute in the following order:

1. The DOS system files load, and then run AUTOEXEC.BAT, which sets up a basic environment and can be set to automatically execute SERVER.EXE.

2. SERVER.EXE runs the NetWare operating system on the computer, which turns the computer into the NetWare server.

3. STARTUP.NCF automates the initialization of the NetWare operating system. It loads disk drivers, loads name space modules to support different file formats (Macintosh or NFS), and may execute some SET parameters that modify default initialization values.

4. AUTOEXEC.NCF loads the server's LAN drivers, specifies the server name and internal network number, mounts volumes, loads any NLMs you want automatically loaded (such as MONITOR), and executes additional SET parameters.

5. Additional .NCF files, if they've been created, can be called from the AUTOEXEC.NCF file or executed from the server's console.

The STARTUP.NCF and AUTOEXEC.NCF files are created automatically during the installation process. They contain commands that reflect the selections you make during installation. (Other types of .NCF files can be created too, depending on the products you install on the server.)

You can edit these .NCF files after installation to add new commands or modify existing ones. Table 3.7 describes the utilities you can use to edit the STARTUP.NCF and AUTOEXEC.NCF files.

T A B L E 3.7	*Utilities Used to Edit Server Startup Files*
UTILITY	**DESCRIPTION**
EDIT.NLM	A text editor on the server that lets you manually edit the files. To use EDIT.NLM, type **EDIT** at the server console, and then enter the name of the desired file.
NWCONFIG.NLM	Lets you modify the same options you set during installation. Automatically updates the appropriate file with the new information you've specified. Also lets you manually edit the files by choosing NCF Files Options.
MONITOR.NLM	Lets you add, delete, or modify SET parameters by selecting them from menus. Automatically updates the appropriate file with the new information you've specified.

Charging Customers for Server Usage

With NetWare, you can charge users for using a server's resources. You can base charges on the following criteria:

▶ The number of minutes they are connected to your server

▶ The number of service requests they make to the server

▶ The total number of blocks they read

▶ The total number of blocks they write to

▶ The total number of blocks of disk storage they use per day

Bear in mind that the accounting feature tracks these items for each individual server. It does not support Novell Directory Services, so if you want to charge for a user's activities across the network, you'll have to set up accounting on each server the user might access.

When you set up accounting services, you will specify a charge rate for each item you want to track. The accounting charge rate is the amount you will charge for each unit used. To obtain the charge rate, you divide the total amount of money you want to accrue (multiplier) by the total number of units you expect to be used (divisor). For example, if you want to charge a total of $1,000 per month for your disk storage, and you expect users to use a total of 50,000 disk blocks per month, the formula would be:

100,000 (cents) / 50,000 (blocks) = 2 cents per block

If you set the multiplier to 0 (the top number in the fraction), the charge amount will be No Charge.

To manage accounting on a server, you use two utilities: the NetWare Administrator utility, which runs in Windows 95/98 and Windows NT, and the ATOTAL utility, which is a command-line utility that runs in DOS.

To set up accounting, use the NetWare Administrator utility from a workstation, as explained in the following steps. (See Chapter 5 for instructions on setting up the NetWare administrator utility on a workstation.)

1. Select the Server object from the NetWare Administrator's Browser.

2. From the Object menu, choose Details.

3. Click the Accounting button at the bottom of the page.

4. (First time only) If this is the first time you've accessed accounting information for this server, answer Yes to confirm that you want to install accounting. Five new page buttons will appear along the right-hand side of the window: Blocks Read, Blocks Written, Connect Time,

Disk Storage, and Service Requests. These pages each represent one of the items you can track and charge for.

5. Open the page for one of the items you want to charge for. A time grid is displayed, along with a list of charge rates. If this is the first time a charge rate will be added to this item, the only charge rate listed is No Charge.

6. Click Add Charge Rate.

7. Enter the Multiplier (top of the fraction) and the Divisor (bottom of the fraction) that will give you the charge rate you want to use, and then click OK. The new charge rate will be added to the list of charge rates.

8. (Optional) If you want to create additional charge rates, repeat Steps 6 and 7. Each charge rate will have its own color.

9. Specify which times of the week this charge rate will apply. To do this, click a charge rate. Move the cursor to the time grid and click any time blocks to which you want to assign this charge rate. You can click individual blocks, or you can click and drag to include rows or columns of blocks. Note that the blocks you select will be color-coded to match the color of the charge rate you are using. You can click additional charge rates (or the No Charge rate) and apply them to different blocks of time. Figure 3.2 shows a time grid for Service Requests, where three different charge rates (including No Charge) were used.

10. When finished, click OK to save your changes.

To display daily and weekly totals for each of the items that are tracked by accounting services, use the ATOTAL utility by entering the command

```
ATOTAL
```

at the workstation's DOS prompt. To redirect the display to a text file that you can read with a text editor, use the following command format:

```
ATOTAL > filename
```

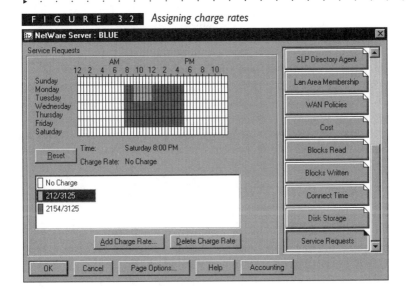

F I G U R E   3 . 2   *Assigning charge rates*

Synchronizing the Servers' Time

Because NetWare 5 maintains a network-wide directory of network objects and information, all servers on the network must maintain a common, relative time so that all updates to that database happen in the correct order, regardless of the server that originated the update.

To ensure that the servers in an NDS tree are keeping the same time, a NetWare feature called TimeSync is implemented on each server. With Time Services, certain servers are designated to be the main timekeepers. The other servers all synchronize their times with these timekeepers.

When you install NetWare 5 on a server, you designate how you want this server to participate in keeping time coordinated with the other servers on the network. The four different time server designations you can give a server are:

▶ *Single Reference.* The sole server that maintains the network time, a Single Reference server is often used on small networks (fewer than 30 servers). All other servers are Secondary time servers. Single Reference servers provide the time to Secondary servers.

▶ *Primary.* A Primary server synchronizes its time by polling one or more Primary or Reference servers. Together, the Primary servers determine an average time, and then each one adjusts its time to approach that average. If a Reference server exists, the Primary servers adjust their time to approach the Reference server's time, because the Reference server won't adjust. Use primary servers on large networks (more than 30 servers) so if one primary server goes down, another can still supply the time to the network. Also, put one primary server in each geographic area, so secondary servers don't have to cross WAN links to obtain the time.

▶ *Reference.* Similar to a Single Reference server, a Reference server is used on larger networks where additional Primary servers are desired. Reference servers participate with other Primary servers to determine the correct time, but they do not adjust their own time. Instead, Primary servers migrate their time to match the Reference server's time. If more than one Reference server exists, they must all be synchronized with the same external time source, such as an atomic clock, or each Reference server's time will drift independently and the network will never be synchronized.

▶ *Secondary.* A Secondary server obtains the time from one of the other time servers. Secondary servers do not participate in determining the time; they merely obtain it for their own use and to provide the time to their workstations.

You will set up TimeSync on the server during installation. TimeSync is controlled by TIMESYNC.NLM, which is loaded automatically when the server is started up.

If your network has fewer than 30 servers, all the servers are in the same time zone, and you have no WAN links between servers, you should use the default settings for TimeSync. TimeSync will automatically set up the first installed server as a Single Reference server, and will set up all subsequent servers in the tree as Secondary servers.

If you want to modify the time synchronization after installation, you can edit the TIMESYNC.CFG file to modify the TimeSync server parameters (also known as SET parameters). You can use MONITOR.NLM to change the server parameters, but MONITOR will not add the parameters to the TIME-SYNC.CFG file. You must still edit the TIMESYNC.CFG file if you want the time synchronization parameters to be in effect the next time you reboot the server.

The time synchronization server parameters enable you to change the type of time server, polling intervals, and so on. For more information about the TimeSync server parameters, see Appendix B.

You can use EDIT.NLM to edit TIMESYNC.CFG.

By default, TimeSync uses SAP broadcasts to keep all time servers synchronized. If you are using an IP only network and do not want SAP traffic on your network, you can turn the SAP synchronization off and tell the server exactly which time servers you want it to use. You can also use this method if you use SAP on your network, but find that the SAP traffic is too heavy or that you frequently have servers joining and leaving the network (for testing or other purposes).

To do this, edit the TIMESYNC.CFG file and add the following commands to it:

```
TYPE= server type
SERVICE ADVERTISING=OFF
CONFIGURED SOURCES=ON
```

For *server type*, specify whether this server is a Reference, Single Reference, Primary, or Secondary server. For example, enter

```
TYPE=PRIMARY
```

and then add the list of the time servers you want this server to contact, in order of priority. Add the following command:

```
TIME SOURCES= server1;server2;server3;
```

For *server1*, *server2*, *server3*, and so on, indicate the name of the time servers you want this server to contact. You can use either the server's NDS name or its IP address. The order in which you list the servers determines the order in which they will be contacted. You can have any number of servers in the list. Be sure to end the list with a semicolon (;) to indicate the end of the server list.

If you have an IP network, you can use another NLM, called NTP.NLM, to synchronize time in conjunction with TIMESYNC.NLM. If you use NTP, TIMESYNC will operate as an NCP responder only, giving NTP the responsibility of setting and managing the network's time clock. All IPX servers running TimeSync become secondary servers when an IP server is running NTP.

NTP.NLM uses a file called NTP.NCF (located in SYS:ETC) to specify the server that should supply the network's time. The server can be the IP server itself, another IP server on the network, or an external server accessed over the Internet.

The default NTP.NCF file supplied with NetWare 5 includes several possible commands that you can choose to synchronize with various external time servers. All of the commands are commented out in the file by default. To activate a command, choose one of the servers listed and remove the # character in front of that command. For example, if you want the server to synchronize with the NASA Ames Research Center, remove the # character from the beginning of the following command:

```
Server ntp.nasa.com
```

If you want the server to use its own internal clock, remove the # character from the beginning of the following command:

```
Server 127.127.1.0
```

You can also add your own commands to this file to select another time source to use. Any command beginning with the word *server* indicates that the local server will be a client and will request the time from the remote server whose address is specified in the command.

If you want the local server to work in symmetric active mode with a remote server, use the word *peer* instead of *server* in the command. For example, to indicate that you want the local server to work in peer mode with a remote server whose IP address is 123.45.6.7, use the following command:

```
Peer 123.45.6.7
```

Additional utilities you can use to work with a server's time are described in Table 3.8.

T A B L E 3.8	*Utilities Used to Manage Time Services*
UTILITY	**DESCRIPTION**
TIME console utility	Displays the server's date, time, Daylight Saving Time status, and time synchronization information.
SET TIME console utility	Lets you change the server's date and time.
SET TIME ZONE console utility	Lets you change the server's time zone information.
SYSTIME workstation utility	Lets you synchronize a workstation's time with the server's time.
DSREPAIR.NLM	Lets you see the TimeSync status of all servers in the tree.

CHAPTER 4

Installing Workstations

Installing

- Each workstation must have Novell client software installed on it. There is a specific version of the client software for Windows 95 and 98, another for Windows NT, and another for DOS/Windows 3.1x.

- Novell frequently updates its client software, so you may want to check its Web site (www.novell.com) for new client software.

- To upgrade workstations to the latest version of the Novell client software, you can use the Automatic Client Upgrade (ACU) feature or the NetWare Application Launcher (part of Z.E.N.works, described in Chapter 6).

Configuring

- To configure the Novell client software on a Windows 95, 98, or NT workstation, use the Novell Client Property pages in the Network Control Panel (accessible through the Control Panel or through the Network Neighborhood).

- To configure the Novell client software on a Windows 3.1x or DOS workstation, edit the NET.CFG file, which contains parameters that configure various aspects of the workstation's software.

Novell Client Software

On a NetWare network, each workstation must have special Novell client software installed on it. (On a NetWare network, workstations are often called *clients* because they request services from the network.) This client software enables the workstation to communicate with the network. This chapter explains how to install and configure Novell client software on the following types of workstations:

- ► Windows 95 (and 98) and Windows NT
- ► DOS and Windows 3.1*x*

It also explains how to remove the client software, should that become necessary. Finally, the chapter describes how to use the Automatic Client Upgrade feature to simplify the process of upgrading numerous clients to the latest NetWare 5 software.

The Novell client installation program automatically copies all necessary NetWare files to the workstation, and edits any DOS or Windows files that require modifications. You must use Novell's client software instead of Microsoft's own client software if you want to take advantage of all the features and benefits of your NetWare 5 network.

You can choose one of three methods for installing the Novell client on your workstation:

- ► You can install the client software directly from the *NetWare 5 Operating System* CD-ROM.

- ► If you are upgrading existing workstations, you can copy the installation files from the CD-ROM into a network directory, and run the installation program from the network directory rather than from the CD-ROM.

- ► You can download the latest Novell client from Novell's Web site on the Internet (www.novell.com). Periodically, Novell releases updated clients with new features, so the client files on the Internet may be newer than the client files on the CD-ROM. Therefore, it's a good idea to check this location for updates.

Now let's look at how to install and configure Novell client software on Windows 95/98 and Windows NT workstations, and on DOS and Windows 3.1*x* workstations.

► · ◄

Windows 95/98 and Windows NT Workstations

The following sections explain how to install, configure, and remove the Novell client software from a Windows 95/98 or Windows NT workstation. Before you can install the client, though, your workstation must meet certain requirements.

To install the client software on a Windows 95 workstation, the computer should have at least 16MB of disk space available on drive C. It must also be running the Windows 95 Service Pack 1 or better. (You can download Microsoft's Service Pack 1 from Microsoft's Web site, at www. microsoft.com.) Windows 98 workstations should meet all the requirements for running Windows 98.

To install the Novell client software on a Windows NT workstation, the computer should meet all the requirements for running Windows NT. In addition, it should be running Windows NT version 4.0, with Service Pack 3 or later installed on it. Again, see Microsoft's Web site for more information about downloading its service packs.

For either platform, you will also need a CD-ROM drive if you're installing the client directly from the CD-ROM, or a connection to the Internet if you're downloading the client. If you're upgrading an existing workstation that already has a connection to the network, you can run the installation program from a network directory instead.

The Novell client software for both Windows 95/98 and Windows NT will work on IP, IPX, or mixed networks. You specify the protocol you want to use during the client installation.

If all these requirements are met, then you're ready to install the client software.

Installing the Client Software

To install the Novell client software on a workstation that is running Windows 95/98 or Windows NT, complete the following steps:

NOTE

You can use the following procedure whether you're installing a network workstation or upgrading an existing one. If you are upgrading an existing workstation, the installation program will detect existing settings (such as the protocol used, the network board, and optional features) and use those same settings as the default settings for the upgraded workstation.

1. Install a network board in the workstation according to the manufacturer's documentation. Record the board's configuration settings, such as its interrupt and port address. (You may want to use a worksheet such as the "Workstation Installation and Configuration" worksheet in Appendix D.)

2. Cable the network board to the network, using the correct cabling hardware, including terminators, hubs, or any other hardware required by your topology. See Chapter 1 and your hardware manufacturer's documentation for more information about limitations and guidelines for installing network hardware.

3. (Optional) If you are planning to upgrade a workstation and want to run the installation program from the network, create a directory called CLIENT under SYS:PUBLIC, and then create a directory called WIN95 (or WINNT) under CLIENT. Then, copy all the files from the PRODUCTS\WIN95\IBM_ENU (or PRODUCTS\WINNT) folder on the CD-ROM to your newly created network directory. Also, copy the WINSETUP.EXE file from the root of the CD-ROM to the new installation directory. (The IBM_ENU folder contains the English version of the client files. If you need another language, use the corresponding IBM_*language* folder.)

4. Run WINSETUP.EXE.

  - If you're installing from the CD-ROM, insert the Client CD-ROM in the workstation's drive. WINSETUP.EXE, which is located at the root of the CD-ROM, will start automatically.

  - If you're upgrading an existing workstation and are running the installation program from the network, run WINSETUP.EXE from the SYS:PUBLIC\CLIENT\WIN95 (or WINNT) directory.

5. Click the language you want to use.

6. Click Windows 95/98 Client (or Windows NT Client).

7. Click Install Novell Client.

8. After you're read the license agreement, choose Yes to accept it.

9. Choose Custom, and then click Next.

10. Choose the protocol you want this workstation to use.

- IP Only — Installs only the IP protocol. The workstation will be able to communicate only with IP servers, and will not be able to communicate with IPX servers.

- IP with IPX Compatibility Mode — Installs the IP protocol, but allows the workstation to communicate with IPX networks if the servers have IPX Compatibility Mode and a Migration Agent installed.

- IP + IPX — Installs both protocols, allowing the workstation to communicate with either type of server.

- IPX Only — Installs only the IPX protocol, allowing the workstation to communicate with IPX servers, but not directly with IP servers.

11. Choose whether you want to log in to NDS or to a bindery, and then click Next. (Only select the bindery option if you need to log in to a NetWare 3.*x* server.)

12. Select any optional components you also want to install. (If the installation program detects that any of these options are already installed on this workstation, those options will be checked.) At minimum, you will probably want to select the Novell Distributed Print Services (NDPS) option. (See Chapter 9 for more information about NDPS.)

13. Click Install.

14. The client installation program can automatically detect and load many LAN drivers for common network boards (which the program calls network adapters). If it cannot detect your network board, it will prompt you to select one. You will need to insert a diskette (or specify another location) for the LAN driver your network board requires.

15. If you are prompted to set a Preferred Tree and Name Context, enter the name of your tree, your name context, and the first network drive. This will make it easier for you to log in later — you won't have to specify this information every time. You do not need to specify a preferred server unless you want to log in to a NetWare 3.*x* server. When you've finished entering this information, click Finish.

16. Choose Reboot to restart the workstation so the Novell client files can take effect.

When the workstation reboots, it will automatically connect to the network and present you with a Login screen. Enter your user name and password, and the client software will authenticate you to the network. When it's finished, your workstation will be connected, and you will be logged in and ready to work.

Configuring the Client Software

After you have installed the Novell client software, you can configure the client software to change some of its aspects, if necessary. You configure the client by modifying its Property pages, which you can access through either the Network Neighborhood or the Network Control Panel:

- ► To use the Network Neighborhood, right-click the Network Neighborhood icon, and select Properties. Then select Novell NetWare Client, and then click Properties. The client software's Property pages will appear.

- ► To use the Control Panel, begin at the Windows Start menu. Choose Settings, and then choose Control Panel. Double-click the Network folder. Select the Novell NetWare Client, and then click Properties. The client software's Property pages will appear.

The client's Property pages enable you to specify information such as login preferences, protocol settings, default capture settings, and so on. The Advanced Settings page enables you to set configuration parameters. These parameters are primarily the same ones you can set in NET.CFG for the Windows 3.1x workstation platform; however, in Windows 95/98 and NT, these parameters are saved in Microsoft's Windows Registry.

When you've finished configuring the client software, click OK to save your settings.

Removing the Client Software

To remove the Novell client software from a Windows NT or Windows 95/98 workstation, you can use the Network Control Panel (which can also be accessed through the Network Neighborhood). This process removes the client components from the workstation, but some client information will remain in the Windows registry. That way, if you reinstall the client, the installation program will be able to use the same settings you had set previously.

To remove the client components, first open the Network Control Panel. You can do this by right-clicking the Network Neighborhood icon and selecting Properties. You can also open the Network Control Panel by opening the

Windows Start menu, and then selecting Settings and then Control Panel. Then, double-click the Network folder.

After you've opened the Network Control Panel, select the Novell NetWare Client, and click Remove. Then click OK, choose Yes to confirm your decision, and reboot the workstation.

► • ◄

Windows 3.1x and DOS Workstations

The following sections explain how to install, configure, and remove the client software on a Windows 3.1x or DOS workstation. Both the Novell client installation program for DOS (INSTALL.EXE) and for Windows 3.1x (WINSETUP.EXE) accomplish the same tasks during installation. You can choose whichever version you prefer. Before you can install the client, however, make sure your workstation meets the following requirements.

To install the client software on a Windows 3.1x or DOS workstation, the computer should have a 386 or better processor, and at least 8MB of RAM. It should also have at least 16MB of disk space available on drive C. In addition, it should be running a memory manager, such as himem.sys, emm386.exe, qemm, or 386max. You will also need a CD-ROM drive if you're installing the client directly from the CD-ROM, or a connection to the Internet if you're downloading the client. If you're upgrading an existing workstation that already has a connection to the network, you can run the installation program from a network directory instead.

The following instructions guide you through the installation steps for each platform.

Installing the Client Software from Windows 3.1x

To install the Novell client software from Windows 3.1x, complete the following steps:

1. Install a network board in the workstation according to the manufacturer's documentation. Record the board's configuration settings, such as its interrupt and port address. (You may want to use a worksheet such as the "Workstation Installation and Configuration" worksheet in Appendix D.)

2. Cable the network board to the network, using the correct cabling hardware, including terminators, hubs, or any other hardware required by your topology. See Chapter 1 and your hardware manufacturer's documentation for more information about limitations and guidelines for installing network hardware.

3. (Optional) If you are planning to upgrade a workstation and want to run the installation program from the network, create a directory called CLIENT under SYS:PUBLIC, and then create a directory called DOSWIN32 under CLIENT. Then, copy all the files from the PRODUCTS\DOSWIN32 folder on the CD-ROM to your newly created network directory. Also, copy the WINSETUP.EXE file from the root of the CD-ROM to the new installation directory.

4. Run WINSETUP.EXE.

   - If you're installing from the CD-ROM, insert the Client CD-ROM in the workstation's drive. WINSETUP.EXE, which is located at the root of the CD-ROM, will start automatically.

   - If you're upgrading an existing workstation and are running the installation program from the network, run WINSETUP.EXE from the SYS:PUBLIC\CLIENT\DOSWIN32 directory.

5. Click the language you want to use.

6. Click Windows 3.*x* Client.

7. Click Install Novell Client.

8. After you've read the license agreement, choose Yes to accept it.

9. Click Next to begin the installation.

10. Select any optional components you also want to install, and then click Next. (If the installation program detects that any of these options are already installed on this workstation, those options will be checked.) At minimum, you will probably want to select the Novell Distributed Print Services (NDPS) option. (See Chapter 9 for more information about NDPS.)

11. Choose the destination directory on the workstation, and then click Next. The default is C:\NOVELL\CLIENT32.

12. The install program displays the disk space required to install your selections. If this is acceptable, click Begin Copy.

13. Select the first network drive letter (a letter that is not already assigned to a local drive or a CD-ROM drive). Then click Next.

14. Choose a Program Group for the client software, and then click Next. The default program group is Novell Client.

15. Choose the manufacturer and model of your network board. Use the pull-down menus to select yours from the list. If yours isn't on the list, click Have Disk and insert the diskette that contains your LAN driver, and then follow the prompts to install it. Then click Next.

16. Choose the settings for your network board (also called a LAN adapter).

17. When asked "Would you like to connect to network servers?" choose Yes. Then enter the name of your tree and your name context. This will make it easier for you to log in later — you won't have to specify this information every time. You do not need to specify a preferred server unless you want to log in to a NetWare 3.*x* server.

18. (Optional) Select any additional protocol you want to use, such as TCP/IP.

19. Remove any diskettes from the workstation's drives, keep the Restart Computer option marked, and click Finish. This will restart the workstation so the Novell client files can take effect.

When the computer reboots, the Novell Login icon will appear in the Novell Client program group on your Windows desktop. To log in to the network, double-click the icon, and then enter your login name and password when prompted. The client software will authenticate you to the network. When it's finished, your workstation will be connected, and you will be logged in and ready to work.

Installing the Client Software from DOS

To install the Novell client software on a DOS computer, complete the following steps:

1. Install a network board in the workstation according to the manufacturer's documentation. Be sure to record the board's configuration settings, such as its interrupt and port address. (You may want to use a worksheet such as the "Workstation Installation and Configuration" worksheet in Appendix D.)

2. Cable the network board to the network, using the correct cabling hardware, including terminators, hubs, or any other hardware required by your topology. See Chapter 1 and your hardware manufacturer's documentation for more information about limitations and guidelines for installing network hardware.

3. (Optional) If you are planning to upgrade a workstation and want to run the installation program from the network, create a directory called CLIENT under SYS:PUBLIC, and then create a directory called DOSWIN32 under CLIENT. Then copy all the files from the PRODUCTS\DOSWIN32 folder on the CD-ROM to your newly created network directory.

4. Run INSTALL.EXE.

- If you're installing from the CD-ROM, insert the Client CD-ROM in the workstation's drive. Then go to the PRODUCTS\DOSWIN32 directory on the CD-ROM, and type **INSTALL**.

- If you're upgrading an existing workstation and are running the installation program from the network, map a drive to the SYS:PUBLIC\CLIENT\DOSWIN32 directory, and then type **INSTALL**.

5. After you've read the license agreement, press Enter to accept it.

6. Select the components you want to install and press F10. At minimum, select the Novell Client for DOS. If this workstation will run Windows 3.1x, also select Novell Client Windows Support and the Novell Distributed Print Services option. Use the Spacebar to mark each option you want to install. Press F10 to save your selections and continue.

7. Specify if you want to use more country codes than the one currently installed on this machine (in most cases, answer No).

8. Network administrators are asked if they want to set the shared Windows path. (In most cases, answer No unless you are an administrator who does want to set up a shared Windows path.) Then press F10 to continue.

9. Choose whether you want to install a 16-bit or 32-bit driver. Select a 32-bit driver if one is available for your network board.

10. Allow the installation program to edit the AUTOEXEC.BAT and CONFIG.SYS files on the workstation.

11. Accept the default client directory (the location on the workstation where the client files should be installed) and the workstation's Windows directory.

12. Select your LAN driver. If the driver you need isn't on the CD-ROM, you will need to have it on a diskette. (Drivers are available from the network board's manufacturer.)

13. Press F10 to accept all the defaults (or your changes) and continue. Client files will now be installed on the workstation.

14. After the installation is complete, restart the computer to make the new client take effect.

After the workstation reboots, you can log in to the network. To log in, type **LOGIN**, and then enter your full login name and password when prompted. The client software will authenticate you to the network. When it's finished, your workstation will be connected, and you will be logged in and ready to work.

You can also add the Login command and your user name to the AUTOEXEC.BAT file, so it will execute the Login command automatically for you whenever you reboot the workstation. For example, if your login name is SWalsh, enter the following command in the AUTOEXEC.BAT file:

```
LOGIN SWALSH
```

You will still have to enter your password each time the workstation reboots, however, for security reasons.

Configuring the Client Software

When the Novell client software is installed on a Windows 3.1x or DOS workstation, the installation program edits or creates several system files that configure the workstation whenever it is booted. You can use any text editor to edit these files to make further changes to the workstation's configuration, if necessary. The following files are the most common ones you may need to edit:

- ► CONFIG.SYS
- ► AUTOEXEC.BAT
- ► STARTNET.BAT
- ► NET.CFG

CONFIG.SYS

CONFIG.SYS is a configuration file that is created at the root of the workstation's boot disk during the operating system's installation. It can also be created or edited with a text editor. CONFIG.SYS configures the workstation's DOS environment. CONFIG.SYS is automatically modified by the NetWare client installation.

AUTOEXEC.BAT

AUTOEXEC.BAT is a batch file created at the root of the disk during DOS installation for most recent versions of DOS. It can also be created or edited with a text editor. It automatically executes when the workstation boots. It can be used to load TSRs (Terminate and Stay Resident programs) that provide added functionality for the workstation, such as CD-ROM support, DOS key buffering, network support, and so on. It can also be used to log the user into the network.

The installation automatically edits AUTOEXEC.BAT to add a line that executes the STARTNET.BAT file. It also adds a DOS search path to the new client directory.

After installation, you may want to add lines to set the user's variables for applications and automatically log the user into the network. (If you want to use the Novell Login icon from Windows to log in, you don't need to add the LOGIN command to this file.) The following is an example of an AUTOEXEC.BAT file with the Login command added:

```
REM ─────────────── WIN
@ECHO OFF
PROMPT $p$g
PATH C:\WINDOWS;C:\DOS;c:\;c:\zip;c:\qemm;C:\mouse2
PATH C:\NOVELL\CLIENT32;%PATH%
SET TEMP=C:\temp
set comspec=c:\command.com
set mouse=C:\mouse2
C:\QEMM\LOADHI /R:1 C:\WINDOWS\MSCDEX.EXE /S /V /D:MSCD001
/M:15 /L:E
@CALL C:\NOVELL\CLIENT32\STARTNET

c:\qemm\loadhi /r:1 C:\mouse2\mouse.com /Y
F:
LOGIN .SWALSH.MKTG.BLUECO
```

STARTNET.BAT

STARTNET.BAT is a batch file created by the NetWare client installation. It is located in the new client directory (NOVELL\CLIENT32) on the workstation. It can be edited with a text editor.

STARTNET.BAT specifies the workstation's language by setting the NWLANGUAGE environment variable, and then it loads Novell client software, the LAN driver, and protocol support files.

In older versions of NetWare client software, called NETX, the commands to load these files were located in the AUTOEXEC.BAT file (instead of in STARTNET.BAT), so if you upgrade a workstation from NETX, you'll need to edit the AUTOEXEC.BAT file to remove those lines.

NET.CFG

NET.CFG is the main configuration file used by the Novell client. It can contain dozens of commands to configure various aspects of your client software, such as 16-bit ODI LAN driver settings, network management settings, and general items for the client software itself. It is created by the NetWare client installation. It is located in the client directory (NOVELL\CLIENT32) and can be edited with a text editor.

Every workstation's NET.CFG file may be different because of the different hardware or software installed on the workstation. Using a text editor, open your workstation's NET.CFG file. Notice that the file is divided by headings.

The Link Driver heading contains indented lines that specify the information for your workstation's LAN driver. If you have two network boards installed in the workstation, the NET.CFG file will have two Link Driver headings.

The NetWare DOS Requester heading contains indented lines that specify general items for the Novell client software. There may also be headings for protocols, network management software, and so on. All the parameters you can set in NET.CFG are explained in Appendix A. They are also explained in the NET.CFG online help.

NET.CFG's help file is named NWCFGDW.HLP, and it is located in the NOVELL\CLIENT32 directory on the workstation. Locate that file from the Windows File Manager, and double-click it to open it. The help file explains all the parameters you can use, divided by categories (which correspond to the headings in the file).

Removing the Client Software

If you want to remove the Novell client software from a Windows 3.1*x* or DOS workstation, you have to manually delete files and edit system files. There is no "uninstall" utility.

If you want to disable the client temporarily, rather than removing it completely, you can simply remove (or comment out) the line in the AUTOEXEC.BAT file that calls STARTNET.BAT.

To remove the client software, complete the following steps:

1. Delete the NOVELL\CLIENT32 directory and all its subdirectories and files from the workstation.

2. In the Windows Program Manager, open the Novell Client window and delete all the icons in that window. Then delete the Novell Client window itself.

3. Using any text editor, open the AUTOEXEC.BAT file.

   a. Delete the line PATH C:\NOVELL\CLIENT32; %path%.

   b. Delete the line @CALL C:\NOVELL\CLIENT32\STARTNET.

   c. Save and close the file.

4. Using a text editor, open CONFIG.SYS.

   a. Delete the line DEVICE=C:\NOVELL\CLIENT32\LOCATION.EXE.

   b. If it's there, delete the line DEVICE=C:\NOVELL\CLIENT32\DIDB.SYS.

   c. Save and close the file.

5. Using a text editor, open SYSTEM.INI.

   a. In the [Boot] section, delete NETWARE.DRV from the line SECONDNET.DRV= or the line NETWORK.DRV=.

   b. From the [Boot.description] section, delete Novell NetWare (or Novell Client) from the line SECONDNET.DRV= or the line NETWORK.DRV=.

   c. In the [386Enh] section, delete VNETWARE.386 from the line NETWORK=.

   d. Also in the [386Enh] section, delete the line DEVICE=VLANINT.386.

   e. Save and close the file.

6. Using a text editor, open WIN.INI.

   a. In the [Windows] section, delete the line LOAD=NWPOP.EXE.

   b. Delete the line RUN=C:\NOVELL\CLIENT32\NWMSTART.EXE.

   c. Save and close the file.

7. Delete the following files from the WINDOWS\NLS*language* directory:

login.dat

login.msg

loginw31.hlp

netware.drv

netware.hlp

8. Delete the following files from the WINDOWS\SYSTEM directory:

calwin16.dll	loginw31.dll	nwgdi.dll	nwuser.exe
clnwin16.dll	ncpwin16.dll	nwipxspx.dll	prtwin16.dll
clxwin16.dll	netware.drv	nwlocale.dll	tli_spx.dll
ctl3dv2.dll	netwin16.dll	nwnet.dll	tli_win.dll
lgnw3116.dll	nwcalls.dll	nwpopup.exe	vlanint.386
locwin16.dll	nwdrvlgo.bmp	nwpsrv.dll	vnetware.386

9. If you installed support for TCP/IP, rename WINSOCK.OLD in the WINDOWS directory to WINSOCK.DLL. Then rename WLIBSOCK.OLD in the WINDOWS\SYSTEM directory to WLIBSOCK.DLL

10. Reboot the computer to make the new configuration take effect.

After you have completed these steps, the Novell client software is no longer installed on this computer.

Simplifying the Upgrade Process with ACU

If you are upgrading many existing NetWare workstations to the new NetWare 5 Novell client software, you can use the Automatic Client Upgrade (ACU) feature to automate this process. With the ACU, you place ACU commands in a profile or system login script to detect if the client software needs to be installed, and then the ACU updates the workstation automatically, if necessary, when the user logs in.

You can also use the ACU process to upgrade workstations that are currently running Microsoft Client for NetWare Networks.

NOTE

Another way to simplify the upgrading process is to use the NetWare Application Launcher (a feature of Z.E.N.works) to set up an icon on each workstation to point to the Novell client installation program. See Chapter 6 for more information about using the Application Launcher.

The ACU feature works best in situations where you have many workstations with similar configurations, because you define a common set of instructions for updating all the workstations in the same way.

To use the ACU process to upgrade a workstation to the Novell Client, complete the following steps:

1. Create a directory called CLIENT under SYS:PUBLIC, and then create a directory called WIN95 (or WINNT, or DOSWIN32, depending on the client software you want to use) under CLIENT. Then copy all the files from the PRODUCTS\WIN95\IBM_ENU (or PRODUCTS\WINNT or PRODUCTS\DOSWIN32) folder on the CD-ROM to your newly created network directory. Also copy the WINSETUP.EXE and WINSETUP.INI files from the root of the CD-ROM to the new installation directory. (The IBM_ENU folder contains the English version of the Windows 95/98 client files. If you need another language, use the corresponding IBM_*language* folder.)

2. (Windows 95/98 only) Copy the Windows 95 (or 98) .cab files from the WIN95 folder on the Microsoft Windows 95 CD-ROM (or the WIN98 folder on the Microsoft Windows 98 CD-ROM) to the new directory.

3. Using the NetWare Administrator utility, create a Group object called ACU. (See Chapter 6 for more information about creating groups.)

4. Give the ACU group Read and File Scan rights to the new directory you created in Step 1. (See Chapter 7 for more information about assigning rights.)

5. Assign users to the ACU group. Assign all users whose workstations you want to upgrade.

6. Edit the WINSETUP.INI file to specify configuration options you want to use during the upgrade. This file is located at the root of the Client CD-ROM, along with WINSETUP.EXE. This file determines whether the workstation's current client software is old and needs to be upgraded to the newer version.

a. By default, the upgrade runs automatically when the user logs in. However, you can set it so that the user can choose whether to upgrade at that time. If the user chooses to skip the upgrade, the upgrade prompt will appear again the next time he or she logs in. To display the screen that lets the user choose whether to upgrade the software, add the following command to the [AcuOptions] heading:

```
DisplayFirstScreen=Yes
```

b. By default, the upgrade will automatically reboot the workstation when it is finished. However, if you want to let the user decide whether to reboot the workstation, add the following command to the [AcuOptions] heading:

```
DisplayLastScreen=Yes
```

7. Edit the login script for the users whose workstations will be upgraded to add the command to launch the WINSETUP.EXE file. You can edit a user's individual script, a container's script, or a profile script, depending on how many users you want to upgrade. (For more information about login scripts, see Chapter 6.) You need to add the following command to the login script, substituting the name of your server for *server*:

```
@\\server\SYS:PUBLIC\WIN95\WINSETUP.EXE
```

If you want the old client configuration to be backed up on the workstation instead of just being replaced by the new client software, you can add the option /RB (for "rollback") to the end of this command. This option will copy the current software configuration to NOVELL\CLIENT32\NWBACKUP.

Now, the next time the users in the group log in, their workstations will be upgraded automatically to the new Novell client.

> **For more information about using ACU, see the Novell online documentation.**
>
> **NOTE**

CHAPTER 5

Managing Novell Directory Services

Managing NDS Objects

▶ To create NDS objects, use the NetWare Administrator utility (which runs in Windows 95/98 and Windows NT).

▶ To change a name context, use the NetWare Administrator or the CX command-line utility.

Managing Replicas and Partitions

▶ To manage replicas and partitions, use the NDS Manager utility (which can be run standalone or as a Tools option in the NetWare Administrator utility).

▶ To manage the NDS schema, use the Schema Manager utility (which is an option under the Object menu in the NDS Manager utility).

Managing Bindery Services

▶ To set a bindery context, use the SET BINDERY CONTEXT parameter, which you can execute as a SET command at the console or choose from the Server Parameters option in MONITOR.NLM.

▶ To display the bindery context, use the CONFIG console utility.

Managing WAN Traffic

▶ To prevent WAN links from being kept open excessively, use the WAN Traffic Manager feature to restrict routine WAN traffic to specific times or days (or to other limits you specify).

Using Catalog Services

▶ To create an easily searchable database of specific object types and information, create a Master Catalog object specifying objects to include in the catalog.

▶ To search through a catalog for information, use the Query Catalog option from the NetWare Administrator utility.

Merging NDS Trees

▶ To merge NDS trees, use DSMERGE.NLM.

Using Additional Services with NDS

▶ Use LDAP Services for NDS to enable LDAP clients to access NDS information.

▶ Use Novell DNS/DHCP Services to integrate DNS and DHCP address management into NDS.

Troubleshooting

▶ To monitor NDS messages, use the SET NDS TRACE console command.

▶ To repair the NDS tree, use DSREPAIR.NLM or the NDS Manager feature of the NetWare Administrator utility, which executes DSREPAIR remotely when necessary.

What Is NDS?

Novell Directory Services (NDS), in simplest terms, is a distributed database of network information. It contains information that defines every object on the network. *Objects* include network resources such as users, groups, printers, print queues, servers, and volumes. For every NDS object, the NDS database describes the type of object it is, where it resides, what level of security the object can exercise, who can access it, and other similar types of information.

In NetWare 3.1x and 2.x, this network information was stored in a database called the bindery. Each server had its own unique bindery. If you wanted a user to access more than one server, you had to create a separate account for that user on each server, because the different binderies couldn't talk to each other to see which users were valid across multiple servers.

With NetWare 4, NDS replaced the bindery. The NDS database is not confined to a single server, as binderies are. Instead, now all the NetWare 4 or NetWare 5 servers in a network tree share a single, distributed database. This way, you only have to create a user or other object once in the network tree; each server will recognize that same user or object. You can allow that user to access different servers simply by granting him or her the appropriate rights to the necessary volumes on each server.

Another difference between binderies and NDS is how the network information can be organized. Binderies use a *flat database structure,* which means all network objects — users, groups, print queues, and so on — exist at the same level. NDS uses a *hierarchical database structure.* With this type of structure, you can group objects together under categories and subcategories. This makes it easier to find the object you're looking for. It also enables you to control objects as a group, such as when you're modifying those objects' security levels.

The NDS database is called the Directory tree, because it can be easily represented as an upside-down tree, with a root at the top and branches and subbranches fanning out below it (see Figure 5.1).

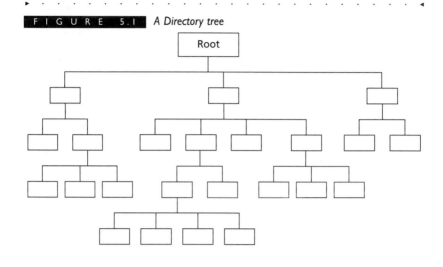

FIGURE 5.1 *A Directory tree*

NDS Objects

For each type of network entity that will operate on the network, you will create an NDS object. This object may represent the real entity, such as a user, or it may represent a service, such as a print server. Each NDS object contains several *properties,* which are the pieces of information that define the object. For example, a User object contains properties that define the user's full name, his or her ID number, an e-mail address, group memberships, and so on. (Properties are also called *attributes.*) Each type of object, such as a Server or Printer object, may have different properties than another type of object.

Each type of object, such as User, Print Queue, or Server, is referred to as an object class.

Categories of Object Classes

Object classes fall into three basic categories:

▶ *Root object.* The Root object is unique and is situated at the very top of the Directory tree.

▶ *Container objects.* These are objects that contain other objects. For example, a container object called Sales could contain all the users who work in the Sales department, their workstations, and their printers. The following are the main container object classes that are available, although you will probably use only one or two of them:

- *Country (seldom used in NDS trees).* You can have only one level of Country objects (if you use them at all), which fall immediately below the Root object. A Country object is often designated by the abbreviation "C," as in "C=US."

- *Locality (seldom used in NDS trees).* The Locality object, if used, can be located under any of the other container objects. It is assigned the abbreviation "L."

- *Organization (always used in NDS trees).* You can have only one level of Organization objects. This falls below the Country object if there is one specified, or the Root object if there isn't one. You need at least one Organization object. During the server installation, you're asked to specify an Organization name for this mandatory object. Organization objects are assigned the abbreviation O, as in O=BlueSky.

- *Organizational Unit (often used in NDS trees).* You can have multiple levels of Organizational Unit objects, which fall below the Organization objects. Organizational Unit objects have the abbreviation OU, as in OU=Sales.

- *License Container.* This container object is created automatically when you install a license certificate or create a metering certificate using NetWare Licensing Services (NLS) technology. This container object contains those certificates, which are leaf objects. (This object is also called the NLS:Product Container object.)

▶ *Leaf objects.* These objects represent the entities on the network. Leaf objects, such as users, servers, and volumes, cannot contain other objects. Unlike container objects, all leaf objects use the same abbreviation, (CN, which stands for Common Name) regardless of the type of objects they may be. This designation is required by the X.500 specifications. Therefore, all leaf objects, such as printers, users, servers, and print queues, use the abbreviation CN, as in CN=ServerA or CN=Fred.

NOTE Country and Locality objects are used primarily for compliance with X.500 naming specifications, but are seldom used in Novell Directory Services trees. The X.500 specifications, which were created by organizations seeking standards for Directory

Services, include a standardized form of naming restrictions for all Directory Services applications. (Some NetWare utilities don't even recognize the Locality object. In most cases, Organization and Organizational Unit objects are all you need to organize your NDS tree.)

You can use these three types of object classes to place your NDS objects into a manageable organization. The Root object resides at the top of the tree. The container objects form branches and sub-branches. The leaf objects are the individual users, printers, servers, and so on that populate those branches.

Figure 5.2 shows how these three categories of object classes appear in the Directory tree.

F I G U R E   5 . 2   *Root, container, and leaf objects in a Directory tree*

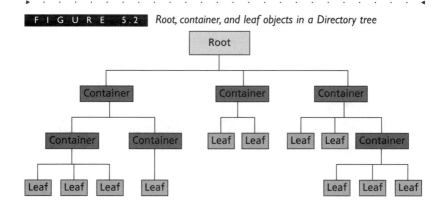

The NDS Schema

The types of NDS objects, their properties, and the rules that govern their creation and existence are called the *NDS schema*. The schema defines which objects and properties are allowed in the NDS database, and determines how those objects can inherit properties and trustee rights of other container objects above it. The schema also defines how the Directory tree is structured and how objects in it are named.

Software developers can expand or change the schema by identifying new classes of objects (say, for example, a database server) or adding additional properties to existing object classes (such as adding a property called Pager Number to a User object).

To see the object classes and properties that are allowed in your current schema, or to change or expand the schema, you can use a utility called the Schema Manager, which is a tool within the NDS Manager utility. NDS Manager and Schema Manager are explained later in this chapter.

 When you install NetWare 5, you may notice messages indicating that the NDS schema is being extended. This is to support some of the features of NetWare 5 that require additional
NOTE objects in the schema.

NDS Object Classes

In NetWare 5, a wide variety of object classes is available. Table 5.1 lists most of the object classes that are available in NetWare 5. The object classes available in your own network environment may vary somewhat from the following list, because some object classes only appear if you install specific features or add-on products. In addition, third-party manufacturers can create their own object classes for their own applications.

T A B L E   5. I   *Object Classes Available by Default*

OBJECT CLASS	DESCRIPTION
Address Range	An object that defines a range of IP addresses used by DHCP. Used with Novell DNS/DHCP Services. See the Novell documentation for more information.
AFP Server	An object that represents an AppleTalk File Protocol (AFP) server that is a node on the network.
Administrator Group	An object that represents a group of users who have access to DNS/DHCP Locator objects. These users can use the DNS/DHCP Administrator utility to create and manage DNS and DHCP objects. Used with Novell DNS/DHCP Services. See the Novell documentation for more information.
Alias	A representation of an object that is really located in another part of the Directory tree. Aliases let you place duplicate icons for an object in multiple locations in the tree so users can find it more easily.

OBJECT CLASS	DESCRIPTION
Application	An object that points to an application installed on the network. An Application object can be "associated" with users or groups. Then that application can easily be executed from each user's Application Launcher (a feature of Z.E.N.works). See Chapter 6 for more information about the Application Launcher.
Application Folder	An object that represents multiple Application objects. Application Folder objects are used with the Application Launcher in Z.E.N.works. See Chapter 6 for more information about the Application Launcher.
Audit File	An object that manages an audit trail's configuration and access rights. Used only if the Auditing feature is used. See the Novell documentation for more information.
Bindery Object	An object that was upgraded from a bindery-based server, but that could not be converted into a corresponding NDS object.
Bindery Queue	An object that represents a print queue that exists outside the NDS tree (either on a NetWare 3.x server or in another NetWare 4 or NetWare 5 tree). This object enables you to manage this queue, even though it's outside your current NDS tree. See Chapter 9 for more information about printing.
Certificate Authority	An object that stores a certificate authority, used with security applications. Used with the Novell's PKI (Public Key Infrastructure) Services. See the Novell documentation for more information.
Computer	An object that represents a computer on the network. It can be any type of computer, such as a server or a workstation.
Country	An optional container object representing the country where a portion of your company is located.
DHCP Server	An object that represents a DHCP server and contains a list of subnet ranges this server can service. Used with Novell DNS/DHCP Services. See the Novell documentation for more information.

(continued)

TABLE 5.1	*Object Classes Available by Default (continued)*
OBJECT CLASS	**DESCRIPTION**
Directory Map	An object that represents a directory path, which typically points to an application or directory. See Chapter 6 for more information.
Distribution List	An object containing a list of e-mail recipients; used if Message Handling Services (MHS) is used by your e-mail package. See the e-mail product's documentation for more information.
DNS Resource Record Set	An object that represents an individual domain name in a DNS zone. Used with Novell DNS/DHCP Services. See the Novell documentation for more information.
DNS Server	An object that represents a DNS server and contains configuration information about the DNS server, such as its IP address and zone list. Used with Novell DNS/DHCP Services. See the Novell documentation for more information.
DNS/DHCP Group	An object representing a group of DNS and DHCP servers that all need rights to DNS and DHCP data in the tree. Used with Novell DNS/DHCP Services. See the Novell documentation for more information.
DNS/DHCP Locator	An object that describes DNS and DHCP information, such as DNS servers, global defaults, DHCP options, subnets, and zones. Used with Novell DNS/DHCP Services. See the Novell documentation for more information.
External Entity	An object that stores information about non-NDS entities for other applications or services; used if Message Handling Services (MHS) is used by your e-mail package. See the e-mail product's documentation for more information.
Group	An object that contains a list of users who have at least some identical characteristics, such as the need for access rights to the same application. Users listed as group members receive a security equivalence to the group. See Chapter 6 for more information about groups.

OBJECT CLASS	DESCRIPTION
IP Address	An object that represents a single IP address on the network. Used with Novell DNS/DHCP Services. See the Novell documentation for more information.
Key Material	An object that stores a server's security information so that security applications can find and use that information. It can store a server's public key, private key, public key certificate, and certificate chain. Used with the Novell's PKI (Public Key Infrastructure) Services. See the Novell documentation for more information.
LAN Area	An object that contains a list of servers that all use the same WAN Traffic Policy (which determines how often NDS traffic is transmitted between those servers). WAN traffic management is discussed later in this chapter.
LDAP Group	An object that stores configuration information for a server or group of servers that provide NDS information to LDAP clients. Used with LDAP Services for NDS. See the Novell documentation for more information.
License	A container object that contains the licenses for NLS-enabled applications. It can also contain metered certificates.
License Catalog	An object that gathers and provides information about licenses that exist on the network, so that the administrator can access that information quickly through the NLS Manager utility.
License Certificate	An object that represents a product license certificate. It contains information about an NLS-enabled application and its licenses. It indicates the product's name, version number, manufacturer, and how many licenses can be used. When an application that uses NetWare Licensing Services is installed, that product's license certificate is added as an object in the License container object.

(continued)

TABLE 5.1	*Object Classes Available by Default (continued)*
OBJECT CLASS	**DESCRIPTION**
List	An object that simply contains a list of other objects. Objects that are list members do not have a security equivalence to the List object.
Locality	An optional container object that represents a location.
LSP Server	An object that represents a License Service Provider server; used only if NetWare Licensing Service is used.
Message Routing Group	An object that represents a group of messaging servers that are connected directly to each other so that e-mail messages can be routed between them; used if Message Handling Services (MHS) is used by your e-mail package. See the e-mail product's documentation for more information.
Messaging Server	An object that represents a server that receives and transfers e-mail messages.
Metered Certificate	An object that records the usage of a software product so you can monitor it.
NDPS Broker	An object that represents the NDPS Broker installed on a server. The NDPS Broker object controls three NDPS printing services: the Resource Management Service, the Event Notification Service, and the Service Registry Service. See Chapter 9 for more information about NDPS printing.
NDPS Manager	An object that represents the NDPS Manager, which is a software program that controls all the printer agents on a server. See Chapter 9 for more information about NDPS printing.
NDPS Printer	An object that represents a network printer that uses the NDPS printing system. See Chapter 9 for more information about NDPS printing.

OBJECT CLASS	DESCRIPTION
NDSCat:Master Catalog	An object that represents a master catalog, which is an easy-to-search database of specified NDS object types and information, such as an employee phone directory. Catalogs are discussed later in this chapter.
NDSCat:Slave Catalog	An object that represents a copy of a master catalog, which can be placed on a server in another geographic location. Catalogs are discussed later in this chapter.
NetWare Server	An object that represents a NetWare server. (Also called an NCP Server object.)
Organization	An object that represents an Organization. Usually named with the organization's name (such as a company name).
Organizational Role	An object that represents a position (such as director, project leader, or recreation coordinator) that various users can occupy. This enables you to assign rights to the position rather than to specific users.
Organizational Unit	A container object that can form a subdivision under an Organization, such as a division, department, project team, or workgroup.
Policy Package	An object that represents a policy package for use with Z.E.N.works. See Chapter 6 for more information about Z.E.N.works.
Print Queue	An object that represents a print queue. Used in queue-based printing. See Chapter 9 for more information about queue-based printing.
Print Server (Non-NDPS)	An object that represents a NetWare print server, which provides print services. Used in queue-based printing. See Chapter 9 for more information about queue-based printing.
Printer (Non-NDPS)	An object that represents a printer attached to the network. Used in queue-based printing. See Chapter 9 for more information about queue-based printing.

(continued)

T A B L E 5.1	Object Classes Available by Default (continued)
OBJECT CLASS	**DESCRIPTION**
Profile	An object whose sole function is to provide a login script that can be used by several users, all of whom do not need to be in the same container. See Chapter 6 for more information about login scripts and profiles.
Root	The object representing the highest point (starting point) of the Directory tree.
Security	A container object that holds security-related objects. See the Novell documentation for more information.
SLP Directory Agent	An object used by the SLP protocol, which manages how services are advertised and located on the network. See the Novell documentation for more information.
SLP Scope Unit	An object used by the SLP protocol. See the Novell documentation for more information.
Subnet	A container object that represents a subnet and holds configuration information that applies to all the IP Address and Address Range objects under the Subnet container object. Used with Novell DNS/DHCP Services. See the Novell documentation for more information.
Subnet Pool	An object that provides support for multiple subnets. Used with Novell DNS/DHCP Services. See the Novell documentation for more information.
Template	An object used to define common characteristics for all users created using this template. See Chapter 6 for more information about user templates.
Unknown	The representation of an object that the server couldn't restore because the object's class is no longer defined in the current schema, or because another mandatory property is missing from the object.
User	An object that represents a network user.
Volume	An object that represents a network volume on a NetWare server.

OBJECT CLASS	DESCRIPTION
Workstation	An object that is created automatically when you register and import workstations for Z.E.N.works (a workstation management program included in NetWare 5). See Chapter 6 and the Novell documentation for more information about Z.E.N.works.
Workstation Group	An object that represents a group of Workstation objects. Used with Z.E.N.works (a workstation management program included in NetWare 5). See Chapter 6 and the Novell documentation for more information about Z.E.N.works.
Zone	A container object that represents a DNS zone and holds all information about that zone. Used with Novell DNS/DHCP Services. See the Novell documentation for more information.

NDS Object Security

If you have used previous versions of NetWare, you know that NetWare uses a set of trustee rights that can be granted to and revoked from users to control what those users can do within specific files and directories.

NetWare 5 uses a similar set of trustee rights to control how NDS objects can work with each other. These NDS object rights are separate from the file system rights, but they operate in a similar fashion. Using NDS object rights, you can allow users to see and manipulate other NDS objects.

NDS object rights are explained in Chapter 7.

Planning the NDS Directory Tree

To plan your Directory tree, take advantage of the container objects to make the tree resemble your company's organization. For example, if your company is quite large, with many divisions and departments, you can use a single Organization object to represent the company's name, and multiple Organizational Unit objects to represent the various divisions and departments.

Individual users, printers, and so on can be placed inside the Organizational Unit that corresponds to their department. (These individual objects are all leaf objects.) Figure 5.3 shows how a large company named RedHawk AeroSpace, Inc. might set up its Directory tree.

If your company is small, you may not need to break up your network into Organizational Units. You may want to have just a single Organization object, representing your company, and then place all leaf objects directly beneath that container. Figure 5.4 shows how a tree for a small company named Rise 'n Shine Clockworks might look.

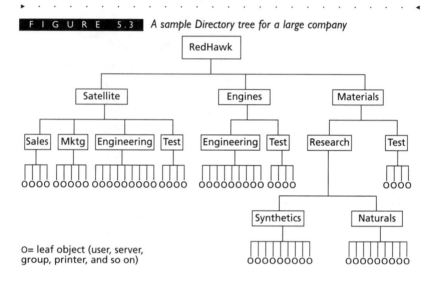

FIGURE 5.3 *A sample Directory tree for a large company*

O= leaf object (user, server, group, printer, and so on)

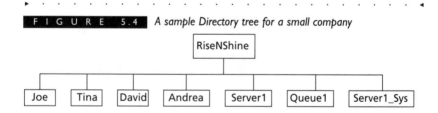

FIGURE 5.4 *A sample Directory tree for a small company*

Name Context — Your Location in the Tree

Each object in the Directory tree exists in a specific location of the tree, which is called the object's *name context*. The name context is really a sort of "address" for that object's location, consisting of the names of any container objects over that object. An object's *full name* (or *full distinguished name*) consists of the object's name plus the list of container names, with the names separated by periods. The name of the object by itself (without the rest of the container names listed) is called its *relative distinguished name*, although it is also often referred to as an object's *common name* (CN).

Within any container, all object names must be unique. For example, you can have only one user with the common name Eric within the container called Mktg. However, there can be other users named Eric on the tree if they are within other containers. Say there's an Eric in Mktg, and another Eric in Sales, both of whom work in the Satellite division of RedHawk AeroSpace, Inc.

The Marketing Eric's full name would be Eric.Mktg.Satellite.RedHawk. Each container name is added to Eric's common name (separated by periods) to spell out his address in the Directory tree, clear back to the Organization's name. His name context, or location in the tree, is Mktg.Satellite.RedHawk.

The Sales Eric's full name would be Eric.Sales.Satellite.RedHawk. Because his full name is different from the other Eric's full name, NDS can keep them both straight.

Specifying objects in the Directory tree is very similar to specifying subdirectories in a DOS file system. In the file system, if you are at the root of the volume or disk or in a completely separate directory path, you have to specify a full directory path to get to the subdirectory you want. If you are at the root of the Directory tree or in a completely different branch of the tree, you have to specify an object's full name to find it.

However, if you are somewhere in the subdirectory's directory path already, you only need to specify the portion of the path that will get you to the desired subdirectory. You don't need to specify the subdirectory's full path. Similarly, if you are already within a container over an object's location, you only need to specify the portion of the Directory tree address that exists between you and the object. You don't need to specify the object's full name, back to the root. This is called specifying a *partial name* (or a *relative distinguished name*).

If you do want to specify an object's full name back to the root, place a period at the beginning of the object's name (in any commands you type) to indicate to the utility you're using that this is a full name and shouldn't be interpreted as a partial name. For example, you would type .Eric.Mktg.Satellite.RedHawk to indicate that this is Eric's full name.

To move around in the Directory tree's context, moving up and down through containers, you can use a NetWare command-line utility called CX. This utility is similar to DOS's CD utility, which enables you to move around in the file system's subdirectory structure. More often, however, you will navigate through the levels of the Directory tree by using the NetWare Administrator utility.

NDS Replicas and Partitions

Because the NDS database is common to all servers on the network, the entire network would be disabled if the database itself were stored on only one server (with all other servers accessing it from that server) and that server went down.

To prevent this single point of failure, NetWare 5 can create *replicas* of the NDS database and store those replicas on different servers. Then, if one server goes down, all the other servers can still access the NDS database from another replica of the database.

If your NDS database is large enough, you may not want to store the entire database on multiple servers. In this case, you can create Directory *partitions,* which are portions of the database that can be replicated on different servers. A Directory partition is a branch of the Directory tree, beginning with any container object you choose. Partitions can also hold subpartitions beneath them (called *child partitions*). If you have a smaller NDS database, the whole database can reside in a single partition. Using partitions can improve network performance, especially if the network spans across a WAN (wide area network). Partitions also can make it easier to manage portions of the tree separately.

When planning your partitions, don't plan to have a partition include servers in more than one geographical location — the extra WAN traffic will be excessive. Instead, keep partitions local to servers connected to the same LAN.

Four types of replicas can be created and stored on servers:

▶ *Master replica.* The master replica is the only replica that can make changes to the Directory partition, such as adding, merging, or deleting replicas. There is only one master replica per partition. By default, the first server installed in the tree will get the master replica. However, you can change this later, if you wish.

▶ *Read-write replica.* Read-write replicas will accept requests to modify NDS objects. Any number of read-write replicas can exist on a network.

▶ *Read-only replica.* The information in a read-only replica can be read, but not modified. Any number of these replicas can exist on a network.

▶ *Subordinate reference replica.* A subordinate reference replica exists on a server if that server holds a replica of a parent partition, but does not hold a replica of the child partition. The subordinate reference replica basically provides pointers to the objects in the real child partition. These replicas are automatically created if necessary. You cannot create these manually.

Novell Directory Services handles the locations of any modifications to the NDS Directory in the background, so you and other network administrators do not need to know which replica to use to make changes to the Directory. Whenever a change is made to a replica, the change is automatically synchronized with all other replicas on the network.

To keep NDS performance optimal, you should have two or three replicas of each partition placed on separate servers. The more replicas of a partition you have, the more synchronization traffic occurs on the network, so you may not want to have more replicas than necessary. Three is the recommended number.

When you install a new server into an existing NDS tree, the installation program determines how many replicas of the partition into which you are installing the server already exist. If there are three or more replicas, the installation program will not create a new replica on the new server by default.

To create, delete, merge, or repair partitions and replicas, you use a utility called NDS Manager, which is explained later in this chapter.

NDS Tools

NetWare 5 includes a variety of tools you can use to manage your NDS tree and objects. With these tools, you can do everything from creating new users to repairing partition replicas to merging two trees into one. The following sections explain these tools.

Using NetWare Administrator to Work with NDS Objects

The primary tool for creating or modifying NDS objects is the NetWare utility called *NetWare Administrator* (sometimes referred to as NWAdmin), which runs in Windows 95/98 and Windows NT.

You can also use the ConsoleOne utility to create or modify NDS objects. ConsoleOne, which can run on the server or on a workstation, provides some of the functionality of NetWare Administrator, but not all of it. For that reason, the NetWare Administrator utility is the primary utility discussed in this chapter. The ConsoleOne utility is explained in Chapter 3.

Typical tasks you can do with NetWare Administrator include:

▸ Creating new NDS objects

▸ Deleting objects

▸ Moving objects

▸ Searching for objects by particular properties (such as all users in a given department)

▸ Changing an object's properties

▸ Renaming objects

To set up NetWare Administrator on a Windows 95/98 or Windows NT workstation, simply create a shortcut or icon on your desktop that points to the file NWADMN32.EXE, located in the SYS:PUBLIC/WIN32 folder.

NOTE If you have upgraded your network from NetWare 4.1 or NetWare 4.11, you will discover that the old version of NetWare Administrator, called NWADMIN.EXE or NWADMN95.EXE, is still in your SYS:PUBLIC directory. If you want to use the new NetWare Administrator utility that comes with NetWare 5, you must first upgrade your workstation to the client software that comes with NetWare 5. The new version of NetWare Administrator requires new .DLL files that will be installed with the new client software. If you don't upgrade your client software, you will have to continue using the older NetWare Administrator utility.

Using NDS Manager to Work with NDS Partitions and Replicas

To create, delete, or merge partitions and to work with replicas, you can use the NDS Manager utility. This utility can be executed by itself, or as a feature of the NetWare Administrator utility under the Tools option. NDS Manager runs on Windows 95/98 and Windows NT workstations.

If problems occur with Directory partitions and replicas, you can also use NDS Manager to analyze them and repair them if necessary. (The NDS

Manager utility automatically executes another utility called DSREPAIR for repair options. DSREPAIR.NLM can also be run by itself from the server's console, but it is usually easier to use NDS Manager from a workstation instead of using DSREPAIR from the console. DSREPAIR is explained in the section "DSREPAIR.NLM," later in this chapter.)

By default, NDS Manager is not part of NetWare Administrator, but you can easily add it. If you don't want to add it to NetWare Administrator, you must add NDS Manager to your workstation desktop as its own icon.

To add the NDS Manager utility to the NetWare Administrator utility on a Windows 95/98 or Windows NT workstation, simply copy the file NMSNAP32.DLL from the SYS:PUBLIC/WIN32 folder to SYS:PUBLIC/WIN32/SNAPINS. The next time you start the NetWare Administrator utility, NDS Manager will appear as an option under the Tools menu.

To set up NDS Manager as a standalone utility on your Windows 95/98 or Windows NT desktop, create a Shortcut or icon on your desktop that points to the file NDSMGR32.EXE, located in the SYS:PUBLIC/WIN32 folder. Then, to launch NDS Manager, double-click its icon on the desktop.

Common NDS Manager Tasks

You can access most NDS Manager options through the menu bar or the button bar, or by right-clicking objects you want to work with.

Documentation for NDS Manager is located in the help file. Open the help file to see a description of all the tasks you can do with NDS Manager.

NOTE

NDS Manager displays two main views of the NDS information. The Tree view shows the containers and servers in the tree, and displays information about the tree's partitions. The Partitions and Servers view is a different way to look at the partitioning information. You can see these views by clicking their respective buttons on the button bar, or by choosing them from the View menu.

Here are some of the partitioning and replication tasks you can do with NDS Manager:

▶ See the partitions on a server. From either the Tree view or the Partitions and Servers view, select a server to display a list of the partitions it holds.

▶ See information about a server or partition (including information about the partition's replicas). From either view, select the server or partition, right-click, and then choose Information. (You can also double-click the server or partition to display the same information.)

▶ Create a partition. You must create new partitions at the container level. From the Tree view, select the container you want to be the root of the partition, and then choose Create Partition.

▶ Merge two partitions. You can merge a child partition into its parent partition. The end result is a single partition that includes all objects from both of the original partitions. To merge partitions, use the Tree view, select the container that is the root of the child partition, and then choose Merge.

▶ Move a partition. You can move a partition and its container object only if it does not have any child partitions. (If you want to move a partition that has a child partition, you can merge the two before you try to move the parent partition.) To move a partition, use the Partitions and Servers view. Select the icon for the partition you want to move, and then choose Move. Specify a destination by clicking the Browser button, browsing through the directory, and selecting a container. Then check Create an Alias for this Container Object. By creating an alias, users will be able to find the partition in the location they're used to. Otherwise, you may have users unable to log in because their startup files specify the wrong name context. Finally, choose Yes, and the partition will be moved.

▶ Stop a partition operation. If you need to stop a creation, deletion, or merge of a partition, you can do so as long as at least one of the replicas involved has not yet completed the operation (as indicated by the State box). To stop an operation, select the partition that is being affected, right-click, and choose Abort Operation.

▶ Create a replica. To create a replica of a partition, right-click the partition you want to replicate, and then choose Add Replica. Select the server on which you want to store the replica, choose the type of replica you want this to be (read/write or read-only), and then click OK.

▶ Delete a replica. To delete a replica, select the partition whose replica you want to delete, choose the replica you want to delete, right-click, and then choose Delete. Master replicas cannot be deleted. If you want to delete a master replica, you must first designate another replica as master. This will automatically change the original master to a read/write replica, which you can then delete.

▶ Change a replica's type. To change a replica to a different type (read-write, master, or read-only), select the partition whose replica you want to change, select the replica you want to change, and then choose Change Replica Type. Select the type you want, and then choose OK.

▶ Delete a server. To delete a server from the Directory tree, select the server object, right-click, and choose Delete. In most circumstances, however, the recommended way to remove a NetWare server from the NDS tree is to "uninstall" NDS instead of deleting the server object.

▶ See the version of NDS on servers. Select the container that holds the servers you want to see. From the Object menu, select NDS Version, and then choose View. Bindery-based servers (NetWare 3.*x* and 2.*x*) will be displayed as Unknown.

▶ Update the version of NDS on a server. Ideally, all replicas of a partition should be stored on servers running the same version of DS.NLM (the NDS database). Periodically, Novell releases an updated DS.NLM on its Web site (www.novell.com). If you install a new version of DS.NLM on a server, update that same version onto other NetWare 5 servers by selecting the updated server object (the server you want to be the source for updating other servers). From the Object menu, select NDS Version, and then select Update. Select the servers you want to update and click the right arrow to move them under the heading Target Servers to be Updated. Then choose OK. It may take 15 to 30 minutes to update the servers.

▶ Check partition continuity. To verify that all of a partition's replicas (called a replica ring) are synchronizing correctly, right-click the partition whose replicas you want to view, and then choose Partition Continuity. If any replica listed has an exclamation point (!), that replica has experienced synchronization errors. Double-click the replica with the error. Then, from the Replica Information screen, click the Help button beside Current Sync Error.

▶ Synchronize replicas. Partition replicas synchronize automatically. If you don't want to wait for the automatic synchronization, however, you can force an immediate synchronization by right-clicking the partition you want synchronized. Then select Partition Continuity, and choose Synchronize Immediately.

▶ Send updates to other replicas. To send updates from one replica to other replicas (including the master), right-click the server whose replica has the information you want to send out, and then select Send Updates.

▶ Receive updates from the master replica. If only one replica is out of sync, you can manually request an update from the master replica. Right-click the partition whose replica you want to update, and choose Receive Updates.

▶ Repair partition and replica problems. Right-click a partition and select Partition Continuity. From the Partition Continuity screen, you can repair several types of problems with your NDS database, such as replica problems, network address problems, and so on. Most of these operations load and run DSREPAIR.NLM on the server automatically.

▶ Print NDS Manager information. You can print out information displayed by NDS Manager. To print from the Tree view or Partitions and Servers view, choose Print from the Object menu. To print from the Partition Continuity screen, choose Print from the File menu.

Using the Schema Manager Tool in NDS Manager

To see the object classes and properties that are allowed in your current schema, or to change or expand the schema, you can use a utility called Schema Manager, which is a tool within the NDS Manager utility. To open Schema Manager, first launch NDS Manager, as explained in the previous sections. Then select a Directory partition. From the Object menu, choose Schema Manager.

Schema Manager enables you to perform the following types of tasks:

▶ View the current schema. You can see all the object classes and properties that are currently allowed in your tree.

▶ Extend the schema. You can add an object class to the schema, or you can add a property to an existing object class.

▶ Compare the schemas on two different trees, and print the comparison.

▶ Delete an object class from the schema.

When you modify or extend a schema, it's best to do so from the root of the tree. That way, all the changes will synchronize cleanly throughout the rest of the tree.

Using Bindery Services to Make NDS Mimic a Bindery

Some applications and network services do not take advantage of NDS's hierarchical database structure. Instead, those applications make requests to a version of NetWare that uses a bindery.

To allow those applications to function with NDS, you can use a feature called *bindery services*. Bindery services makes the objects within a container appear as a bindery located on a particular server. That way, both bindery-based applications and NDS-aware applications can find the objects they need.

Bindery services also enables NetWare 3.*x* users to log in to a NetWare 4 or NetWare 5 server and use its resources.

If you want to set up bindery services on a NetWare 5 server, you have to tell the server which *portion* of the tree you want to appear as its bindery. By default, the server installation process sets the container in which the server was installed as the bindery context for the server. This portion of the tree consists of any container you choose and its objects. You can specify up to 16 different containers to look like a single bindery on a server. To the bindery-based application, the objects in all 16 containers will look like objects in a single flat database. By specifying these containers, you are setting the server's *bindery context*.

To set a server's bindery context, you use the SET command. To set a server's bindery context to be a single container — for example, Sales.Satellite.RedHawk — you would type the following command at the server's console:

```
SET BINDERY CONTEXT=Sales.Satellite.RedHawk
```

To set the bindery context to consist of two or more different containers, use the same command, and separate the name of each container by a semicolon, as follows:

```
SET BINDERY CONTEXT=Satellite.RedHawk;Engines.RedHawk
```

For a server to be able to use bindery services after you've set its bindery context to a container, you need to make sure the server has a read-write replica of the partition that holds that container. If the container specified in the bindery context is not in a replica on the given server, NetWare still allows the container to be specified. However, the objects in that container will not be available for bindery services on that server until a replica of the container's partition is created on the server.

To see the current bindery context that is already specified for a server, type **SET BINDERY CONTEXT** at the server console. This displays the string of containers that you've assigned to this server's bindery context, but does not show you if any of the containers are invalid.

To see the "effective" bindery context for a server, use the CONFIG console utility. This utility displays the containers that are currently valid and being used by that server as its bindery context. It does not display any container that may have been specified to be part of the bindery context, but whose partition replica doesn't exist on the server.

To set the bindery context to "nothing" (effectively preventing any objects from being available for bindery services on that server), type **SET BINDERY CONTEXT=**. (Don't put anything after the equal sign.)

NOTE Instead of using the SET command at the server console, you can use MONITOR.NLM to set the bindery context parameter. From MONITOR's main menu, choose Server Parameters, and then choose the Directory Services category to find the Bindery Context parameter.

Using WAN Traffic Manager to Control NDS Traffic

If your network spans geographical areas, and you have WAN links that use phone lines, you may want to use the WAN Traffic Manager feature in NetWare 5 to control how often NDS information is synchronized across the network. Ordinarily, NDS synchronization can take place anytime an NDS event occurs. On a locally contained network, the traffic generated by this synchronization isn't usually noticeable. However, if your network uses phone lines, the synchronization traffic can keep the phone lines very busy, causing excessive phone costs.

WAN Traffic Manager enables you to control when routine NDS synchronization takes place, so that the traffic is minimized and confined to less-used times of day.

WAN Traffic Manager is an optional feature of NetWare 5. If you want to use it, you must install it on the server. You can install it at the end of the regular server installation, as one of the products listed in the final Install Other Products screen. You can also install it later by loading NWCONFIG on the server, choosing Product Options, and then choosing Install Other Novell Products.

You need to install Wan Traffic Manager on each server that will be communicating across a WAN link, and whose traffic you want to control. If servers that share replicas of the same partition are on opposite sides of a WAN link, all those servers should have WAN Traffic Manager installed if you want to control their traffic.

To control the NDS traffic, you need to create a WAN Traffic Policy, which defines the rules that control how the traffic goes out on the network. This policy is stored as a property of each Server object. If you have several servers that all require the same policy, you can create a LAN Area object, which contains a list of all the affected servers. Then you can assign the policy to that single LAN Area object, instead of to multiple individual servers.

NetWare 5 includes several predefined policies that may suit your situation. For example, one commonly used policy specifies that all routine updates should be performed between 1:00 and 3:00 a.m. You can also edit those policies to create customized policies for your network. For more detailed information about these predefined policies, see the Novell online documentation. The following predefined policies are available in NetWare 5:

- ▶ 1-3AM Group — These policies limit NDS traffic to be sent between the hours of 1:00 a.m. and 3:00 a.m.

- ▶ 7AM-6PM Group — These policies limit NDS traffic to be sent between the hours of 7:00 a.m. and 6:00 p.m.

- ▶ COSTLT20 Group — These policies only allow traffic to be sent if the cost factor is less than 20. You can assign cost factors to destinations, in units such as dollars per hour or cents per minute.

- ▶ IPX Group — These policies allow only IPX traffic.

- ▶ NDSTTYPS Group — These policies are sample policies for limiting traffic to specific types of NDS traffic and events.

- ▶ ONOSPOOF Group — These policies allow NDS traffic to be generated only across existing WAN links that are already open.

- ▶ OPNSPOOF Group — These policies allow NDS traffic to be generated only across existing WAN connections that are already opened, unless the connection hasn't been used for at least 15 minutes. (It assumes the connection is being used for another purpose and is not available.)

- ▶ SAMEAREA Group — These policies allow traffic only between servers in the same network section (servers sharing a common network address).

- ▶ TCPIP Group — These policies allow only TCP/IP traffic.

- ▶ TIMECOST Group — These are additional policies that cover different types of time and cost restrictions.

The following sections explain how to set up a LAN Area object and how to assign a WAN policy to a server or LAN Area object.

Creating a LAN Area Object

If you want to assign a single WAN policy to multiple servers, you can save time by creating a LAN Area object that contains a list of all the servers, and then assigning the policy to the LAN Area object. Complete the following steps to create a LAN Area object.

I. Start up NetWare Administrator.

2. From the Browser window, select the container object that will contain the LAN Area object.

3. From the Object menu, choose Create.

4. Select LAN Area, and then click OK.

5. Enter a name for the new LAN Area object.

6. Mark the checkbox beside Define Additional Properties, and then click Create.

7. If you wish, enter any specific information about this LAN Area object, such as a description or location.

8. Open the page titled Servers Belonging to LAN Area.

9. Click Add.

10. From the screen that appears, browse the NDS tree to locate and select a server, and then click OK. Repeat this step for all the servers you want to add to this LAN Area object.

I I. When finished adding servers to the LAN Area object, click OK.

Assigning a WAN Policy to Servers

Complete the following steps to assign a WAN policy to a single Server object, or to a LAN Area object:

I. Start up NetWare Administrator.

2. From the Browser window, double-click the Server object or the LAN Area object to which you want to assign the WAN policy (or select the object and choose Details from the Object menu).

3. Open the WAN Policies page.

4. To assign a predefined policy, click Predefined Policy Groups and choose a policy group from the pull-down menu that appears.

5. Click the Load Group button. The individual policies available in that group appear in the Load Group Results window, showing whether any errors were encountered in the policies.

6. (Optional) To edit one of these policies to customize it to your situation, click Advanced. Select the policy you want to change, and then click Edit. If you make any changes and want to save the edited policy, choose Save As from the Policy menu, and give the policy a new name. (It's recommended that you keep the original policy unchanged, in case you need to revert to it later.)

7. When finished selecting the policy you want to use, click OK.

Now the new policy will take effect for the server (or for all servers in the LAN Area object), and NDS traffic will be restricted accordingly.

Using Catalog Services to Search the Tree

One of the benefits of NDS is that you can search the NDS tree for objects you want to locate. One method of searching the tree is to simply use the NetWare Administrator's Browser screen and navigate your way through the tree, opening containers and looking for your desired object.

Another way to search for objects is to use Catalog Services. Catalog Services is a feature of NDS that enables you to group together specific types of objects and information into a smaller database, so you can quickly locate the objects you want. A good example of this would be an employee phone directory—you could define a "catalog" that would gather an up-to-date list of all the User objects in the tree and their telephone number properties. Then, you could search that catalog and see a list of all those employees without having to navigate the tree itself.

By default, such catalogs are updated daily by a process called a *dredger*, which simply goes through the NDS tree looking for new information that should be added to the catalog. (You can manually update a catalog at any time, or you can change the automatic update interval.)

Applications, such as e-mail packages, can also create catalogs of information for their own use.

There are two types of catalogs: a master catalog and a slave catalog. The master catalog is the main catalog. Slave catalogs are copies of the master. The slave catalogs can be placed on remote servers so users in those locations can quickly access the same information as in the master catalog.

The following sections explain how to create master and slave catalogs, and how to query (search) a catalog.

Creating a Master Catalog

Complete the following steps to create a master catalog in the NDS tree:

1. Start up NetWare Administrator.

2. From the Browser screen, select the container you want to hold the master catalog.

3. From the Object menu, choose Create.

4. Select NDSCat:Master Catalog, and then click OK.

5. Enter a name for the new Master Catalog object.

6. Mark the checkbox beside Define Additional Properties, and then click Create.

7. Choose a host server for this catalog. (The host server will contain the dredger process for this catalog.) You can click the Browse button to navigate the tree and locate the server you want.

8. (Optional) If you wish, enter any additional information about the catalog, such as a description or organization.

9. Click the New button, and specify both a primary and secondary label for the catalog. The primary label is often the company or department name, and the secondary label is used to further describe the catalog. Use any labels you wish.

10. Open the Filter page and enter a filter statement (indicating which objects you want to include in your catalog). For example, to list user objects in your catalog, type:

    ```
    "object class" = "user"
    ```

11. Define how deeply the catalog will search in the tree. You can specify whether you want to search the entire subtree beneath this context or only search the immediate subordinates (only one level below this context).

12. Open the Schedule page and specify when the dredger should update the catalog. You can choose to manually update the catalog now, or you can specify an automatic interval and start time.

13. Open the Attributes/Indexes page. Click Selected Attributes. From the Available column, choose the properties you wanted listed in the catalog, and then click Add. When finished selecting attributes, click OK.

14. Click Select Indexes to specify by which property the catalog should be indexed. Again, choose the property from the Available column, and then click OK.

15. Click OK to save the new master catalog object.

NOTE

Make sure the master catalog object has browse and read rights to any container object that holds objects you want the catalog to include. See Chapter 7 for more information about assigning rights to an object.

Creating a Slave Catalog

Complete the following steps to create a slave catalog in the NDS tree:

1. Start up NetWare Administrator.

2. From the Browser screen, select the container you want to hold the slave catalog.

3. From the Object menu, choose Create.

4. Select NDSCat:Slave Catalog, and then click OK.

5. Enter a name for the new Slave Catalog object. The name must be different from the master catalog's name.

6. Mark the checkbox beside Define Additional Properties, and then click Create.

7. In the Master field, specify the master catalog to which this slave will belong. (You can click the Browse button to locate the master catalog by navigating through the tree.)

8. (Optional) If you wish, enter any additional information about the catalog, such as a description or organization, and then click OK.

9. Click OK to save the new Slave Catalog object.

Searching Through a Catalog

Complete the following steps to search for information in a catalog (also called *querying a catalog*):

1. Start up NetWare Administrator.

2. From the Tools menu, choose Query Catalog.

3. Enter the name of the catalog you want to query, or click the Browse button to locate one in the tree.

4. In the Indexed By field, specify whether you want the query's results listed by the object name (the object's full name), a canonical name (a different way to show a name, specified by the network administrator), or the base class (the type of object, such as user, printer, and so on).

5. In the Attribute Names field, specify the properties from which to retrieve information. (Click the Select Attributes button to add or remove properties from the list.)

6. (Optional) In the Where field, indicate any restrictions on where to search for the information.

7. Click Query. The results of the search are displayed.

Using DSMERGE to Merge Multiple NDS Trees

If you have two or more NDS trees, you can merge them into a single tree by using DSMERGE.NLM. (Do not use this utility to try to merge Directory partitions. This utility should only be used for merging two Directory trees.) You can also use this utility to rename a tree.

DSMERGE merges both trees at their roots. The tree from which you are running DSMERGE is the *local source tree*. The tree you are merging your source tree into is called the *target tree*. The target tree's Root object will become the Root object for the new merged tree, and the target tree's name is the new tree's name as well. Objects that were located immediately under the root of the source tree will be located immediately under the new tree's root.

Ordinarily, merging two trees doesn't change any contexts or NDS names. All containers in the original two trees are retained, along with their respective objects. The only exception to this is if both trees have container objects with the same name — in that case, one of the containers must be renamed before the merge, so the objects within the renamed container will have new contexts and full names.

During the merge, all replicas of the source tree's root partition are removed from all servers. Then the server that contained the master replica of the source tree will receive a read-write replica of the new tree's root partition. In addition, DSMERGE will create new partitions for each container below the source tree's root.

The following are the preliminary steps you must take to merge two trees:

1. Remove any leaf objects or alias objects from the root of the source tree. Either move these objects to a container, or delete them for now and re-create them later. If you've enabled auditing at the root level, you must disable auditing from the root and remove any auditing objects that were created at the root before starting the merge process.

2. Make sure there are no similar names between the two trees. For example, if each tree has a container called Mktg immediately beneath the root, those two names will conflict. Rename one or the other before trying to merge them.

3. Make sure all users are logged out of both trees, and close all connections.

4. Verify that both trees are running the same version of NDS and are using the same NDS schema. (DSMERGE.NLM will check this for you, too.)

5. Make sure all servers that have a replica of either tree's root partition are up and running.

6. After the merge, only one Reference or Single Reference time server can exist. Therefore, before the merge, make sure only one of the trees has such a server. Convert the other tree's server to a Primary time server, if necessary. Ensure that all servers in both trees are synchronized to within two seconds of each other and that they are using only one time source. You can view the time synchronization information with DSMERGE before you begin the merge process.

7. From a server on the source tree, load DSMERGE.NLM.

8. If both trees have the same tree name, use the Rename this tree option to change the source tree's name.

9. Use the Check servers in this tree option to verify that each server's status is listed as Up.

10. When satisfied that you can safely merge the trees, choose Merge Two trees.

11. Enter the administrator's name and password for the source tree.

12. Choose Target Tree and select the target tree from the list.

13. Enter the administrator's name and password for the target tree.

14. Press F10 to start the merge process.

15. Evaluate the new partitions and replicas that exist. You may want to merge some or split others to make the partitions more useful in the new tree.

16. If necessary, re-create any leaf or Alias objects you deleted from the source tree's root, and also re-enable auditing and re-create auditing objects.

NDS Troubleshooting

There are two utilities and some SET parameters you can use to diagnose and repair any suspected problems with your NDS database: DSREPAIR.NLM, NDS Manager, and the SET NDS TRACE commands.

NOTE Most of NDS Manager's repair features execute DSREPAIR.NLM. Because NDS Manager can execute from a workstation, you may prefer to use it rather than DSREPAIR.NLM. NDS Manager was discussed earlier in this chapter.

NDS TRACE

NDS TRACE is a set of server SET commands that enables you to monitor NDS status and error messages. To turn on the NDS TRACE screen, type the following command at the server console:

```
SET NDS TRACE TO SCREEN = ON
```

You can also use the following command to do the same thing:

```
SET DSTRACE = ON
```

NOTE If you want NDS TRACE to display WAN Traffic Manager messages too, type the following command:

SET DSTRACE = +WANMAN

To stop displaying WAN Traffic Manager messages, type:

SET DSTRACE = -WANMAN

If you want to send the messages to a file so that they are saved for later reference, type:

```
SET NDS TRACE TO FILE = ON
```

You can also use the following shorter command:

```
SET TTF=ON
```

The file that will receive these messages is called DSTRACE.DBG, and is located in the SYS:SYSTEM directory. This file will grow to a maximum size of 1MB by default. When the file reaches its maximum size, it will wrap to the beginning of the file and overwrite older information. You should only need to send the information to a file if you are trying to capture an error condition for diagnostic purposes. There's no need to save this information on a routine basis.

As you read the information displayed by NDS TRACE, if you see the following message:

```
All processed = YES
```

it means that all of the pending NDS activities have been successfully completed for the specified partition.

Not all messages displayed on the screen will be errors. Many will simply indicate the current status of NDS. Therefore, you need to look up the messages in the System Messages manual (located online) to see if any of the messages require an action on your part.

To turn off the NDS tracing feature, type one of the following commands:

```
SET NDS TRACE TO SCREEN = OFF
```

or

```
SET DSTRACE = OFF
```

If you sent the NDS Trace information to a file, be sure you turn it off when you're finished with it, by typing one of the following commands:

```
SET NDS TRACE TO FILE = OFF
```

or

```
SET TTF = OFF
```

NOTE

Instead of using the SET command at the server console, you can use MONITOR.NLM to set the NDS Trace parameters. From MONITOR's main menu, choose Server Parameters, and then choose the Directory Services category to find the NDS Trace parameters.

DSREPAIR.NLM

If you discover a problem with your NDS database, you may be able to fix it using DSREPAIR.NLM.

You use DSREPAIR.NLM to repair the NDS database on individual servers. You have to run it on each server that has a problem. Most DSREPAIR.NLM features are specific to the local server. DSREPAIR will also perform replica synchronization operations and enable you to see the current status of this server's view of the network or Directory. For example, DSREPAIR.NLM enables you to see a list of servers known to the given server. Not all DSREPAIR features are necessarily repair functions, but they can be used to help diagnose or verify the health of your NDS Directory.

NOTE   The NDS Manager utility, which runs on a workstation, executes DSREPAIR automatically to perform many partition and replica problems. Therefore, you may find it easier or more convenient to use NDS Manager from the workstation instead of running DSREPAIR.NLM on the server console.

With DSREPAIR.NLM, you can do tasks such as:

- ► Check the local Directory database records for consistency, and repair them if necessary
- ► Verify volume trustees and eliminate invalid trustees
- ► Update the NDS schema
- ► View the status of the Directory tree's replica synchronization and repair replicas
- ► Verify external references to objects in subordinate reference replicas
- ► View information about the network's time synchronization

DSREPAIR also lets you create a log file of DSREPAIR operations. If necessary, you can use DSREPAIR to create a *dump file* of a damaged NDS database that you can send to Novell Technical Support technicians for use in diagnosing a problem.

To use DSREPAIR, load the NLM on the server whose database you want to examine or repair. The options described in Table 5.2 are available for DSREPAIR.

T A B L E 5 . 2	DSREPAIR.NLM Options
OPTION	**DESCRIPTION**
Unattended Full Repair	Repairs everything it can in the database without asking for user intervention.
Time Synchronization	Contacts all servers in this server's partition to display time synchronization information.
Report Synchronization Status	Displays the status of each replica's synchronization.
View Repair Log File	Sends messages about DSREPAIR activities to a log file, and lets you view the file.
Advanced Options Menu	Lets you manually perform repair options on the NDS tree (rather than choosing Unattended Full Repair). It can also display diagnostic information about the NDS database, let you configure the log file, create a database dump file, and so on.

Using Additional Services with NDS

There are two additional services you can use with NDS to extend it to use a broader range of addressing protocols:

- ▸ LDAP Services for NDS
- ▸ Novell DNS/DHCP Services

Using LDAP Services for NDS

LDAP (Lightweight Directory Access Protocol) is a communications protocol currently being developed for use on the Internet. The goal is for LDAP to eventually become the standard protocol for accessing directory information over the Internet. NDS provides a strong directory service for LDAP to access and use.

LDAP Services for NDS is an optional feature of NetWare 5. You can install it during the server installation as an additional product. LDAP Services enables LDAP clients to access information stored in NDS. You can specify what types of information are available to those LDAP clients.

For more information about using LDAP with your network, see the Novell documentation.

Using Novell DNS/DHCP Services

Novell DNS/DHCP Services is an optional feature of NetWare 5 that integrates DNS and DHCP addressing and management into NDS. DNS (Domain Name System) and DHCP (Dynamic Host Configuration Protocol) manage the assignment and discovery of IP addresses on a network. By integrating this information into NDS, network administrators can now manage both DNS/DHCP information and regular NDS information from a single, centralized location. The DNS/DHCP information is stored in NDS database, so it is distributed and replicated just like other NDS data, making it easier to access and manage.

When you install DNS/DHCP Services as an optional product during the server installation, the NDS schema is extended to include a variety of DNS and DHCP-related objects. These objects help keep track of IP addresses, DNS and DHCP servers, configurations, host addresses, zones, and the like.

With DNS/DHCP Services installed on the network, an IP client can establish a connection with the network by using DHCP. A DHCP server sends the address of an NDS server to the client, along with an IP address and NDS context that the client can use to log in. DHCP enables a workstation to "lease" an IP address from a pool of available addresses, rather than requiring that the workstation be assigned a fixed address individually. This can make the maintenance of IP addresses much easier on a network.

You can manage DNS/DHCP objects through a utility called the DNS/DHCP Administrator. This utility can be run directly from a Windows 95/98 or Windows NT workstation desktop, or it can be executed from the Tools menu of the NetWare Administrator utility.

For more information about DNS/DHCP Services, see the Novell documentation.

Keeping Up to Date

Periodically, Novell releases updated versions of DS.NLM (the NDS database program) and its management utilities on the Novell Web site (www.novell.com). These updates may add minor features or fix problems. You should try to keep your network updated with these new versions whenever possible.

If you obtain an updated version of DS.NLM, install it on all the NetWare 5 servers in your network. All servers in a partition's replica ring must be running the same version of DS.NLM in order to use any new features of DS.NLM. Keeping all of your servers running the same version will help simplify your support of the Directory tree.

For more information about Novell's Web site, see Appendix C.

CHAPTER 6

Managing Users and Groups

Instant Access

Creating Users and Groups

▸ To create User objects and Group objects, use the NetWare Administrator utility (which runs in Windows 95/98 or Windows NT).

▸ To set up a template so all users you create receive a set of common characteristics, use the NetWare Administrator utility to create a Template object.

User Tasks

▸ To log in, users can use the LOGIN command-line utility; the Login program that runs in Windows 3.1, 95/98, and NT; the Network Neighborhood; or the NetWare User Tools utility (which runs in Windows 3.1).

▸ To log out, users can use the LOGOUT command-line utility, the Network Neighborhood, or the NetWare User Tools utility.

▸ To specify a default name context (location in the NDS tree) for logging in, users can put the NAME CONTEXT command in their NET.CFG files or change the Novell Client software property pages.

▸ To change the name context after they are logged in, users can use the NetWare User Tools utility or the CX command-line utility.

▸ To control print jobs, users can use the NetWare User Tools utility, the NetWare Administrator utility, or the Novell Printer Manager (for NDPS printing).

▸ To send brief messages to other network users, users can use the NetWare User Tools utility.

▸ To map drives to network directories, users can put MAP commands in their login scripts, or they can use the NetWare User Tools utility, the Network Neighborhood, or the MAP command-line utility.

▸ To change their passwords, users can use the NetWare User Tools utility or the SETPASS command-line utility.

Managing Users' Work Environments

▶ To create login scripts, use the NetWare Administrator, select a container object, Profile object, or User object (depending on the type of login script you want to create), select Details from the Object menu, and then open the Login Script page.

▶ To allow users to launch applications from their desktop without having to know what drives to map or where to find the application, use the Z.E.N.works Starter Pack. Once Z.E.N.works is installed, use the NetWare Administrator utility to create an Application object, and then set up the Application Launcher on the user's desktop.

What Do Users Need?

Once you've set up the hardware and software, it's time to start managing the human elements of your network: users. After a brand new installation, the only User object that will exist in the tree is the Admin User object.

Before your users can begin using the network, you have to create user accounts for each of them. In addition, you may want to organize the users into groups to more easily manage security, printer assignments, and other issues that may affect many or all of the users in the same way.

To make the network easier to use, you can also create login scripts. Login scripts can automatically set up the users' workstation environments with necessary drive mappings and other types of useful environmental settings.

In addition, you can use the Application Launcher feature of Z.E.N.works to set up an icon on users' desktops that points directly to network applications. Then the users can simply launch the application from their desktops without having to know where the application is, which drives to map, and so on.

After the user has logged in to the network, there are a few common tasks that the user may want to perform, such as logging in and out, of course, redirecting the workstation's printer port to a network print queue, or mapping a drive to a directory. NetWare User Tools is a Windows 3.1-based NetWare utility that is geared toward end users. They can use this utility to perform most of these common tasks. Most Windows 95/98 and Windows NT users will use the regular Windows features, such as the Windows Explorer and the Network Neighborhood, to do these tasks.

Creating a user's account involves more than just creating a new object for the user in the NDS tree. Before a user can really work on the network, you need to set up many of the following tools or characteristics (some are optional, depending on your situation):

- ▶ The user's NDS account (which is an object for the user with its associated properties filled in, such as the user's last name, full name, telephone number, and so on)
- ▶ The user's group memberships
- ▶ A home directory for the user's individual files
- ▶ A login script that maps drives to the directories and applications to which the user will need access

- ▸ NDS trustee rights (to control how the user can see and use other NDS objects in the tree)

- ▸ File system trustee rights to the files and directories the user needs to work with (to regulate the user's access and activities in those files and directories)

- ▸ Account restrictions, if necessary, to control when the user logs in, how often the user must change passwords, and so on

- ▸ An e-mail account, if necessary

- ▸ Access to the network printers

The following section describes how to create user and group accounts on the network.

Creating Users and Groups

Users, of course, are the individual people who have accounts on the network. You can assign users to groups, so that you can manage things such as security and login script commands for many people simultaneously, rather than one by one. A group is really a Group object, which contains a list of users who are assigned to that group.

NOTE Because you can use container objects to assign rights and login scripts to all the users in those containers, you may find that you don't need to use as many groups as you may have in previous versions of NetWare. For example, users in a container gain a security equivalence to that container by default. Therefore, granting rights at the container level is a quick way to grant identical rights to all users in the container, eliminating the need to create a separate group object to grant those same users the same rights.

To create a new user or group on the network, you use the NetWare Administrator utility from a workstation. The NetWare Administrator is a NetWare utility that can run on either Windows 95/98 or Windows NT. (If you have not yet installed the NetWare Administrator on your workstation, see Chapter 5 for instructions.)

Creating a User

To create a user, complete the following steps:

1. Create a directory for all users' home directories. For example, you may want to create a network directory called Users on volume VOL1.

2. Start up NetWare Administrator.

3. Select the container object that will hold the new user.

4. From the Object menu, choose Create.

5. From the New Object dialog box that appears, choose User, and then choose OK.

6. In the Create User dialog box, enter the user's login name and last name. The login name is the name you want this user to type when he or she logs in.

7. Create a home directory for this user.

   a. Mark the checkbox next to Create Home Directory.

   b. Click the Browse button above the Home Directory field.

   c. From the panel on the right, double-click the container if necessary, and then the volume that will hold the user directories.

   d. When the directory you created in Step 1 appears in the left panel, select that directory and click OK. The path to that directory should now appear in the Create User dialog box.

8. To specify additional, optional properties for the User object, mark the Define Additional Properties checkbox.

9. Choose Create. The user's Identification page appears. The Identification page will appear every time you look at this object in the future. Along the right side of the screen are large rectangular buttons with turn-down corners. Each of these buttons represents a different page of information about the user. You can fill in some, none, or all of the information on these pages, depending on your needs. If you have entered new information in one of these pages that needs to be saved, the turn-down corner will appear black. Fill in any information you want to specify, and then choose OK when finished.

10. Create another user by following the same steps.

Assigning Identical Properties to Multiple Users

If you plan to assign many of your users some identical properties, you can use a user Template object. The Template object will automatically apply default properties to any new user you create using the Template. (It will not, however, apply those properties to any users that existed before you created the user Template.) Network administrators often use a Template to grant default NDS and file system rights to users automatically.

To create a user Template object, complete the steps in the following checklist:

1. Create a directory for all users' home directories. For example, you may want to create a directory called Users.

2. Start up NetWare Administrator.

3. Select the container object that will hold the new user Template object.

4. From the Object menu, choose Create.

5. From the New Object dialog box that appears, choose Template, and then choose OK.

6. When the Template object's dialog box appears, enter a name for the Template.

7. If you want this Template to specify some or all of the same information that appears in another Template object or User object, check the Use Template or User box and use the Browser button to select the Template or User object.

8. Check the Define Additional Properties box, and then click Create.

9. Enter any additional information (or edit existing information) that you want assigned to each user, and then click OK when you're finished.

10. The next time you create a new user and want to use the information in this Template, mark the Use Template checkbox and select this Template object from the Browser button.

Editing Information for Several Users at Once

With NetWare, it's easy to edit the same information for several users simultaneously. For example, suppose a whole department moves to a different floor in the building. If you've entered the Location or Address information in those users' Details pages, you can update the information quickly.

From the NetWare Administrator Browser, select all of the user objects you want to update, and then choose Details on Multiple Users from the Object menu. Any information you enter in this screen will be applied to all the users you selected.

To select multiple objects at once from the Browser, use Shift+Click or Ctrl+Click.

NOTE

Creating Groups and Assigning Group Membership to a User

Creating a group is very similar to creating a user. The following checklist outlines the steps to create a group and assign group membership to a user.

I. Start up NetWare Administrator.

2. Select the container object that will hold the new group.

3. From the Object menu, choose Create.

4. From the New Object dialog box that appears, choose Group, and then choose OK.

5. Enter the group's name.

6. Mark the checkbox next to Define Additional Properties.

7. Choose Create. The group's Identification page appears. Enter any information you desire under the Identification page.

8. Open the Members page and click Add.

9. Specify any existing users who should be members of this group. From the right panel, open the container that holds the user you want. From the left panel, select the user, and then choose OK. The user's name now appears as a member of the group. (To select multiple users, use Shift+Click or Ctrl+Click.)

If the group already exists, you can also assign a user to that group by selecting the user object, opening the user's Group Membership page, and adding the group.

► • ◄

User Network Activities

Once users have been created, they can begin working on the network. In most cases, users on a network will notice very little difference from working on a standalone computer. They still use the applications they were using before. They still open, save, and delete files the same way. They can still play the same games — if they can get away with it.

The primary differences for most users are the following: They have to enter a login name and password; they have more drives and directories available to them; there are some files that are restricted to them; and their print jobs go to the same printer as everyone else's. Whether or not you want them to be able to control most of these network activities themselves is up to you.

For most users, the following NetWare and Windows utilities will take care of their networking tasks:

- ▶ LOGIN (from either the DOS command line or from Windows 3.1, 95/98, or NT) lets users log in to the network.

- ▶ LOGOUT (from either the DOS command line or from Windows 3.1, 95/98, or NT) lets users log out of the network.

- ▶ NetWare User Tools (from Windows 3.1) lets users perform many networking tasks, such as logging in and out, mapping drives, and changing passwords.

- ▶ Windows Network Neighborhood (from Windows 95/98 or NT) lets users perform many network tasks, such as logging in and out, mapping drives, and changing passwords.

- ▶ Novell Printer Manager (from Windows 3.1, 95/98, or NT) lets users manage NDPS printers.

- ▶ NetWare Administrator (from Windows 95/98 or NT) lets users browse the NDS tree, see information about network objects, manage their printers, and so on.

Logging In

To log in to the network, the user uses the LOGIN utility and specifies a login name and a password. LOGIN authenticates the user to the network and executes login scripts to set up the user's work environment.

There are two versions of this utility: a DOS-based version and a Windows-based version. The DOS-based version is the LOGIN.EXE utility, which the user executes at the DOS prompt of the workstation. The LOGIN.EXE utility is located in SYS:LOGIN. For DOS, the user types the following command, replacing *tree* with either a Directory tree name or a server name (this is not necessary if the user wants to log in to the default tree or server), and replacing *username* with the login name:

```
LOGIN tree/username
```

From Windows 3.1, Windows 95/98, or Windows NT workstations, the user can log in to the network using the graphical version of LOGIN. The Login program for Windows 3.1, Windows 95/98, and Windows NT is installed as part of the NetWare client software. To log in using the graphical Login program, use one of the following methods (depending on the workstation's OS):

▶ To log in to the network from Windows 3.1, double-click the Novell Login icon (located in the Novell Client program group), and specify a login name and a password.

▶ From Windows 95/98 or NT, the Login program is usually set to execute automatically whenever the workstation is rebooted. Enter a login name and password when the utility appears.

▶ From Windows 95/98 or NT, you can also log in from the Network Neighborhood. Open the Network Neighborhood by either double-clicking the Network Neighborhood icon or double-clicking the N logo in the system tray. Then right-click the desired tree or server, click either Authenticate or Login to NDS Tree, and then enter a login name and password. You can also open the Login program by opening the Windows Start menu, then selecting Programs, then Novell, and then NetWare Login.

Which login name the user enters depends on whether you've modified the user's startup information to specify the user's name context.

For DOS and Windows 3.1 workstations, you specify the user's name context in NET.CFG. For Windows 95/98 and Windows NT workstation, you specify the user's context in the Novell Client Properties. These steps are explained in the following sections.

Specifying a Name Context for DOS and Windows 3.1

If the workstation is using the default NET.CFG file that was created when you installed the workstation, the Login utility doesn't know the context in which the user was created. It assumes the default context is at the root of the tree. If you've created the user in a container beneath the root, which is most likely the case, Login won't find the user in the tree if the user enters only his or her common name and will deny the user access to the network.

There are two ways to make sure Login finds the user's correct name context. The first way is for the user to specify a complete name, all the way back to the root of the tree. Obviously, this can be a little cumbersome for the user. For example, Eric would have to log in using the following command:

```
LOGIN .Eric.Mktg.Satellite.RedHawk
```

The period at the beginning of Eric's full name indicates that this name is the object's full context, going clear back to the root of the tree. The other way to make sure Login finds the user's context is to specify the context in the NET.CFG file under the NetWare DOS Requester heading. For example, to specify Eric's context, put the following command in the NET.CFG file:

```
NAME CONTEXT = "Mktg.Satellite.RedHawk"
```

Then, Eric can simply log in using his common name, Eric, which is obviously going to be easier for him to remember.

To simplify the user's life even more, you may also want to put the Login command in the user's AUTOEXEC.BAT file so it executes every time the user boots the workstation.

Specifying a Name Context in Windows 95/98

To set Windows 95/98 users' default name contexts so they don't have to enter a full name each time they log in, use the Network Neighborhood. Right-click the Network Neighborhood and select Properties. Select the Novell NetWare Client, and then click the Properties button.

Under the Client tab, put the user's context in the Name Context field. If it isn't already filled in, also indicate a Preferred Tree for the user. When finished, click OK twice. Now the user can simply enter his or her login name instead of a full name whenever the Login screen appears.

Specifying a Name Context in Windows NT

To set Windows NT users' default name contexts so they don't have to enter a full name each time they log in, use the Control Panel. From the Windows NT Start menu, choose Settings, then Control Panel, then Network, and then Services. From the Network Services list, choose Novell Client for Windows NT, and then click Properties.

Put the user's context in the Name Context field. If it isn't already filled in, also indicate a Preferred Tree for the user. When finished, click OK. Now the user can simply enter his or her login name instead of a full name whenever the Login screen appears.

Logging Out

How you log out of the network depends on the operating system you're using on your workstation:

▶ If you're using a DOS workstation, simply type the following command at the DOS prompt:

```
LOGOUT
```

▶ If you're using a Windows 3.1 workstation, you can either go to DOS and type **LOGOUT** at the DOS prompt, or you can use the NetWare User Tools utility to log out. Double-click NetWare User Tools, select NetWare Drive Connections, choose the server or tree from which you want to log out, and choose Logout.

▶ If you're using a Windows 95/98 or NT workstation, double-click the Network Neighborhood icon (or open the Network Neighborhood by clicking the N logo in the system tray), right-click the NDS tree or server from which you want to log out, and choose Logout.

Network Tasks from Windows 3.1

NetWare 5 includes a utility, called NetWare User Tools, that enables Windows 3.1 users to perform their most common network tasks. With this utility, Windows 3.1 users can do the following:

▶ Set up print queues and control how their print jobs are printed on the network

▶ Send short messages to other network users

▶ Map drive letters to network directories

▶ Change passwords

▶ Log in to and out of Directory trees and network servers (but without a login script executing)

▶ Change their own name context in the Directory tree

▶ Edit user login scripts (DOS version only)

NOTE

Most Windows 95/98 users use the Windows Explorer and Network Neighborhood instead of the NetWare User Tools to complete network tasks.

To use NetWare User Tools, double-click the NetWare User Tools icon, which is automatically placed in the Novell Client program group when the Novell client software is installed.

This utility doesn't allow you to edit a login script. Instead, you can set up drive mappings and printer port redirection right in the utility, and click the

Permanent button to make those assignments permanent. This has the same effect as placing the corresponding commands in a login script. Every time you log in, NetWare User Tools will automatically map the drives and capture printer ports the way you specified. Use the Help button to read about the tasks you can perform with this utility.

Network Tasks from Windows 95/98 and Windows NT

Most Windows 95/98 and Windows NT users will use the Network Neighborhood to accomplish most common networking tasks, such as logging in and out of the network and mapping drives. Users can also right-click the N logo in the system tray to choose network tasks from a menu. (The system tray usually appears at the bottom right-hand corner of the Windows screen.)

For example, to map a drive from the Network Neighborhood, open the Network Neighborhood and double-click a server to display its volumes. Open a volume, and keep opening folders until you find the one to which you want to map a drive. Then right-click the folder and select Novell Map Network Drive. Choose a drive letter and mark the options you want, such as Reconnect at Logon (which maps the drive permanently so it continues to be mapped every time you log in), Map Search Drive, or Map Root. Then click Map. The new drive mapping will appear when you open My Computer.

To map a drive from the N logo in the system tray, right-click the N logo. From the menu that appears, choose Novell Map Network Drive. The same Map screen appears as in the procedure from Network Neighborhood. You choose the drive letter, mark the options you want, and click Map.

To delete a drive mapping, open My Computer. Right-click the drive mapping, and choose Disconnect.

Managing Printers and Print Jobs

Users who want to see information about queue-based printers and their print jobs can use the NetWare Administrator utility. Users who want to see information about NDPS network printers and their print jobs can use either NetWare Administrator or the Novell Printer Manager utility.

With these utilities, users can see the status of their print jobs. They can also change certain aspects of their own print jobs, such as canceling them or putting them on hold. Printer users can only change their own jobs. Printer Operators can change print jobs for any users on a printer.

For more information about the two different types of printing setups, and about using these utilities, see Chapter 9.

► · ◄

Making Applications Easy to Access

NetWare 5 includes a feature called the Z.E.N.works Starter Pack, which you can use to make your applications easier to access. This is a subset of the full-featured Z.E.N.works, which can be purchased separately. The Starter Pack includes primarily the Application Launcher, which existed in NetWare 4.11, but which has been enhanced for NetWare 5. The Starter Pack also includes some basic workstation management functionality.

NOTE

The full-featured Z.E.N.works product includes advanced workstation management features, such as Help Request management tools and workstation registration tools so you can remotely access a user's workstation to diagnose problems. The full-featured product is available separately. Only the Starter Pack is included in NetWare 5.

Once you have the Z.E.N.works Starter Pack installed on a server and the Application Launcher set up on each user's workstation, you can use NetWare Administrator to make an application become an object in the NDS tree. Then, the icon for the Application object will appear automatically on the desktop of each user you assign to that application.

The users don't need to know where the application is, they don't need to map drives or enter launch parameters, and you don't need to update login scripts. When you update the application, the icons in all the desktops will continue to point to the new application. You can make an application simply run from the network, or you can even make the application install itself automatically on each workstation.

To install Z.E.N.works on the server, you need to run the installation program on the Z.E.N.works CD-ROM. This is the same CD-ROM that contains the Novell Client software. When Z.E.N.works is installed, it extends the NDS schema to add Application objects (and other related objects). In addition, it automatically adds a snap-in module to the NetWare Administrator utility so you can manage Application objects.

After you've installed Z.E.N.works on the server, you can create an Application object to represent a particular application. Then, you put a command in each user's login script to execute the Application Launcher (for Windows 3.1) or Application Explorer (for Windows 95/98 or NT). The Application Launcher/Explorer is a window that appears on the user's desktop. This Window contains any Application objects you assign to that user.

For Windows 95/98 and NT, you can also specify that the Application object appears on the user's desktop, in Windows Explorer, or in the System Tray.

If you want the application to install itself automatically on the workstation, you can run the application's installation program on a single representative workstation and capture all the installation information and settings with a program called snAppShot. Then you can use that captured information when you create the Application object. The object will use that captured information to run the installation program on every other workstation. This captured information is stored in a file with an .AOT extension (Application Object Template). You can also create a text file with this type of information, and store it in a file with the extension .AXT; however, in most cases it is easier to use the .AOT file.

Z.E.N.works requires that each workstation using the Application object must be running the Novell client software that came on the Novell Client and Z.E.N.works CD-ROM. Earlier versions of the client software won't work with Z.E.N.works.

In addition, you must use the NetWare Administrator utility that came with NetWare 5 (NWADMN32.EXE). The same utility is included on the Novell Client and Z.E.N.works CD-ROM, for your convenience.

The following sections explain how to:

▶ Install Z.E.N.works on the server.

▶ Run snAppShot to create an .AOT file to capture installation options and settings if you want the application to install itself on workstations.

▶ Create an Application object and assign it to users, groups, or containers.

Installing Z.E.N.works on the Server

To install Z.E.N.works on the server, complete the following steps:

1. From a workstation, insert the Novell Client and Z.E.N.works CD-ROM. The installation program should start up automatically.

2. Choose English.

3. Choose Install Z.E.N.works.

4. At the Welcome screen, click Next.

5. At the License Agreement screen, read it and click Yes.

6. Choose Typical to install application management software, desktop management software, and NetWare Administrator. If you only want to install one or two of these options, choose Custom and select the ones you want. Click Next to continue.

7. Choose the tree and server upon which you want to install Z.E.N.works. Click Next to continue.

8. Choose the language you want to install, and click Next.

9. Confirm the installation summary, which shows the components you've selected. If you want to keep the selections, click Next. To change some selections, choose Back.

10. Select a context to which all users will have rights, so they can write a workstation registration entry to their container. Select the default, or specify another container. Then click OK to continue.

11. When a message appears saying rights were successfully set up, click OK.

12. If you want to view the readme file and the setup log file, leave the boxes next to those options checked, and click Finish. If you don't want to view them, unmark the boxes, and click Finish.

13. When you receive an informational message telling you to distribute new client software on all workstations, click the Exit button (at the bottom right corner of the screen) to exit the installation program.

The Z.E.N.works Starter Pack has now been installed on the server. If you go into NetWare Administrator, you can see that Z.E.N.works has successfully been installed, by choosing Tools — you'll see Application Launcher Tools listed as an option.

Running snAppShot

If you want the application to install itself on workstations, you can use snAppShot to capture all the installation options and parameters in an .AOT file. Many applications make modifications to a variety of workstation files while being installed. For example, an application may modify the Windows Registry file, .INI files, system configuration files, and so on. SnAppShot captures all those modifications by running twice — once before the application's installation program runs, and once after. Then snAppShot compares the two images of the workstation and creates a template file (with the extension .AOT) showing the differences.

SnAppShot also captures all the files that the application installs on the workstation, and copies them to a network directory that you specify. It renames all the files numerically and gives them the extension .FIL. The Application object will use these files when it installs itself on other workstations.

Then, when you create the Application object, you can tell it to use the .AOT file, and it will automatically know which changes to make to all subsequent workstations.

NOTE
An .AOT file will work best on applications that don't require specific hardware choices that may vary between workstations on your network. If your application requires that you choose a video driver, for example, and your workstations have different video drivers, you may not be able to run a single .AOT file for all your workstations. You may need to set up different application objects, using different .AOT files, for each different type of workstation.

To run snAppShot, complete the following steps. You will need to run snAppShot on a workstation that adequately represents the other workstations on which the Application object will run later. You will install the application on this workstation as part of the snAppShot process.

1. From a representative workstation, log in to the network.

2. Run the file SNAPSHOT.EXE from the SYS:PUBLIC\SNAPSHOT folder.

3. (Optional) When the introductory screen appears, you can click Getting Started if you want to read an overview of snAppShot. When finished reading the overview, close the online help screen to return to the introductory snAppShot screen.

4. Choose the type of discovery process you want to use. In most cases, choose Standard, which runs the discovery process using default settings. (After you have become familiar with using snAppShot, you may want to choose one of the other options instead. The Custom option lets you specify the particular drives, files, folders, Registry hives, and shortcuts that snAppShot discovers. The Express option lets you scan for any changes using a snAppShot Preferences file created during a previous discovery session.)

5. Enter the name you are going to give the Application object, and then enter an Application Icon Title (the name of the icon that will appear on users' workstations). Then click Next.

6. Enter the location where you want the application files to be captured. The default path will be to the C: drive on the workstation, but change the path to a network directory on the server, so that all workstations will be able to access those files. (You should create a unique network directory for each application you install.) Click Next when finished.

7. Accept the filename and location for the .AOT file. (The location should be the same as the directory you specified in Step 6.) Click Next to continue.

8. Choose the drives you want snAppShot to scan for installation changes. Click Add if you want to add more drives than those that are listed. Then click Next to continue.

9. Review the summary of your selections, and click Next to continue. (If you want to make changes, click Back.)

10. When snAppShot finishes scanning the workstation for the preinstallation image, click Run Application Install. You will now run the application's regular installation program. Browse for the application's installation (or Setup) program, and go through the normal installation procedures. When the installation is finished, be sure you note the location of the application's executable file on the workstation.

11. When the installation finishes, you are returned automatically to snAppShot. Enter the path to the executable, and then click Next to continue. SnAppShot will now rescan the workstation to capture the post-installation image. Then it will compare the two images to create a template of the changes.

12. When snAppShot is finished, review the Completion Summary to see where snAppShot put the installation files.

Now you are ready to create the Application object.

Creating an Application Object

To create an Application object for a network application, complete the following steps:

1. Start up NetWare Administrator.

2. Select the container object that will hold the Application object.

3. From the Object menu, choose Create.

4. From the New Object dialog box that appears, choose Application and then choose OK.

5. Choose whether to create the object using an .AOT file, and then click Next.

6. If you chose to create the object using an .AOT file, enter the path to the .AOT file.

7. When the Application object's dialog box appears, enter its name, source path (the network directory that contains the application files), and the target path on the workstation (where you want the application installed).

8. Review your choices, and mark the checkbox next to Display Details After Creation. Then click Finish.

9. Open the Application object's Associations page. In this page, click Add to assign this Application object to users, groups, or containers that you want to have access to this application.

10. Open the System Requirements page, and choose the platforms on which this application will run.

11. Enter any additional information necessary on other pages for this application. When finished, click OK to save your changes and exit the object's property pages.

12. From the NetWare Administrator Browser, select the user, group, or container object that will use this application, and choose Details from the Object menu.

13. (Optional) Open the Launcher Configuration page. In this page, you can click Edit to specify any particular settings you want for the Application Launcher or Application Explorer when it appears on this user's (or group's) desktop.

14. Open the Login Script page. Add a command to the login script that will execute the Application Launcher or Application Explorer. Use one of the following sets of login script commands:

   • For Windows 3.1 workstations, add this command to launch the Application Launcher, substituting the name of the server for *server*:

     ```
     @\\server\sys\public\nal.exe
     ```

- For Windows 95/98 and NT workstations, add these commands to launch the Application Explorer, substituting the name of the server for *server* (and change "w95" to "w98" if you are using Windows 98):

```
if platform = "w95" then
        @\\server\sys\public\nalexpld.exe
end
if platform = "wnt" then
        if os_version = "v4.00" then
                @\\server\sys\public\nalexpld.exe
        end
end
```

15. (Windows 95/98 and Windows NT only) Open the Applications page. Here, you can change where the Application object appears on Windows 95/98 and NT workstations. Click Add if necessary to add an application to the list. Then, in the list, mark the checkbox under each location option: Force Run, Application Launcher (marked by default), Start Menu, Desktop, or System Tray.

16. Click OK to save all your changes and exit the object's property pages.

Now, when the user boots the workstation, the Application object should appear in the Application Launcher (or Application Explorer) window, and in any other location you may have specified in Step 15.

NOTE

For more information about using Z.E.N.works Starter Pack and its application management and desktop management features, see the Novell online documentation or the Z.E.N.works help file. To read the Z.E.N.works help file from the Z.E.N.works CD-ROM, browse to locate the file called DMPOLICY.HLP, located in the PRODUCTS\ZENWORKS\PUBLIC\NLS\ENGLISH folder. You can also read the help file by opening the NetWare Administrator utility, choosing Help, opening Help Topics, and selecting Z.E.N.works.

Login Scripts

Login scripts are tools similar to batch files that you can use to automatically set up users' workstation environments. Each time a user logs in, the LOGIN utility executes the login scripts, which can set up frequently used drive mappings, capture the workstation's printer port to a network print queue, display connection information or messages on the screen, or do other types of tasks for the user.

In previous versions of NetWare (3.1*x* and 2.*x*), there were two types of login scripts: user login scripts and system login scripts. The system login script was a file on the server. It executed for every user who logged in to that server, so it was a good place to store drive mappings or other information that was common to all users. The user login script was a separate file for each user, stored in users' MAIL subdirectories. In the user login script, you could create drive mappings or other items that were specific to that user only.

In NetWare 5, there are three types of login scripts:

- *User Login Scripts.* User login scripts are the same in NetWare as in previous versions, except that they are not stored as text files. Instead, they are actual properties of the User object. You still store user-specific drive mappings, and so on, in the user login script. If the user does not have a specific user login script, a default login script will execute instead, setting up the most basic drive mappings.

- *Container Login Scripts.* Instead of belonging to a server, a system login script belongs to a container object. Because users no longer log in to a server, and because all the users in a container may access different servers for files, keeping a server-specific login script seems useless. However, a script that applies to all users within a given container makes much more sense. Therefore, the system login script (now called a container login script) is a property of a container object. It applies to every user in that container.

- *Profile Login Scripts.* With a profile script, you can create a script that will apply to several users who don't necessarily have to be in the same container. It's kind of a group login script. The profile login script is a property of a Profile object, which defines a list of users who belong to the Profile. A user can have only one profile login script execute upon login.

These three types of login scripts work together to set up each user's environment upon login. They execute in the following order:

► Container login script

► Profile login script

► User login script (or default login script, if a user login script doesn't exist)

All three are optional. If you don't create one of them, LOGIN will skip to the next in the list.

Because up to three different login scripts can execute for a given user, conflicts between the login scripts may occur. If they do, the final login script to execute wins. Therefore, if the container login script maps a directory to drive letter G, and then the user script maps a different directory to drive letter G, the user script's mapping overwrites the container script's mapping.

Container login scripts only apply to the users immediately within that container. They don't apply to users in a child container. If the container that holds user Andrea doesn't have a login script, no container login script will execute when Andrea logs in, even if a container higher up in the tree has a login script.

To simplify administration of login scripts, try to put as much common information as possible, such as drive mappings to application directories, in the container and profile login scripts. It's much easier to change a drive mapping in one script and have it apply to all your users than to make the same change dozens or hundreds of times for every user script.

If you upgrade NetWare 2.*x* or 3.*x* to NetWare 5, the user login scripts are automatically transferred into the Login Script property of each User object. Server-specific system login scripts, however, are not upgraded. You will need to re-create the system login script, if needed, as a property of a container object. (The server-specific system login script in previous versions of NetWare is a text file in the SYS:PUBLIC directory called NET$LOG.DAT. You can print out this file to refer to while creating a container login script.)

NOTE

If you want to log in to the network without executing a login script, add the /NS option to the login command. For example, user Lauren would type LOGIN LAUREN/NS.

Creating a Login Script

You use the NetWare Administrator utility to create login scripts, just as you assign any other properties to NDS objects. Open the object's Details page, and then click the button for the Login Script page.

When you open up the Login Script property for a User, Profile, or container object, you are presented with a blank screen (or the previous login script, if one already exists). In this screen, you type any commands you want the login script to hold: drive mappings, printer port captures, messages, environment settings, and so on.

To create or edit a login script, you must have the Write NDS right to the object that will contain the script.

When creating login scripts, keep the following conventions and rules in mind. (Login script commands mentioned here are explained in the next section.)

- ▸ Begin each command in the login script on its own line. (Commands that wrap automatically to another line are considered a single line. Commands are limited to 150 characters per line.)

- ▸ To make multiline WRITE commands display better and to avoid having a line misinterpreted by LOGIN, begin each line of the displayed message with the word WRITE.

- ▸ If you use the pound sign (#) to execute an external program, note that some programs may require that the user have drives mapped to particular directories. If so, make sure the MAP commands that map drives to those directories are placed in the login script ahead of the command that executes the external program.

- ▸ Enter commands in the general order you want them to execute. If order isn't important, group similar commands together (such as MAP and CAPTURE commands) to make the login script easier to read.

- ▸ Remember that most commands are case-insensitive. The only exception is identifier variables enclosed in quotation marks and preceded by a percent sign (%); they must be uppercase.

- ▸ Use identifier variables to make generic commands useful to specific users. When a user logs in, his or her specific information is substituted for the identifier variable in the generic command. Identifier variables (explained later in the section "Using Identifier Variables") make it possible to put most necessary commands in the container or profile script, rather than in a user login script.

▶ Use blank lines to separate groups of commands in the script, if it makes it easier to read. Blank lines don't affect the execution of the login script.

▶ Use remarks in the login script to explain what commands in the script are doing, for future reference. Lines in the login script beginning with the word REM, an asterisk, or a semicolon are remarks, and they don't display when the login script executes.

▶ Copy portions of a login script by using the mouse to highlight the desired text and pressing Ctrl+C. To paste the text, either elsewhere in the script or in another object's script, press Ctrl+V.

Assigning Profile Login Scripts to Users

To create a profile login script, you create a Profile object just as you create any other NDS object. Create its script in the Profile object's Login Script property. After you've created the script, you must assign it to individual users. To do this, complete the steps in the following checklist:

1. Use the Browser to select a User object.

2. Choose Details from the Object menu, and then open the Login Script page.

3. Enter the name of the Profile object in the Profile field beneath the login script text window.

4. Save the information and return to the Browser.

5. From the Browser, select the Profile object.

6. From the Object menu, choose Trustees of This Object.

7. Click the Add Trustee button and enter the name of the user who will use this profile login script.

8. Make sure the Browse object right and Read property right are checked, and then choose OK to assign those rights to the user.

Login Script Commands

The many commands you can use in NetWare login scripts are explained in the following sections. Many of these commands are unique to NetWare login scripts. Some commands may work similarly to DOS commands or may actually execute DOS commands you might be familiar with, such as the SET and DOS BREAK ON commands. All of them are optional. You only need to use the commands that accomplish tasks you want performed for the user.

Command

This command executes an external command or program, such as a NetWare utility, from the login script. To execute the program, use the pound (#) symbol at the beginning of the command. When the program is finished executing, the login script will take over again and continue running. (If you want to execute a Windows-based application that will remain running for an extended period of time, use the @ command instead of #. The @ command will allow the login script to finish while letting the application continue running.)

When this command is used on a DOS workstation to execute another program, the LOGIN utility may be swapped out of conventional memory and into extended or expanded memory (if available) or onto the hard disk, to allow both LOGIN and the program to execute at the same time. If you do not want LOGIN to be moved out of conventional memory, use the NOSWAP login script command, covered later in this chapter.

The # command is commonly used with the CAPTURE utility (explained in Chapter 6). For example, to capture a user's LPT1 port to use a network print queue named LaserQ, you might put the following command in the login script:

```
#CAPTURE L=1 Q=.LaserQ.Satellite.RedHawk NB NT NFF TI=5
```

@ Command

This command executes an external command or program, such as a NetWare utility or a Windows-based application, from the login script. Use this command only on Windows-based workstations. To execute the program, use the @ symbol at the beginning of the command. (The @ command will allow the login script to finish while letting the application continue running.)

For example, to execute the NetWare Administrator utility from within the login script, include the following command in the script:

```
@SYS:\PUBLIC\WIN32\NWADMN32
```

ATTACH Command

This command attaches the user to a NetWare 4.11 or NetWare 5 server using bindery services. It can also be used to attach the user to a NetWare 3.1x or 2.x server. ATTACH doesn't execute a login script for that server; it simply attaches you to the server so you can access its resources. Do not use ATTACH if you want to use Novell Directory Services on a NetWare 4.11 or NetWare 5 server (there is no need to attach to a NetWare 4.11 or NetWare 5 server if you're already logged in to the NDS tree).

To use ATTACH, put the following command in the login script, replacing *server* with the server's name and *username* with the user's login name:

```
ATTACH server/username
```

BREAK ON Command

BREAK OFF is the default. This command lets you abort the login script while it is executing by pressing Ctrl+C or Ctrl+Break.

BREAK ON only lets you break out of the login script. To break out of programs other than the login script, use the DOS BREAK ON command, explained later in this chapter.

To use BREAK ON, put the following command in the login script:

```
BREAK ON
```

CLS Command

Use this command to clear the workstation's screen of any commands that have been displayed by the login script up to the point where this CLS command occurs. (This command is useful only on DOS workstations.)

To use CLS, put the following command in the login script:

```
CLS
```

COMSPEC Command

If you have set up your workstations to run DOS from a network directory instead of from a local disk, use this command. The COMSPEC command lets you tell the workstation that the DOS command processor (COMMAND.COM) is located on the network. If your workstations are running DOS locally, don't use this command. (This command is useful only on DOS workstations.)

To use COMSPEC, put the following command in the login script:

```
COMSPEC=path COMMAND.COM
```

For example, if DOS is located in the directory SYS:PUBLIC\ %MACHINE\%OS\%OS_VERSION, and you have mapped search drive S2 to that directory, you would enter the following command in the login script:

```
COMSPEC=S2:COMMAND.COM
```

CONTEXT Command

Use this command to set the user's name context. CONTEXT works in the login script much like the CX workstation utility works when typed at the workstation's DOS prompt. This command changes the context the user sees after he or she logs in. To change the context before the user logs in, use the NET.CFG file instead of the login script.

To use CONTEXT, put the following command in the login script:

```
CONTEXT context
```

Replace *context* with the user's new name context, such as .Satellite.RedHawk.

DISPLAY Command

This command displays an ASCII text file on the workstation screen during login. If you want to display a word-processed file that has word-processing and printer codes embedded in it, use FDISPLAY instead. (FDISPLAY is covered later in this chapter.)

To use DISPLAY, put the following command in the login script, replacing *path\filename* with the directory path and name of the file you want to display:

```
DISPLAY path\filename
```

DOS BREAK ON Command

This command lets you abort a program (other than the login script) while it is executing, by pressing Ctrl+C or Ctrl+Break. DOS BREAK OFF is the default.

To break out of the login script, use the BREAK ON command instead (explained earlier in this chapter).

To use DOS BREAK ON, put the following command in the login script:

```
DOS BREAK ON
```

DOS VERIFY ON Command

Use this command to make DOS's COPY command verify that files can be read after they are copied. You do not need to use this command if you use only the NetWare NCOPY utility, because NCOPY verifies the copies automatically. (This command is useful only for DOS and Windows 3.1 workstations.)

The default is DOS VERIFY OFF.

To use DOS VERIFY ON, put the following command in the login script:

```
DOS VERIFY ON
```

DRIVE Command

This command lets you change to a different default network drive while the login script is executing. Be sure to place this command in the login script after the MAP command that maps a drive to the desired directory.

For example, to map drive H to SYS:USERS\PAULINE\STATUS, and then make drive H the default drive, put the following commands in the login script:

```
MAP H:=SYS:USERS\PAULINE\STATUS
DRIVE H:
```

EXIT Command

Use this command at the end of a login script to stop the script and go immediately into another program, such as a menu program or an application.

EXIT stops the current login script, which is why you must place it at the end of the script. In addition, it prevents any other login scripts from executing. If you put an EXIT command at the end of the container system login script, the profile and user scripts will not execute, so be sure you place the EXIT command at the end of any scripts you do want to execute.

To use EXIT, put the following command in the login script:

```
EXIT "program"
```

Inside the quotation marks, replace *program* with the command that executes the program you want the user to enter. For Windows workstations, the string of letters inside the quotation marks can be as many characters long as is necessary. However, for DOS workstations, the string inside the quotation marks can't exceed the number of the workstation's keyboard buffer length (typically 15) minus 1. (In other words, most DOS workstations are limited to 14 characters inside the quotation marks.)

For example, to exit to a menu program called DATA, use the following command at the end of the login script:

```
EXIT "NMENU DATA"
```

If you have changed the workstation's long machine name in the NET.CFG file, you need to execute the PCCOMPATIBLE login script command before the EXIT command.

FDISPLAY Command

This command displays, on the workstation screen during login, a word-processed file that has word processing and printer codes embedded in it. It removes these embedded codes and displays just the text of the file. If you want to display an ASCII text file, you can use DISPLAY instead (covered earlier in this chapter).

To use FDISPLAY, put the following command in the login script, replacing *path\filename* with the directory path and name of the file you want to display:

```
FDISPLAY path\filename
```

FIRE PHASERS Command

On a DOS workstation, this command makes the workstation emit a phaser sound. You can specify how many times (up to nine) the phaser sound occurs. On a Windows workstation, this command makes the workstation execute a sound file (such as a .WAV file). You can use this command to draw attention to a displayed message during login.

To use FIRE PHASERS, put the following command in the login script:

```
FIRE x filename
```

For *x*, substitute the number of times you want the sound to occur (1 to 9). For a DOS workstation, don't include a *filename*. For a Windows workstation, substitute the name of a sound file, such as a .WAV file or other platform-compatible sound file, for *filename*.

GOTO Command

Use this command to make the login script skip to another portion of the script. To use this command, label the part of the login script you want to execute with a single word of your choice, and then put the following command in the login script, substituting the word you used in the script for *label*.

```
GOTO label
```

IF...THEN Command

Use this command to indicate that a command should execute only if certain conditions are met. For example, you could use IF...THEN to make a message display only on a particular day of the week.

The IF...THEN command uses this basic format:

```
IF something is true THEN
execute this command
ELSE execute this command
END
```

The ELSE portion of the command is optional. You only use it when you have two or more commands that you want to execute at different times, based on different circumstances.

For example, to display the message "Friday's here at last!" on Fridays, you would use the following commands:

```
IF DAY_OF_WEEK="Friday" THEN
WRITE "Friday's here at last!"
END
```

No message will appear on any other day of the week.

Suppose you want to make the same message appear on Fridays, and on all other days you want to display the message, "Customers are our first priority." To do this, use the same command, but add an ELSE portion:

```
IF DAY_OF_WEEK="Friday" THEN
WRITE "Friday's here at last!"
ELSE
WRITE "Customers are our first priority."
END
```

The first line of the IF...THEN command (IF *something is true*) is called a conditional statement, because this is the condition that makes the rest of the command execute. To use a conditional statement, you use a variable, and you indicate what value that variable has to have before it can execute the command.

These variables are called *identifier variables*. The identifier variables you can use in login scripts are explained later in this chapter, in the section "Using Identifier Variables."

For example, if you specify the DAY_OF_WEEK variable, you can also indicate the value you need the variable to have, such as "Friday." Then, whenever the day's value matches the one you indicated in the command, the command will execute. (In other words, on every Friday, the command will execute.)

In conditional statements, the value must be enclosed in quotation marks.

INCLUDE Command

This command lets you execute another text file or another object's login script as part of the login script currently executing. The other file or login script, called a *subscript*, must contain regular login script commands. The users who will be receiving the subscript must have rights to the subscript file or object.

To call a subscript, put one of the following commands in the main login script at the point where you want the subscript to execute:

INCLUDE *path\filename*

or

INCLUDE *object*

Replace *path\filename* with the directory path and name of the text file that contains the login script commands, or replace *object* with the name of the object whose login script you want to execute. (If the object is in another context, be sure to use the object's full name.)

LASTLOGINTIME Command

This command simply displays the time of the user's last login on the workstation screen.

To use LASTLOGINTIME, put the following command in the login script:

LASTLOGINTIME

LOGOUT

Use this command to log out of the network or a specific server. To log out of the entire network and disconnect all drive mappings and network connections, type:

LOGOUT

To log out of a specific server, while leaving other network connections and drive mappings intact, type the following command, substituting the name of the server for *server*:

LOGOUT *server*

MACHINE Command

Use this command to set the workstation's DOS machine name. The default is IBM_PC. Some programs, such as NetBIOS, may need this command if they were written to run under PC DOS, but in most cases, you shouldn't have to use this command. (Use this command only with DOS and Windows 3.1 workstations.)

This command is different from the MACHINE identifier variable. That variable, which can be used in MAP and WRITE login script commands, gets its value from the NET.CFG file.

The machine name can be up to 15 characters long.

To use MACHINE, put the following command in the login script, replacing *name* with the machine name:

```
MACHINE=name
```

MAP Command

Use this command to map drive letters to network directories. When you put a MAP command in a login script, that command will be executed every time the user logs in.

Use the MAP login script command just as you use the MAP utility at the DOS prompt, with the following command format:

```
MAP letter:=path
```

For example, to map drive L to VOL1:APPS\WP, the command would be as follows:

```
MAP L:=VOL1:APPS\WP
```

Because your users probably have home directories in which they store their individual files, you may want to map a drive to the user's home directory. You can do that generically in a system or profile script by using the LOGIN_NAME identifier variable. For example, if all your users have a subdirectory under the directory USERS, and you want the first available drive to be mapped to this subdirectory, you can put the following mapping in the system or profile login script:

```
MAP N VOL1:USERS\%LOGIN_NAME
```

%LOGIN_NAME is the identifier variable. When user Tina logs in, her name will automatically be substituted for this variable, and the first available network drive will be mapped to VOL1:USERS\TINA.

You can also use MAP to map search drives. Search drives are used to indicate directories that contain applications or utilities. Search drives let users execute an application without having to know where the application is; the network searches through the designated search drives for the application's executable file when the user types the program's execution command.

To map a search drive, you use the letter S, followed by a number, rather than designating a drive letter. The search drive will assign its own letters in reverse order, starting with the letter Z. (You can have up to 16 search drives mapped.) For example, to map the first search drive to the SYS:PUBLIC directory, enter the following line in the login script:

```
MAP S1:=SYS:PUBLIC
```

Search drive mappings are added to the workstation's DOS PATH environment variable. This means that if you specify that a search drive is S1, as in the preceding example, the mapping to SYS:PUBLIC will overwrite the first DOS path that had already been set. To avoid overwriting a path setting, use the INS option. By entering

```
MAP INS S1
```

instead of

```
MAP S1
```

the search drive mapping will be inserted at the beginning of the DOS path settings, moving the path setting that was previously first to the second position.

In login scripts, some drives should be mapped in a particular order. In the system login script, the following search drives should be mapped first:

```
MAP INS S1:=SYS:PUBLIC
MAP INS S2:=SYS:PUBLIC\%MACHINE\%OS\%OS_VERSION
```

The SYS:PUBLIC directory contains the NetWare utilities and other NetWare files that users need. The second mapping maps a search drive to the DOS directories. If you want your users to run DOS from the network instead of from their local disks, use this command, which points to the network directories that contain DOS. (This command uses identifier variables for some directory names. For example, the identifier variable %OS represents the workstation's operating system. Therefore, if a workstation requires MS-DOS version 5.0, the search drive would be mapped to SYS:PUBLIC\IBM_PC\MSDOS\50.)

After these two search drives, you can map additional search drives in any order you want.

NOTE

Instead of mapping search drives in order (S3, S4, S5, and so on), use MAP S16 for all subsequent mappings that don't require an exact position (as do the first two mappings, mentioned above). Each MAP S16 command will insert its drive mapping at the end of the list, pushing up the previous mappings. This just makes the list of search drives more flexible, so if you delete one, the others will reorder themselves automatically. Also, you don't run the risk of overwriting a search drive that may have been specified in another login script.

You can use several variations of the MAP command to accomplish different tasks, as shown in Table 6.1.

TABLE 6.1	*MAP Command Options*
TASK	**DESCRIPTION**

Map drives in order, without your specifying drive letters	If you don't want to specify exact drive letters, you can map each available drive, in order. This is useful if you don't know which drive letters have already been mapped in a system or profile login script. To assign drive letters this way, use an asterisk, followed by a number. For example, to get the first and second available drives, you could use the following commands:
	
	`MAP *1:=VOL1:APPS\WP`
	
	`MAP *2:=VOL1:DATA\REPORTS`

Map the next available drive	To map the next available drive, use the letter N (without a colon), as in the following command: `MAP N=VOL1:APPS\WP`
Delete a drive mapping	To delete a mapping for drive G, for example, use the following command: `MAP DEL G:`
Turn off MAP's display	Whenever a MAP command is executed in the login script, it will display the new drive mapping on the workstation screen unless you specify otherwise. To turn off this display, use the following command: `MAP DISPLAY OFF`

Turn on MAP's display	At the end of the login script, you may want to turn MAP's display back on and show a listing of all the completed drive mappings. To do this, put the following commands at or near the end of the login script:
	
	`MAP DISPLAY ON`
	`MAP`

TASK	DESCRIPTION
Map a fake root	Some applications must be installed at the root of a volume or hard disk. If you would rather install the application in a subdirectory, you can do that, and then map a fake root to the application's subdirectory. You can map a fake root in a regular drive mapping or in a search drive mapping. To map drive H as a fake root to the VOL1:APPS\CAD subdirectory, use the following command: `MAP ROOT H:=VOL1:APPS\CAD`
Map a drive to a Directory Map object	You can create an NDS object, called a Directory Map object, that points to a particular directory. Then, you can map drives to that object instead of to the actual directory path. This way, if you later move the directory to another part of the file system, you can just change the Directory Map object's description instead of updating all the affected login scripts. Preferably, use Directory Map objects in the user's current context. If the Directory Map object is in another part of the NDS tree, you can either use the Directory Map object's full context name in the mapping command, or you can create an Alias object for the Directory Map object in the user's current context. To map a search drive to a Directory Map object named Database, use the following command: `MAP S16:=DATABASE`

NOTE

In Windows NT, all drive mappings are automatically created as fake root mappings. Therefore, if you want to prevent drive mappings from being automatically mapped to fake roots, you must set the Windows NT environment variable MAP ROOT OFF = 1. Then all drives are mapped as you specify them with the MAP command: either regular drive mappings, search drive mappings, or explicit fake root mappings.

NO_DEFAULT Command

Use this command at the end of a system or profile login script if you do not want the default script to execute for a user who doesn't have a user login script.

To use NO_DEFAULT, put the following command in the login script:

```
NO_DEFAULT
```

NOSWAP Command

Use this command, on DOS workstations only, to keep LOGIN from being moved out of conventional memory into higher memory.

When the # command is used to execute another program, the LOGIN utility may be swapped out of conventional memory and into extended or expanded memory (if available) or onto the hard disk, to allow both LOGIN and the program to execute at the same time. This happens by default. If you do not want LOGIN to be moved out of conventional memory, use the NOSWAP login script command. If the workstation doesn't have enough memory to run both LOGIN and the external program, the external program will fail, but the rest of the login script will execute.

To use NOSWAP, put the following command in the login script:

```
NOSWAP
```

PAUSE Command

This command makes the login script pause in its execution. The message "Strike any key when ready . . ." appears on the workstation's screen. When the user presses a key, the login script continues executing.

To use PAUSE, put the following command in a login script, wherever you want the pause to occur:

```
PAUSE
```

PCCOMPATIBLE Command

Use this command only if you are using the EXIT command and have changed the workstation's long machine name in the NET.CFG file to something other than IBM_PC.

To use this command, place it before the EXIT command, as in the following example (which exits the login script and goes into a program called CAD):

```
PCCOMPATIBLE
EXIT "CAD"
```

PROFILE Command

Use this command in a container login script to set or override a user's assigned profile script. To use this command, replace *name* in the command shown here with the Profile object's name:

```
PROFILE name
```

REMARK Command

Use REMARK — or its equivalents REM, an asterisk (*), or a semicolon (;) — to indicate that the rest of the line in the login script is a comment and should not be displayed or executed. Use comments to describe commands in the login script so you or others will recall why certain commands are there when you read the script later.

For example, the following lines in the login script indicate that a MAP command follows them:

```
REM The next drive mapping is for students' temporary use.
REM Delete the mapping at end of quarter.
```

SCRIPT_SERVER Command

This command specifies a home server from which the workstation can read a bindery login script. This command does not apply to NetWare 4.11 or NetWare 5 servers.

To use SCRIPT_SERVER, put the following command in a login script, replacing *server* with the bindery server's name:

```
SCRIPT_SERVER server
```

SET Command

Use SET to set DOS environment variables. The variables remain in effect after the login script is finished (unless you change them from the DOS command line at some point after login — but then the variables will be reset when the login script is executed again). You can use any of the regular DOS variables in this command.

Use the SET login script command just as you would use regular DOS SET variables, with one exception: for a login script command, you must enclose the value you are setting in quotation marks.

For example, to set the prompt to display the current directory, add the following command to the login script:

```
SET PROMPT= "$P$G"
```

If you use SET PATH, the path will overwrite any previous path settings established in AUTOEXEC.BAT or earlier in the login script.

To use a SET variable as an identifier variable in another login script command, enclose the variable in angle brackets, as in <path>. For example, the following MAP login script command uses the path variable:

```
MAP S16:=%<PATH>
```

If you want the variable to be set for a DOS workstation only while the login script is executing, and you want it to return to its original state after execution, add the word TEMP to the beginning of the SET command, as in the following example:

```
TEMP SET PROMPT= "$P$G"
```

SET_TIME OFF Command

By default, when a workstation logs in, it sets its time to the time of the first server it connects to. To prevent the workstation from adopting the server's time, use the command SET_TIME OFF. To allow the workstation to adopt its time from the server after all, use SET_TIME ON (the default).

To use SET_TIME OFF, put the following command in the login script:

```
SET_TIME OFF
```

SHIFT Command

This command changes the order in which variables entered at the LOGIN command line are interpreted. You can use special variables, called %n variables, as placeholders in a login script command. Then, when a user logs in, the values the user enters at the command line are substituted for the %n variable.

The SHIFT command lets you change the order in which the %n variables are executed. In the SHIFT command, specify a positive or negative number to indicate that you want to shift the variables one direction or the other. For example, the following command moves each %n variable one position to the right:

```
SHIFT +1
```

Using %n variables is described later in this chapter.

SWAP Command

Use this command, on DOS workstations only, to move LOGIN out of conventional memory into higher memory.

When the # command is used to execute another program, the LOGIN utility may be swapped out of conventional memory and into extended or expanded memory (if available) or onto the hard disk, to allow both LOGIN and the program to execute at the same time. This happens by default. However, if you do not want LOGIN to be moved out of conventional memory, you can use the NOSWAP login script command. If NOSWAP has been used earlier in the login script, you can use SWAP to make LOGIN able to swap into higher memory again.

To use SWAP, put the following command in the login script:

```
SWAP
```

TERM Command

Use this command only with Novell Application Launcher login scripts. This command stops the login script and returns an error code. It is often used in conjunction with IF...THEN commands, so that the login script stops and returns an error code only if a certain condition is encountered.

If you put the TERM command in a login script, it will stop the script at that point, and it will also prevent any subsequent login scripts (such as a profile or user script) from executing.

To use TERM, put the following command in the login script, substituting any error number between 000 and 999 for *nnn*:

```
TERM nnn
```

TREE Command

Use this command to attach to another NDS tree after you've already established a connection with one tree. After the TREE command executes, all subsequent MAP commands and other commands will affect the new tree.

To use the TREE command, put the following command in the login script, substituting the new NDS tree name for *tree* and the user's full NDS name for *username*:

```
TREE tree/username
```

WRITE Command

Use WRITE to display short messages on the workstation screen during login. To use WRITE, enter the command

```
WRITE
```

followed by quotation marks enclosing the text you want to appear on the user's screen. For example, to display the message "Have a nice day," enter the following command:

```
WRITE "Have a nice day"
```

To display a message that is too long for a single line, use the word WRITE at the beginning of each line. For example, suppose you want to display the following message:

```
Please attend today's weekly staff meeting in
Conference Room B.

Be prepared to discuss your client call status and
success stories.

Remember to bring your expense reports.
```

To get these sentences to appear correctly on five lines, you should enter the following commands:

```
WRITE "Please attend today's weekly staff meeting in"
WRITE "Conference Room B."

WRITE "Be prepared to discuss your client call status and
WRITE "success stories."

WRITE "Remember to bring your expense reports."
```

For information about using identifier variables in WRITE commands, see the next section, "Using Identifier Variables."

There are a few special characters you can enter in a WRITE command to make the command appear as you want. These are shown in Table 6.2.

TABLE 6.2   *Special Characters for the WRITE Command*

CHARACTER	DESCRIPTION
;	Links two WRITE commands together so they appear as a continuous sentence or paragraph. Can also be used to link text within quotation marks to an identifier variable that isn't included in the quotation marks.
\r	Causes a carriage return when used inside the text string.
\n	Begins a new line of text when used inside the text string.
\"	Makes a quotation mark display inside the text message when used inside the text string.

CHARACTER	DESCRIPTION
\7	Causes a beep sound to occur when used inside the text string.

Using Identifier Variables

In login scripts, an identifier variable is simply a placeholder for information that is substituted whenever a user logs in. Using identifier variables in login scripts is effective for two reasons:

▸ It's an efficient way to make generic commands work for most users.

▸ It enables you to make different commands execute only at certain times or in particular situations.

An identifier variable may be replaced by specific user information, such as the user's login name or full name, or it may be replaced by information about the user's workstation, such as its address or machine type. It may also be replaced by general information that has nothing to do with the user, such as the day of the week, time, or network address.

You can use identifier variables in many different login script commands. You can use them in WRITE commands to display the value that is provided. For example, suppose you add the following command to the system login script:

```
WRITE "GOOD %GREETING_TIME, %LOGIN_NAME."
```

When user Eric logs in at 8:00 a.m., the following message displays on his screen:

```
Good MORNING, ERIC.
```

When user Maude logs in at 1:30 p.m., she receives this message:

```
Good AFTERNOON, MAUDE.
```

You can also use identifier variables in other types of commands, such as IF...THEN commands, to allow a particular command to execute only under certain conditions. For example, the following IF...THEN command will execute a WRITE command only on Wednesdays:

```
IF DAY_OF_WEEK="Wednesday" THEN
WRITE "Don't forget staff meeting today at 3:00."
END
```

For more about the IF...THEN command, see the section in this chapter titled "IF...THEN Command."

Syntax for Using Identifier Variables

In the previous examples, you may have noticed that sometimes a percent sign (%) is added to the beginning of the variable, and sometimes it isn't. Ordinarily, in a WRITE command, everything inside the quotation marks is displayed. However, the percent sign indicates that the following word is not to be displayed as is; rather, it is an identifier variable, and the variable's value should be displayed instead.

In other commands, when the identifier variable is not enclosed in quotation marks, do not use the percent sign.

The basic syntax rules for identifier variables are as follows:

▶ Identifier variables should be typed in uppercase.

▶ If you want the variable's value to be displayed in a WRITE command, precede the variable with a percent sign and enclose it in quotation marks.

▶ To use a variable in any other command, do not use a percent sign.

▶ In an IF...THEN command, if you specify a desired value for the variable, enclose the value in quotation marks, as in IF DAY_OF_WEEK="Monday".

You can specify how an identifier variable matches a particular value in six different ways, as shown in Table 6.3.

T A B L E 6.3	Operators for Assigning Values to Identifier Variables
OPERATOR	**EXAMPLE**
= (equals)	IF LOGIN_NAME = "David" means *If the user is David*
<> (doesn't equal)	IF LOGIN_NAME <> "Admin" means *If the user isn't Admin*
> (is greater than)	IF HOUR > "9" means *If the hour is 10:00 or later*
>= (is greater than or equal to)	IF HOUR >= "9:00" means *If the hour is 9:00 or later*
< (is less than)	IF HOUR < "5" means *If the hour is 4:00 or earlier*
<= (Is less than or equal to)	IF HOUR <= "5" means *If the hour is 5:00 or earlier*

Using the %n Identifier Variable

When users log in, they type a LOGIN command that usually includes at least two parameters: their login names, and either a tree name or a server name. If there is only one tree or server available, a user may only have to specify the login name parameter, but the other parameter is implied.

In addition, a user can add more parameters to the LOGIN command, such as an application name or other keyword he or she wants to use. This enables the user to have different login script commands execute depending on the parameter the user specifies in the LOGIN command.

In login scripts, you can insert a special type of identifier variable to use and display these LOGIN parameters. It is called the %n variable (where n is a number, such as 0, 1, and so on).

To use a %n variable, you insert it into a command just like any other identifier variable, except that it is always preceded by a percent sign and enclosed in quotation marks. Then, whenever a user logs in, the parameters he or she enters are substituted for the %n variable in the login script command.

The first two variables, %0 and %1, must always have the following values:

%0   The server or tree name, depending on how the user logs in
%1   The user's login name

Subsequent numbers, such as %2 and %3, can be fulfilled by whatever additional parameters the user enters with the LOGIN command.

The following is an example of how %n variables can be used in login script commands:

```
IF "%1"="Jessica" THEN
MAP *3:=VOL1:APPS\DB
IF "%2"="wp" THEN
MAP *4:=VOL1:APPS\WP
END
```

In this example, two %n variables are used: %1 and %2. Because %1 is always a user login name, the first line of the command is specifying that the following commands execute only if the login name is Jessica.

The second variable, %2, will be whatever variable user Jessica enters after her login name. If she enters

```
WP
```

after her login name, she will get an additional drive mapping to the WP subdirectory. She would enter the following command when she logs in:

```
LOGIN JESSICA WP
```

In this command, the first variable, %0, wasn't supplied but is implied to be the server to which she attaches, because %0 is always the server. The second variable, %1, is the user login name (Jessica, in this case). The third variable, %2, is the WP parameter she entered after her login name. Whenever she uses this command to log in, Jessica will receive two drive mappings — one to the DB subdirectory, and one to the WP subdirectory.

If Jessica logs in using the following command:

```
LOGIN JESSICA
```

she will receive only a drive mapping to the DB subdirectory.

If anyone other than Jessica logs in, that person will not receive either drive mapping.

The SHIFT login command lets you actually shift the position of the parameters to the right or left, depending on whether you enter a positive or negative number. (See the description of the SHIFT login script command, earlier in this chapter.)

Identifier Variables

The identifier variables can be grouped into the following categories:

- ► User
- ► Workstation
- ► Network
- ► Date
- ► Time
- ► Miscellaneous

Table 6.4 lists each of the available user identifier variables.

TABLE 6.4	User Identifier Variables	
IDENTIFIER VARIABLE	**DESCRIPTION**	**EXAMPLE**
FULL_NAME	The user's full name, if defined in the User object's properties. (Spaces are replaced by underscores.)	Eric_V._McCloud
LAST_NAME	The user's last name in NDS (or full name on the bindery servers).	McCloud

IDENTIFIER VARIABLE	DESCRIPTION	EXAMPLE
LOGIN_ALIAS_ CONTEXT	Displays "Y" if the requester context is an alias.	
LOGIN_CONTEXT	The user's name context in the NDS tree.	Mktg.Satellite.RedHawk
LOGIN_NAME	The user's login name (same as common name).	Eric

MEMBER OF "*group*"	The group a user might belong to. Can also use the word NOT with this variable.	`IF MEMBER OF`
		`"Design" THEN`
		`. . .`
		`IF NOT MEMBER OF`
		`"Design"`
		`THEN. . .`

PASSWORD_EXPIRES	Displays how many days before the user's password expires.	`WRITE "Your`
		`password`
		`expires in`
		`%PASSWORD_`
		`EXPIRES days."`

REQUESTER_ CONTEXT	The context from which LOGIN was started. This may not necessarily be the same context the user will be in after login.	`IF REQUESTER_`
		`CONTEXT =`
		`"RedHawk"`
		`THEN. . .`

USER_ID	Unique number assigned to each user.	12345678

Table 6.5 lists each of the available workstation identifier variables.

T A B L E 6.5	*Workstation Identifier Variables*	
IDENTIFIER VARIABLE	**DESCRIPTION**	**EXAMPLE**
MACHINE	The workstation's computer type	IBM_PC (This is the default.)
NETWARE_REQUESTER	Version of the NetWare client software for OS/2 or Novell VLM client software	V1.20

(continued)

TABLE 6.5	*Workstation Identifier Variables (continued)*	
IDENTIFIER VARIABLE	**DESCRIPTION**	**EXAMPLE**
OS	The workstation's type of operating system	MSDOS
OS_VERSION	The version of the workstation's operating system	V6.20
P_STATION	The workstation's node address	000106FFACDE (12-digit hexadecimal number)
PLATFORM	The workstation's operating system	DOS, OS2, WIN (for Windows 3.1), W95 (for Windows 95), WNT (for Windows NT), etc.
SHELL_TYPE	The version of the workstation's DOS shell	V4.20A
SMACHINE	The workstation's short machine name	IBM (This is the default.)
STATION	The workstation's connection number	14
WINVER	The version number of the workstation's Windows operating system	v3.01

Table 6.6 lists each of the available network identifier variables.

TABLE 6.6	*Network Identifier Variables*	
IDENTIFIER VARIABLE	**DESCRIPTION**	**EXAMPLE**
FILE_SERVER	The NetWare server name	Sales1
NETWORK_ADDRESS	The IPX external number of the cabling system attached to the server's network board	00120FED (eight-digit hexadecimal number)

Table 6.7 lists each of the available date identifier variables.

TABLE 6.7	Date Identifier Variables	
IDENTIFIER VARIABLE	**DESCRIPTION**	**EXAMPLE OR VALUES**
DAY	The day's date	Values: 01 through 31
DAY_OF_WEEK	The day's name	Example: Tuesday
MONTH	The month's number	Values: 01 through 12
MONTH_NAME	The month's name	Example: October
NDAY_OF_WEEK	The number of the day of the week	Values: 1 through 7 (1=Sunday)
SHORT_YEAR	The last two digits of the year	Example: 96
YEAR	All four digits of the year	Example: 1996

Table 6.8 lists each of the available time identifier variables.

TABLE 6.8	Time Identifier Variables	
IDENTIFIER VARIABLE	**DESCRIPTION**	**VALUES**
AM_PM	Morning or afternoon	AM or PM
GREETING_TIME	General time of day	Morning, Afternoon, or Evening
HOUR	Hour on a 12-hour scale	1 through 12
HOUR24	Hour on a 24-hour scale	00 through 23 (00=Midnight)
MINUTE	Minute	00 through 59
SECOND	Second	00 through 59

Table 6.9 lists each of the miscellaneous identifier variables.

TABLE 6.9 Miscellaneous Identifier Variables

IDENTIFIER VARIABLE	DESCRIPTION	EXAMPLE OR VALUES
<DOS variable>	Any DOS variable, such as PATH, PROMPT, etc. Must be enclosed in angle brackets. If in a MAP command, must also be preceded by a percent sign (%).	Example: MAP S16:= %<PATH>
%n	Variable for LOGIN parameters, such as server name and user name	Example: IF %1 = "Joel" THEN...
NDS property name	Any NDS property name, such as GIVEN NAME, TITLE, etc. Use to display the property value in WRITE commands. If the property name contains spaces, it must be the last item in the quoted string.	Example: WRITE "Hello, %GIVEN_NAME"
ACCESS_SERVER	Displays whether the access server is online.	Values: TRUE (functioning) or FALSE (not functioning)
ERROR_LEVEL	An error number	Values: Any error number (0=No errors)

Login Script Example

The following is an example of a container login script.

```
MAP DISPLAY OFF
IF "%1"="ADMIN" THEN
MAP *1:=SERVER1_SYS:SYSTEM
ELSE MAP *1:=SERVER1_VOL1:USERS\%LOGIN_NAME
END
```

```
MAP INS S1:=SERVER1_SYS:PUBLIC
MAP INS S2:=SERVER1_SYS:PUBLIC\%MACHINE\%OS\%OS_VERSION
COMSPEC=S2:COMMAND.COM
MAP S16:=VOL1:APPS\WORD
MAP S16:=VOL1:APPS\DATAB
IF MEMBER OF "Design" THEN
MAP ROOT S16:=VOL1:APPS\CAD
MAP *2:=VOL1:DESIGNS\PROJECTA
MAP *3:=VOL1:DESIGNS\PROJECTB
END
IF MEMBER OF "Field" THEN
MAP S16:=VOL1:APPS\CDBASE
MAP *4:=VOL1:REPORTS\CLIENTS\NEW
END

#CAPTURE L=1 Q=.LaserQ.Satellite.RedHawk NB NT NFF TI=5

MAP DISPLAY ON
MAP
WRITE "Good %GREETING_TIME, %LOGIN_NAME."

IF DAY_OF_WEEK="Monday" THEN
WRITE "It's a great week to design satellites!"
FIRE 3 TIMES
END
```

The first line in the script:

```
MAP DISPLAY OFF
```

turns off the display of any MAP commands as they're being executed during the login process. This simply keeps the screen from looking too busy and from distracting or concerning the user.

The next group of four lines:

```
IF "%1"="ADMIN" THEN
  MAP *1:=SERVER1_SYS:SYSTEM
ELSE MAP *1:=SERVER1_VOL1:USERS\%LOGIN_NAME
END
```

maps the first network drive to a network directory. If the user who logs in is user Admin, then the first drive mapping is to the SYS:SYSTEM directory on server SERVER1. All other users who log in will get a drive mapped to their home directories on volume VOL1 instead.

The next line:

```
MAP INS S1:=SERVER1_SYS:PUBLIC
```

maps the first search drive to the SYS:PUBLIC directory for all users. This is the directory where all NetWare utilities are stored, so it's important for users to have access to it.

The next two lines:

```
MAP INS S2:=SERVER1_SYS:PUBLIC\%MACHINE\%OS\%OS_VERSION
COMSPEC=S2:COMMAND.COM
```

map a search drive to the directory that contains DOS, so users can run DOS from the network instead of from the local hard disk. For every version of DOS your users will run on their machines, you should create a unique DOS directory, named with the workstation's machine type, DOS type, and DOS version, and load that version of DOS in the version subdirectory. For example, if your user is running an IBM-compatible computer, with MS-DOS version 6.2 on it, the DOS directory would be

```
SYS:PUBLIC\IBM_PC\MSDOS\6.20
```

The login script command, which uses identifier variables in the directory path, will gather the workstation's particular information and map a drive to the correct directory.

The next two lines:

```
MAP S16:=VOL1:APPS\WORD
MAP S16:=VOL1:APPS\DATAB
```

map search drives to two application directories so users can access them.

The next five lines only execute if the user logging in is a member of the group called "Design." If so, then a fake root search drive is mapped to the CAD subdirectory, and regular network drives are mapped to two subdirectories: PROJECTA and PROJECTB.

```
IF MEMBER OF "Design" THEN
MAP ROOT S16:=VOL1:APPS\CAD
MAP *2:=VOL1:DESIGNS\PROJECTA
MAP *3:=VOL1:DESIGNS\PROJECTB
END
```

The next four lines:

```
IF MEMBER OF "Field" THEN
MAP S16:=VOL1:APPS\CDBASE
MAP *4:=VOL1:REPORTS\CLIENTS\NEW
END
```

only execute if the user logging in is a member of the group called "Field." These users, who are field sales people, get a search drive mapped to their CDBASE application and a regular network drive mapped to the NEW subdirectory, where they log new clients.

The next line:

```
#CAPTURE L=1 Q=.LaserQ.Satellite.RedHawk NB NT NFF TI=5
```

captures the workstation's LPT1 port to a network print queue named LaserQ. Its full NDS name is given in this case (.LaserQ.Satellite.RedHawk). The full name isn't necessary if the print queue is in the same context as the user logging in. The NB parameter means "No Banner," the NT parameter means "No Tabs," NFF means "No Form Feed," and TI=5 means that the capture will time out after five seconds, if necessary.

The next line turns MAP's display back on:

```
MAP DISPLAY ON
```

The next line displays a list of all the drive mappings that have been successfully mapped during the login process:

```
MAP
```

The next line displays a greeting to the user, such as "Good MORNING, ERIC."

```
WRITE "Good %GREETING_TIME, %LOGIN_NAME."
```

The final four lines:

```
IF DAY_OF_WEEK="Monday" THEN
```

```
WRITE "It's a great week to design satellites!"
FIRE 3 TIMES
END
```

execute only on Mondays. They display a supposedly inspirational message to the user and make the phaser sound three times as the login script ends.

CHAPTER 7

Network Security

Instant Access

Using Login Security

- To create account restrictions, use the NetWare Administrator utility (which runs in Windows 95/98 and Windows NT).

- To set or change passwords, use the NetWare Administrator utility, the LOGIN utility, or SETPASS (a command-line utility).

Using NDS Security

- To view or change NDS rights, use the NetWare Administrator utility.

Using Directory and File Security

- To view or change file system rights, use the NetWare Administrator utility or RIGHTS (a command-line utility).

- To view or change directory and file attributes, use the NetWare Administrator utility or FLAG (a command-line utility).

Securing the Network from Intruders

- To use NCP Packet Signature, use the SET command on the server. Then use either the NET.CFG file on Windows 3.*x* workstations, or the Advanced Settings parameters of the Network Neighborhood's Novell NetWare Client property page on Windows 95/98 and Windows NT workstations.

- To set Intruder Detection, use the NetWare Administrator utility.

- To lock the server console, use SCRSAVER.NLM.

- To remove DOS and prevent NLMs from being loaded from insecure areas, use the SECURE CONSOLE console utility.

The Keys to NetWare Security

One of the aspects of NetWare that sets it apart from other network operating systems is its high levels of security. How you implement this security is up to you. You can make your NetWare network as open as you need or as secure as Fort Knox.

NetWare uses several different types of security mechanisms to enable you to have control over your network's security. Those types of security are as follows:

- ▶ Login security, which ensures that only authorized users can log in to the network

- ▶ NDS security, which controls whether NDS objects, such as users, can see or manipulate other NDS objects and their properties

- ▶ File system security, which controls whether users can see and work with files and directories

- ▶ Intruder detection, which automatically detects someone trying to break into an account and locks them out

- ▶ NCP Packet Signature, which prevents fraudulent packets from being forged on a network

- ▶ Server protection, which includes ways to prevent unauthorized users from accessing the server

Each of these types of security is described in this chapter.

Login Security

Login security ensures that only authorized users can get into the network in the first place. Login security means that users are required to have valid user accounts and valid passwords. You can also use account restrictions to limit the times that users can log in, the workstations they can use, and other things such as the length of their passwords and how frequently they must change their passwords.

Account Restrictions

With account restrictions, you can limit how a user can log in to the network. Table 7.1 shows the four different types of account restrictions you can implement.

TABLE 7.1	Account Restrictions
RESTRICTION	**DESCRIPTION**
Login Restrictions	Control whether the account has an expiration date (which might be useful in situations such as schools, where the authorized users will change with each semester) and whether the user can be logged in from multiple workstations simultaneously.
Password Restrictions	Control whether passwords are required, how often they must be changed, whether they must be unique so that users can't reuse them, and how many grace logins a user can have before being locked out of the account.
Login Time Restrictions	Control the times of day by which users must be logged out of the network. By default, users can be logged in at any time; there are no restrictions.
Network Address Restrictions	Control which network addresses (workstations) a user can use to log in. By default, there are no restrictions on addresses.

You can set each of these types of account restrictions for individual users, or you can set them in a user template so they apply to all users you create in a particular container. If you set them up in a user template, the restrictions will apply to any new users you create from that point on. They aren't retrofitted to users that already exist. Managing account restrictions for all new users in a user template can save you time if all your users need the same types of restrictions.

To set account restrictions, use the NetWare Administrator utility. (For instructions on setting up the NetWare Administrator utility on a workstation, see Chapter 5.)

To set account restrictions for a single user, use the NetWare Administrator utility and select the User object. Then select Details from the Object menu, open the appropriate information pages, and specify the restrictions you want. (Each type of account restriction has its own Information page.)

To set account restrictions for all new users you create, use the NetWare Administrator utility and select the appropriate Template object. Then select Details from the Object menu, open the appropriate restriction pages, and specify the correct restrictions. (Changes to the Template object apply only to users you subsequently create. These changes do not apply to users that already exist.) For more information about using Template objects, see Chapter 6.

Passwords

If passwords are to be a useful form of security, you should ensure that they are being used, that users are changing them frequently, and that users aren't choosing easily guessed passwords.

The following tips can help preserve password security:

- ▶ Require that passwords be at least five characters long (seven or eight is better). Five characters is the default minimum.

- ▶ Require that passwords be changed every 30 days or less.

- ▶ Require unique passwords so that users can't reuse a password they've used before.

- ▶ Do not allow unlimited grace logins. Limit the number of grace logins to three.

- ▶ Tell users to avoid choosing passwords that can be easily guessed, such as birthdays, favorite hobbies or sports, family member names, pet names, and so on.

- ▶ Remind users not to tell others their passwords or allow others to use their accounts.

- ▶ Tell users to mix words and numbers together to form words that can't be found in a dictionary, such as BRAVO42 or STAR2CLOUD.

To set password restrictions for a user or a user template, use the NetWare Administrator utility and select the User (or Template) object. Then open the Details screen, select the Password Restrictions page, and enter the restrictions you want to apply to the user or the template.

Users can change their own passwords by entering the command

SETPASS

at the DOS prompt or by using the Password Restrictions page in the NetWare Administrator utility. More often, however, users change their passwords when the LOGIN utility informs them that their passwords have expired and offers them the opportunity to type in new passwords.

NDS Security

Once you've created your NDS Directory tree, you've probably invested a fair amount of time in making sure that the objects you've created contain all the right information in their properties. Now you can decide who gets to see that information and who can change it.

To make the information about the objects in your tree secure, you can use NDS trustee rights to control how objects in the tree can work with other objects and their properties. *NDS trustee rights* are permissions that allow users or objects to perform tasks such as viewing other objects, changing their properties, deleting them, and so on.

When you assign a user enough NDS trustee rights to work with another object, you've made that user a *trustee* of the object. Each object contains a property called the Access Control List (ACL), which is a list of all the trustees of this particular object.

When the network is first installed, the user Admin has all NDS trustee rights to all objects in the tree. This means that when you log in as user Admin, Admin's NDS trustee rights enable you to create and delete other objects, see them, read and modify all their properties, and so on. Admin is the only user who has full NDS rights to everything in the network immediately after installation. However, while logged in as Admin, you can grant other users the same NDS rights, so that they can have the same privileges as Admin. By default, users are granted only a subset of NDS rights, so they have limited capabilities to work with other objects. You can add to or remove these NDS rights to customize your users' capabilities.

For security reasons, you should be frugal with NDS rights. NDS rights are a tool to protect your network objects from both accidental and intentional tampering. You may want to assign two users to have full NDS rights to the network, such as Admin and another user account that only you can use. This way, there is a backup account you can use if, for example, you forget the Admin's password or delete the Admin user.

There are two types of NDS trustee rights. *Object rights* control how the user works with the object. These are listed in Table 7.2.

Property rights control whether the user can see and work with an object's properties. These are listed in Table 7.3.

To change object or property rights, refer to "Seeing and Changing an Object's NDS Rights" later in this chapter.

TABLE 7.2 *NDS Object Rights*

NDS OBJECT RIGHT	DESCRIPTION
Supervisor	Grants the trustee all NDS rights to the object and all of its properties. It can be blocked by the Inherited Rights Filter (explained in the next section).
Browse	Allows the trustee to see the object in the NDS tree.
Create	Allows the trustee to create a new object in this container. (This right only appears if you're looking at the trustee assignments for a container object.)
Delete	Allows the trustee to delete an object.
Rename	Allows the trustee to change the object's name.

TABLE 7.3 *NDS Property Rights*

NDS PROPERTY RIGHT	DESCRIPTION
Supervisor	Grants the trustee all NDS rights to the property. It can be blocked by the Inherited Rights Filter (explained in the next section).
Compare	Allows the trustee to compare the value of this property to a value the user specifies in a search. (For example, with the Compare right to the Department property, a user can search the tree for any object that has Marketing listed in its Department property.)

(continued)

T A B L E 7.3	NDS Property Rights (continued)
NDS PROPERTY RIGHT	**DESCRIPTION**
Read	Allows the trustee to see the value of this property. (The Read right automatically grants the Compare right, as well.)
Write	Allows the trustee to add, modify, or delete the value of this property. (The Write right automatically grants the Add Self right, as well.)
Add Self	Allows trustees to add or remove themselves as a value of this property. This right only applies to properties that list User objects as values, such as group membership lists or the Access Control List.

Inheriting NDS Rights

NDS object and property rights can be inherited. This means that if you have NDS rights to a parent container, you can inherit those rights and exercise them in an object within that container, too. Inheritance keeps you from having to grant users NDS rights at every level of the Directory tree.

However, it is sometimes desirable to block inheritance. For example, you may want to allow a user to delete objects in a parent container, but not let that user delete any objects in a particular subcontainer. Inheritance can be blocked in three ways:

▶ By granting a new set of NDS rights to an object within the container. Any new assignment will cause the inherited NDS rights from a parent container to be ignored. You can grant a new set of rights using the NetWare Administrator utility, as explained later in this chapter.

▶ By marking a container's trustee assignments as either inheritable or not. If you specify that a container's trustee assignments are not inheritable, none of the rights will be inherited at lower levels.

▶ By removing individual rights from an object's Inherited Rights Filter (IRF). Every object has an Inherited Rights Filter, specifying which NDS rights can be inherited from a parent container. By default, an object's IRF allows all NDS rights to be inherited. You can change the

IRF, however, to revoke one or more NDS rights. Any rights that are revoked from the IRF cannot be inherited.

NOTE The NetWare Administrator utility prevents a user from cutting off all supervisor access to a branch of the NDS tree by searching for an object with supervisor rights to the given container. If an object with supervisor rights isn't found, NetWare Administrator warns you and prevents you from blocking rights.

You can only inherit an NDS right if you've been assigned that right at a higher level. If you don't have the Supervisor right in the parent container, for example, you can't inherit it and use it in another object, even though that right is allowed in the IRF. The IRF doesn't grant NDS rights; it just allows you to inherit them if they've already been assigned to you.

When you assign a user property rights to an object's properties (by using the NetWare Administrator utility), you can click the All Properties button, which is a quick way to give the user the same property rights to all the properties of that object. Alternatively, you can choose Selected Properties and give the user different property rights to each individual property. If you select All Properties, those property rights can be inherited. Property rights assigned only to specific properties cannot be inherited.

NDS Security Equivalence

You can assign one object to have the same NDS rights as another object by using the Security Equal To property. With security equivalence, you can make user Lila have the same NDS rights to the same NDS objects as user Erica, for example. (In fact, Lila will also receive the same file system rights as Erica, too. File system rights are explained later in this chapter.)

When you add a user to a Group object's membership list or to an Organizational Role object's list, the user really becomes security equivalent to that Group or Organizational Role object.

When you are given *security equivalence* to another user, you only receive the same NDS rights that the other user was explicitly granted. You do not get equivalences to that other user's equivalences. In other words, security equivalence doesn't travel. If Lila is equivalent to Erica, and Erica is equivalent to Jess, Lila doesn't end up being equivalent to Jess, too. Lila only receives whatever rights Erica received explicitly.

Effective NDS Rights

Because a user can be given NDS rights to an object and its properties through a variety of methods (explicit assignment, security equivalence, and inheritance), it can be confusing to determine exactly which NDS rights the user really has. A user's *effective NDS rights* are the NDS rights the user can ultimately execute. The user's effective rights to an object are determined in one of two ways:

▶ The user's inherited NDS rights from a parent container, minus any rights blocked by the object's IRF.

▶ The sum of all NDS rights granted to the user for that object through direct trustee assignments and security equivalences to other objects. The IRF does not affect direct trustee assignments and security equivalences.

For example, suppose user Joanna has been given the Browse right to a container object. Joanna has also been given a security equivalence to user Eric, who has Create, Delete, and Rename rights to the same container. This means Joanna's effective NDS rights to this container are now Browse, Create, Delete, and Rename. Even if the container's IRF blocks the Delete right, Joanna still has that right. This is because the IRF affects only inherited rights, and inherited rights are completely ignored if the user has explicit trustee assignments to an object or a security equivalence that gives her NDS rights to that object.

Seeing and Changing an Object's NDS Rights

To see the trustees of an object, use the NetWare Administrator utility (which runs in Windows 95/98 or NT). From the NetWare Administrator's Browser, select the object whose list of trustees you want to see, and then choose Trustees of This Object from the Object menu. (You can also right-click the object to bring up a menu that contains some of the more frequently used tasks, and select Trustees of This Object from that menu.)

The Trustees of This Object screen appears, and you can see all the trustees of this object, as shown in Figure 7.1. If you click each trustee, you can see the specific NDS object and property rights belonging to that trustee. You can also add or delete NDS rights from that trustee by marking the checkboxes next to each right.

F I G U R E   7.1
Trustees of This Object screen

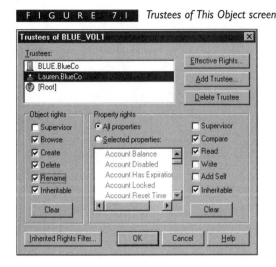

Also, in this screen you can see the object's Inherited Rights Filter. By default, any object or property rights can be inherited from the parent object. If you want to block an NDS right from being inherited, click the checkbox next to the right to clear its box.

If you want to see all the objects to which a particular object has NDS rights, use the NetWare Administrator's Browser and select the object. Then, from the Object menu, choose Rights to Other Objects (or click the right mouse button and select the same option from the menu that appears). Specify the name context (location in the NDS tree) that you want to search for other objects. Then, the Rights to Other Objects screen appears, as shown in Figure 7.2.

To see or change a user's security equivalence, use the NetWare Administrator's Browser and select the user. Then, from the Object menu, select Details, and then choose the Security Equal To page. There, you can add or delete other objects to which this user has a security equivalence.

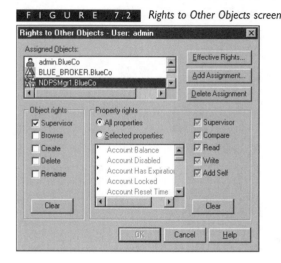

F I G U R E 7.2 *Rights to Other Objects screen*

File System Security

File system security ensures that users can only access and use the files and directories you want them to see and use. You can implement two different types of security tools in the file system, either together or separately, to protect your files:

▶ File system trustee rights, which you assign to users and groups. Just as NDS object rights and NDS property rights control what users can do with other objects, file system trustee rights control what each user or group can do with the file or directory.

▶ Attributes, which you can assign directly to files and directories. Unlike file system rights, which are specific to different users and groups, attributes belong to the file or directory, and they control the activities of all users, regardless of those users' file trustee rights.

The next few sections explain file system trustee rights. File and directory attributes are explained later in this chapter, in the section "File and Directory Attributes."

File System Trustee Rights

File system trustee rights allow users and groups to work with files and directories in specific ways. Each right determines whether a user can do things such as see, read, change, rename, or delete the file or directory. When a file system right is assigned to a file, the right affects the user's allowable actions in that file only. When a file system right is assigned to a directory, the right affects the user's allowable actions on that particular directory, as well as all the files within that directory.

Although file system rights are similar in nature to the NDS rights for objects and properties (described earlier in this chapter), they are not the same thing. File system rights are separate from NDS rights. They affect only how users work with files and directories. NDS rights affect how users work with other NDS objects.

There are eight different file system trustee rights. You can assign any combination of those file system rights to a user or group, depending on how you want that user or group to work.

Table 7.4 lists the available file system rights and explains what each right means when assigned for a directory and for a file.

T A B L E 7 . 4   *File System Rights*

FILE SYSTEM RIGHT	ABBREVIATION	DESCRIPTION
Read	R	Directory: Allows the trustee to open and read files in the directory.
		File: Allows the trustee to open and read the file.
Write	W	Directory: Allows the trustee to open and write to (change) files in the directory.
		File: Allows the trustee to open and write to the file.
Create	C	Directory: Allows the trustee to create subdirectories and files in the directory.
		File: Allows the trustee to salvage the file if it was deleted.

(continued)

| T A B L E 7.4 | *File System Rights (continued)* |

FILE SYSTEM RIGHT	ABBREVIATION	DESCRIPTION
Erase	E	Directory: Allows the trustee to delete the directory and its files and subdirectories.
		File: Allows the trustee to delete the file.
Modify	M	Directory: Allows the trustee to change the name, directory attributes, and file attributes of the directory and its files and subdirectories.
		File: Allows the trustee to change the file's name or file attributes.
File Scan	F	Directory: Allows the trustee to see the names of the files and subdirectories within the directory.
		File: Allows the trustee to see the name of the file.
Access Control	A	Directory: Allows the trustee to change the directory's IRF and trustee assignments.
		File: Allows the trustee to change the file's IRF and trustee assignments.
Supervisor	S	Directory: Grants the trustee all rights to the directory, its files, and its subdirectories. It cannot be blocked by an IRF.
		File: Grants the trustee all rights to the file. It cannot be blocked by an IRF.

Inheriting File System Rights

Just like NDS rights, file system rights can be inherited. This means that if you have file system rights to a parent directory, you can inherit those rights and exercise them in any file and subdirectory within that directory, too. Inheritance keeps you from having to grant users file system rights at every level of the file system.

Inheritance can be blocked by granting a new set of file system rights to a subdirectory or file within the parent directory. Any new assignment will cause the inherited rights from a parent directory to be ignored.

You can also block inheritance by removing the right from a file's or a subdirectory's Inherited Rights Filter. Every directory and file has an Inherited Rights Filter, specifying which file system rights can be inherited from a parent directory. By default, a file's or directory's IRF allows all rights to be inherited. You can change the IRF, however, to revoke one or more rights. Any file system rights that are revoked from the IRF cannot be inherited.

You can only inherit a file system right if you've been assigned that right at a higher level. If you don't have the Create right in the parent directory, for example, you can't inherit it and use it in another subdirectory even though that right is allowed in the IRF. The IRF doesn't grant rights; it just allows you to inherit file system rights if they've already been assigned to you at a higher level.

For instructions on assigning file system rights or changing the IRF, refer to "Seeing and Changing a User's File System Rights" later in this chapter.

File System Security Equivalence

Security equivalence for file system rights works the same way as security equivalence for NDS rights (explained earlier in this chapter). You can assign one user to have the same NDS rights and file system rights as another user by using the Security Equal To property. With security equivalence, you can make user Lila have the same rights to the same NDS objects, files, and directories as user Erica, for example.

When you add a user to a Group object's membership list or to an Organizational Role object's list, the user becomes security equivalent to that Group or Organizational Role object.

When you are given security equivalence to another user, you only receive the same rights that the other user was explicitly granted. You do not get equivalences to that user's other equivalences. Security equivalence doesn't travel. If Lila is equivalent to Erica, and Erica is equivalent to Jess, Lila doesn't end up being equivalent to Jess, too. Lila only receives whatever rights Erica received explicitly.

Effective File System Rights

Just as with NDS rights, determining which file system rights a user can actually exercise in a file or directory can be confusing at first. A user's *effective file system rights* are the file system rights that the user can ultimately execute in a given directory or file. The user's effective rights to a directory or file are determined in one of two ways:

- ► The user's inherited rights from a parent directory, minus any rights blocked by the subdirectory's (or file's) IRF.

- ► The sum of all rights granted to the user for that directory or file, through direct trustee assignment and security equivalences to other users.

A file's or directory's IRF does not affect direct trustee assignments and security equivalences. Therefore, if you have been given an explicit trustee assignment in a file or directory, any rights you might have inherited from a parent directory will be completely ignored. On the other hand, if you have not been given an explicit trustee assignment or security equivalence that specifically gives you rights in a file or directory, you will automatically inherit any rights you had in a parent directory, minus any rights blocked by the IRF.

Seeing and Changing a User's File System Rights

To see a user's file system rights, you can use either the NetWare Administrator utility (from Windows 95/98 or Windows NT) or the RIGHTS command-line utility from DOS.

To use the NetWare Administrator utility, you can either select a user and see the user's trustee assignments (a list of the files and directories of which that user is a trustee), or you can select a file or directory and see a list of all its trustees.

To see or change a user's trustee assignments, complete the following steps:

1. From the NetWare Administrator's Browser, select the user and choose Details from the Object menu.

2. Open the Rights to Files and Directories page.

3. To see the user's current file system rights, you must first select a volume that contains directories to which the user has rights. To do this, click the Show button. Then, in the Directory Context panel on the right side, navigate through the Directory tree to locate the desired volume. Select the volume from the Volumes panel on the left side, and then click OK.

4. Now, under the Files and Directories panel, a list appears showing all of the files and directories of which the user is *currently* a trustee, as shown in Figure 7.3. To see the user's assigned file system rights to one of these directories or files, select the directory or file, and then look at the list of rights below. An "X" in the checkbox next to each right means that the user has rights to this file or directory. To change the user's rights, click each desired checkbox to either mark it or clear it.

Rights to Files and Directories

5. To see the user's effective file system rights to this file or directory, click the Effective Rights button.

6. To assign the user file system rights to a *new* file or directory, click the Add button. In the Directory Context panel on the right side, navigate through the Directory tree to locate the desired volume or directory. Then, select the volume, directory, or file from the left panel, and click OK. Now the newly selected file, directory, or volume appears under the Files and Directories panel. Make sure the new file, directory, or volume is selected, and then assign the appropriate file system rights by marking each desired checkbox.

7. To see or change a user's security equivalence, open the user's Security Equal To page. There, you can add or delete other objects to which this user has a security equivalence. Remember that security equivalence affects both NDS and file system rights.

To use the NetWare Administrator utility to see all the trustees of a directory (or a file or volume), complete the following steps:

1. From the NetWare Administrator's Browser, select the directory and choose Details from the Object menu.

2. Open the Trustees of This Directory page. This page shows the containers and users that have trustee rights to this directory, as shown in Figure 7.4. This page also shows the directory's IRF. By default, the IRF allows any file system rights to be inherited from the parent directory.

FIGURE 7.4 *Trustees of This Directory*

3. To change the IRF to block a file system right from being inherited, click the checkbox next to that right to clear its box.

4. To see a particular trustee's effective file system rights to the directory, click the Effective Rights button, and then select the trustee. (You can either type in the trustee's name or click the Browse button next to the Trustee field to navigate the NDS tree and select the trustee that way.) That trustee's effective rights will appear in bold type.

5. To add a trustee to the directory, click the Add Trustee button. Navigate through the Directory tree in the right panel, and then select the user you want from the Objects panel on the left side. That user now appears in the Trustees list. Select that user, and then mark the checkboxes next to the file system rights you want the user to have.

To use the RIGHTS command-line utility to see a list of all the trustees with rights to a directory or file, use the following command format at the workstation's DOS prompt, replacing *path* with the path to the directory or file:

RIGHTS *path* /T

To use RIGHTS to see or change a user's current file system rights to a file or directory, use the following command:

RIGHTS *path rights* /option

For *path*, insert the path to the directory or file you want. To indicate the current directory, use a single period (.).

For *rights*, insert the list of rights you want to assign. (Use the rights' abbreviations, and separate each one with a space.) If you want to add some rights to the existing rights already assigned, you can use the plus (+) sign in front of the abbreviation. To delete a right, leaving the others intact, use a minus (-) sign. To replace all existing rights with those you specify, don't use either sign. If you want to assign all available rights, use the word ALL instead of specifying individual attributes. If you want to revoke all rights from the specified trustee, use the letter N (for No Rights) instead of specifying individual attributes. To completely remove the trustee from the file or directory, use the word REM (for Remove).

For *options*, insert the options you want. The available options are listed in Table 7.5.

TABLE 7.5	RIGHTS Options
RIGHTS OPTION	**DESCRIPTION**
/C	Scrolls continuously through the display.
/F	Displays the IRF.
/I	Displays where the inherited rights are coming from.
/NAME=name	Displays or changes the rights for the specified user or group. (If the user or group is in a different name context in the NDS tree than is the volume, you need to specify the user's complete NDS name.)
/S	Displays or changes all subdirectories below the current directory.
/T	Displays the trustee assignments for a directory.
/VER	Displays the version number of the RIGHTS utility.
/?	Displays help screens for the RIGHTS utility.

For example, if you want to see the list of trustees for the SYS:PUBLIC directory, which is mapped to search drive Z, you could use the following command:

```
RIGHTS Z: /T
```

at the workstation's DOS prompt.

To assign user Paul all available rights to the directory that is currently mapped to drive G (assuming Paul is in your own current name context), use the following command:

```
RIGHTS G: ALL /NAME=PAUL
```

To grant user Teresa (who is in a different name context than you) the Create, Erase, Modify, and File Scan rights to the REPORTS.2 file in the current directory, use the following command, specifying Teresa's full name:

```
RIGHTS G:REPORTS.2 CEMF /NAME=.TERESA.MKTG.OUTVIEW
```

For more examples of how to use RIGHTS, display the help screens for the utility with the following command:

```
RIGHTS /? ALL
```

File and Directory Attributes

Another important NetWare security tool for securing files and directories is attributes. *Attributes* are properties of files and directories that control what can happen to those files or directories. Attributes, which are also called *flags,* are different from trustee rights in several ways:

▶ Attributes are assigned directly to files and directories, whereas rights are assigned to users.

▶ Attributes override rights. In other words, if that directory has the Delete Inhibit attribute, you can't delete the directory even if you've been granted the Erase right.

▶ Likewise, attributes don't grant rights. Just because a file has the Read-Write attribute doesn't mean you can write to it if you don't have the Write right.

▶ Attributes affect all users, including the Admin user.

▶ Attributes affect some aspects of the file that rights do not, such as determining whether or not the files in a directory can be purged immediately upon deletion.

Types of File and Directory Attributes

There are eight attributes that apply to either files or directories. There are an additional eight that apply only to files. These attributes are listed in Table 7.6. The table also shows the abbreviations used for each attribute (when using the FLAG command), and whether the attribute applies to both directories and files or only to files. The FLAG command is discussed in the next section ("Assigning File and Directory Attributes").

TABLE 7.6   *File and Directory Attributes*

ATTRIBUTE	ABBREVIATION	FILE	DIRECTORY	DESCRIPTION
Delete Inhibit	Di	X	X	Prevents users from deleting the file or directory.
Hidden	H	X	X	Hides the file or directory so it isn't listed by the DOS DIR command or in the Windows File Manager, and can't be copied or deleted.
Purge (Also Purge Immediate)	P	X	X	Purges the file or directory immediately upon called deletion. Purged files can't be salvaged.
Rename Inhibit	Ri	X	X	Prevents users from renaming the file or directory.
System	Sy	X	X	Indicates a system directory that may contain system files (such as DOS files). Prevents users from seeing, copying, or deleting the directory. (However, does not assign the System attribute to the files in the directory.)
Don't Migrate	Dm	X	X	Prevents a file or directory from being migrated to another storage device.
Immediate Compress	Ic	X	X	Compresses the file or directory immediately.
Don't Compress	Dc	X	X	Prevents the file or directory from being compressed.
Archive Needed	A	X		Indicates that the file has been changed since the last time it was backed up.

ATTRIBUTE	ABBREVIATION	FILE	DIRECTORY	DESCRIPTION
Execute Only	X	X		Prevents an executable file from being copied, modified, or deleted. Use with caution! Once assigned, it cannot be removed, so assign it only if you have a backup copy of the file. You may prefer to assign the Read-Only attribute instead of the Executable Only attribute.
Read-Write	Rw	X		Allows the file to be opened and modified. Most files are set to Read-Write by default.
Read-Only	Ro	X		Allows the file to be opened and read, but not modified. All NetWare files in SYS:SYSTEM, SYS:PUBLIC, and SYS:LOGIN are Read-Only. Assigning the Read-Only attribute automatically assigns Delete Inhibit and Rename Inhibit.
Shareable	Sh	X		Allows the file to be used by more than one user simultaneously. Useful for utilities, commands, applications, and some database files. All NetWare files in SYS:SYSTEM, SYS:PUBLIC, and SYS:LOGIN are Shareable. Most data and work files should not be Shareable, so that users' changes do not conflict.
Transactional	T	X		When used on database files, allows NetWare's Transactional Tracking System (TTS) to protect the files from being corrupted if the transaction is interrupted.

(continued)

T A B L E 7.6 *File and Directory Attributes (continued)*

ATTRIBUTE	ABBREVIATION	FILE	DIRECTORY	DESCRIPTION
Copy Inhibit	Ci	X		Prevents Macintosh files from being copied. (Does not apply to DOS files.)
Don't Suballocate	Ds	X		Prevents a file from being suballocated. Use on files, such as some database files, that may need to be enlarged or appended to frequently. (See Chapter 8 for information on block suballocation.)

Assigning File and Directory Attributes

To assign attributes to a file or directory, you can use either the NetWare Administrator utility (which runs in Windows 95/98 or Windows NT) or the FLAG command-line utility from DOS.

To use NetWare Administrator, select the file or directory and choose Details from the Object menu. Then select the Attributes page. The marked check boxes show which attributes have been assigned to the file or directory. To change the attributes, click the checkboxes to mark or unmark them. Figure 7.5 shows the attributes for a directory.

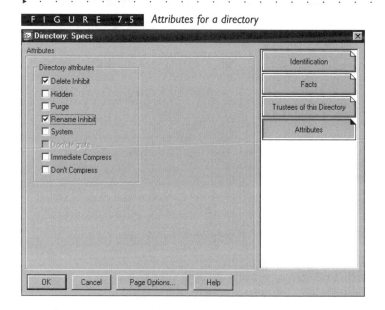

F I G U R E   7.5   *Attributes for a directory*

To use the FLAG utility, use the following command format at the workstation's DOS prompt:

FLAG *path attributes* /*options*

For *path*, indicate the path to the directory or file whose attributes you're changing.

For *attributes*, insert the list of attributes you want to assign. Use the attributes' abbreviations, and separate each one with a space. If you want to add an attribute to the existing attributes already assigned, you can use the plus (+) sign in front of the abbreviation. To delete an attribute from the file or directory, leaving the others intact, use a minus (-) sign. To replace all existing attributes with those you specify, don't use either sign. If you want to assign all available attributes, use the word ALL instead of specifying individual attributes. If you want to reset the attributes to the default settings, use the letter N (for Normal) instead of specifying individual attributes.

For *options*, insert the options you want. The available options are listed in Table 7.7.

TABLE 7.7 *FLAG Options*

FLAG OPTION	DESCRIPTION
/C	Scrolls continuously through the display.
/D	Displays details about the file or directory.
/DO	Displays or changes attributes for all subdirectories (no files) in the specified path.
/FO	Displays or changes attributes for all files (no subdirectories) in the specified path.
/M=*mode*	Changes the search mode for executable files. (Using FLAG to set search mode is explained in Appendix E.)
/NAME=*name*	Changes the owner of the file or directory.
/OWNER=*name*	Displays all files and directories owned by the specified user.
/S	Searches all subdirectories in the specified path.
/VER	Displays the version number of the FLAG utility.
/?	Displays help screens for the FLAG utility.

For example, to assign the Read-Only and Shareable attributes to the TEST.BAT file in the current directory, use the following command:

```
FLAG TEST.BAT RO SH
```

To add the Purge Immediate attribute to this same file, without removing the Read-Only and Shareable attributes, use the following command:

```
FLAG TEST.BAT +P
```

To reset the TEST.BAT file to its normal setting (the Read-Write attribute), use the following command:

```
FLAG TEST.BAT N
```

To see the attributes for the directory currently mapped to drive G, use the following command:

```
FLAG G: /DO
```

To see the help screens for FLAG (which contain more examples), use the following command:

```
FLAG /? ALL
```

Intruder Detection

NetWare can detect if a user is trying unsuccessfully to log in to the network. You can set the network so that users are locked out after a given number of failed login attempts. This helps ensure that users don't try to break into the network by simply guessing another user's password or by using programs that automatically generate passwords.

To set up intruder detection, you use the NetWare Administrator utility and assign intruder detection for a container. Then any user account within that container is subject to being locked if login attempts fail. To enable intruder detection, complete the following steps:

1. From the NetWare Administrator's Browser, select the container for which you want to set up intruder detection, and then choose Details from the Object menu.

2. Open the Intruder Detection page (shown in Figure 7.6).

3. To detect intruders, mark the Detect Intruders checkbox. Then, specify the intruder detection limits. The Incorrect Login Attempts and Intruder Attempt Reset Interval enable you to specify how many incorrect login attempts will be allowed in a given time. If you mark the Detect Intruders checkbox, the default values that appear allow seven incorrect attempts within a 30-minute interval. You may want to reduce the number of attempts to four or five, depending on how likely your network is to have such an intruder.

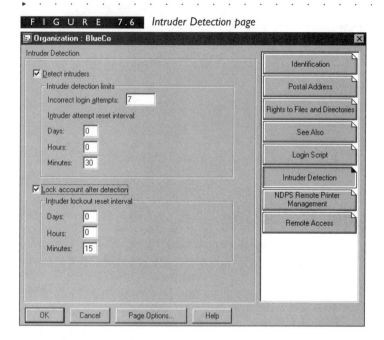

FIGURE 7.6 *Intruder Detection page*

4. If you want the user's account to be locked after an intruder is detected, mark the Lock Account After Detection checkbox. Then, specify how long you want the account to remain locked. The default locks the account for 15 minutes after the given number of failed login attempts. After 15 minutes, the account will be reopened automatically (intruder detection for that account will be reset). You may want to increase this time if you are concerned about intruders.

To see if a user's account has been locked, use the NetWare Administrator and select the user in question. Choose Details from the Object menu, and then open the user's Intruder Lockout page. This page shows whether the account is locked, as shown in Figure 7.7. If the Account Locked checkbox is marked, the account is locked. To unlock it, click the checkbox to clear it.

This page also shows the number of incorrect login attempts within the specified interval, when a user's account was locked, and the address of the workstation from which the failed login attempts were tried.

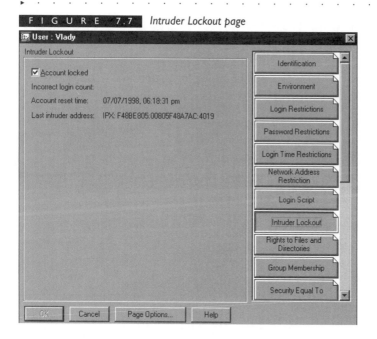

Intruder Lockout page

NCP Packet Signature

NCP Packet Signature is another feature designed to thwart intruders of a more persistent and knowledgeable type. NCP Packet Signature makes it impossible for someone to forge packets and access network resources through these forged packets. This feature requires workstations and servers to automatically "sign" each NCP packet with a signature and to change the signature for every packet.

NCP Packet Signature is an optional security feature. It can slow down network performance on busy networks, so you may prefer not to use packet signatures if your network is operating in a trusted environment with little threat of intruders stealing sensitive information.

There are four levels of NCP Packet Signature, which must be set on both workstations and servers. If the levels on the workstation and server don't form an allowable combination, the two computers will not be able to communicate with each other.

To set the signature level on a server, use MONITOR.NLM and select Server Parameters, and then choose the NCP category. If you prefer, you can type the following SET command at the server's console prompt:

SET NCP PACKET SIGNATURE OPTION=*number*

Replace *number* with the signature level (0 through 3) you want the server to use. After the server has been booted, you can execute the SET command to increase the signature level. If you want to decrease the level, however, you have to reboot the server. Table 7.8 shows the NCP Packet Signature levels for servers.

T A B L E 7.8   *Server Levels for NCP Packet Signature*

LEVEL	DESCRIPTION
0	Server does not sign packets.
I	Server signs packets only if workstation requests signature.
2	Server prefers to sign packets, but will allow access from workstations that cannot sign.
3	Server and workstation must both sign packets.

To set the signature level on DOS or Windows 3.1 workstations, add the following command to the NET.CFG file:

SIGNATURE LEVEL=*number*

Replace *number* with the signature level (0 through 3) you want the workstation to use. Table 7.9 shows the NCP Packet Signature levels for workstations.

For Windows 95/98 or Windows NT workstations running the NetWare Client software, right-click the Network Neighborhood and choose Properties. Then select the Novell NetWare Client, choose Properties, and open the Advanced Settings tab. There you can select Signature Level and specify the level you want to use.

T A B L E 7.9   *Workstation Levels for NCP Packet Signature*

LEVEL	DESCRIPTION
0	Workstation does not sign packets.
I	Workstation signs packets only if server requests signature.
2	Workstation prefers to sign packets, but will access a server that cannot sign.
3	Workstation and server must both sign packets.

Figure 7.8 shows how the signature levels on servers and workstations combine to either allow unsigned packets, force signed packets, or deny login.

NCP Packet Signature levels combine to allow or deny login

Workstation Level

		0	1	2	3
	0	Unsigned	Unsigned	Unsigned	Login Denied
Server Level	1	Unsigned	Unsigned	Signed	Signed
	2	Unsigned	Signed	Signed	Signed
	3	Login Denied	Signed	Signed	Signed

Server Protection

An important aspect of network security is to make sure the server itself is secure from tampering. This is a simple task but is often overlooked, leaving the network vulnerable to either deliberate or accidental damage.

If the server is sitting in an area that is easily accessible and isn't protected with a keyboard lock or password, a malicious user can easily access the server and wreak havoc. Less dramatic, but potentially just as damaging, is the accidental tampering that could occur. A janitorial employee could unplug the server to plug in the vacuum cleaner; a helpful employee could try to load a virus-infected file directly on the server; another employee could try to "fix" a printing problem while you're not around and end up with a worse problem than the original one.

The following are some of the simple ways you can secure your server:

▶ Lock the server in a separate room. Just putting the server in a locked room can prevent much of the potential tampering that could occur.

▶ Lock the server's console with SCRSAVER.NLM, which loads a screen saver on the server. To do this, type **SCRSAVER** at the server's console. By default, this module will lock the server's console when the screen saver activates. To unlock the console while the screen saver is displayed, press any key, and then enter a user name and password. The user name must have valid access rights to the server, such as Admin. The default time for the screen saver to activate is 10 minutes of inactivity. You can change this time delay, and you can specify whether or not the screen saver locks the console. For more information, see the SCRSAVER.NLM section in Appendix E.

▶ Prevent loadable modules from being loaded from anywhere but the specified search paths (by default, SYS:SYSTEM only) by using the SECURE CONSOLE command at the server's console. Then make sure that only authorized users have rights to SYS:SYSTEM. Without SECURE CONSOLE enabled, an intruder could create an NLM that breaches security and load that NLM from the server's diskette drive or another directory where he or she has more rights than in SYS:SYSTEM. SECURE CONSOLE also prevents anyone from accessing the operating system's debugger and from changing the server's date and time. To remove SECURE CONSOLE, you must down the server and reboot it. (To set a server's search paths, use the SEARCH console command. See Appendix E for more information about SEARCH.)

▶ Use a secure password for the Remote Console feature. When you load REMOTE.NLM, you're asked to enter a password (it can be any password you make up at this time). To use Remote Console, then, you have to enter that same password. Make sure the REMOTE.NLM password is secure, and change the password periodically by reloading REMOTE.NLM.

▶ Protect the server from electrical problems by installing an *uninterruptible power supply* (UPS). Because the UPS enables the server to close all its files safely before shutting itself down in the event of a power problem, the UPS can prevent excessive damage to the server's files.

▶ Use disk mirroring or disk duplexing to protect the network data in case one disk fails.

▶ Keep a regular, up-to-date series of backups, so that all server and network files are archived and can be readily restored, and practice restoring files to make sure that the backups are accurate. See Chapter 8 for more information about performing backups and restores.

▸ Maintain updated virus protection software, and regularly scan for viruses.

Following these practices can help protect your server and, therefore, your entire network.

Additional NetWare 5 Security Features

There are two additional NetWare 5 security features you may want to take advantage of, depending on your situation:

▸ Novell Public Key Infrastructure (PKI) Services, which enables your network to use public key cryptography and public key certificates in an NDS network. This service can be integrated into NDS, and can be used with various security applications.

▸ Auditing, which enables independent auditors to audit network events. Auditing is two-way security: independent auditors can access event information without compromising network security, and network administrators can't access auditing information, thus preventing audited data from being compromised.

For more information about either of these security features, see the Novell online documentation.

CHAPTER 8

File Management

Instant *Access*

Managing Disk Space

- To manage file compression, use MONITOR.NLM to set file compression SET parameters.
- To limit users' disk space, use the NetWare Administrator utility (which runs in Windows 95/98 or Windows NT).

Managing Files

- To purge or salvage files that have been deleted, use the NetWare Administrator utility or PURGE (a command-line utility).
- To display information about files and directories, use the NetWare Administrator utility.

Creating a Fake Root

- To create a fake root for an application that needs to be installed at the root of the volume, use MAP (a command-line utility).

Backing Up and Restoring Files

- To back up and restore network files, use Enhanced SBACKUP, which can run from either a server (SBCON.NLM) or a workstation (NWBACK32.EXE). You can also use a third-party backup product.

Managing Volumes

- To create, delete, or enlarge a traditional NetWare volume, use NWCONFIG.NLM.
- To create, delete, or enlarge an NSS volume, use either NWCONFIG.NLM or the NSS administration console utility.
- To mount either a traditional or an NSS volume, use either NWCONFIG.NLM or MOUNT (a console utility).
- To dismount either a traditional or an NSS volume, use either NWCONFIG.NLM or DISMOUNT (a console utility).
- To mount a server's DOS partition as an NSS volume, load NSS support with the DOSFAT module.
- To repair a corrupted traditional NetWare volume, use VREPAIR.NLM.

- To repair a corrupted NSS volume, use REBUILD (which can be run from the NSS administration console utility).

- To add name space support to a volume, load the name space module on the server, and then use the ADD NAME SPACE *module* TO *volume* command at the server console.

Protecting Database Transactions

- To manage the NetWare Transaction Tracking System (TTS), use MONITOR.NLM to change the appropriate SET parameters.

- To flag a file with the Transactional file attribute, use the NetWare Administrator utility or FLAG.

- To reenable TTS after it's been disabled, use the ENABLE TTS console utility.

▶ • ◀

Understanding the NetWare File System

NetWare enables you to manage files in many different ways. How you manage your files can contribute significantly to how well users can find files, how well your disk space is conserved, and how easy it is to restore the network files when something goes wrong with them.

When you first set up your server, you need to take into account how your file system will be structured. Several factors can affect how you organize your network files and applications. Careful planning can make it easier to back up and restore needed files, and can also make it easier to assign trustee rights to large numbers of users.

The first step toward planning and managing an effective file system is to understand how NetWare uses volumes.

NetWare Volumes

A volume is the highest level in the file system hierarchy, and it contains directories and files. Each NetWare server has at least one volume, SYS, which contains all of the NetWare files and utilities. You can have additional volumes on a server if you want. Volumes help you organize files on the server.

With NetWare 5, you can choose to create two different types of volumes: a traditional volume or a Novell Storage Services (NSS) volume. NSS is a new feature in NetWare 5. NSS volumes use a new type of NetWare file system that allows NSS volumes to mount much faster than traditional volumes. However, NSS volumes currently don't support some of the features that traditional NetWare volumes support.

The SYS volume, which is required on all NetWare servers, must be created as a traditional volume. Any other volumes on the server can be created as either type of volume, depending on your needs. You can even have both types of volumes on the same server. If you plan to have very large volumes that you want to mount quickly, NSS may be the right choice. If you need to use some of the traditional volume features of NetWare, however, you may want to use the traditional volume format instead.

The following sections explain the differences between traditional NetWare volumes and NSS volumes.

Traditional NetWare Volumes

If you have used previous versions of NetWare, you're familiar with traditional NetWare volumes. In NetWare 5, traditional volumes function exactly as they do in previous versions. Traditional volumes can support space-saving features such as block suballocation and file compression, as well as data preservation features such as TTS (Novell's Transactional Tracking System) and disk mirroring. (These features are explained later in this chapter.)

A NetWare server can support up to 64 traditional volumes. In NetWare 5, volume SYS is always a traditional volume, because it requires some of the traditional volume features.

When a traditional volume is created on a disk, a "segment" is also created on the disk to hold the volume. If you create two volumes on the disk, the disk will have two segments (also called volume segments). If you later decide to merge the two volumes into one, you will discover that the new single volume contains two segments. If you create a volume that spans multiple hard disks, the portion of the volume on each disk will be contained in a different segment.

Each volume can have up to 32 volume segments, which can all be stored on the same hard disk or scattered across separate disks. Letting volume segments reside on different disks enables you to increase the size of a volume by adding a new hard disk. In addition, by putting segments of the same volume on more than one hard disk, different parts of the volume can be accessed simultaneously, which increases disk input and output. However, the more segments a volume has, the slower the performance may be, so use this option carefully.

If you spread volume segments across disks, it is important to mirror the disks so a single disk's failure won't shut down the entire volume. (For more information about disk mirroring, see Chapter 3.)

One hard disk can hold up to eight volume segments that belong to one or more volumes. However, a single segment cannot span multiple disks.

When you create a traditional volume using the installation program or NWCONFIG.NLM, a Volume object is automatically created in the NDS tree at the same time. The Volume object is placed in the same context as the server. By default, the Volume object is named with the server's name as a prefix. For example, if the server's name is Sales, the Volume object for volume SYS is named Sales_SYS.

NSS Volumes

NSS (Novell Storage System) is a new file system in NetWare 5 that is ideally suited for networks that require extremely large volumes, extremely large files, or huge numbers of files. NSS volumes can handle up to 8 trillion files, or a single file up to 8 terabytes in size.

In addition, NSS supports up to 255 volumes per server rather than the limit of 64 volumes supported by the traditional NetWare file system. NSS also allows up to 1 million files to be open simultaneously.

Aside from the large capacity provided by NSS volumes, another beneficial feature is the quick mounting and access times provided by NSS volumes. Volumes of any size, including 8-terabyte volumes, can mount in less than one minute. NSS volumes are also frugal with memory — an NSS volume requires only 1MB of RAM to mount.

NSS also enables you to mount both CD-ROMs and the server's own DOS partition as NSS volumes.

The version of NSS that is included in NetWare 5 has some limitations, however. Some of the features available in traditional NetWare volumes are not available in NSS volumes at this time. However, many of them are slated to be delivered in future releases of NSS and NetWare. Currently, NSS volumes do not support the following features:

- ► File compression
- ► Block suballocation
- ► Data migration
- ► Novell Transaction Tracking System (TTS)
- ► NFS (Network File System, used in UNIX)
- ► FTP (file transfer protocol)
- ► Disk mirroring and duplexing
- ► Auditing
- ► File name locks
- ► Disk striping (although NSS does support disk spanning)

How NSS Uses Free Space

Like traditional NetWare volumes, NSS uses partitions, volumes, directories, and files to make up its file structure. However, instead of "segments," NSS uses *storage groups* of free space to make up its volumes.

When creating an NSS volume, you can use either unpartitioned free space or free space that is available within a traditional NetWare volume. It's best not to mix the two types of free space together into a single NSS volume, however. If you create an NSS volume out of free space within a traditional NetWare volume, the NSS volume will look like a file within the NetWare volume. Then the two volumes will be joined together for most activities; for example, you must mount both volumes simultaneously, and if you delete the traditional NetWare volume, you automatically delete the NSS volume, too. For this reason, you may find it easiest to create NSS volumes only out of unpartitioned free space.

Let's look at how NSS turns free space into a volume. Figure 8.1 illustrates the following process:

1. First, an NSS feature called a *storage provider* identifies any free space on the hard disk. This free space is sometimes referred to as a *storage deposit*.

2. Next, NSS claims ownership of the free space. This section of claimed free space is now called a *managed object*.

3. Now, a *storage group* can be created out of one or more of the managed objects. (Storage groups can also be merged into a single storage group.)

4. Finally, from a storage group, one or more volumes can be created. (A new storage group, such as one created when a new hard disk is installed, can also be added to an existing volume to increase that volume's size.)

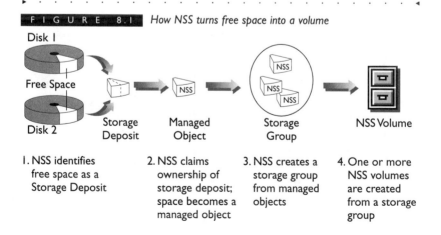

FIGURE 8.1 *How NSS turns free space into a volume*

Disk 1				
Free Space	Storage Deposit	Managed Object	Storage Group	NSS Volume
Disk 2				

1. NSS identifies free space as a Storage Deposit

2. NSS claims ownership of storage deposit; space becomes a managed object

3. NSS creates a storage group from managed objects

4. One or more NSS volumes are created from a storage group

When Can You Create NSS Volumes?

When you install the NetWare 5 server, you are asked to set up the volumes you want. At that time, you set up SYS as a traditional NetWare volume. If you want, you also can create additional volumes at that point. You can choose to create either traditional volumes or an NSS volume, or both. If you created an NSS volume at that time, the installation program took all the free, unpartitioned space it found and created a single NSS volume for you.

If you want to create new NSS volumes after installation, or if you want to modify one you may have created during installation, you can do that at any time using either NWCONFIG.NLM or the NSS administration console utility. You can create an NSS volume out of free space on an existing volume, or you can add a new hard disk and create the NSS volume from the new disk's free space.

NOTE IBM-compatible hard disks only support four partitions per hard disk. Therefore, whether you can create a new NSS volume on a disk may depend on how many volumes you've already created on that disk.

Loading NSS Support

To use NSS volumes, you need to load NSS support on the server. To load NSS support, simply type **NSS** at the server console. (You can also add the NSS command to the AUTOEXEC.NCF file to ensure that NSS support is loaded each time the server is rebooted.) Loading NSS will load the necessary NLMs. In addition, it will make available the NSS administration console utility, which you can use to create and manage NSS volumes.

To see all the commands that are available after you've loaded NSS support, type the following command at the server console:

```
NSS HELP
```

To bring up the main NSS administration utility, type:

```
NSS MENU
```

Loading NWCONFIG.NLM will automatically load NSS support, too.

You can use either the NWCONFIG.NLM utility or the NSS administration console utility to create and modify NSS volumes at any time after the server installation. Both utilities accomplish the same tasks. (However, the NSS administration utility also provides two additional utilities that let you rebuild and verify NSS volumes that have become corrupted.)

Planning the File System

Now that you understand both traditional NetWare volumes and NSS volumes, you can plan your entire file system. This section offers tips for planning your file structure. Instructions for creating and managing both traditional and NSS volumes appear later in this chapter.

The following list includes some tips that may help you plan an accessible, easy-to-manage file system:

▸ You may want to reserve volume SYS for NetWare files and utilities. Try to avoid putting other types of files in SYS, such as applications or users' daily work files.

▸ Decide if you want to create only traditional NetWare volumes, or if you want to use NSS volumes, too.

▸ You may want to plan a separate volume for storing Macintosh files. To store Macintosh files on a volume, you have to load the Macintosh name space module (called MAC.NAM) on the server, and then add the name space to that particular volume. The name space allows the Macintosh file's resource fork, long filename, and other characteristics to be preserved. Likewise, if you plan to store UNIX files on the server, you may want to create a separate volume and load the NFS.NAM module on it, to support those files. By default, the NetWare server is loaded with the LONG.NAM name space module, which supports the OS/2, Windows 95/98, and Windows NT formats. For more information about Macintosh and other name spaces, see the "Adding a Name Space to a Volume" section later in this chapter.

▸ To simplify backups, create a separate volume for applications and other non-NetWare utilities. That way, you only need to back up the volume containing applications occasionally, while you back up the volume with the users' daily work files more frequently. If an application and users' work files need to be stored in the same volume, this strategy won't work, of course. In this case, try to store the applications and the users' work files in separate branches of subdirectories in the same volume. For more information about backing up files, see the "Backing Up and Restoring Files" section later in this chapter.

▶ If different applications will be available to different groups of users, try to organize the applications' directory structures so you can assign comprehensive rights in a parent directory. This may help prevent you from having to create multiple individual rights assignments at lower-level subdirectories. For more information about file system rights, see Chapter 7.

▶ If you want to use file compression to compress less frequently used files, try to group those types of files into directories separate from other files that are used more often. That way, you can turn on compression for the less-used directories and leave it turned off for the frequently used directories. For more information about file compression, see the "File Compression" section later in this chapter.

▶ Decide whether you want users' daily work files to reside in personal directories, in project-specific directories, or in some other type of directory structure. Allow for ample network directory space for users to store their daily work files. Encourage your users to store their files on the network so those files can be backed up regularly by the network backup process, and so the files can be protected by NetWare security.

▶ Decide if you want users to have their own individual home directories. You can have home directories created automatically when you create a new user, as explained in Chapter 6.

These tips can help you effectively plan your file system. In addition, you should take into consideration the directories that NetWare creates automatically during installation, as well as planning for directories that will contain applications. These issues are described in the following sections.

Directories That Are Created Automatically

When you first install NetWare 5 on the server, some directories are created automatically in the SYS volume. These directories contain the files needed to run and manage NetWare 5. You can create additional directories and subdirectories in volume SYS, or if you created additional volumes during installation, you can create directories for your users in the other volumes.

The following directories are created automatically on volume SYS:

▶ LOGIN contains a few files and utilities that will let users change their name context (location) in the NDS tree and log in to the network.

- ► SYSTEM contains NLMs and utilities that the network administrator can use to configure, manage, monitor, and add services on the NetWare server.

- ► PUBLIC and its subdirectories contain all of the NetWare utilities and related files that users and administrators may need to access. It also contains .PDF files (printer definition files) if you choose to install them on the server. You can add utilities or other software to this directory if you want users to have access to them. For example, you could create client subdirectories under PUBLIC. These client subdirectories could contain the files required for installing NetWare client software on workstations.

- ► MAIL is empty when it is first created. It may be used by e-mail programs that are compatible with NetWare. In NetWare 3.1x and NetWare 2.x, the MAIL directory contained subdirectories for each individual user. Each of these subdirectories, named with the user's object ID number, contained the user's login script file. If you upgrade a NetWare 3.1x or 2.x server to NetWare 5, those existing users will retain their MAIL subdirectories in NetWare 5, but the login scripts will become properties of their User objects instead.

- ► DELETED.SAV is used to store files that have been deleted, but have not been purged from the server. DELETED.SAV only stores deleted files whose directories have also been deleted; if the original directory still exists, the deleted file remains in that directory.

- ► ETC contains files used for managing protocols and routers.

Because these directories contain the files required for running and managing your NetWare network, do not rename or delete any of them without making absolutely sure they're unnecessary in your particular network's situation.

Application Directories

When planning your file system, decide where you want to put the directories that will contain applications and program files. It may be easier to assign file system trustee rights if you group all multiuser applications on the network under a single volume or parent directory. By installing, for example, your word-processing, spreadsheet, and other programs into their own subdirectories under a parent directory named APPS, you can assign all of your users the minimum necessary rights to APPS, and then the users will inherit those rights in each individual application's subdirectory. For more information about file system rights, see Chapter 7.

If you install applications into subdirectories under a common parent directory, you can then usually designate that users' daily work files be stored in their own home directories elsewhere on the network.

When planning network subdirectories for your applications, follow any special instructions from the manufacturer for installing the application on a network. Some applications can be run either from a local hard disk on the workstation or from a network directory. Be sure to follow the instructions supplied by the manufacturer.

In some cases, the instructions may indicate that the application has to be installed at the root of a volume. If your application requires this, you can still install it in a subdirectory under the APPS directory if you want, and then map a "fake root" to the application's subdirectory. A fake root mapping makes a subdirectory appear to be a volume, so that the application runs correctly.

For example, suppose you want to install an application called ABC into a subdirectory under a directory called APPS on the volume called VOL1, but the application's instructions say that ABC must be installed at the root of the volume. Create a subdirectory called ABC under VOL1:APPS, and install the application into ABC. Then, you can map a fake root to the ABC subdirectory and assign it to be a search drive at the same time by using the command

```
MAP ROOT S16:=VOL1:APPS\ABC
```

You can type this command at the workstation's DOS prompt if you only need the mapping to be in effect until the user logs out. If you want it to be in effect each time the user logs in, put the command in a login script. For more information about login scripts, see Chapter 6.

When you install an application, you may want to flag the application's executable files (usually files with the extension .COM or .EXE) with the Shareable and Read Only file attributes. This will allow users to simultaneously use the applications, but will prevent users from deleting or modifying them. (This is more typically controlled by assigning restrictive trustee rights to users in those applications' directories, however.) You can use either the NetWare Administrator utility or the FLAG utility to assign file attributes. File and directory attributes are covered at length in Chapter 7.

Working with Traditional NetWare Volumes

When you install the server, you will create at least one traditional volume that will be used to store network files. You can, however, create and modify traditional NetWare volumes after installation, if you choose. The following sections explain how to work with traditional volumes. Instructions for working with NSS volumes appear later in this chapter.

Creating and Mounting Traditional Volumes

To create new traditional NetWare volumes after the initial server installation, use NWCONFIG.NLM. You can create a new volume out of any free space on the disk. The free space may be space that was never assigned to a volume before, or it may be free space on a new hard disk that's just been added.

After you've created a volume, you must mount it before network users can access it.

To create a volume, complete the following steps:

1. If you're installing a new hard disk, install the hard disk according to the manufacturer's instructions.

2. Load NWCONFIG.NLM, select Standard Disk Options, and then choose Modify Disk Partitions and Hot Fix. This option enables you to create a new NetWare partition for the disk, which will become the new volume.

3. Choose Create NetWare Disk Partition to display information about the free space currently available.

4. Enter the size you want the partition to be (in megabytes) and accept the default values for the Hot Fix data and redirection area sizes. Then Press F10 and answer Yes to save your changes. Press Esc to return to the Disk Options menu.

5. Choose NetWare Volume Options.

6. Press the Insert key to see a list of existing volume segments and free disk space. The disk space you just configured as a NetWare partition should now appear listed as Free Space.

7. From the list, select the existing free space and press Enter.

8. Choose Make This Segment a New Volume.

9. Enter a name for the new volume (up to 15 characters long), and then press Enter. The name can be made up of letters or numbers.

10. If you don't want the new volume to use all the available disk space, type in a new volume size in megabytes.

11. Press F10 several times as needed to save the new volume information.

12. Enter the administrator user's full name and password so you can authenticate to the NDS tree.

13. To mount the volume, choose Mount All Volumes.

To mount a volume later, you can load NWCONFIG, choose Standard Disk Options, and then choose NetWare Volume Options. Then select the volume and press Enter. Highlight the Status field, and press Enter. Then you can select to Mount or Dismount the volume.

You can also mount a volume by using the MOUNT console command. For example, to mount the volume named VOL1, use the following command:

```
MOUNT VOL1
```

To mount all volumes on the server, use the following command:

```
MOUNT ALL
```

Dismounting and Deleting Traditional Volumes

Deleting a volume deletes all the files and directories on that volume as well, so be sure you only delete a volume if you don't need the files anymore, or if you have a reliable backup.

Before you delete a volume, you must dismount it so that its files are unavailable to users. You can dismount the volume you want to delete by typing the following console command at the server's console (substitute the volume's name for *name*):

```
DISMOUNT name
```

You can also dismount a volume from within NWCONFIG.NLM, as explained in the following procedure.

To dismount and then delete a volume, complete these steps:

1. Back up all files on the volume or move them to a different volume, if you want to keep them.

2. Load NWCONFIG.NLM and choose Standard Disk Options, and then choose NetWare Volume Options.

3. Select the volume you want to delete. (Do not delete volume SYS.)

4. To dismount the volume, press Enter, and then at the Status field press Enter and choose Dismount. Then press F10 to return to the NetWare Volume Options screen.

5. Select the volume again and press the Delete key, and then press Enter at the warning message.

6. When asked if you want to delete the volume, answer Yes.

Increasing the Size of a Traditional Volume

To increase the size of a volume, you can add a volume segment to an existing volume. First, you will configure the free space as a NetWare partition, and then you will add that segment to an existing volume. To do this, complete the following steps:

1. Load NWCONFIG and select Standard Disk Options, and then choose Modify Disk Partitions and Hot Fix.

2. Choose Create NetWare Disk Partition to display information about the free space currently available.

3. Enter the size you want the partition to be (in megabytes) and accept the default values for the Hot Fix data and redirection area sizes. Then Press F10 and answer Yes to save your changes. Press Esc to return to the Disk Options menu.

4. Choose NetWare Volume Options.

5. Press the Insert key to see a list of existing volume segments and free disk space. The disk space you just configured as a NetWare partition should now appear listed as Free Space.

6. From the list, select the existing free space and press Enter.

7. Choose Make This Segment Part of Another Volume.

8. Choose the volume to which you want to add this segment and then press Enter.

9. If you don't want the volume to use all the available disk space you just added to it, select the new partition and modify the size of the segment. Any leftover space will be listed as free space in the volume list.

10. Press F10 several times as needed to save the new volume information.

I I. Enter the administrator user's full name and password so you can authenticate to the NDS tree.

12. To mount the volume, choose Mount All Volumes.

Repairing a Corrupted Traditional Volume with VREPAIR

Occasionally, a server's hard disk problems may cause minor problems with one or more of the server's volumes. If a volume won't mount, the primary File Allocation Table (FAT) or Directory Entry Table (DET) may be corrupted. VREPAIR.NLM can usually repair these types of volume problems.

NetWare keeps two copies of the FAT and DET. VREPAIR compares the two tables for inconsistencies. If it finds an inconsistency, it uses the most correct table entry to update the incorrect one. Then VREPAIR writes the corrected entry to both the primary and the secondary tables.

VREPAIR can also be used in the following circumstances:

► When a power failure corrupts the volume

► When a hardware problem causes a disk read error

► When bad blocks on the volume cause read or write errors, "data mirror" mismatch errors, multiple allocation errors, or fatal DIR errors

► When you want to remove a name space from a volume

If a volume doesn't mount when you boot the server, VREPAIR will run automatically and try to repair the volume. If the volume fails while the server is running, you can run VREPAIR manually. (A volume must be dismounted before you can run VREPAIR on it.)

Most volume problems that VREPAIR can fix are hardware related. Therefore, if you repeatedly have to repair the same volume, you should consider replacing the hard disk.

To use VREPAIR.NLM manually, load it at the server's console. VRE-PAIR.NLM is located on the server's DOS partition. If you are repairing a volume that has a non-DOS name space loaded (or if you're removing a name space from the volume), VREPAIR needs to load another NLM for that name space support. The VREPAIR name space modules are named V_*namespace*.NLM.

For example, for the MAC name space, VREPAIR looks for a module named V_MAC.NLM. If this module is located in the server's DOS partition (where it is installed by default), VREPAIR automatically loads it. If this module is in a different location, you'll have to load it manually before running VREPAIR.

Again, in many cases VREPAIR will run automatically. If you want to run VREPAIR manually, however, you should complete the following steps:

1. Make sure the volume you want to repair is dismounted.

2. At the server's console, load VREPAIR.

3. Choose 1 (Repair a Volume) to begin trying to fix the volume. If more than one volume is currently dismounted, you'll have to choose the volume you want to repair.

4. If you want to change how VREPAIR is displaying errors as it finds them, press F1. Then select option 1 if you don't want VREPAIR to pause after each error. Select 2 if you want the errors logged in a text file. Select 3 to stop the repair. Select 4 to resume the repair.

5. When the repair is finished, choose Yes when asked if you want to write repairs to the disk.

6. If VREPAIR found errors, run it again. Continue running VREPAIR repeatedly until it finds no more errors.

7. When VREPAIR finds no more errors, remount the volume.

8. If the volume still won't mount, delete the volume, re-create it, and then restore all of its files from backups.

VREPAIR may have to delete some files during the repair operation. If it does, it stores those deleted files in new files named VR*nnnnnn*.FIL (where *n* is any number). These files are stored in the directories in which the original files were stored when they were found during VREPAIR's operation.

Files may be deleted if VREPAIR finds problems such as a file with a name that is invalid in DOS, or two files with the same filename.

Working with NSS Volumes

You may have created an NSS volume when you first installed the server. In addition, you can create and modify NSS volumes after installation, if you choose. The following sections explain how to work with NSS volumes. Instructions for working with traditional NetWare volumes appear earlier in this chapter.

Creating and Mounting NSS Volumes

To create new NSS volumes after the initial server installation, you can use either NWCONFIG.NLM or the NSS administration console utility. You can create a new volume out of any free space on the disk. The free space may be space that was never assigned to a volume before, or it may be free space on a new hard disk that's just been added.

If you want to take all unpartitioned free space on all available hard disks in the server, and then assign it all into one single NSS volume, the easiest way is to use the NSS utility's One-Step Configuration feature. If you want to make multiple NSS volumes or want more flexibility in specifying the size of the volume, you can use either the NSS utility's Advanced Configuration feature or NWCONFIG.NLM. Both utilities go through identical steps. The following sections explain each procedure.

Using the NSS Utility's One-Step Configuration

In this procedure, NSS will gather all available, unpartitioned free space from all storage devices on the server, and assign it all into a single NSS volume. After you've created the volume, you must mount it before network users can access it. Because NSS volumes created in the NSS administration utility don't automatically appear in the NDS tree, you may also want to manually create a Volume object for the new volumes and add it to the NDS tree.

To create the NSS volume, complete the following steps:

1. If you're installing a new hard disk, install the hard disk according to the manufacturer's instructions.

2. If NSS isn't already loaded, load NSS on the server by typing:

   NSS

3. Launch the NSS administration utility on the server by typing:

   NSS Menu

4. Choose Configure.

5. Choose Create.

6. Choose One-Step Configuration.

7. Enter a name for the new volume, or accept the default (NSSVOL).

8. When asked to confirm that you want to create the volume, answer Yes.

9. Press Esc to exit the NSS utility.

10. Now you've created the volume, but users can't access it until you mount it. Mount the new volume by typing the following command at the server's console (if you used a different volume name, substitute that name for NSSVOL):

    MOUNT NSSVOL

11. (Optional) If you want a Volume object for this new volume to appear in the NDS tree, complete the following steps:

   a. Load NWCONFIG.NLM on the server by typing:

     NWCONFIG

   b. Choose Directory Options, and then choose Upgrade Mounted Volumes Into the Directory.

   c. Enter your user name and password.

   d. Choose the NSS volume from the list of volumes that appears, and confirm that you want to add the volume to the Directory.

   e. When you are finished, press Esc to exit NWCONFIG.NLM.

Now the new NSS volume is mounted and ready to be accessed by users. It also appears in the NDS tree as a Volume object.

Using the NSS Utility's Advanced Configuration

In this procedure, NSS will identify available free space from all storage devices on the server. Then you will assign NSS ownership to the free space, turning it into a managed object. Next, you will assign the managed object to an NSS storage group. Finally, you will turn the storage group into a volume.

After you've created the volume, you must mount it before network users can access it. Because NSS volumes created in the NSS administration utility don't automatically appear in the NDS tree, you also may want to manually create a Volume object for the new volumes and add it to the NDS tree.

To create the NSS volume, complete the following steps:

1. If you're installing a new hard disk, install the hard disk according to the manufacturer's instructions.

2. If NSS isn't already loaded, load NSS on the server by typing:

   NSS

3. Launch the NSS administration utility on the server by typing:

   NSS Menu

4. Choose Configure.

5. Choose Create.

6. Choose Advanced Configuration.

7. Choose Update Provider Information, and then choose NSS Media Manager Provider. (The NSS provider is the program that finds and manages free space. This step ensures that NSS knows about any free space available.) Press any key to return to the Options menu.

8. Choose Assign Ownership, and select the space you want to use. (The unpartitioned space you want to choose will be labeled "Fixed.") This space will become a "managed object." Enter the size you want the new managed object to be, and answer Yes to confirm your choice.

9. Choose Create a New Storage Group, and then select a managed object (this is the space you selected in Step 8). Answer Yes to confirm your choice.

10. Choose Create a New NSS Volume, and then select a managed object (this is the storage group you just created in Step 9). Then enter the size you want the new NSS volume to use and a name for the new volume. The default name is NSSVOL, but you can choose another name if you want. Answer Yes to confirm your choices. At the summary screen, press any key to return to the Options menu.

11. Press Esc multiple times to exit the NSS utility.

12. Now you've created the volume, but users can't access it until you mount it. Mount the new volume by typing the following command at the server's console (if you used a different volume name, substitute that name for NSSVOL):

```
MOUNT NSSVOL
```

13. (Optional) If you want a Volume object for this new volume to appear in the NDS tree, complete the following steps:

    a. Load NWCONFIG.NLM on the server by typing:

    ```
    NWCONFIG
    ```

    b. Choose Directory Options, and then choose Upgrade Mounted Volumes Into the Directory.

    c. Enter your user name and password.

    d. Choose the NSS volume from the list of volumes that appears, and confirm that you want to add the volume to the Directory.

    e. When you are finished, press Esc multiple times to exit NWCONFIG.NLM.

Now the new NSS volume is mounted and ready to be accessed by users. It also appears in the NDS tree as a Volume object.

Using NWCONFIG.NLM

In this procedure, NSS will identify available free space from all storage devices on the server. Then you will assign NSS ownership to the free space, turning it into a managed object. Next, you will assign the managed object to an NSS storage group. Finally, you will turn the storage group into a volume.

After you've created the volume, you must mount it before network users can access it. Unlike the NSS utility, NWCONFIG automatically creates a Volume object for new NSS volumes, so you don't need to add the volume to the NDS tree manually.

To create the NSS volume, complete the following steps:

1. If you're installing a new hard disk, install the hard disk according to the manufacturer's instructions.

2. Load NWCONFIG.NLM on the server by typing:

   NWCONFIG

3. From the main menu, choose NSS Disk Options.

4. Choose Storage.

5. Choose Update Provider Information, and then choose NSS Media Manager Provider. (The NSS provider is the program that finds and manages free space. This step ensures that NSS knows about any free space available.) Press any key to return to the Available NSS Storage Options menu.

6. Choose Assign Ownership, and then select the space you want to use. (The unpartitioned space you want to choose will be labeled "Fixed.") This space will become a "managed object." Enter the size you want the new managed object to be, and answer Yes to confirm your choice. At the summary screen, press any key to return to the Available NSS Storage Options menu.

7. Press Esc to return to the Available NSS Options menu.

8. Choose NSS Volume Options.

9. Enter the administrator user's full name and password.

10. Choose Create.

11. Choose Storage Group, and then select a managed object (this is the space you selected in Step 6). Answer Yes to confirm your choice, and then press Esc to return to the Available NSS Volume Options menu.

12. Choose NSS Volume, and then select a managed object (this is the storage group you just created in Step 11). Then enter the size you

want the new NSS volume to use and a name for the new volume. The default name is NSSVOL, but you can choose another name if you want. Answer Yes to confirm your choices. When you receive a confirmation message, press any key to continue.

13. Select Return to the Previous Menu, then press Esc as necessary to exit NWCONFIG.

14. Now you've created the volume, but users can't access it until you mount it. Mount the new volume by typing the following command at the server's console (if you used a different volume name, substitute that name for "NSSVOL"):

```
MOUNT NSSVOL
```

Now the new NSS volume is mounted and ready to be accessed by users. It also appears in the NDS tree as a Volume object.

Mounting a DOS Partition as an NSS Volume

With NSS, you can mount a server's DOS partition as a volume, so that you can access its files like any other network volume. To do this, you need to specify that you want to load the DOSFAT.NSS modules when you load NSS support on the server. Type the following command at the server console:

```
NSS DEFAULTNLMS DOSFAT
```

This command loads NSS support with the default NLMs required, and simultaneously loads the DOSFAT.NSS module to turn the DOS partition into an NSS volume.

Dismounting and Deleting NSS Volumes

Deleting a volume deletes all the files and directories on that volume as well, so be sure you only delete a volume if you don't need the files anymore, or if you have a reliable backup.

Before you delete a volume, you must dismount it so that its files are unavailable to users. To dismount and delete an NSS volume, complete the following steps.

1. Back up all files on the volume or move them to a different volume, if you want to keep them.

2. Dismount the volume you want to delete by typing the following console command at the server's console (substitute the volume's name for *name*):

```
DISMOUNT name
```

3. Load the NSS administration utility on the server by typing:
NSS MENU

4. Choose Configure.

5. Choose Delete.

6. Select the delete option that will accomplish what you want to do:

- If you select Release Ownership, the entire block of disk space (a storage deposit) will revert back to the free-space state it was originally in. All volume and storage groups that were created from this storage space will be destroyed. Choose the storage deposit you want to delete and confirm your choice.

- If you select Destroy Storage Group, a single storage group will be removed from the storage deposit, and that storage group's NSS volumes will be destroyed. If there are other storage groups in that storage deposit, they will be unaffected. Choose the storage group you want to delete and confirm your choice.

- If you select Remove Volume From NSS Storage, the NSS volume will be destroyed, but the storage group will remain. Choose the volume you want to delete and confirm your choice.

You can also dismount and delete an NSS volume from within NWCONFIG.NLM, as explained in the following procedure.

I. Back up all files on the volume or move them to a different volume, if you want to keep them.

2. Dismount the volume you want to delete by typing the following console command at the server's console (substitute the volume's name for *name*):
DISMOUNT *name*

3. Load NWCONFIG.NLM on the server by typing:
NWCONFIG

4. Choose NSS Disk Options, and then choose NSS Volume Options.

5. Enter the administrator's full user name and password.

6. Choose Delete.

7. Select the delete option that will accomplish what you want to do:

- If you select Storage Group, a single storage group will be removed from the storage deposit, and that storage group's NSS volumes will be destroyed. If there are other storage groups in that storage deposit, they will be unaffected. Choose the storage group you want to delete and confirm your choice.

- If you select NSS Volume, the NSS volume will be destroyed, but the storage group will remain. Choose the volume you want to delete and confirm your choice.

Increasing the Size of an NSS Volume

To increase the size of a volume, you can create a new NSS managed object from free space, and add that space to an existing volume. You can use either the NSS administration utility or NWCONFIG.NLM, as explained in the following sections.

Using the NSS Utility

To use the NSS administration utility to increase the size of a volume, complete the following steps:

1. If you're installing a new hard disk whose space you want to add to an existing volume, install the hard disk according to the manufacturer's instructions.

2. Launch the NSS administration utility on the server by typing:

   NSS Menu

3. Choose Configure.

4. Choose Create.

5. Choose Advanced Configuration.

6. Choose Update Provider Information, and then choose NSS Media Manager Provider. (The NSS provider is the program that finds and manages free space. This step ensures that NSS knows about any free space available.) Press any key to return to the Options menu.

7. Choose Assign Ownership, and select the space you want to use. (The unpartitioned space you want to choose will be labeled "Fixed.") This space will become a "managed object." Enter the size you want the new managed object to be, and answer Yes to confirm your choice. Then press any key to return to the Options menu.

8. Choose Create a New Storage Group, and then select a managed object (this is the space you selected in Step 7). Answer Yes to confirm your choice, and then press Esc to return to the Options menu.

9. Press Esc twice to return to the main NSS Administration window.

10. Choose Modify.

11. Choose Increase NSS Volume Size.

12. Select the volume you want to increase.

13. Select the storage group you want to add to the volume.

14. Confirm your choice, and press Esc multiple times to exit the NSS utility when you're finished.

Using **NWCONFIG.NLM**

To use NWCONFIG to increase the size of a volume, complete the following steps:

1. If you're installing a new hard disk whose space you want to add to an existing volume, install the hard disk according to the manufacturer's instructions.

2. Load NWCONFIG.NLM on the server by typing:

```
NWCONFIG
```

3. From the main menu, choose NSS Disk Options.

4. Choose Storage.

5. Choose Update Provider Information, and then choose NSS Media Manager Provider. (The NSS provider is the program that finds and manages free space. This step ensures that NSS knows about any free space available.) Press any key to return to the Available NSS Storage Options menu.

6. Choose Assign Ownership, and then select the space you want to use. (The unpartitioned space you want to choose will be labeled "Fixed.") This space will become a "managed object." Enter the size you want the new managed object to be, and answer Yes to confirm your choice. Then press any key to return to the Available NSS Storage Options menu.

7. Press Esc to return to the Available NSS Options menu.

8. Choose NSS Volume Options.

9. Enter the administrator user's full name and password.

10. Choose Modify.

11. Choose Increase NSS Volume Size.

12. Select the NSS volume whose size you want to increase.

13. Select the storage group to add to the volume, and confirm your choice.

14. Press Esc multiple times to exit the utility.

Repairing a Corrupted NSS Volume with REBUILD

Volumes on a NetWare server can sometimes become corrupted, due to a variety of hardware errors. If an NSS volume won't mount, or if the volume begins generating numerous read/write errors or similar types of problems, you can try repairing the volume using the REBUILD utility.

NOTE The VREPAIR utility, with which you may be familiar from previous versions of NetWare, only works on traditional NetWare volumes. VREPAIR does not work on NSS volumes. Use REBUILD on NSS volumes instead. (Similarly, REBUILD does not work on traditional NetWare volumes.)

To run the REBUILD utility, launch the NSS administration utility by typing the following command at the server console:

```
NSS MENU
```

Then, from the Utilities menu, select Rebuild NSS Volume. Select the volumes you want to rebuild, and confirm your choice. The REBUILD utility goes through the volume, checking and repairing any errors it finds. REBUILD keeps an error log of any errors it finds and records. This file is located in the SYS volume, and is named with the volume's name, followed by the extension .RLF. For example, if your NSS volume is named NSSVOL, the error log will be named NSSVOL.RLF.

If you want to check the integrity of the NSS volume after REBUILD has run, you can choose Verify NSS Volume from the Utilities menu in the NSS administration utility.

Saving Disk Space

NetWare 5 contains several features that will help you to conserve disk space:

► File compression, which compresses less frequently used files, typically can conserve up to 63 percent of your hard disk space. This feature is available only on traditional volumes.

► Block suballocation allows several files to share a single block to avoid wasting space unnecessarily. This feature is available only on traditional volumes.

► Restricting users' disk space enables you to decide how much disk space users can fill up on a volume.

► Purging files lets you free up disk space by removing files that have been deleted but were still retained in a salvageable state. (You can also salvage deleted files, instead of purging them, but of course that doesn't free up any disk space.)

The following sections explain each of these features.

File Compression

File compression typically can save up to 63 percent of the server's hard disk space by compressing unused files. Compressed files are automatically decompressed when a user accesses them, so the user doesn't necessarily know that the files were compressed. (This feature is not available on NSS volumes.)

It takes only two steps to make file compression occur on the server:

► First, during installation, you choose whether to enable the volume for file compression, which simply means that you let the volume handle file compression if needed. The default is to enable the volume, but you can choose not to enable it if you want.

► Second, you must decide whether you want file compression turned on or off. By default, file compression is turned on, so that any volumes enabled for compression will use file compression. However, you can easily turn off compression by changing the SET Enable File Compression parameter to Off. This SET parameter will affect file compression for all enabled volumes on the server.

Disabling and Reenabling Compression

By default, all NetWare volumes are enabled for file compression. Because you can easily turn on and off file compression using a SET parameter, there is really no reason to disable compression for a particular volume, especially because the only way to disable the volume is to delete and re-create it.

If the volume was disabled for compression and you want to reenable it, use NWCONFIG.NLM. Load NWCONFIG, select Standard Disk Options, and then select NetWare Volume Options. Then choose the volume you want, go to the File Compression field, and press the Enter key, which will toggle the field from Off to On. Press the Esc key to save the new setting.

Managing Compression

By default, once the volume is enabled and compression is turned on, files and directories are compressed automatically after they've been untouched for seven days.

You can change several aspects of file compression, however, such as how long the files wait before being compressed, the time of day the compression activity occurs, and which files never get compressed. To control file compression, you can use two file and directory attributes and several SET parameters.

To specify compression for specific files or directories, you can assign them the following file and directory attributes:

▶ The Immediate Compress attribute compresses the file or directory immediately, without waiting for the standard duration of inactivity.

▶ The Don't Compress attribute prevents the file or directory from ever being compressed, even if compression is turned on for a parent directory.

To assign a file or directory one of these attributes, you can use the NetWare Administrator utility or the FLAG utility (covered in Chapter 7).

The SET parameters that affect file compression let you control compression characteristics for all enabled volumes on the server. You can set options such as when compression happens, how many files can be compressed at the same time, how many times a file must be accessed before it is decompressed, and so on. The easiest way to change these parameters is to use MONITOR. NLM, but you can also type the SET command at the server's console. If you change a SET parameter, the change will affect all files and directories in all volumes on the server that have been enabled for compression.

To change the SET parameters, load MONITOR on the server and choose Server Parameters. Then, from the Select a Parameter Category menu, choose File System, and change the parameters you want. When you are finished, press Esc multiple times to exit MONITOR. You do not need to reboot the server, because the values have already taken effect. The following are the SET parameters that affect compression:

▶ **Compression daily check stop hour=*hour*** Specifies the hour when the file compressor stops searching volumes for files that need to be compressed. If this value is the same as the Compression Daily Check Starting Hour value, then the search starts at the specified starting hour and goes until all compressible files have been found. Default: 6 (6:00 a.m.). Values: 0 (midnight) to 23 (11:00 p.m.).

▶ **Compression daily check starting hour=*hour*** Specifies the hour when the file compressor begins searching volumes for files that need to be compressed. Default: 0 (midnight). Values: 0 to 23 (11:00 p.m.).

▶ **Minimum compression percentage gain=*number*** Specifies the minimum percentage that a file must be able to be compressed in order to remain compressed. Default: 20. Values: 0 to 50.

▶ **Enable file compression=*on/off*** When set to On, file compression is allowed to occur on volumes that are enabled for compression. If set to Off, file compression won't occur, even though the volume is still enabled for compression. Default: On.

▶ **Maximum concurrent compressions=*number*** Specifies how many volumes can compress files at the same time. Increasing this value may slow down server performance during compression times. Default: 2. Values: 1 to 8.

▶ **Convert compressed to uncompressed option=*number*** Specifies how a compressed file is stored after it has been accessed. Default: 1. Values: 0 = always leave the file compressed; 1 = leave the file compressed after the first access within the time frame defined by the Days Untouched Before Compression parameter; then leave the file uncompressed after the second access. 2 = change the file to uncompressed after the first access.

▶ **Decompress percent disk space free to allow commit=*number*** Specifies the percentage of free disk space that is required on a volume before committing an uncompressed file to disk. This helps you avoid running out of disk space by uncompressing files. Default: 10. Values: 0 to 75.

▶ **Decompress free space warning interval=*time*** Specifies the interval between warnings when the volume doesn't have enough disk space for uncompressed files. Default: 31 min 18.5 sec. Values: 0 sec (which turns off warnings) to 29 days 15 hours, 50 min 3.8 sec.

▶ **Deleted files compression option=***number* Specifies how the server handles deleted files. Default: 1. Values: 0 = don't compress deleted files; 1 = compress deleted files during the next day's search; 2 = compress deleted files immediately.

▶ **Days untouched before compression=***days* Specifies how many days a file or directory must remain untouched before being compressed. Default: 14. Values: 0 to 100000.

▶ **Allow unowned files to be extended=***on/off* When set to On, files can be changed even if their owner has been deleted. Default: On.

Block Suballocation

A block is a unit that is allocated to store a file. A file may take up more space on the disk than its actual size because NetWare allocates the disk into uniformly sized blocks that are used to store pieces of files. The default block size depends on the volume's size, as shown in Table 8.1. In general, larger block sizes are better for large database records, because they can help speed up access. Smaller block sizes require more server memory, but help prevent disk space from being wasted. In versions of NetWare before NetWare 4.1*x*, there was nothing you could do to prevent the inefficient use of disk space if you wanted to use larger block sizes. For example, if your block size was 32K, a 35K file would take two 32K blocks, using a total of 64K of disk space.

T A B L E   8 . I   *Default Block Sizes for Storing Files*

VOLUME SIZE	BLOCK SIZE
0 to 31MB	4K
32 to 149MB	8K
150 to 499MB	16K
500MB to 1999MB	32K
2000MB or more	64K

However, NetWare 5 includes a feature for traditional volumes called block suballocation. (This feature is not available on NSS volumes.) Block suballocation lets the file system break a block into suballocation blocks as small as 512 bytes, so that several files (or pieces of files) can share a single block. With block suballocation turned on, the 35K file will use up one 32K block, plus enough suballocation blocks required, for a total of only 35K of disk space.

Block suballocation is turned on by default when NetWare 5 is installed. You do not need to do anything to use or manage block suballocation.

Restricting Users' Disk Space

You can restrict how much disk space a user can fill up on a particular volume. This can help prevent individual users from using an excessive amount of disk space. To limit the space individual users can use, use the NetWare Administrator and select a Volume object. Choose Details from the Object menu, and then choose the User Space Limits page.

On the User Space Limits page, you can see which users have restricted disk space allowances on this volume. You can see what their restrictions are, and how much space they still have available. You can also modify these limits or add other users and restrict their disk space, too.

Purging and Salvaging Files

When files are deleted from a NetWare server, they are not actually removed from the server's hard disk. Instead, they are retained in a salvageable state.

Deleted files are usually stored in the same directory from which they were originally deleted. If, however, the directory itself was also deleted, the deleted files are stored in a special directory called DELETED.SAV at the volume's root.

Deleted files are stored in this salvageable state unless one of the following occurs:

- ► The file is salvaged, restoring it to its original form.
- ► The server runs out of free space on the disk and begins to overwrite files that have been deleted for a specified period of time. The oldest deleted files are overwritten first. You can use a SET parameter to set the amount of time the file must have been deleted before it can be overwritten.
- ► The file is purged by the administrator or user. (When purged, a file is completely removed from the disk and cannot be recovered.) You can purge a file either manually, by using the NetWare Administrator utility or PURGE (a command-line utility), or you can use the Purge directory and file attributes to mark a file or directory to be purged immediately upon deletion.

▶ The Purge directory attribute is assigned to the volume that contains files you want purged as soon as they are deleted. If you use this attribute, you cannot salvage files you delete from that volume.

▶ The administrator sets the SET parameter called Immediate Purge of Deleted Files to On. All volumes on that server will immediately purge deleted files. (The default for this parameter is Off.)

Purging and Salvaging Files with NetWare Administrator

To use the NetWare Administrator utility to either purge or salvage a deleted file or directory, complete the following steps:

1. From the NetWare Administrator's Browser, select the directory containing the files or directories you want to salvage or purge.

2. From the Tools menu, select Salvage. (This option lets you both salvage and purge files.)

3. In the Include field of the Salvage dialog box that appears, indicate which files you want to see displayed. Specify a filename or use wildcards to indicate several files.

   A blank line or the wildcard symbols *.* will display all the deleted files in the selected directory.

4. From the Sort Options drop box, specify how you want the displayed files to be sorted: by Deletion Date, Deletor, File Name, File Size, or File Type.

5. From the Source drop box, choose whether you want to see deleted files in your current directory or in a deleted directory.

6. Click the List button to display the files you've specified. Figure 8.2 shows an example of the Salvage dialog box with deleted files listed.

7. From the displayed list, select the files you want to purge or salvage.

8. Click either the Salvage button or the Purge button, depending on what you want to do. If you salvage files from an existing directory, the files are restored to that directory. If you salvage files from a deleted directory, the files are restored into the DELETED.SAV directory under the root of the volume.

9. When finished, click the Close button.

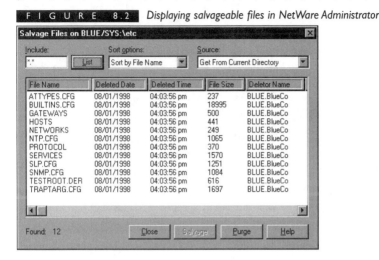

FIGURE 8.2 *Displaying salvageable files in NetWare Administrator*

Purging Files with PURGE

To purge deleted files, you can also use the PURGE command-line utility. To purge files using PURGE, use the following command:

```
PURGE path\filename /option
```

Replace *path* with the path to the files you want to purge, and replace *file-name* with a filename for the specific files. Wildcards are acceptable. The following options can be used with PURGE:

/A   Purges all files in the current directory and all of its subdirectories.

/VER   Displays the version number of PURGE.

/?   Displays help screens for PURGE.

For example, to purge all the deleted files with the extension .BAT in the current directory only, use the following command:

```
PURGE *.BAT
```

Adding a Name Space to a Volume

By default, NetWare 5 servers support DOS, OS/2, Windows NT, and Windows 95/98 file formats. (Previous versions of NetWare only supported the DOS filename format by default.) If you want a volume to store Macintosh,

UNIX, or FTAM files, you need to add name space support for those file formats to the volume. Name space support is a feature that extends the volume's storage characteristics, enabling the volume to store the longer filenames and additional information that different file formats may contain.

For example, Macintosh name space support enables the volume to store a Macintosh file's resource fork and long filename.

The following name spaces are available for NetWare 5:

► MAC.NAM for Macintosh files

► LONG.NAM for OS/2, Windows NT, and Windows 95/98 files (installed by default). This module replaces the OS2.NAM and NT.NAM modules available for previous versions of NetWare.

► NFS.NAM (Network File System) for UNIX files

► FTAM.NAM (File Transfer, Access, and Management), which supports the FTAM protocol for remote file access (available separately).

A volume with support for a non-DOS name space requires twice as much memory as a volume with DOS-only files, because the name spaces use twice as many directory entries that have to be cached.

To add name space support to a volume, complete the following steps:

I. Load the name space loadable module on the server. For example, to load the Macintosh name space, type

```
LOAD MAC
```

2. Add the name space support to the desired volume by using the ADD NAME SPACE console command. To add the Macintosh name space to the volume VOL1, type the following command:

```
ADD NAME SPACE MAC TO VOL1
```

Once you've added the name space support to a volume, the only ways you can remove the name space support are to run VREPAIR.NLM or delete and re-create the volume.

To see a list of all the volumes on a server and their name spaces, use the VOLUMES console command.

► . . . . ◄

Backing Up and Restoring Files

Files can be lost or damaged in a variety of ways. They can be corrupted by viruses, accidentally deleted by users, overwritten by other applications, or destroyed when a hard disk fails. Despite all the best precautions, you can't always prevent files from being lost.

What you can do, however, is make sure that you always have current backup copies of your network data, so you can restore files. If you have a carefully planned and executed backup strategy, you can minimize the amount of work that will be lost if you have to restore a file from your archives.

Many different backup products are available on the market. NetWare 5 includes a backup solution called Enhanced SBACKUP that you can use, or you can purchase a third-party product that may provide additional features you need. Backup products can back up data onto a variety of storage media, such as tapes and optical disks.

Backing up network files involves more than just making a copy of the files. It's important to use a backup product, such as NetWare's Enhanced SBACKUP, that backs up not just the files, but also the NetWare information associated with those files, such as trustee rights, Inherited Rights Filters, and file and directory attributes.

It's important to make sure you have a solid backup strategy, as explained in the following section.

Planning a Backup Strategy

Planning an efficient backup strategy is one of the most beneficial tasks you can do as part of network management. With a good backup strategy, you can limit the time it takes to do backups, ensure that the least amount of working time is lost by your users, and avoid unnecessary headaches from searching for lost files.

Backup strategies can be different for every network. What works for someone else may not work well for you, and vice versa. When planning a backup strategy, you need to consider the following questions:

- ▶ What type of backup medium do you need to use?
- ▶ What backup schedule should you follow?
- ▶ How frequently should you rotate your backup medium?
- ▶ Where should the backups be stored?
- ▶ How often will you test the restore procedure?

The tips and suggestions in the next few sections can help you decide on your own backup strategy.

Whenever possible, avoid restoring the NDS tree from a backup tape. Instead, use partition replication to restore the NDS tree. See Chapter 5 for more information on partition replication.

NOTE

Choosing Your Backup Medium

Before purchasing a backup device, you must decide what kind of backup medium you want to use, such as tapes or optical disks. Many manufacturers' backup products can back up data onto a variety of storage media, but it's a good idea to know what you want before you buy something that limits your choices. The medium you choose will probably depend on the following factors:

- ► How much you're willing to spend
- ► How large your network is
- ► How long you need to retain your backed-up data (some media deteriorate after a few years; other media may have a 100-year guarantee)

Tape is probably the most common backup medium in use today, especially in small- to medium-sized businesses. Tapes are relatively easy to use, can be used in any size network, and are fairly inexpensive.

One of the downsides of tape is that backup manufacturers tend to use different, proprietary tape formats that aren't compatible with each other. Two tape standards have been established (one from Novell, and another from Microsoft), so some efforts have been made to standardize on one or the other, but there are still differences between manufacturers. Be sure any backup product you buy will be compatible with any other system with which you may need to share tapes.

TIP

Currently, the two most affordable and popular tape formats used in smaller businesses are:

- ► DAT (Digital Audio Tape)
- ► QIC (Quarter-Inch Cartridge)

A newer tape format, called Digital Linear Tape (DLT), has much higher performance and capacity than DAT or QIC, but it is also much more expensive. Its higher, more expensive performance makes it better suited for large networks. Another tape format, 8mm, is also faster and has more capacity than DAT and QIC, but isn't quite as expensive as DLT.

Tape, while easy to use and relatively affordable, is not necessarily suited to long-term storage of data. Like any magnetic medium, tape can oxidize or otherwise deteriorate over time; therefore, for long-term storage, you may want to consider some of the different types of optical disks. Some optical disks that are available currently include:

- ▶ CD-R (Compact Disk-Recordable)
- ▶ DVD
- ▶ Magneto-optical
- ▶ Floptical disks

These technologies are constantly being improved with innovative features and compatibility with earlier or existing products. Talk to your reseller about your network's specific needs, and choose the medium that best suits your network.

NOTE

NetWare's Enhanced SBACKUP product supports quarter-inch tape, 4mm tape (DDS-certified, computer grade), and 8mm tape formats.

Planning a Backup Schedule

A good way to determine how often to back up critical data is to calculate how long you could afford to spend re-creating the information if it was lost. If you can't afford to lose more than a day's worth of work, you should perform daily backups of that information. If losing a week's worth of work is more of a nuisance than a devastating blow, perhaps you don't need to do daily backups and can rely on weekly backups instead.

Most backup products, including NetWare's backup product, let you determine not only when to back up your network, but also what types of information you back up each time. In many cases, you'll find that there's no point in backing up your entire network every night if only a few of the files change during the day.

With most products, you can choose between doing a full backup and an *incremental* backup. In an incremental backup, only the files that have been changed are detected and backed up. With a little careful planning, you can create a schedule that staggers complete backups with incremental backups, so you still get full coverage without spending more time and money than necessary.

For example, you can do a full backup of the network once a week. Then, once a day, do incremental backups of only those files that have changed (the backup product can usually detect changed files for you). In the event of a total loss of files, you can restore all the files from the weekly backup, and then restore each of the daily tapes to update the files that changed during that week. In this way, you can cover all of your files while minimizing the time each backup session takes during the week.

TIP

Any good backup product can detect changed files when performing an incremental backup. It does this by looking for a special file attribute called the *Archive Needed* attribute (also called the Modify bit). When a file is changed, this attribute is assigned to it. Then, the backup product detects this attribute and knows to back up this file.

In many cases, you can specify whether the backup product should then remove the attribute. (This is done so the file isn't backed up unnecessarily during the next incremental backup.) You can also choose to leave the attribute set so it still appears to be a changed file.

Another tip for minimizing backup time is to organize your directory (folder) structure so that often-changed files are separate from seldom-changed files. For example, there's no point in wasting your time by frequently backing up files such as applications and utilities, which seldom change. If you put applications in one directory and work files in another, you can skip the application directory completely during incremental backups, making the process go faster.

Finally, be sure to document your backup schedule and keep a backup log. A written record of all backups and your backup strategy can help someone else restore the files if you aren't there.

Planning the Medium Rotation

It's important to plan a rotation schedule for your backup medium. You should decide in advance how long you will retain old files, and how often you will reuse the same tapes or disks.

Assume you're using tapes (although any rewritable medium gives you the same situation). If you have only one backup tape that you use every week, you could unknowingly back up corrupted files onto your single tape each time you replace the previous week's backup with the new one. In short, you're replacing your last good copy with a corrupted one.

To prevent this type of problem, plan to keep older backup tapes or disks on hand at all times. Many network administrators use four or more tapes or disks for the same set of files, cycling through them one at a time. Each week, the most outdated tape or disk is used for the new backup. This way, three or more versions of backups are available at any given time. How many tape or disk sets you'll need depends on your rotation schedule. If you want to keep four weeks' worth of daily and weekly backups, you'll need at least 20 sets of tapes or disks—five for each week.

Some backup products offer preset rotation schedules for you. They will automatically prompt you for the right set of media and keep track of the schedule.

Decide Where to Store the Backups

Another important aspect of your backup strategy is to plan where to store your backups. If you have backups of noncritical data, you may be comfortable keeping them onsite. However, when storing backups onsite, you should at least store them in a room separate from the server's room. If an electrical fire breaks out in the server room, your backup tapes won't do you much good if they burn right beside the server.

For mission-critical data, you may need to keep backups in an offsite location. That way, if a physical disaster occurs (such as a fire, flood, or earthquake), they'll be safe. If the data is critical enough to store offsite, but you also want to have immediate access to it, consider making two backups and storing one offsite and the other onsite.

Test the Restore Process

Test the restore process to make sure your backups can be restored.

A backup is only useful if the data in it can be restored successfully. Too many people discover a problem with their backups when they're in the middle of an important restoration process. Practice restoring files before you need to do so. By practicing, you may identify problems you didn't realize you had. Don't wait until it's too late.

Preparing to Use Enhanced SBACKUP

Enhanced SBACKUP, the backup utility included in NetWare 5, can be used either from the server console or from a workstation. With this product, you can back up all the different types of files that can be stored on your server: DOS, Macintosh, OS/2, Windows NT, Windows 95 and 98, and UNIX.

Enhanced SBACKUP enables you to select the type of backup you want to perform. There are three choices (all of which can be customized for your particular needs):

▶ *Full backup.* This option backs up all network files. It removes the Archive Needed file attribute from all files and directories. (This attribute is also called the *modify bit.* It is assigned to a file whenever the file is changed. When the file is backed up, most backup products can remove the attribute so the next time the file is changed, the attribute is once again assigned.)

▶ *Differential backup.* This option backs up only files that were modified since the last full backup. It does not remove the Archive Needed attribute from these files.

▶ *Incremental backup.* This option backs up only files that were modified since the last full or incremental backup. It removes the Archive Needed attribute from these files.

To use Enhanced SBACKUP to back up files, you first need to install a backup device and load the device's drivers on a server. Then you need to load some necessary backup NLMs on this server. This server is called the *host server.* Next, you load Target Service Agents (TSAs), which also come in the NetWare 5 product, on any servers or workstations whose files you want to back up. These servers and workstations are called *targets.* (TSAs are NetWare Loadable Modules.)

Finally, you need to launch the NetWare backup utility on either the host server or a workstation. The server-based version of the backup utility is called SBCON.NLM. The workstation-based utility is called NWBACK32.EXE. Both utilities accomplish the same tasks, enabling you to back up and restore network files. It doesn't matter which utility you choose, so select the utility most convenient for you.

Before you can use either SBCON.NLM or NWBACK32.EXE, you must prepare the host server and then set up target servers or workstations, as explained in the following sections.

Setting Up the Host Server and Targets

Before you can run the NetWare Backup utility, you must first prepare the host server and any targets you want to back up, by completing the following steps:

1. Attach the backup device (tape or disk drive) to the host server.

2. Load the necessary backup device drivers on the host server. Then enter the command

```
SCAN FOR NEW DEVICES
```

at the console to register the device with the server. Check the manufacturer's documentation to find out which drivers you need. Place the commands that load the backup device drivers in the server's STARTUP.NCF file if you want them to load automatically when the server is rebooted.

3. At the server console, load SMDR.NLM. This module loads the SMS Data Requester on the server, and automatically creates an SMS SMDR Group object in the server's context. This Group object will contain each server and workstation that will be backed up by this host server. Load SMDR.NLM by typing:

```
SMDR
```

(If you want to create a new SMDR Group object, type **SMDR NEW** at the console instead, and enter a new name and context for the SMDR Group object.)

4. Load the SMS Device Interface module, which will let the SBACKUP program communicate with the backup device, by typing:

```
SMSDI
```

5. Load the SMS Queue Manager, which will create a job queue for the backup program to use. The backup queue is an object named "*Server* Backup Queue" (with the server's name substituted for *Server*). To load the Queue Manager on this server, type:

```
QMAN
```

(If you want to create a new Queue object, type **QMAN NEW** at the console instead, and enter a new name and context for the job queue.)

6. Load the SBACKUP Communication module on this server by typing:

```
SBSC
```

7. (Optional) If you are going to back up the network files that reside on this server (in other words, this server is both the host and the target), load the NetWare 5 TSA on this server by typing:

```
TSA500
```

8. (Optional) If you are going to back up Windows 95/98 or Windows NT workstations from this host server, load TSAPROXY.NLM on this server by typing:

```
TSAPROXY
```

9. If you are going to back up another server from this host server, go to that server and load the appropriate TSA. Once the TSA is loaded on a server, that server is called a *target server*. You can use the following TSAs, depending on the type of server you want to back up:

- TSA500 — Load on NetWare 5 servers
- TSA410 — Load on NetWare 4 servers
- TSANDS — Load on a server whose NDS tree you want to back up (it's usually best to load this on a server that contains a replica of the tree's largest Directory partition)
- TSADOSP — Load on a server if you want to back up its DOS partition

At this point, the host server is prepared, and the target server is ready to be backed up. If you want to back up a Windows 95/98 or Windows NT workstation, you must take extra steps to configure TSAs on those workstations, as explained in the following sections. If you are ready to back up or restore files, skip to "Backing Up Files" or "Restoring Files" later in this chapter.

Preparing to Back Up Workstations

Although most people use Enhanced SBACKUP to back up files from network servers, you can also use it to back up files from the hard disks of Windows 95/98 or Windows NT workstations. To do this, you must load and configure TSA software on the workstations. TSA software is an optional set of software that you can install as part of the Novell client software. During the client installation, be sure you check the Target Service Agent option to install the TSA support.

After the TSA software is installed, you must configure it, as described in the following sections.

Configuring the Windows 95/98 TSA   Before you try for the first time to back up files that reside on a Windows 95/98 workstation, you must configure the TSA. If you have installed the TSA software during the client installation, a small, round, shield-shaped icon will appear in the Windows 95/98 system tray (usually at the bottom right-hand corner of the screen). When you put the cursor over this icon, the words "Novell TSA (Not Registered)" will appear. If the words "Novell TSA (Listening)" appear, this workstation has already been configured, and you can skip this section and go straight to "Backing Up Files."

To configure the TSA and register it with the host server, complete the following steps:

I. Double-click the shield icon in the workstation's system tray. The Properties page for the Novell Target Service Agent for Windows 95 appears, as shown in Figure 8.3.

2. Enter your username and password.

3. If necessary, choose the protocol you want to use (IPX or IP).

4. Enter the name of the host server that will back up this workstation's files.

5. Under the Resources Available to TSA heading, choose the local drives you want to back up.

6. Check Auto Register, to automatically register this workstation with the host server.

7. Make sure the option to Show TSA Icon on Taskbar is checked.

8. Click OK.

9. Reboot the workstation to make the changes take effect.

After the workstation is rebooted, the TSA's icon in the system tray should display the words "Novell TSA (Listening)." Now the workstation is ready to be backed up. Skip to the section "Backing Up Files" later in this chapter.

F.IGURE   8.3   *The Property page for the Windows 95 TSA*

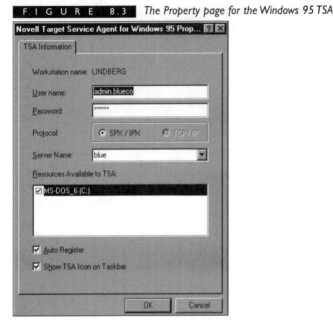

Configuring the Windows NT TSA   Before you try for the first time to back up files that reside on a Windows NT workstation, you must configure the TSA. Make sure you installed the TSA software during the client installation.

To configure the TSA and register it with the host server, complete the following steps:

1. Open the Properties page for the Windows NT TSA.

2. Open the Preferences tab.

3. In the Workstation field, enter the name of this workstation.

4. In the Preferred Server field, enter the name of the host server that will back up this workstation's files.

5. In the Protocol field, choose the protocol you want to use (IPX or IP).

6. In the Events to Log field, check the items you want to log.

7. Check Allow Backup User to grant the backup user rights.

8. Check Auto Register to automatically register this workstation with the host server.

9. Open the Registration tab. If all the information shown is correct, click Register. If some of the information is incorrect, click Withdraw and return to the Preferences page to make any necessary changes.

10. Open the Connections tab. If you need to change or add information to these fields, make the changes and click Apply. If all the information is correct, click OK.

11. Reboot the workstation to make the changes take effect.

After the workstation is rebooted, it is ready to be backed up, as explained in the following section.

Backing Up Files

After you've loaded the necessary NLMs on the host server and loaded a TSA on the target server or workstation, you can use the NetWare backup program (Enhanced SBACKUP) to back up the target's files. You can use either the server-based backup program (SBCON.NLM) or the workstation-based backup program (NWBACK32.EXE). Both programs accomplish the same tasks, so choose the program that is most convenient for you to use. The following sections explain how to use these programs.

Using the Server-based Utility (SBCON)

To use the server-based SBCON.NLM to back up files, complete the following steps:

1. At the host server, load SBCON.NLM by typing:

```
SBCON
```

2. From the main menu, choose Job Administration, and then choose Backup.

3. At the Target Service field, press Enter.

4. Choose the target server you want to back up. If you're backing up a workstation, choose the workstation's host server.

5. Choose whether you want to back up the server's file system or a workstation attached to the server.

6. Enter a user name and password for the target. (Use the user's full context name, beginning with a period.)

7. Choose What to Back Up.

8. From the Resource List that appears, choose the directories and files you want to back up. If the list is blank, or if you want to make changes, press Ins. Then select whether you want to back up the server, only server-specific information, or a volume. You can also specify directories and files within a volume by choosing the volume and then pressing Ins again. When you select a directory, press Esc to make it appear in the Resource List box. When finished selecting what you want to back up, press Enter to save the information and return to the Backup Options page.

9. In the Description field, enter a descriptive name for this backup session.

10. Choose the backup device and medium you will use. If only one device is available, the backup program will choose it for you. (The wildcard characters *.* will select the default device.)

11. At the Advanced Options field, press Enter. From the screen that appears, you can select the backup type (full, differential, or incremental), the subset of directories you want to back up, scan options, the time to execute the backup session, and scheduling options. When finished selecting these Advanced Options, press Esc to save the information and return to the Backup Options menu.

NOTE

The Advanced Options screen lets you use *include* and *exclude* options to customize what you want to back up. Use exclude options when you want to back up most of the file system while omitting only a small part. Everything that you don't specifically exclude is backed up. Use include options when you want to back up only a small portion of the file system. Everything you don't specifically include is excluded.

When specifying subsets to back up, two options enable you to exclude or include Major TSA resources. A *Major TSA resource* is simply a server or volume. You can choose to include or exclude volumes, directories, or files.

12. If your backup device enables you to put multiple sessions on a single tape, and if a session is already on the tape you're using, select Append Session and answer Yes to add the new session to the tape. To overwrite any existing sessions, choose No. When finished, press Esc to save the information and return to the Backup Options menu.

13. Press Esc to return to the main SBCON menu.

14. When asked if you want to submit a job, answer Yes to begin the backup session.

Using the Workstation-based Utility (NWBACK32)

To use the workstation-based NWBACK32.EXE from a Windows 95/98 or Windows NT workstation to back up files, complete the following steps:

1. From the workstation you are using to run the backup program, log in to the host server.

2. Create a shortcut to NWBACK32.EXE, which is located in the SYS volume, under the Public directory.

3. Launch NWBACK32.

4. The first time you run NWBACK32, you will be asked to enter NDS information. Enter the tree name, and then the contexts for the SMDR and the SMDR Group objects. You must enter the context for these objects using the format O=*container* or OU=*container*.O=*container*. The O= and OU= designations are required in this release. If you are using IPX on your network, make sure SAP is checked. Then click OK to save the information. To make sure the changes take effect, exit and then relaunch NWBACK32.

5. Click Backup.

6. Double-click What to Backup.

7. Double-click the item you want to back up: NDS, NetWare servers, workstations, or a DOS partition on a NetWare server. A list of servers appears beneath the item you double-clicked, as shown in Figure 8.4.

8. Double-click a server, and then enter a user name and password for that server.

9. Click the information you want to back up (NetWare server, server-specific information, or volumes), so that an X appears in the box next to the item you want.

10. Double-click Where to Backup.

11. Double-click the context. (If you need to change contexts, click the Change to Context button on the toolbar.)

12. Double-click Queues to open a list of backup queues.

FIGURE 8.4 *Choosing What to Backup*

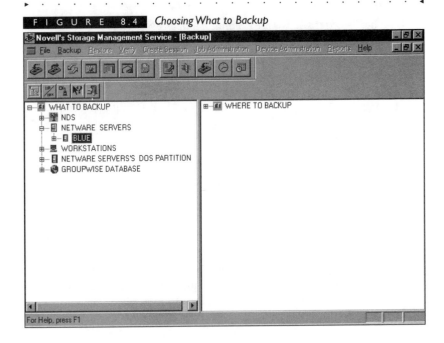

13. Right-click a queue and choose Submit the Job. The screens that appear enable you to choose the backup type (full, differential, or incremental), subsets of directories you want to back up, filtering options, the time to execute the backup session, and other scheduling options. At the last screen, indicate whether you want to append this session to a tape that already contains previous sessions, then enter a description of this session and indicate whether you want to keep this job. Then press Finish.

NOTE

These screens let you use *include* and *exclude* options to customize what you want to back up. Use exclude options when you want to back up most of the file system while omitting only a small part. Everything that you don't specifically exclude is backed up. Use include options when you want to back up only a small portion of the file system. Everything you don't specifically include is excluded.

When specifying subsets to back up, two options enable you to exclude or include Major TSA resources. A *Major TSA resource* is simply a server or volume. You can choose to include or exclude volumes, directories, or files.

14. When asked if you want to submit the job, answer Yes to begin the backup session.

Restoring Files

To restore files from a backup, you need to prepare the host server and targets the same way you did for the backup procedure. (See the section "Setting Up the Host Server and Targets" earlier in this chapter.)

After you've loaded the necessary NLMs on the host server and loaded a TSA on the target server or workstation, you can use the NetWare Enhanced SBACKUP program to restore files to the target. You can use either the server-based backup program (SBCON.NLM) or the workstation-based backup program (NWBACK32.EXE) to restore files. Both programs accomplish the same tasks, so choose the program that is most convenient for you to use. The following sections explain how to use these programs.

Using the Server-based Utility (SBCON)

To use the server-based SBCON.NLM to restore files, complete the following steps:

1. At the host server, load SBCON.NLM by typing:

    SBCON

2. From the main menu, choose Job Administration, and then choose Restore.

3. At the Target Service field, press Enter.

4. Choose the target server to which you want to restore. If you're restoring to a workstation, choose the workstation's host server.

5. Choose whether you want to restore the server's file system or a workstation attached to the server.

6. Enter a user name and password for the target. (Use the user's full context name, beginning with a period.)

7. In the Description field, enter a descriptive name for this restore session.

8. Choose the backup device and medium you will use. If only one device is available, the backup program will choose it for you. (The wildcard characters *.* will select the default device.)

9. In the Session to Restore field, press Enter, and then choose a backup session from the list that appears.

10. At the Advanced Options field, press Enter. From the screen that appears, you can select to rename the data sets (which will send the restored files to a different location that you specify), the subset of directories you want to restore, and Open Mode options (which let you pick the types of information about files and directories to restore). You can also specify whether you want to overwrite "parents" (which are simply servers, volumes, or directories) if they exist, and whether to overwrite "children" (which are files). Finally, you can specify the time to execute the restore session and other scheduling options. When finished selecting these Advanced Options, press Esc to save the information and return to the Restore Options menu.

11. Press Esc to return to the main SBCON menu.

12. When asked if you want to submit the job, answer Yes to begin the restore session.

Using the Workstation-based Utility (NWBACK32)

To use the workstation-based NWBACK32.EXE from a Windows 95/98 or Windows NT workstation to restore files, complete the following steps:

1. From the workstation you are using to run the backup program, log in to the host server.

2. Launch NWBACK32.EXE, which is located in the SYS volume, under the PUBLIC directory.

3. Click Restore.

4. Double-click What to Restore.

5. Double-click the context. (If you need to change contexts, click the Change to Context button on the toolbar.)

6. In succession, double-click Queues, then the queue object, then Servers, then the server object, then Devices, and then the backup device you want to restore from.

7. From the list of backup media, choose the one that has the files you want to restore.

8. Double-click Where to Restore.

9. Double-click the item you want to restore: NDS, NetWare servers, workstations, or a DOS partition on a NetWare server. A list of servers appears beneath the item you double-clicked.

10. Double-click a server, and then enter a user name and password for that server.

11. Right-click the server and choose Submit the Job. The screens that appear enable you to choose filtering options and scheduling options. Then press Finish.

12. When asked if you want to submit the job, answer Yes to begin the restore session.

Protecting Databases with TTS

Transaction Tracking System (TTS) is NetWare's feature for protecting database transactions. With TTS turned on, the transaction is completely backed out so the database isn't corrupted if a transaction is caught only half-completed when a problem such as a power outage occurs.

When a transaction is backed out, the database is restored to the original state it was in before the transaction began. TTS protects data by making a copy of the original data before it is overwritten by new data. Then, if a failure of some component occurs in the middle of the transaction, TTS restores the data to its original condition and discards the incomplete transaction.

TTS protects the NDS database and the queuing database files from corruption. In addition, you can use it to protect your own database files. If your database application doesn't offer its own form of transaction tracking, NetWare's TTS can provide protection for it. If your database application does offer its own transaction tracking, NetWare's TTS may still benefit you by tracking the transactions in the server. Tracking the file writes in the server means less data is transferred across the network, and NetWare's disk caching system increases performance.

TTS can be used with any application that stores information in records and allocates record locks. It can't be used with applications such as word processors, which don't store data in discrete records.

Because TTS is used to protect the NDS database, TTS is enabled by default. You should not disable TTS. TTS may become disabled on its own if the SYS volume becomes full, because the SYS volume is the volume TTS uses for its backout data. In addition, TTS may become disabled if the server runs out of memory to run TTS. You can see if TTS has been disabled by using a text editor to read the TTS$LOG.ERR file at the root of the volume.

If TTS has been disabled, you can use the ENABLE TTS console utility to reenable TTS after you correct the problem that caused it to become disabled.

Table 8.2 shows the tasks you can use to manage how TTS works.

TABLE 8.2	TTS Tasks
TASK	**HOW TO DO IT**
Make TTS track a file	Use FLAG or NetWare Administrator to assign to the file the Transactional file attribute.
Reenable TTS	Use the console command **ENABLE TTS.**
Make the server automatically back out incomplete transactions without prompting you for input	Load MONITOR.NLM. Choose Server Parameters, and then choose the Transaction Tracking category. Set the Auto TTS Backout Flag to On. (Default: On)
Keep an error log for TTS data	Load MONITOR.NLM. Choose Server Parameters, and then choose the Transaction Tracking category. Set the TTS Abort Dump Flag to On. (Default: Off)

► . . . . ◄

Managing Files and Directories

The most common way to work with files and folders on your workstation is to use the commands or features of your regular workstation operating system, such as DOS commands, the Macintosh Filer program, the Windows File Manager, or the Windows 95/98 Explorer or Network Neighborhood. However, there are also NetWare utilities you can use to work with files and folders.

With NetWare Administrator, for example, which runs in Windows 95/98 and Windows NT, you can use the Browser to select files and directories and view information about them, as explained in earlier sections of this chapter. Some of the types of information about files and directories you can see with the NetWare Administrator utility include the following:

- ► Name spaces
- ► Size restrictions of directories

- Creation dates and times
- Trustees
- Effective rights
- Inherited Rights Filters
- File and directory attributes
- File owners

For more information about accessing and using the NetWare Administrator utility, see Chapter 5.

NOTE

You can also use the following NetWare utilities to work with files and directories. For more information on how to use these utilities, see Appendix E.

- The FLAG command-line utility, as explained in Chapter 7, can be used to view and assign attributes to files and directories. It can also be used to assign search modes for executable files.
- The NCOPY command-line utility lets you copy files and directories from one drive or disk to another.
- The NDIR command-line utility lets you list a directory's files, subdirectories, and related information, such as file owners, sizes, attributes, and so on.

CHAPTER 9

Setting Up NetWare Print Services

Instant *Access*

Installing NDPS

▸ During the server installation, set up the NDPS Broker on a server, and add printer drivers to it if necessary.

▸ To set up printers on the network, use the NetWare Administrator utility to create an NDPS Manager object, and load NDPSM.NLM on the server. Then use NetWare Administrator to create a public access printer or a controlled access printer (controlled access printers can also be configured to service print queues).

▸ Automatically install printer support on workstations by using NetWare Administrator and opening the NDPS Remote Management page for an NDPS Printer object.

Installing Queue-Based Printing

▸ To install queue-based print services using default options (the quick and easy way), use the Print Services Quick Setup feature of the NetWare Administrator utility (which runs in Windows 95/98 and Windows NT), and then load PSERVER.NLM on the NetWare server.

▸ To connect a network printer to a DOS or Windows 3.1 workstation, load NPRINTER.EXE on the workstation.

▸ To connect a network printer to a Windows 95 or 98 workstation, load NPTWIN95.EXE on the workstation.

▸ To connect a network printer to a NetWare server, load NPRINTER.NLM on the NetWare server.

▸ To redirect LPT1 to a print queue, put a CAPTURE command in a login script, use NetWare User Tools (which runs in Windows 3.1*x* only), or configure the application for network printing.

Defining Print Options

▸ To tell the printer how to print a job (paper form to use, format, and so on), define printer configurations with the NetWare Administrator utility.

Printing Jobs

▸ To print files from within an application, simply follow the application's normal printing procedures (make sure the application is configured to print to a network printer).

▸ In NDPS, to cancel or move a print job, use the NetWare Administrator utility or the Printer Manager utility, select the printer, and then open that printer's list of print jobs.

▸ In queue-based printing, to cancel or move a print job that's already in a print queue, use PCONSOLE (select Print Queues, select the queue, and then choose Print Jobs) or the NetWare Administrator utility (select the Print Queue object, choose Details from the Object menu, and then open the Job List page).

How NetWare Printing Works

NetWare print services allow your network users to share printers that are connected to the network. With NetWare print services loaded, you can increase productivity and save on hardware expenses by allowing users to share a smaller number of printers than you would have to buy if each user had a standalone printer. (You may also be able to buy a single, more sophisticated printer instead of multiple lesser-quality printers.) In addition, users don't have to waste time waiting for printers to complete their print jobs before they can resume using an application, as they often do when printing to a directly connected standalone printer.

Another benefit is that users can send their print jobs to different printers for different purposes, without having to copy the file they want to print onto a diskette and then physically moving to a different workstation.

NetWare print services also enable you to prioritize print jobs, so important print jobs are sent to the printer ahead of less-important print jobs.

In standalone printing, a printer is connected directly to the serial or parallel port (usually LPT1) on the workstation. When the user prints a file, the print job goes from the application to the print driver, which formats the job for the specific printer. (The print driver is software that converts the print job into a format that the printer can understand.) Next the print job goes to the LPT port, and then directly to the printer. Often, the application has to wait until the print job is finished before it can resume working.

With NetWare print services, the print job goes to the network instead of directly to the printer, though this process is transparent to users. Then the network takes care of sending the print job to the correct printer.

NetWare 5 provides two different ways to set up your printing services: NDPS (NetWare Distributed Print Services) and queue-based printing. NDPS is the preferred method.

NDPS is a new printing system designed by Novell, Hewlett-Packard, and Xerox that provides advanced printing features. Queue-based printing is the older system used in all previous versions of NetWare.

If you have been using earlier versions of NetWare, you're familiar with queue-based printing. If you would like to continue using queue-based printing, you can. NetWare 5 fully supports queue-based printing, and you can keep using this system if you'd like.

The newer printing service, NDPS, is fully compatible with existing queue-based printing. You can install NDPS and have it support existing print queues. Or, if you prefer, you can install only NDPS, so that all of your printing is handled through this newer architecture.

The first half of this chapter explains NDPS. The second half of this chapter explains queue-based printing.

NDPS Printing

Novell Distributed Print Services (NDPS) is the newest printing system that Novell has developed in conjunction with Hewlett-Packard and Xerox. In addition to providing normal network printing capabilities, NDPS also includes the following new features that weren't available in queue-based printing:

▸ Bidirectional communication so you can communicate with the printer and the printer can communicate with you

▸ Event notification, so the printer can notify appropriate personnel when something occurs (such as the printer running out of toner)

▸ Automatic downloading of printer drivers and other printing resources to workstations that need them (such as fonts, banners, or printer definition files)

In addition, NDPS software can be embedded directly into a printer by the printer manufacturer. That way, future printers can be smarter, providing more customized features to communicate with users effectively. These printers will be called "NDPS-aware" in this chapter, to distinguish them from existing printers that do not have NDPS software embedded.

NDPS is fully compatible with older queue-based network printing, so you can easily support existing queues and printers if you're installing NetWare 5 into an existing network.

Understanding NDPS Printing

Before installing NDPS printing, it's important to have a good understanding of the components that make up NDPS. The following sections explain the NDPS components, how to use those components with the types of printers you have, and the difference between public access and controlled access printers.

NDPS Components

In a NetWare network, you can have multiple printers all working at the same time, and users from all over the network may be sending print jobs to those printers simultaneously. To take care of all that traffic and potential conflicts, NDPS uses the following software components, which are explained in the following sections:

▶ Printer agents

▶ Gateways

▶ The NDPS Manager

▶ The NDPS Broker

NDPS Printer Agents A printer agent is a software entity that manages a printer. Every printer must have its own unique printer agent. An NDPS-aware printer has a printer agent embedded in the printer itself. (While few printers like this will be available when NetWare 5 first ships, more should be released soon.) All other printers must have a printer agent created on the server.

The printer agent for a printer performs the following tasks:

▶ It manages the printer's print jobs.

▶ It answers client queries about print jobs or printer attributes (such as whether the printer supports color printing).

▶ It receives notification from the printer when something goes wrong, or when a requested event occurs.

▶ It services existing queues from queue-based printing setups, so the NDPS printer can print jobs from those queues.

Gateways If a printer requires that a printer agent be installed on the server (in other words, if the printer is not NDPS-aware), the printer also must have a gateway installed. The gateway is software that translates NDPS commands into language the printer can interpret.

Eventually, most printer manufacturers may have their own specific gateways to support their existing non-NDPS printers. At this point, there are three available inside NetWare 5: one from HP, one from Xerox, and a generic gateway from Novell. Manufacturer-specific gateways will offer more features customized for their specific printers. Novell's generic gateway will work for all printers, but may provide fewer features.

For more information about the Hewlett-Packard and Xerox gateways included in NetWare 5, see the Novell online documentation.

Gateways aren't necessary for NDPS-aware printers (those that have their own printer agents embedded).

NDPS Manager The NDPS Manager is the software program that controls all the printer agents on a server. (If you're familiar with queue-based printing, the NDPS Manager is similar to the print server.)

You load the NDPS Manager by loading an NLM on the server. Then you create an NDS object for it so you can manage it from the NetWare Administrator utility.

If all of your printers are NDPS-aware and have embedded printer agents, you will not need this NDSP Manager. It's only required for printer agents that reside on the server.

NDPS Broker The NDPS Broker is an NLM loaded on the server. The Broker NLM is loaded and a corresponding NDS object is created during the NetWare server's installation. The Broker manages centralized printing services for all the printers on the network. It provides three services:

▶ *Resource Management Service.* This service stores printing resources (mainly printer drivers, fonts, banners, and printer definition files) in a central location on the network. When a workstation needs a new printer driver, for example, the Broker automatically downloads that driver from this central location.

▶ *Event Notification Service.* This service receives the event notifications that come from the printer agents, and sends the notification out to users via predetermined methods. Users (or the administrator, or anyone else that has been specified) can be notified of printer events by NetWare pop-up messages on a workstation screen, in log files, via GroupWise e-mail, or by other delivery methods that can be defined or developed.

▶ *Service Registry Service.* This service enables public access printers to advertise themselves and their attributes (such as make, model, and address) so users can locate them. Public access printers are described later in this chapter.

NDPS Brokers are created automatically by the regular NetWare server installation. However, because a Broker doesn't need to exist on every single server in the network, the installation program analyzes each server to determine whether the Broker needs to be installed.

If an existing Broker is within three hops of the server you're currently installing, the installation program will not install a Broker automatically on this server. If the nearest existing Broker is four or more hops away, the installation program will install a Broker on this server. (A *hop* is simply the connection between two servers.) Figure 9.1 illustrates this concept.

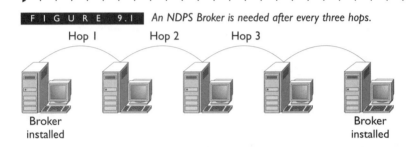

| F I G U R E   9 . 1 | *An NDPS Broker is needed after every three hops.* |

Hop 1   Hop 2   Hop 3

Broker   Broker
installed   installed

In addition to the "three-hop" guideline, there may be other situations where you want to have the installation program create a Broker. For example, you may want to have two Brokers on a network for reliability — if one server goes down, the Broker will still exist on the other server.

If your network is spread across a large geographical area and is connected by phone lines, you should plan to have a Broker at each site. This lets the Broker handle local network traffic more efficiently.

Which NDPS Components Do You Need?

To quickly summarize, if all the printers on your network are NDPS-aware, meaning they have NDPS printer agents embedded in them, the only NDPS software component you need on your network is an NDPS Broker. The Broker handles event notification, service registry to advertise public access printers, and automatic downloading of printer drivers and other resources. (You may need more than one Broker, depending on the size of your network.)

If at least some of your printers are non-NDPS printers, you need to create:

- ▶ A printer agent for each non-NDPS printer
- ▶ A gateway so the non-NDPS printer can communicate with NDPS
- ▶ An NDPS Manager to manage the printer agents on the server
- ▶ An NDSP Broker

Public Access Printers versus Controlled Access Printers

When you install a printer with NDPS, you can choose to make the printer available to users in one of two ways. You can make the printer a public access printer, or you can make it a controlled access printer.

A public access printer doesn't have an object in the NDS tree. It only has a printer agent. As soon as the printer agent is created for this printer, the printer is immediately available to anyone on the network. Because there is no printer NDS object for this printer, it isn't subject to the same security measures and other controls as NDS objects. This public access printer advertises itself to users through the Broker, and users can locate it by using the Novell Printer Manager utility from their workstations.

You create a public access printer by using the NDPS Manager object in NetWare Administrator to create a printer agent for the printer.

Because they are installed so simply and don't exist in the NDS tree, public access printers are also limited in the NDPS features they support. For example, they are only capable of job notification, rather than the full gamut of event notifications.

If you want a printer to support all the features of NDPS, you can create it as a controlled access printer. To do this, you create an NDPS Printer object for the printer in the NDS tree. When you create this printer object, the printer agent is created automatically. Once the printer has its own object, it can be controlled by NDS trustee rights and managed through NetWare Administrator's Browser like any other object. It can also take advantage of all NDPS features. A controlled access printer can also be configured to service existing print queues.

You can easily convert a public access printer to a controlled access printer at any time, just by creating an NDPS Printer object for the printer.

To summarize, a public access printer does not have an object in the NDS tree and doesn't take advantage of all NDPS features, but it's available to everyone on the entire network, regardless of their trustee rights. A controlled access printer is represented in the NDS tree by an NDPS Printer object, supports all NDPS features, and can only be accessed by users with appropriate NDS trustee rights.

Planning NDPS Printing

As you plan your NDPS printing setup, keep in mind the following information about NDPS:

▸ NDPS supports IP, IPX, and mixed networks. If both protocols are available, NDPS will default to using IP.

▸ NDPS is fully compatible with queue-based printing. If you already have queues created from an existing system, you can assign a printer agent to accept jobs from one or more of those queues.

▸ To take advantage of NDPS printing, workstations must use the version of NetWare client software included in your NetWare 5 package (or download the new client software from Novell's Web site). See Chapter 4 for more information about installing updated NetWare client software.

▸ Only Windows 3.1, Windows 95/98, and Windows NT clients have been updated to support NDPS features at this time. Macintosh, OS/2, and DOS workstations must continue to send jobs to queues. (Of course, because NDPS printing supports queues, you can still install NDPS on your network — you'll just need to keep the queue-based printing system in place simultaneously.)

▸ You can perform some NDPS activities from more than one tool. For example, you can create a printer agent from the server console (using NDPSM.NLM), from an NDPS gateway, or from the NetWare Administrator utility. In general, this chapter explains how to accomplish tasks from the NetWare Administrator utility, because that is usually the most common and easiest way.

If you consider each of the following suggestions before beginning the installation process, your NDPS installation may go more smoothly:

▸ If you're upgrading a network from a previous version of NetWare, you may find it easiest to install NDPS, and then make sure that all of the existing queues are assigned to new NDPS printer agents. That way, all of your users can continue to print normally using their existing client software on their workstations. Then you can upgrade those workstations to the new NDPS-aware client software at your leisure.

▸ Although NDPS doesn't use print queues, you may still want to configure each printer agent so it has space on a volume to store files that are waiting to be printed. (This is called *job spooling*.)

▸ Decide which printers you want to make public access printers, and which ones you want to make controlled access printers.

▸ Decide which printers you want to be "installed" on users' workstations automatically (which basically consists of automatically downloading the appropriate printer driver to the workstations). You will need to make sure those printers' drivers are added to the Broker's

Resource Management database. (If a user needs a printer driver that isn't in the database, he or she can install the driver from a diskette or other site, just as users have done in the past.)

▶ Plan which servers need to have an NDPS Broker installed. Plan for at least one Broker per geographic site (two Brokers per site is better, in case one server goes down). Also, any server should be no more than three hops away from a Broker.

▶ Create an NDPS Manager object on each server that will control NDPS printers. (One NDPS Manager can support an unlimited number of printer agents.) You may want to assign printer agents on one server to multiple NDPS Manager objects (on other servers) to make sure that if one server goes down, network users can still print. Assigning printer agents to multiple NDPS Managers also helps balance the load of printing traffic. (However, you should keep printer agents assigned to NDPS Managers within the same geographical site, so that printing traffic isn't going across phone lines unnecessarily.)

▶ After NDPS has been fully implemented and you no longer need to support print queues on your network, remove all CAPTURE commands from batch files, login scripts, AUTOEXEC.BAT files, or other locations. (Do not remove CAPTURE commands until all of the workstation's dependencies on queues have been removed, however.)

▶ Decide which roles you want your users to fulfill. Users can be assigned three separate roles for working with NDPS printers: Manager, Operator, and User. A Manager has full control over printing, and can change or delete Printer objects, assign other Managers, Operators, or Users, configure event notification, and so on. An Operator can control assigned printers, but can't modify NDS objects. A User can send print jobs to a printer, and can modify or delete his or her own print jobs only.

The following sections explain how to install and manage NDPS printing on your network.

Installing NDPS Printing

Several steps are involved with installing NDPS printing on your NetWare 5 network. The following sections explain how to:

▶ Set up the NDPS Broker on a server, and add printer drivers to it if necessary.

▶ Create the NDPS Manager.

▶ Create a public access printer or a controlled access printer (controlled access printers can also be configured to service print queues).

▶ Install printer support on workstations.

Setting Up the NDPS Broker

The easiest way to set up the NDPS Broker on a server is to do it while you're installing the server itself. At the end of the server installation program, you are given the option to install "additional products." One of the products listed is NDPS.

If you choose to install NDPS, the installation program will copy all the necessary NDPS files to the server and, by default, create an NDPS Broker object in the NDS tree. All three of the Broker's services (Resource Management Service, Event Notification Service, and Service Registry Service) are enabled.

NOTE If you want to turn off one or more of the Broker's services, or if you want to prevent the Broker from being installed on this server, click the Customize button at the end of the server installation. From there, you can choose NDPS, and make these modifications before the installation is finished. Chapter 2 explains more fully how to customize the server installation.

After the server is installed, the server's ConsoleOne screen appears. Press Alt+Esc to toggle between the ConsoleOne screen and other active screens on the server. One of the active screens will be the NDPS Broker screen. This screen shows you that the Broker NLM is loaded and active, and that all three services are enabled.

During installation, a command to load the Broker NLM is automatically added to the server's AUTOEXEC.NCF file so it will be loaded every time the server is rebooted.

If you did not install NDPS when you first installed the server, you can install it at any time. Load the NWCONFIG.NLM on the server by typing the following command at the server's console:

```
NWCONFIG
```

Then, from the list of options that appears, select Product Options. Then select Choose an Item or Product Listed Above. Next, select Install Other Novell Products. You will need to insert the *NetWare 5 Operating System* CD-ROM and specify the path to the CD-ROM to install NDPS. The screen will then display a list of available products you can install. Select NDPS, click Next, and follow the prompts to install it.

NOTE

You can move a Broker object to a different container, if necessary, by using the NetWare Administrator utility to move the object to the container you choose. (To move an object, hold down the Ctrl key while dragging the object to the new container.) If you move a Broker object and want a different server to load BROKER.NLM, you need to manually edit the new server's AUTOEXEC.NCF file to include the LOAD BROKER command. (You also need to edit the old server's AUTOEXEC.NCF file to delete the same command.)

Adding Printer Drivers or Other Resources to the Broker NetWare 5 ships with many printer drivers for common printers. However, this is not a complete set of all available printer drivers that exist in the market, so you should make sure that the printer drivers you need for your printers are included. If they are not in the Broker's database, you can add them from the manufacturer's diskette (or some other source).

You can also add other resources, such as banner pages, to the Broker using the same procedure.

To see the list of existing printer drivers (or other resources), and to add a driver to the list, complete the following steps:

1. From any workstation, log in to the network as user Admin, and launch the NetWare Administrator utility.

2. From the NetWare Administrator's Browser window, double-click the Broker object (or select the Broker object and choose Details from the Option menu).

3. Open the Resource Management (RMS) page, shown in Figure 9.2.

4. Click the Add Resources button.

5. Choose the icon for the type of resource (such as Windows 95/98 Printer Drivers) you want to see (or add). A list appears, showing all resources of that type that are currently loaded.

6. If the driver you need does not appear, click Add. You can click the Browse button to search for the location of the driver you want to add.

7. Enter the appropriate information about the printer driver, and follow prompts as they appear. You need to supply the driver on a diskette or from some other location.

8. Click OK.

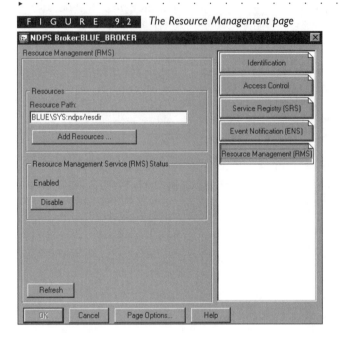

F I G U R E 9.2 *The Resource Management page*

Now the new printer driver will appear in the list of available printer drivers in the Resource Management database.

Disabling a Broker Service By default, all three of the Broker's services are enabled when the Broker is installed. If you want to disable (or re-enable) a service, you can disable it from the Broker NLM's console screen on the server.

You can also use the NetWare Administrator utility to disable (or re-enable) a Broker service. From the NetWare Administrator's Browser window, select the Broker object. Open the page for the service you want to disable, and then click the Disable button.

Only disable a Broker service if you're sure you do not need that service on your network, or if that service is available on another server that is no more than three hops away.

Creating the NDPS Manager on a Server

To create an NDPS Manager on your server, you have to create an NDPS Manager object in the NDS tree, and then load NDPSM.NLM on the server. To do this, complete the following steps:

1. From any workstation, log in to the network as user Admin, and launch the NetWare Administrator utility.

2. To create the NDPS Manager object in the NDS tree, open the NetWare Administrator's Browser screen and select the container object that will contain the NDPS Manager.

3. From the Object menu, choose Create.

4. Select NDPS Manager from the list of class objects that appears.

5. In the Create NDPS Manager Object screen, enter the name you want to give this NDPS Manager object. (If you have a queue-based print server running on the network, be sure you don't give the NDPS Manager object the same name as the print server, or both will be advertising the same name, creating a conflict.) See Figure 9.3.

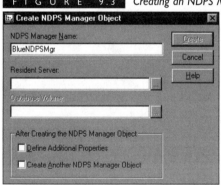

FIGURE 9.3 *Creating an NDPS Manager object*

6. In the Resident Server field, enter the server where this NDPS Manager and its database of information will be located. (Click the Browse button to search for the server in the tree.)

7. In the Database Volume field, enter the name of the volume that will hold the NDPS Manager's database. (This volume must be located on the Resident Server you selected in Step 6.) The volume you select should have at least 5MB of disk space available for this database.

8. Click Create. The NDPS Manager object has now been created, and will appear in the Browser window the next time you open it.

9. Go to the server and load NDPSM.NLM on the server by typing the following command, substituting the new NDPS Manager object's full name for *name*:

LOAD NDPSM *name*

(If the NDPS Manager's object name contains spaces, use underscores instead of the spaces in the name.)

10. To make sure NDPSM.NLM loads every time the server is rebooted, add the same command to the server's AUTOEXEC.NCF file.

NOTE

When you load the NDPSM module on the server, a console screen will appear, showing any created printer agents. You can manage the NDPS Manager from this screen if you like. However, you can also manage the NDPS Manager from the NetWare Administrator utility, which is often easier to use. For consistency, this chapter discusses only the NetWare Administrator approach to managing NDPS printing.

Creating Network Printers

When you are ready to create network printers, you must first decide whether to create public access printers or controlled access printers. (You can convert a public access printer to a controlled access printer at any time.) The following sections explain how to create each type of printer, and how to convert a public access printer to a controlled access printer.

Creating a Public Access Printer To create a public access printer, you will use the NDPS Manager object to create a printer agent and select a gateway for the printer. Use the NetWare Administrator utility, as explained in the following steps:

1. From any workstation, log in to the network as user Admin, and launch the NetWare Administrator utility.

2. From the NetWare Administrator's Browser window, double-click the NDPS Manager object (or select the NDPS Manager object and choose Details from the Option menu).

3. Open the Printer Agent List page. (If asked to choose a printer agent list, select the one you need to use.) A list of any current printer agents is displayed.

4. Click New.

5. In the Printer Agent (PA) Name field, enter a name for the new printer agent you are creating.

6. Choose the Gateway Type you want to use. Hewlett-Packard and Xerox have provided gateways in NetWare 5 for use with some of their printers. The generic Novell printer gateway is provided for all other printers. See the Novell online documentation for more information about the HP and Xerox gateways if you have one of their printers.

7. Click OK.

8. Choose the printer type and port type for your printer, and select any other information necessary for your printer (such as the connection type). This information varies depending on the gateway you selected. (If you are installing a printer that attached directly to the network, such as a JetDirect printer, and you have to choose between installing it in Queue Server mode or in Remote Printer mode, choose Remote Printer mode.)

9. Choose the printer drivers necessary for each workstation operating system that your users may be using (Windows 3.1, Windows 95/98, or Windows NT). You can choose more than one driver if necessary. If you select None, users will have to provide the printer driver on a diskette the first time they install this printer on their workstation. (If the printer driver you want is not in the driver list, you can add it to the Broker's Resource Management Service, as explained earlier in this chapter.)

10. Click Continue. A new printer agent has now been created for this printer, and the printer is now available to anyone on the network.

NOTE You can also create a public access printer by using a gateway provided by a printer manufacturer, or by using NDPSM.NLM at the server console. See the Novell online documentation or the manufacturer's documentation for more information about these methods.

To manage a public access printer, use the Tools menu from the NetWare Administrator utility.

You can convert a public access printer to a controlled access printer at any time. To do this, refer to the section "Converting a Public Access Printer to a Controlled Access Printer," later in this chapter.

Creating a Controlled Access Printer To create a controlled access printer, you need to create an NDPS Printer object in the NDS tree. (You must have already created an NDPS Manager object.) You can configure an NDPS Printer object so that it services existing print queues.

Use the NetWare Administrator utility to create a controlled access printer, as explained in the following steps:

1. From any workstation, log in to the network as user Admin, and launch the NetWare Administrator utility.

2. Open the NetWare Administrator's Browser screen and select the container object that will contain the NDPS Printer object.

3. From the Object menu, select Create.

4. Choose NDPS Printer from the list that appears and click OK.

5. In the NDPS Printer Name field, enter a name for this Printer object.

6. Under Printer Agent Source, click Create a New Printer Agent, and then click Create.

7. Choose the name you want to use for the new printer agent. The default name is the same as the new Printer object you're creating. See Figure 9.4.

► • ◄

F I G U R E   9 . 4   *Specifying information for an NDPS Printer object*

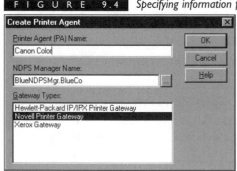

8. Assign the printer agent to an NDPS Manager object. (Click the Browse button to search the tree for the NDPS Manager you want to use.)

9. Choose the gateway you want to use. Hewlett-Packard and Xerox have provided gateways in NetWare 5 for use with some of their printers.

The generic Novell printer gateway is provided for all other printers. See the Novell online documentation for more information about the HP and Xerox gateways if you have one of their printers.

10. Click OK.

11. Choose the printer type and the port type for your printer. (The Novell port handler may be adequate for most printers.)

12. Select any other information necessary for your printer. This information varies depending on the gateway you selected. If asked to select the connection type, choose Local Printer only if the printer is attached directly to the server where the NDPS Manager is loaded. Choose Manual only if you want to manually build the port handler string. Choose Queue-based to support printers and print systems that require print jobs to be sent to queues. If you are installing a printer that is attached directly to the network, such as a JetDirect printer, and you have to choose between installing it in Queue Server mode or in Remote Printer mode, choose Remote Printer mode (and specify whether you're using IPX or TCPIP). When finished making selections, click Finish.

13. Choose the printer drivers necessary for each workstation operating system that your users may be using (Windows 3.1, Windows 95/98, or Windows NT). You can choose more than one driver, if necessary. If you select None, users will have to provide the printer driver on a diskette the first time they install this printer on their workstation. (If the printer driver you want is not in the driver list, you can add it to the Broker's Resource Management Service, as explained earlier in this chapter.)

14. Click Continue. The new controlled access printer is now available on the network for anyone with the appropriate NDS trustee rights to access it.

15. Make sure the new printer's job spooling area on the server's volume is set up the way you want it to be. Double-click the new NDPS Printer object in the Browser window. Click Jobs, and select Spooling Configuration. You can change the location of the spooling area (the default is the same volume as the NDPS Manager information), the maximum size of the spooling area's disk space, and the schedule that determines the order in which jobs are printed.

16. If you want this printer to service print queues, go to the same Spooling Configuration screen (described in Step 15). Under Service Jobs from NetWare Queues, click Add. Then choose the print queues you want this printer to service. Click OK. Now this printer can service those existing print queues.

Converting a Public Access Printer to a Controlled Access Printer
You can convert a public access printer to a controlled access printer at any time. To do this, you create an NDPS Printer object in the NDS tree, and assign it to the printer agent that was created when you first installed this public access printer. Use the NetWare Administrator utility, as explained in the following steps:

1. From any workstation, log in to the network as user Admin, and launch the NetWare Administrator utility.

2. Open the NetWare Administrator's Browser screen and select the container object that will contain the NDPS Printer object you are about to create for this printer.

3. From the Object menu, select Create.

4. Choose NDPS Printer from the list that appears, and then click OK.

5. In the NDPS Printer Name field, enter a name for this Printer object.

6. In the Printer Agent Source field, click Public Access Printer, and then click Create. (You'll receive a message warning you that you will have to reinstall this printer support on every workstation that has used it. Click OK to continue.)

7. From the list of public access printers that appears, choose the public access printer you want to convert, and click OK. The new controlled access printer is now available on the network for anyone with the appropriate NDS trustee rights to access it.

8. Make sure the new printer's job spooling area on the server's volume is set up the way you want it to be. Double-click the new NDPS Printer object in the Browser window. Click Jobs, and select Spooling Configuration. You can change the location of the spooling area (the default is the same volume as the NDPS Manager information), the maximum size of the spooling area's disk space, and the schedule that determines the order in which jobs are printed.

9. If you want this printer to service print queues, go to the same Spooling Configuration screen (described in Step 8). Under Service

Jobs from NetWare Queues, click Add. Then choose the print queues you want this printer to service. Click OK. Now this printer can service those existing print queues.

Installing Printer Support on Workstations

With NDPS, you can designate specific printer drivers to be automatically downloaded and installed on users' workstations, so the users don't have to worry about installing their own printer support. The printers you specify will appear automatically on the user's installed printers list. The feature that lets you designate the printers that should be installed automatically on workstations is called Remote Printer Management. You can also use Remote Printer Management to designate which printer should be a user's default printer, and to remove printers from workstations.

You aren't required to designate printers to download and install automatically. Users can also install printer support manually. However, you will probably find that it saves time to designate automatic downloads instead.

With Remote Printer Management, you configure printer drivers and other information you want to be installed. When a user logs in, the workstation software checks the user's container object for any new printer information. If new printer information (such as a new driver to be downloaded) exists, the workstation is automatically updated.

Automatically Installing Printer Support You can access Remote Printer Management in one of three ways, depending on how many printers you want to manage for a given task:

- ▶ To manage all of the printers in a single container, select the container object in NetWare Administrator, and choose Details from the Object menu. Then open the NDPS Remote Printer Management page.

- ▶ To manage a single controlled access printer, select that NDPS Printer object in NetWare Administrator, and choose Details from the Object menu. Then open the NDPS Remote Printer Management page.

- ▶ To manage a single public access printer, use the Tools menu in NetWare Administrator and select NDPS Public Access Printers. Select the printer, and choose Details from the Object menu. Next, open the NDPS Remote Printer Management page.

After you access the Remote Printer Management feature for the container or printer you selected, you can designate the printers you want to automatically download and install on workstations. You can also specify default printers for the users.

Manually Installing Printer Support If a required printer driver isn't automatically downloaded, users can still install the printer support on their workstations manually. They can either install a printer driver from a diskette, or they can install a public access or controlled access printer that resides on the network (the drivers for these printers will be in the NDPS Broker's database).

There are two ways to install printer support manually on a workstation:

- ► Using the Add Printers feature in Windows 95/98 and Windows NT. (Windows 3.1 workstations can't use this option.)
- ► Using a Novell utility called Novell Printer Manager.

To use the Windows Add Printers feature, click Start, then Settings, and then Printers. Then click the Add Printers icon and follow the instructions to load the printer driver on the workstation.

To use the Novell Printer Manager utility to manually install printer support on the workstation, complete the following steps:

1. Launch the Printer Manager utility by using the Windows Run command. For a Windows 3.1 workstation, run the file called NWPMW16.EXE, located in the PUBLIC folder on volume SYS. For Windows 95/98 and Windows NT workstations, run the file called NWPMW32.EXE, located in the WIN32 folder, which is in the PUBLIC folder on volume SYS.

2. From the Printer menu, select New. A list appears, showing any printers that are already installed on this workstation. It also shows this workstation's default printer.

3. Click Add. A list appears, showing all available public access printers and all of the controlled access printers in your context. To see controlled access printers in other parts of the NDS tree, click the Browse button.

4. Choose the printer you want to install on your workstation, and click Install.

5. If you wish, change the printer name and choose a printer configuration that matches your needs.

6. Click OK. The printer driver for the printer should download automatically. If the printer driver is not available, you will need to provide a diskette or alternate location for the driver.

7. Click Close to finish.

Managing NDPS Printers

After NDPS printers have been installed, managing them is relatively easy.

To manage controlled access printers, use the NetWare Administrator utility and double-click the NDPS Printer object. When the Details page for the printer opens, you can add or modify information about it, such as assigning operators or users, filling in a description of the printer, and so on. You can also configure the printer so that print job owners are notified of events that occur with their print jobs. In addition, you can use the Access Control Notification feature to enable notification to be sent to "interested parties," such as the printer's Manager or Operator.

To manage a public access printer, you also use the NetWare Administrator utility. However, instead of opening a printer object (because there's no printer object for a public access printer), you pull down the Tools menu, and select NDPS Public Access Printers. Select the printer you want to manage, and then choose Details from the Object menu.

Users who want to see information about network printers can use the Novell Printer Manager utility. Users can launch the Printer Manager utility by using the Windows Run command. (Windows 95/98 and NT users may want to create a shortcut to the Printer Manager utility.) The executable file a user must run depends on the workstation's operating system:

▶ For a Windows 3.1 workstation, run the file called NWPMW16.EXE, located in the PUBLIC folder on volume SYS.

▶ For Windows 95/98 and Windows NT workstations, run the file called NWPMW32.EXE, located in the WIN32 folder, which is in the PUBLIC folder on volume SYS.

The main Printer Manager window displays all the NDPS printers currently installed on the workstation. From here, users can add more printers to their workstation, if necessary.

In addition, the Printer Manager utility displays information about the printer, such as its status, its attributes (such as whether it prints in color), any problems with the printer (such as a paper jam or low toner), and so on. Users can also use the Printer Manager utility to see and change the status of their print jobs, as explained in the next section.

Managing NDPS Print Jobs

Users can use either the NetWare Administrator utility or the Printer Manager utility to see the status of their print jobs. They can also change certain aspects of their own print jobs, such as canceling them or putting them on hold. Printer users can only change their own jobs. Printer Operators can change print jobs for any users on a printer.

From either the NetWare Administrator or the Printer Manager, select the printer whose jobs you want to see and select Details from the Object menu to open the main Printer Control page. Then click Jobs and select Job List.

When the list of all active jobs appears, you can perform any of the following tasks:

- ▶ To see information about the print job, highlight the job, and click Information. This displays the job's status, details, owner, submission date and time, and size.

- ▶ To see which print jobs have been processed but retained (put on hold), click Show Retained Jobs.

- ▶ To copy or move a job to another location, select the job, and click Job Options. Then choose Copy (or Move) and specify the new location.

- ▶ To see or change the properties of a job, select the job, click Job Options, and then click Configuration. Click each tab to see the different properties of this job.

- ▶ To delete a job, select the job, and click Job Options. Then choose Cancel Printing.

- ▶ To change the order of print jobs waiting to be printed, select Job Options, and then select Reorder. Select the job you want to move and specify the position to which you want to move it (you can only move jobs down the list).

Queue-Based Printing

Queue-based printing is the printing system that has been used in NetWare for years. Although NDPS is the newest printing system created by Novell, queue-based printing is still a strong, reliable printing option. If you have been using queue-based printing in previous versions of NetWare and don't feel the need for the newer features offered by NDPS, rest assured that you can safely retain queue-based printing in NetWare 5.

Understanding Queue-Based Printing

Before planning and installing queue-based printing, let's look at the components and processes that make up NetWare queue-based printing. The following sections explain how queue-based printing works.

Print Queues and Print Servers

In queue-based printing, NetWare employs two features, called print queues and print servers, to move the print job from the workstation to the printer. The *print queue* is a special network directory that stores print jobs temporarily before they are printed. Multiple network users can have their jobs stored in the same print queue. The print queue receives all incoming print jobs from various users, and stores them in a first-come, first-served order.

The *print server* is a software program, called PSERVER.NLM, that runs on the NetWare server. The print server controls how the print queues and printers work together. The print server takes the jobs from the print queue and forwards them on to the printer when the printer is available.

You can have more than one print queue on a network. Further, you can set up one print queue so that it services several printers (although this can be confusing because you never know which printer will print the job you send). You can also set up a single printer so that it services several print queues. However, it generally simplifies your administration tasks and reduces your users' confusion if you use a one-to-one correspondence between print queues and printers, so that each print queue sends jobs to its own printer.

When you set up NetWare queue-based print services, you assign a printer, a print server, and a print queue to each other. Then you redirect the workstation's parallel port to point to a network print queue instead of to a directly attached printer.

To redirect the workstation's LPT port, you can use the NetWare utility called CAPTURE (usually placing the CAPTURE command in a login script so it is executed automatically). You can also use the NetWare User Tools utility (which runs under Windows 3.1) to assign LPT1 to a print queue.

Alternatively, most network-aware applications let you set them up so they redirect print jobs to a print queue themselves. In many cases, you can simply specify a printer in the application, and because the printer, print queue, and print server are all assigned to each other, the job is sent automatically to the correct print queue.

Where Can Printers Be Attached?

NetWare queue-based print services allow printers to be attached directly to the server, attached to various workstations on the network, or attached directly to the network cabling (this last option is currently the most common).

If you attach printers directly to the NetWare server, the server must run an NLM called NPRINTER.NLM. This NLM is a port driver, which is software that routes jobs out of the print queue, through the proper port on the server, and to the printer.

If you attach printers to workstations on the network, those workstations must also be running a port driver, called NPRINTER.EXE (for DOS and Windows 3.1), and NPTWIN95.EXE (for Windows 95 and Windows 98). The workstation's version of NPRINTER or NPTWIN95 works the same way as the server's version, sending print jobs through the port on the workstation to the printer.

Workstations that have printers attached can still be used by workstation users to do regular, day-to-day work. The workstation simply acts as a connection to the network for that printer.

The workstation attached to the printer should still redirect its own LPT1 port to the network so that it uses network printing services like all the other workstations instead of printing directly to the printer. Even if there is a printer attached directly to the workstation, it is usually more efficient to send the print job from the workstation to a network print queue, and then back to the printer. This also allows other workstations to use the printer.

Currently, the most common type of printing connection is to use printers that connect directly to the network cabling, rather than to a server or a workstation. These types of printers, often called *network-direct printers*, may run in either remote printer mode or queue server mode.

Remote printer mode lets the printer function as if it were running its own NPRINTER port driver. It doesn't need to be connected to a workstation; its internal NPRINTER-like software lets it be controlled by the NetWare print server and allows it to take advantage of NDS functionality.

The bindery-based *queue server mode* is used when the printer device has not been designed to work with NDS. This means that you must take care to install the printers, print queues, and the network-direct print devices in the same bindery context. In addition, there may be other restrictions that affect these devices. Be sure to read the manufacturer's documentation for more information about installing these devices.

The Print Job's Journey

With NetWare queue-based print services, the journey of a print job follows this path:

▸ The application works with the print driver to format the print job, just as it does in standalone mode.

▸ Instead of going through the LPT port directly to a printer, the print job is redirected to a print queue. If you specify that one print job goes to one printer and another job goes to a second printer, they will both be redirected from the LPT port to the correct print queues.

▸ When the printer is available, the print server takes the print job from the print queue and sends it to the port driver (such as NPTWIN95.EXE, NPRINTER.EXE, or NPRINTER.NLM) running wherever the printer is connected.

▸ The port driver then sends the print job to the printer, and the job is printed.

Figure 9.5 illustrates the path a print job takes through the network. In this particular example, the printer is attached to a workstation that is running NPRINTER.EXE.

Planning Queue-Based Printing

When you plan how to set up NetWare queue-based print services, keep the following guidelines and restrictions in mind:

▸ In general, PSERVER.NLM uses about 27K of server RAM for each configured printer.

▸ PSERVER.NLM can service DOS, UNIX, and Macintosh printers.

▸ A single print server can service up to 255 printers, although performance begins to degrade after about 60 printers or so.

▸ If you need more than one print server in your network, you can load PSERVER.NLM on additional NetWare servers, and those print servers can service more network printers.

▸ Printers, print queues, and print servers are all created as NDS objects in the Directory tree.

▸ To set up and manage print services, you can use the NetWare Administrator utility, which runs on Windows 95/98 and Windows NT.

FIGURE 9.5 *A print job's path through the network*

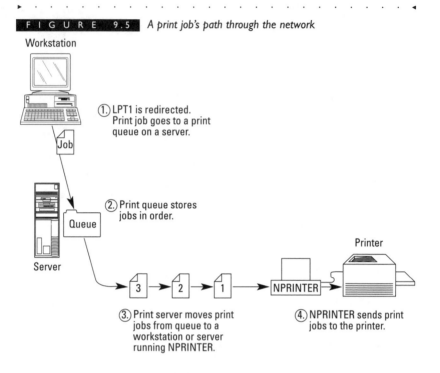

Workstation

1. LPT1 is redirected. Print job goes to a print queue on a server.

2. Print queue stores jobs in order.

Queue

Server

Printer

3 → 2 → 1 → NPRINTER →

3. Print server moves print jobs from queue to a workstation or server running NPRINTER.

4. NPRINTER sends print jobs to the printer.

► When you use the CAPTURE utility to redirect an LPT port to a network print queue, you can also use CAPTURE to specify options such as whether or not to print a banner page, whether to use tabs, and so on.

► Instead of using CAPTURE, you may prefer to set up print job configurations. A print job configuration can simplify a user's task of selecting print options by predefining settings such as the designated printer, whether to print a banner page, and the paper form to print on. Print job configurations are stored in databases. Global (or public) print job configuration databases are properties of container objects, and they can be used by multiple users. A private print job configuration database is a property of a user object and can be used only by that user. To create a print job configuration, you can use the NetWare Administrator.

▶ To define print devices and paper forms to be used in print job configurations, you can use the NetWare Administrator utility. (If the application you are using supports your printer, you do not need to define a print device.)

▶ To print a job from outside of an application (such as printing an ASCII file or a workstation screen), you can use a command-line utility called NPRINT, which runs in DOS.

As you plan your printing setup, decide how many printers you need and where you want to locate them. If you are going to attach printers to workstations, you may want to choose workstations that are not used as heavily as others are. In addition, it will be important for the users of those workstations to remember not to turn off the workstation when other users are using the network. Instead, those users should just log out of the network when they've finished using the workstation.

Installing NetWare Queue-Based Printing

There are two different ways to set up NetWare queue-based print services for your network:

▶ Use the Print Services Quick Setup option in the NetWare Administrator utility. This is the quickest, easiest way to set up print services. If you want to set up each printer to service a single print queue, which simplifies printing administration greatly, this is the installation option to use. This option also assigns printers, print servers, and print queues to each other automatically so there is no chance for you to miss a connection and end up with a broken link somewhere in the print communication chain. After you've set up printing using this quick option, you can modify the setup later.

▶ Use the NetWare Administrator utility to set up a custom print configuration for a more complex situation.

Using the Quick Setup Option

The Print Services Quick Setup option in the NetWare Administrator utility is a fast, efficient way to set up queue-based print services.

NOTE

The NetWare Administrator utility runs under Windows 95/98 or Windows NT. For instructions on setting up the NetWare Administrator utility on a workstation, see Chapter 5.

To set up print services using the Quick Setup option, complete the following steps:

1. Decide where you want to locate your printers and attach them to the server, workstations, or network cabling.

2. From any workstation, log in to the network as user Admin.

3. Launch the NetWare Administrator utility on the workstation.

4. Select the container object that will contain the print server, printers, and print queues. Quick Setup will put them all in the same container, which will be especially beneficial if users have to access the objects in bindery mode.

5. From the Tools menu, select the Print Services Quick Setup (Non-NDPS) option. The screen that appears shows the default names and information that NetWare Administrator will assign to the print server, printer, and print queue. See Figure 9.6 for an example of the Quick Setup screen.

6. If necessary, change the name of the print server, printer, or print queue.

► . . . . ◄

F I G U R E   9 . 6 *Print Services Quick Setup screen*

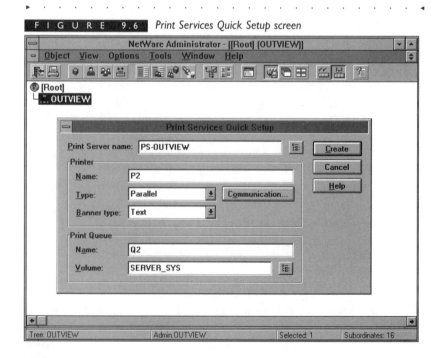

7. Choose the printer type you are using (parallel, serial, UNIX, AppleTalk, or AIO) and fill in any necessary information about that printer type. (If the printer will be attached directly to the network or to an OS/2 workstation, choose Other/Unknown.)

8. If necessary, choose a different volume in which to store the print queue.

9. Click Create.

10. Go to the network server that will run the print server (or use Remote Console to access that server's console) and load the print server software using the following command:

    ```
    LOAD PSERVER printserver
    ```

    where *printserver* is the name of the newly created print server. (Later, you can put the PSERVER command, along with the print server's name, in the NetWare server's AUTOEXEC.NCF file so it automatically loads when the server is rebooted.)

11. If the printer is attached to a network server that is not running PSERVER, load the NPRINTER.NLM on the network server, specifying the print server name and printer number in the NPRINTER command. (This command can also be placed in the NetWare server's AUTOEXEC.NCF file.) If you have more than one printer attached to this server, load NPRINTER multiple times, specifying a different printer number (and print server if necessary) for each printer. For example, to load NPRINTER for printer number 0, which uses print server PS-Tech, use the following command:

    ```
    LOAD NPRINTER PS-Tech 0
    ```

12. If the printer is attached to a workstation, run NPRINTER.EXE (for DOS and Windows 3.1) or NPTWIN95.EXE (for Windows 95/98) on that workstation.

    a. For DOS and Windows 3.1: Type **NPRINTER,** followed by the print server name and printer number in the command. (You can include this command in the workstation's AUTOEXEC.BAT file, after the login command.) For example, to load NPRINTER for printer number 0, which uses print server PS-Tech, use the following command:

       ```
       NPRINTER PS-Tech 0
       ```

b. For Windows 95/98: Start up the NetWare Client software on the workstation. From the Network Neighborhood, locate the NPTWIN95.EXE file in SYS:PUBLIC\WIN95. Fill in the Add Network Printer dialog box. (To make sure NPTWIN95 loads every time the workstation reboots, add this file to the Startup folder. Choose Start, then Settings, then Taskbar, and then select the Start Menu Programs tab. Choose Add, and then Browse to find NPTWIN95.EXE. Choose Next, and then Startup. Enter a name for the icon, such as NPRINTER, and choose Finish.)

13. If you have applications that may not redirect workstation ports to a print queue automatically, add a CAPTURE command to the system, profile, or user login script, so that DOS and Windows 3.1 users' LPT ports will be redirected to a network print queue. You may need to specify the queue's full name. For example, to redirect users' LPT1 ports to the queue named Q1, with no banner page, no tabs, no form feed, and a five-second timeout interval, add the following command to the system login script:

```
#CAPTURE L=1 Q=.Q1.Sales.Satellite.RedHawk NB NT NFF
TI=5
```

(This command should normally be on a single line. It's shown on two lines here because of space constraints.) To capture a port on a Windows 95/98 workstation, use the Network Neighborhood. Double-click the printer, and then specify that you want to capture the port. Fill in any necessary information.

14. Configure your applications for printing, specifying queues, and so on. Follow the manufacturer's instructions for setting up the application for network printing.

15. If you want to specify different kinds of paper for different print jobs, set up definitions of paper forms. This is helpful if you use applications that print on different types of paper — such as paychecks, invoices, and so on — and the printer doesn't reset correctly after each type of job.

To do this, select the container object and choose Details from the Object menu. Then open the Printer Forms page and give the form a name and ID number, and indicate its size (width in characters and length in lines). Now, the print server operator will be notified when a print job requires a different form to be mounted.

To mount a form, change the paper in the printer, select the Printer object, open Details from the Object menu, open the Printer Status page, and then select Mount Form.

16. If your application isn't designed for network printing, set up print job configurations. Print job configurations tell the printer how the print job should be printed on the paper form you set up in Step 15. Print job configurations can specify items such as whether a banner page will be printed, to which queue the job should be sent, and what paper form to use. To create a print job configuration, select a container object for public configurations or a user object for private configurations. Then, choose Details from the Object menu, and open the Print Job Configurations page.

17. If your applications don't recognize your printer (meaning they don't have a printer driver for that type of printer), you may be able to use a printer definition file from Novell, or you may have to create your own printer definition file. See the "Print Device Definitions" section later in this chapter for more information.

18. If you want to modify any information for the printing objects you've created, simply select the object from the NetWare Administrator Browser, choose Details from the Object menu, and edit the fields you want to change.

Setting Up Custom Print Services

If you want to set up a custom queue-based printing environment, such as designating multiple queues that will be serviced by a single printer or multiple printers that will service a single queue, use the NetWare Administrator utility.

To set up custom printing services, complete the following steps:

1. Decide where you want to locate your printers and attach them to the server, workstations, or network cabling.

2. From any workstation, log in to the network as user Admin.

3. Run the NetWare Administrator utility on the workstation by double-clicking its icon.

4. From NetWare Administrator's Browser, select the container object that you want to contain the printing objects.

5. From the Object menu, choose Create.

6. Select Print Queue. The screen that appears lets you specify information about the print queue you want to create. Choose Directory Service Queue, and then fill in a name for the queue and the volume that will store the queue.

7. Click the Define Additional Properties option. Define any additional information for the queue at this time by opening pages and specifying the appropriate information. For example, you can assign users and queue operators to the queue. By default, the container in which this print queue resides is assigned as a user, so all objects within the container are also users of the queue. The user Admin is the default queue operator (a person assigned to manage the queue). When finished, click OK, and then click the Create button to actually create the queue, and you'll return to the Browser.

8. Again, select the container in which you're creating the printing objects, and then choose Create from the Object menu.

9. Select Printer. Enter a name for this printer.

10. Click the Define Additional Properties option. A print queue must be assigned to a printer before the printer can take print jobs from the network. Assign this printer to a print queue by selecting the Assignments page. Click the Add button. Then navigate through the NDS tree using the Directory Context panel, and select the print queue you want from the Objects panel.

11. Open additional pages to specify more information for the printer, such as configuration information. When finished, click OK. Then click the Create button to actually create the printer, and you'll return to the Browser.

12. Again, select the container in which you're creating the printing objects, and then choose Create from the Object menu.

13. Select Print Server. Enter a name for this print server.

14. Click the Define Additional Properties option. A printer must be assigned to a print server before network printing will work. Assign this print server to a printer by selecting the Assignments page. Click the Add button, navigate through the NDS tree using the Directory Context panel, and then select the printer you want from the Objects panel.

15. Open additional pages to specify more information for the print server as necessary. When finished, click OK. Then click the Create button to actually create the printer, and you'll return to the Browser.

16. Go to the network server that will run the print server (or use Remote Console to access that server's console) and load PSERVER.NLM by typing the following command:

```
LOAD PSERVER printserver
```

where *printserver* is the name of the newly created print server. (Later, you can put the PSERVER command, along with the print server's name, in the NetWare server's AUTOEXEC.NCF file so it loads automatically when the server is rebooted.)

17. If the printer is attached to a network server that is not running PSERVER, load NPRINTER.NLM on the network server, specifying the print server name and printer number in the NPRINTER command. (This command can also be placed in the NetWare server's AUTOEXEC.NCF file.) If you have more than one printer attached to this server, load NPRINTER multiple times, specifying a different printer number (and print server if necessary) for each printer.

18. If the printer is attached to a workstation, run NPRINTER.EXE (for DOS and Windows 3.1) or NPTWIN95.EXE (for Windows 95/98) on that workstation.

    a. For DOS and Windows 3.1: Type **NPRINTER,** followed by the print server name and printer number in the command. (You can include this command in the workstation's AUTOEXEC.BAT file, after the login command.) For example, to load NPRINTER for printer number 0, which uses print server PS-Tech, use the following command:

```
NPRINTER PS-Tech 0
```

    b. For Windows 95/98: Start up the NetWare Client software on the workstation. Then, from the Network Neighborhood, locate the NPTWIN95.EXE file in SYS:PUBLIC\WIN95. Fill in the Add Network Printer dialog box. (To make sure NPTWIN95 loads every time the workstation reboots, add this file to the Startup folder. Choose Start, then Settings, then Taskbar, and then select the Start Menu Programs tab. Choose Add, and then Browse to find NPTWIN95.EXE. Choose Next, and then Startup. Enter a name for the icon, such as NPRINTER, and choose Finish.)

19. If you have applications that may not redirect workstation ports to a print queue automatically, add a CAPTURE command to the system, profile, or user login script, so that DOS and Windows 3.1 users' LPT ports will be redirected to a network print queue. You may need to specify the queue's full name. To capture a port on a Windows 95/98 workstation, use the Network Neighborhood. Find and double-click the printer, specify that you want to capture the port, and fill in any necessary information.

20. Configure your applications for printing. In many cases, you may be able to simply configure the application to use a particular printer, because NetWare will automatically associate the printer with a print queue. Follow the manufacturer's instructions for setting up the application for network printing.

21. If you want to specify different kinds of paper for different print jobs, set up definitions of paper forms. This is helpful if you use applications that print on different types of paper — such as paychecks, invoices, and so on — and the printer doesn't reset correctly after each type of job.

To do this, select the container object and choose Details from the Object menu. Then open the Printer Forms page and give the form a name and ID number, and indicate its size (width in characters and length in lines). Now, the print server operator will be notified when a print job requires a different form to be mounted.

To mount a form, change the paper in the printer, and then select the Printer object. Open Details from the Object menu, open the Printer Status page, and then select Mount Form.

22. If your application isn't designed for network printing, set up print job configurations. Print job configurations tell the printer how the print job should be printed on the paper form you set up in Step 21. Print job configurations can specify items such as whether a banner page will be printed, to which queue the job should be sent, and what paper form to use. To create a print job configuration, select a container object for public configurations or a user object for private configurations. Then, choose Details from the Object menu, and open the Print Job Configurations page.

23. If your applications don't recognize your printer (meaning they don't have a printer driver for that type of printer), you may be able to use a printer definition file from Novell, or you may have to create your own printer definition file. See the "Print Device Definitions" section for more information.

Print Device Definitions

After you install queue-based printing, you may need to install printer drivers for your printers. Printer drivers are software programs that control printer functions, regulating how printers handle print jobs. Many network-aware applications contain printer drivers for a variety of common printers. If your application doesn't recognize your type of printer, you will either have to use a Novell print device definition (also called a printer definition file), or you will have to create your own.

To see if NetWare came with a printer definition file that you can use, look at the files with the .PDF extension in the SYS:PUBLIC directory. If yours is there, you can import that file into the device database.

To import one of Novell's printer definition files so you can use it, use the NetWare Administrator utility. Choose the container object, and then choose Details from the Object menu. Open the Print Devices page (shown in Figure 9.7), click Import, and select the correct .PDF file from the SYS:PUBLIC directory.

If the driver you need isn't in the SYS:PUBLIC directory, you need to create your own printer definition file. To do this, select the container object, and then choose Details from the Object menu. Open the Print Devices page. Enter a name for the printer definition, and then choose OK. Now click the Modify button. Click the Create Function or Create Mode buttons to specify the control sequences used by your printer. You will have to refer to the manufacturer's documentation for the control sequences (or printer commands) to use.

After you've created your own printer definition file, you can export it to the SYS:PUBLIC directory (or another location) so you can then import it to other container objects. To export the definition file, return to the Print Devices page, select the definition you just created, and click Export. Locate the directory where you want to place the file, and then choose OK. The file is named with the first eight characters from the definition's name, plus the .PDF extension. This file can now be imported to other containers' or users' databases.

FIGURE 9.7 *The Print Devices page*

Verifying Your Queue-Based Printing Setup

After you've set up your queue-based printing services, you can use the NetWare Administrator utility to see a graphical representation of your printing setup. Using this feature, you can see if all your printing objects are assigned to each other correctly.

To see this printing layout diagram, select the container that holds the printing objects, or select the specific print server that interests you. Choose Details from the Object menu, and then open the Print Layout page. Figure 9.8 shows an example of a print layout diagram.

If all you see is a list of print servers, click a print server to expand the view to show its assigned printers and queues. Lines connecting the printing objects indicate that the objects are assigned to each other correctly. A dashed line connecting them indicates that the connection is only good for this session. When the server is rebooted, the connections will be removed.

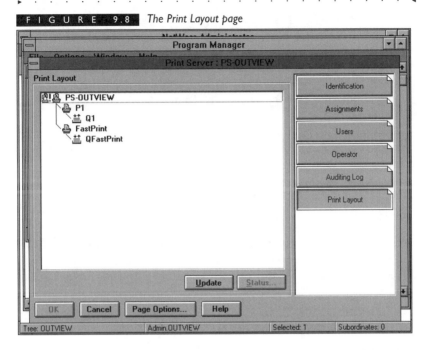

FIGURE 9.8 *The Print Layout page*

If any printing object has an icon with an exclamation mark (!) beside it, there's a problem with that object. (Notice the print server object in Figure 9.8 has an exclamation mark.) Go back through the instructions and see if you missed any steps assigning print queues, print servers, and printers to each other.

You can also right-click any of the objects to see more information about that particular object.

In addition, you can see the print jobs in a queue by double-clicking the queue object. However, you cannot modify the print jobs from this screen. To modify the print jobs, you have to go back to the NetWare Administrator Browser, select a print queue, and open its Print Jobs page.

Managing Queue-Based Print Jobs

After NetWare print services are set up on the network, users can send their jobs to network print queues as long as they have access to those printers.

A user has access to a queue if he or she is assigned as a print queue user. By default, the container in which a print queue resides is assigned as a user, so all objects within the container are also users of the queue. A print queue user can add jobs to a print queue, see the status of all jobs in the queue, and delete his or her own job from the queue. A queue user cannot delete other users' print jobs from the queue.

A print queue operator is a special type of print queue user who has the capability to manage the print queue. A queue operator can delete other users' print jobs, put them on hold, and so on. The user Admin is the default queue operator.

You can add or remove users and operators from the list of print queue users by using the NetWare Administrator utility. You can also use the same utility to look at the current print jobs in the print queue.

To use the NetWare Administrator utility to change users and operators, select the Print Queue object, choose Details from the Object menu, and then open the Users or Operator page.

To see the current print jobs in the queue, open the Job List page. Here, users can delete their own print jobs or put them on hold. Queue operators can put on hold or delete any users' print jobs. Press the F1 key to read help on each of the available fields in the Job List screen. Figure 9.9 shows the Print Jobs page.

Unloading PSERVER.NLM

At some point, you may need to unload the print server (PSERVER.NLM) from the server. (For example, if you are changing your printing system to NDPS, you will need to unload the queue-based print server when you're finished.) Unloading PSERVER.NLM is very easy. From the NetWare Administrator utility, select the print server object. Then, from the Object menu, choose Details and click Unload.

To reload PSERVER, type the following command at the network server's console:

PSERVER *printserver*

where *printserver* is the name of the newly created print server.

F I G U R E   9 . 9 *Print jobs in a print queue*

CHAPTER 10

Installing and Using Online Documentation

Instant *Access*

Installing the Documentation

▸ To set up the online documentation so network users can access it, install the NetWare documentation on a network directory by inserting the documentation CD-ROM in a workstation's drive, and then choosing Install Documentation.

▸ Install the Netscape Communicator browser on each workstation by inserting the documentation CD-ROM and selecting Workstation Install.

Using the Documentation

▸ Any workstation browser can access and read the documentation. However, to take full advantage of advanced searching and printing features, you should use Netscape Communicator 4.x (included on the NetWare 5 documentation CD-ROM) or Microsoft Internet Explorer 4.x or higher.

▸ To access the documentation from a workstation, double-click the Netscape (or other browser) icon, and then select the NetWare 5 documentation's location. (If you set up the Netscape browser using the documentation CD-ROM's Workstation Install option, you can choose the NetWare 5 documentation from Netscape's bookmark list.)

Novell's Online Documentation

In an effort to save trees, bookshelf space, and the administrator's time, most of the documentation for NetWare 5 is online, located on a CD-ROM. The only printed documentation that is included in the NetWare package is the documentation you'll need to get your server up and running. The rest of the documentation is located on the CD-ROM.

Having the documentation online enables you to access the documentation from anywhere on the network. Obviously, this is more handy than having to tote three dozen manuals with you to a user's office. In addition, the online documentation's search features can help you locate the information you need quickly.

You can read the online documentation directly from the CD-ROM, or you can install the documentation onto a network directory so you and other users can access it from anywhere on the network. (You can also install the documentation directly onto a workstation's local hard disk.)

The Novell online documentation is in HTML format, which means it can be read using any browser. However, to use the searching and printing features of the online documentation, you will need to use Netscape 4.*x* (or higher) or Microsoft Internet Explorer 4.*x* (or higher). The Novell documentation CD-ROM comes with the correct version of Netscape Navigator on it, so if you choose to read the documentation directly from the CD-ROM, the Navigator browser will open automatically for you.

To read the online documentation directly from the CD-ROM, insert the CD-ROM in your workstation's drive, open the CD-ROM, and select View Documentation from the main Product Documentation window that appears. The online documentation will automatically open, and you can select topics from the table of contents.

To install the documentation on a network so additional users can view it, you first use the installation program on the CD-ROM to install the documentation files into a network directory. Then you run the Workstation Install program from the CD-ROM on each workstation to set up the browser to point to the documentation files.

The following sections describe how to install the online documentation files onto the server and how to set up the workstation browsers.

NOTE

A full set of printed documentation, which you can purchase separately, is also available. To order the printed documentation, send in the order form that came in your NetWare box or call 800-336-3892 (in the United States) or 512-834-6905.

Installing the Online Documentation Files

Use the following steps to install the online documentation files into a network directory, or onto a workstation's hard disk. (If you install the files into a network directory, users can access the files from anywhere on the network, as long as they have trustee rights to do so.)

NOTE

While installing the documentation, you will also be required to install a browser on the workstation you're using for the installation, if one doesn't already exist. The following instructions include steps for installing both the documentation and the Netscape browser, because Novell has integrated the two procedures into a single, convenient program. If you install the documentation into a network directory, you need to install only the browser on additional workstations. Instructions for installing the Netscape browser alone are in the next section.

1. From a workstation, log in as a user who has sufficient rights to copy files into the network directory that will contain the online documentation.

2. Close all programs that are running on the workstation, so the installation program won't encounter any file conflicts.

3. Insert the Novell online documentation CD-ROM for NetWare 5 into the workstation's drive, and open the CD-ROM. (It may open automatically, displaying the main Product Documentation window.)

4. Choose Install Documentation. The Product Documentation Setup program begins running.

5. At the Welcome screen, click Next to continue.

6. Choose the destination where you want to install the documentation. (The default may be a location on the hard disk. If you want to install

the files into a network directory, click Browse to locate and select the appropriate directory.) When finished selecting the destination, click Next to continue.

7. Select the language you want to install. (This screen also enables you to select which "services" you want to install. Click Services if you want to install only some of the documentation — you can specify which portions of the documentation you want to ignore.) When finished selecting the language and, if necessary, the services you want to install, click Next to continue.

8. At the confirmation screen that displays your choices, click Next to continue (or click Back to make changes). The installation program begins copying files to the destination you specified.

9. A message appears indicating that the Novell Search Engine installation will now begin. Click OK.

10. At the Search Engine Welcome screen, click Next.

11. The installation program now checks this workstation for Netscape 4.x. If you have already installed the Netscape 4.x browser on this workstation, a message appears telling you that bookmarks to the Novell documentation are being added to your browser. Skip to Step 12. If you do not have Netscape 4.x on this workstation, the installation program will install it now.

    a. When asked if you want to install Netscape, click Yes.

    b. A message appears telling you not to reboot the computer automatically if prompted. Click OK. The Netscape browser installation begins. (Note: The Search Engine Welcome screen may still appear on your screen. Ignore it.)

    c. At the Netscape Communicator Welcome screen, click Next.

    d. At the license agreement screen, click Yes.

    e. Select whether you want to do a Typical installation or a Custom installation. A Typical installation installs Netscape's Communicator (which includes the Navigator browser), Conference, Netcaster, and Multimedia support. If you choose the Custom installation, you can choose not to install one or more of these components.

f. From the same screen, also select the destination for the Netscape software on this workstation. If the folder you select doesn't yet exist, you will be asked if you want to create it. Choose Yes.

g. Select the program folder for the Netscape software, and then click Next.

h. At the confirmation screen, confirm your selections and click Install to continue (or click Back to make changes).

i. When asked if you want to view the readme file for Netscape Communicator, choose either Yes or No.

j. A message appears indicating the setup is complete. Click OK.

k. When asked if you want to restart the computer now, choose No.

12. If you want to install Adobe Acrobat, click Yes when prompted. (If Adobe Acrobat is already installed on this workstation, skip to Step 13.)

a. At the Adobe Acrobat Welcome screen, click Next.

b. At the license screen, click Yes.

c. Choose the destination folder for Acrobat files on this workstation, and click Next. The Acrobat files are decompressed and copied to the workstation.

d. When the setup is complete, decide if you want to read the readme file. If you do, click Finish. If you don't want to read the readme now, unmark the box beside Display Acrobat Reader 3.01 Readme File before clicking Finish.

13. When prompted to select the HTML Browser's location, make sure you select the location of the Netscape browser on this workstation, and then click Next.

14. Select the location of the NetWare 5 documentation you installed earlier (such as SYS:\PUBLIC\NOVDOCS), and then click Next.

15. At the confirmation screen, verify your selections, and then click Next. The installation program copies files and makes system modifications.

16. A message appears telling you to reboot your server. Click OK.

17. Another message appears telling you that bookmarks for the NetWare documentation are being added to your Netscape browser. Click OK.

18. When the installation is complete, decide if you want to read the readme file. If you do, click Finish. If you don't want to read the readme now, unmark the box beside the option to view the readme before clicking Finish.

19. At the main Product Documentation screen, choose Exit.

20. Reboot the workstation to make all the new settings take effect.

Now you need to make sure that every workstation that needs to access the online documentation has a browser available to read the documentation. The next section explains how you can use the NetWare documentation CD-ROM to set up the Netscape Communicator on any workstation and automatically add bookmarks to the documentation you installed.

Setting Up the Browser on a Workstation

As mentioned before, you can use any browser to read the NetWare 5 online documentation. However, to use the search and print features of the documentation, you need to use Netscape 4.x or Microsoft Internet Explorer 4.x. The 4.x version of Netscape is included on the NetWare 5 documentation CD-ROM so you can easily install it on your workstations. The installation program for the Netscape browser also installs Adobe Acrobat, which is used to read some portions of the documentation.

If you've installed the online documentation into a network directory, all you need to do is install the browser on each workstation that will access the documentation. To install Netscape 4.x on a workstation, complete the following steps:

1. Close all programs that are running on the workstation, so the installation program won't encounter any file conflicts.

2. Insert the Novell online documentation CD-ROM for NetWare 5 into the workstation's drive, and open the CD-ROM. (It may open automatically, displaying the main Product Documentation window.)

3. Choose Workstation Install. The Novell Search Engine Setup program begins running.

4. At the Search Engine Welcome screen, click Next.

5. The installation program now checks this workstation for Netscape 4.*x*. If you have already installed the Netscape 4.*x* browser on this workstation, a message appears telling you that bookmarks to the Novell documentation are being added to your browser. Skip to Step 6. If you do not have Netscape 4.*x* on this workstation, the installation program will install it now.

  a. When asked if you want to install Netscape, click Yes.

  b. A message appears telling you not to reboot the computer automatically if prompted. Click OK. The Netscape browser installation begins. (Note: The Search Engine's Welcome screen may still appear on your screen. Ignore it.)

  c. At the Netscape Communicator Welcome screen, click Next.

  d. At the license agreement screen, click Yes.

  e. Select whether you want to do a Typical installation or a Custom installation. A Typical installation installs Netscape's Communicator (which includes the Navigator browser), Conference, Netcaster, and Multimedia support. If you choose the Custom installation, you can choose not to install one or more of these components.

  f. From the same screen, also select the destination for the Netscape software on this workstation. If the folder you select doesn't yet exist, you will be asked if you want to create it. Choose Yes.

  g. Select the program folder for the Netscape software, and then click Next.

  h. At the confirmation screen, confirm your selections and click Install to continue (or click Back to make changes).

  i. When asked if you want to view the readme file for Netscape Communicator, choose either Yes or No.

  j. A message appears indicating the setup is complete. Click OK.

  k. When asked if you want to restart the computer now, choose No.

6. If you want to install Adobe Acrobat, click Yes when prompted. (If Adobe Acrobat is already installed on this workstation, skip to Step 7.)

  a. At the Adobe Acrobat Welcome screen, click Next.

  b. At the license screen, click Yes.

    c. Choose the destination folder for Acrobat files on this workstation, and click Next. The Acrobat files are decompressed and copied to the workstation.

    d. When the setup is complete, decide if you want to read the readme file. If you do, click Finish. If you don't want to read the readme now, unmark the box beside Display Acrobat Reader 3.01 Readme File before clicking Finish.

7. When prompted to select the HTML Browser's location, make sure you select the location of the Netscape browser on this workstation, and then click Next.

8. Select the location of the NetWare 5 documentation you installed earlier (such as SYS:\PUBLIC\NOVDOCS), and then click Next.

9. At the confirmation screen, verify your selections, and then click Next. The installation program copies files and makes system modifications.

10. A message appears telling you to reboot your server. Click OK.

11. Another message appears telling you that bookmarks for the NetWare documentation are being added to your Netscape browser. Click OK.

12. When the installation is complete, decide if you want to read the readme file. If you do, click Finish. If you don't want to read the readme now, unmark the box beside the option to view the readme before clicking Finish.

13. At the main Product Documentation screen, choose Exit.

14. Reboot the workstation to make all the new settings take effect.

Now the workstation's browser is set up and ready to access the NetWare 5 documentation.

Launching the Netscape Communicator

The first time you launch the Netscape Communicator from a workstation, you will need to create a new *profile* for yourself, to store your personal settings and files that Netscape will use. If several people use this workstation, each user should have his or her own profile to make logging in to the browser easier. You can also create more than one profile for yourself if you want to log in using different settings for different situations. Complete the following steps to set up a profile:

1. Launch the Netscape Communicator by double-clicking its icon.

2. A message appears telling you to create a new profile for yourself. Click Next.

3. Enter your name and e-mail address, and then click Next.

4. Enter a name for this profile and a location in which to store the settings. Then click Next.

5. A screen appears asking for information relating to your outgoing mail. This information is optional, and is used if you are connected to the Internet and expect to send and receive mail through the Internet. You can add it now or later. To add it now, verify your name and e-mail address, and then specify the name of your outgoing mail server. Then click Next.

6. Now a screen appears asking for incoming mail information. Again, this information is optional. If you wish, enter your user name, the name of your incoming mail server, and the type of mail server. Then click Next.

7. A screen appears asking for information relating to discussion groups. This information is also optional at this time. If you wish, enter the name of the news server and port you will use. Then click Finish.

Your Netscape profile is now stored, and the browser opens. From Netscape's Bookmarks menu, select the Novell documentation to open the NetWare 5 information.

► . . . . ◄

Viewing the Novell Online Documentation

After the browser is installed on the workstation and the documentation is installed on the network, you can access the online documentation. To do this, double-click the browser icon from your workstation to start up the browser, and then open the Novell documentation from the Netscape list of bookmarks.

NOTE

You can also read the Novell documentation directly from the CD-ROM without having to install either the documentation or a browser on the workstation. The only difference between running the documentation from a CD-ROM and running it from the network or a local hard disk is that the CD-ROM tends to be a little slower.

The NetWare 5 documentation's home page appears. The left-hand panel indicates the types of information included in the documentation. Click one of the related buttons to see a table of contents for that information. Click a heading in the table of contents to go to that piece of documentation.

Throughout the documentation, the left-hand panel usually displays the table of contents for the section of documentation you're in currently. The right-hand panel shows the actual documentation.

As you read through the manual's text, you will see references to related information. These references appear in a different color and are underlined. If you click those references, they take you instantly to the location of the related information.

To search for a particular word or phrase in the documentation, click the magnifying glass icon at the bottom of the browser screen. The Netscape Search Console appears, enabling you to type in the word or phrase for which you want to search.

To print a page from the online documentation, click the printer icon at the bottom of the Netscape screen. Clicking the home icon will return you to the initial screen of the NetWare 5 documentation.

If you install the documentation on the network and receive an error message when trying to search or print the documentation, verify that the workstation was set up correctly by completing the following steps:

1. First, make sure you are using either Netscape Communicator 4.*x* or Microsoft Internet Explorer 4.*x* or higher. Other versions or other browsers do not support the search and print features of the Novell documentation.

2. Make sure your workstation has a drive mapping to the volume that contains the NOVDOCS folder.

3. Go to the MS-DOS prompt and type **SET** to make sure that a PATH statement has been set to the directory that contains the KSERVER folder (such as F:\NOVDOCS\KSERVER), and that a CLASSPATH statement has been set to the NVCLASS.ZIP file in the KSERVER folder. These commands should have been added to your AUTOEXEC.BAT file during the documentation installation.

4. Make sure Java and JavaScript are enabled in the browser. In Netscape Communicator, choose Preferences under the Edit menu, check Advanced in the Category window, and then make sure Enable Java and Enable JavaScript are both checked.

5. For more information, read the documentation's README.TXT file, which is located in the NOVDOCS folder on the online documentation CD-ROM, and in the NOVDOCS folder on the network directory.

Netscape FastTrack Server for NetWare

Instant *Access*

Installing the FastTrack Server

▶ To install the FastTrack Server, run SETUP.EXE from a Windows 95/98 or NT workstation.

Managing the FastTrack Server

▶ To manage the FastTrack Server, use the Admin Server.

▶ To manage the Admin Server, set global settings, and manage users and groups, use the General Administration section of the Admin Server.

▶ To set server preferences, manage Web application development programs, monitor server status, and manage Web site content, use the Servers Supporting General Administration section of the Admin Server.

The FastTrack Server

The Netscape FastTrack Server for NetWare is a robust, high-performance, industry-leading Web server included in NetWare 5. It was made available to Novell through a partnership between Netscape and Novell called Novonyx, a research and development division of Novell.

The FastTrack Server is based on open standards. It supports many leading Internet application development languages, and enables NetWare 5 to be a powerful Web development platform. The FastTrack Server is very different from the Novell Web Server, which you may currently be using. It has many features that were not available with the Novell Web Server.

The FastTrack Server is easy to install and use. Tight integration with NDS and the use of LDAP makes the FastTrack Server excellent for use with intranets or the Internet.

The FastTrack Server includes an Administration Server that allows browser-based management of FastTrack and other Netscape servers. The Netscape Administration Server (also called the Admin Server) enables you to manage the Netscape FastTrack Server and any other Netscape servers you may be using. The Admin Server is a Web server of its own and operates on a port separate from the FastTrack Web Server. This enables you to change, load, and unload other Netscape servers remotely. Because the Admin Server is always up, you always have control of your Web servers.

You access the Admin Server through a Netscape browser (version 3.01 or higher). Older versions of Netscape's browser, Microsoft Internet Explorer 4.0, and other browsers do not support all of the JavaScript functions that are required for administration.

This chapter discusses the Netscape FastTrack Server's installation procedure, features, and functionality.

Installing the FastTrack
Server for NetWare

The installation of the FastTrack Server is one of its best features. You run the installation program from a workstation, and the installation program sets up the entire configuration for you. Before you can install FastTrack Server, however, be sure that your workstation and server meet the minimum hardware and software requirements for installation.

Client requirements include:

- ▶ Window 95/98 or Windows NT
- ▶ Novell's Client software
- ▶ A CD-ROM drive if you are installing the FastTrack Server from the CD-ROM
- ▶ A minimum of 100MB of free space on the workstation's hard disk
- ▶ Administration rights to the SYS volume

Server requirements include:

- ▶ A minimum of 100MB free on the SYS volume
- ▶ 64MB of memory

Complete the following steps to install the FastTrack Server on a NetWare 5 server:

1. From a Windows 95/98 or NT workstation, open the Start menu and choose Run. Browse the NetWare 5 Operating System CD-ROM to the \products\webserv folder, and then select the SETUP.EXE file.

2. When an information screen appears, click the Finish button to continue.

This unpacks the necessary installation files onto your workstation. If you do not have sufficient disk space, the installation will fail. (These files will be automatically deleted after the installation completes.)

3. At the Welcome screen, click Next to continue.

4. Read the Software License Agreement and click Yes to continue.

5. Select the server and SYS volume where you want to install the FastTrack Server. (You must select the root of the SYS volume.) When finished, click OK and then click Next to continue.

6. The installation procedure will now verify long filename support and will verify that you have IP properly configured. Enter the IP address of the server you selected in Step 5. Then enter the hostname for your server. If there is no DNS entry for the IP address you are using, enter the IP address of the server in the hostname field. When finished, click Next to continue.

7. Enter the port for the Web server. By default, this will be 80. Then click Next to continue.

8. Enter an admin port number and click Next to continue. (It is very important that you remember the port number. This is the number you will use to access the Admin Server. If you forget the port number, it is located in the ns-admin.conf file located in the sys:\novonyx\ suitespot\admin-serv\config\ directory. This number should only be known to network administrators.)

9. An information screen appears. Click OK to continue.

10. When prompted, enter a user name for the SuperUser, and then enter a password and confirm the password. (Remember the SuperUser name and password.) Click Next to continue.

11. When the installation program displays LDAP (Lightweight Directory Access Protocol) information, click Next to continue. (LDAP is a protocol for accessing network information directories.)

12. Select whether to add the NSWEB.NCF command to your NetWare server's AUTOEXEC.NCF file. If you choose not add this command, you will be required to manually start the FastTrack Web Server any time you restart your NetWare server.

13. When the summary of the server's configuration appears, check the information to make sure it is correct, and click Next to continue.

14. After all files have been copied, you have the option of automatically launching the FastTrack Web Server and viewing the ReadMe file. If you elect not to launch the Web server now, you can type NSWEB at the server console later to launch the FastTrack Server.

15. Click Finish to complete the installation.

The FastTrack Web Server is now installed.

Connecting to the Administration Server

Once you have FastTrack up and running, you can connect to the Admin Server by opening your Netscape browser and entering your server's URL and administration port number.

A login box appears and requires you to enter the name and password of the SuperUser that you entered during the installation process. After you enter this information, the Netscape Server Administration page appears.

There are two different sections of the Server Administration page, as shown in Figure 11.1: General Administration and Servers Supporting General Administration.

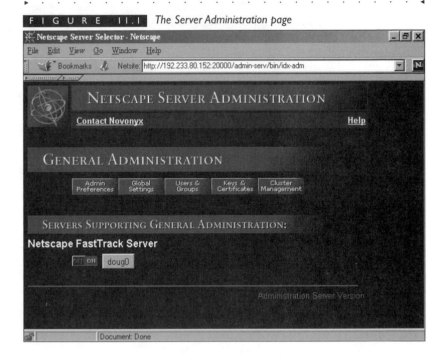

FIGURE 11.1 *The Server Administration page*

General Administration Options

The General Administration section contains buttons for configuring the Admin Server and general configuration for all installed Netscape servers. Any changes you make in this section will affect the Netscape FastTrack Server and any other Netscape servers that have been installed on your NetWare server.

The following options are available under the General Administration section of the Server Administration page:

- ▸ Admin Preferences
- ▸ Global Settings
- ▸ Users and Groups
- ▸ Keys and Certificates
- ▸ Cluster Management

These options are explained in the following sections.

Using the Admin Preferences Page

The first button under General Administration is Admin Preferences. This button enables you to configure the Admin Server itself. Click the Admin Preferences button to see the following options listed down the left side of the screen:

- ▶ Shutdown — This option enables you to shut down the Admin Server. Clicking the Shutdown The Administration Server button will unload ADM-SERV.NLM from your NetWare server. After this NLM has been unloaded, you can restart the Admin Server by typing NVXADMUP.NCF at the server console prompt. All other Netscape servers can be shut down and restarted through the Admin Server interface.

- ▶ Network Settings — This option configures the Admin Server port that was chosen during the installation process. To change this number, enter the change and click OK. If you change this value, you will have to shut down and then restart the Admin Server for the changes to take effect.

- ▶ SuperUser Access Control — This option enables you to configure SuperUser access for your Admin Server. You can limit access to the Admin Server by hostname or individual IP address. By limiting hostnames or IP addresses, you require that all administration be done from a specific location. Some administrators allow administration from any location on the network, whereas others may choose to require that the machine that is connected to the Admin Server be located within a certain IP segment. This adds an extra level of security. This page also enables you to change the SuperUser name and password.

- ▶ Turn On/Off SSL — This option allows you to disable or enable SSL (Secure Sockets Layer). Netscape servers use the SSL communication system to ensure privacy when communicating with other SSL-enabled products, such as other servers, Netscape Navigator, and Netscape Communicator.

- ▶ Security Preferences — This option enables you to make choices about SSL connections.

- ▶ Logging Options — This option enables you to specify the location of Admin Server log files. You can use these log files to monitor your server and troubleshoot problems.

- ▶ View Access Log — This option lets you view the Admin Server's log files, which are stored on your NetWare server.

- ▶ View Error Log — This option lets you view the Admin Server's error log file.

Using the Global Settings Page

The Global Settings page specifies which directory service you want to use with your FastTrack Server. This directory service stores all of your user and group information. It also handles all authentication and access control for the FastTrack Server. You can choose from three directory services: Local Database, LDAP Directory Server, and Novell Directory Services (NDS). Each option requires careful consideration, because there are significant differences between each choice.

- ▶ The Local Database option stores all information in a local LDAP-based directory on your NetWare server The local database is the simplest of the directory service choices. This option works well for a small number of users who do not need access to resources located anywhere else on the network. Keep in mind, though, that the local database information is available only to Netscape servers running on that specific NetWare server. Other Netscape servers will not be able to access the information in the local database.

- ▶ The LDAP Directory Server option enables you to choose from any directory that supports LDAP access, including Netscape's Directory Server running on another platform or a connection to Novell Directory Services via Novell's NLDAP Gateway (which provides LDAP access to NDS). You may also connect to any other directory that has an LDAP interface. After you have installed the NLDAP Gateway on a NetWare server on your network, you can use LDAP for all user and group authentication for your Netscape servers. Figure 11.2 shows the LDAP Directory Server Configuration page.

- ▶ The Novell Directory Services option enables the FastTrack Server to make a native connection to NDS. (Figure 11.3 shows the NDS configuration page.) If you select NDS, you will be required to use the NetWare Administrator utility to manage all access control for the FastTrack Server. All user, group, and ACL management features in the FastTrack Server and the Admin Server will be disabled. This allows you to use the NetWare Administrator utility to assign trustee rights through the NetWare file system. This gives users the same access to files, whether they are accessing a file through the browser or mapping a drive and opening a file through some other application. The advantage of this is that you have a single point of administration. Once access control has been set for the file system, it has been set for the Web server, too. A possible disadvantage is that you have given users the capability to access the file through both the Internet Web server and a workstation on the local network. If you use either of the LDAP options instead of the NDS option, you are only exposing files through the Web server. Another limitation of native NDS is that you cannot limit access by IP address or hostname. If you need IP access control, use the LDAP option.

FIGURE 11.2 *The LDAP Directory Server Configuration page*

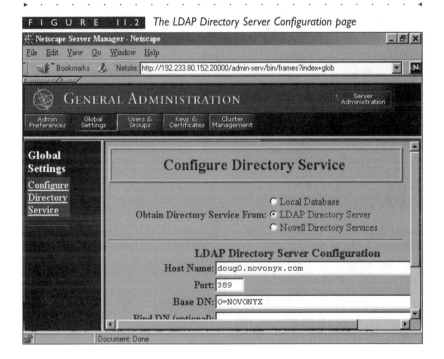

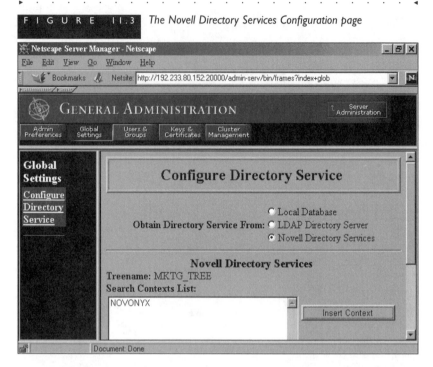

If you choose to use the Local Database or Novell Directory Services, select the appropriate radio button and restart your Admin Server. If you decide to use an LDAP Directory Server, you will need to enter information about your server. For Host Name, you can enter the hostname or IP address. The standard LDAP port is 389; be sure to check your LDAP server so you use the same port. For connections to NDS through LDAP, Base DN is required. You must enter the full LDAP distinguished name.

Using the Users and Groups Page

The Users and Groups page enables you to add new users, groups, or Organizational Units. You can also edit existing users, groups, or Organizational Units, and import or export directory information.

If you decided to use Native NDS for your directory, this page will be disabled and you will need to use the NetWare Administrator utility for user and group administration.

NOTE

The following options are available for managing your user and group information:

▶ New User, Group, or Organizational Unit — These options enable you to enter all information about your new object. When you select Create, the object information you have entered will be added into the directory. Figure 11.4 shows the New User screen.

▶ Manage Users, Groups, or Organizational Units — The Manage options give you simple query options for finding specific objects in the directory. You can select objects by different properties. You also can search for objects that sound like the information entered. This can be helpful in a very large organization. Once you find the object you are looking for, you can make changes and update the information.

▶ Import/Export — These options let you import or export LDIF files. LDIF files can be very helpful in moving large amounts of directory information from one location to another.

FIGURE 11.4 *The New User Entry page*

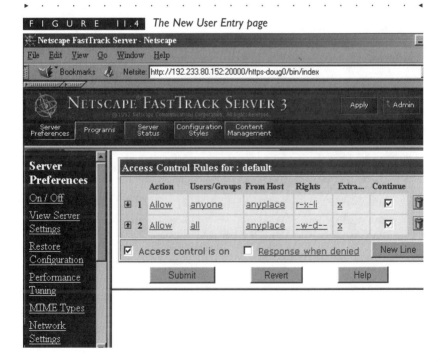

Using the Keys and Certificates Page

One of the biggest concerns about the Internet today is security. Because the Internet is a collection of connected systems, the information sent from one computer to another can pass through any number of computers before it reaches its target destination. Most of the intermediary computers will just route the Internet traffic that comes to them, but a dishonest person could intercept your private data. The eavesdroppers might even replace your information with incorrect or harmful data, and send it on its way. Because of the architecture of the Internet and intranets, there will always be opportunities for people to commit dishonest acts.

Most information does not need to be secure, but as companies begin to do business on the Internet, they want to be reasonably sure the information they are sending or receiving has not been tampered with or viewed by unauthorized parties. The Secure Sockets Layer (SSL) supported by the FastTrack Server is the protocol that keeps your data safe. SSL preserves data security on three levels: confidentiality, integrity, and authentication:

- ► Confidentiality is ensured through encryption. Encryption converts your data into a format that cannot be read by anyone other than the intended recipient. Your data is sent across the Internet in this format and is then decrypted by the recipient when it arrives at the intended location.

- ► Integrity is also ensured through encryption. If someone does intercept your encrypted data, changes are not possible without alerting the recipient.

- ► Authentication is provided through digital certificates. These certificates act as a digital identity or passport for your computer. Certificates can be purchased from a company that both parties trust. The location from where the certificate was obtained is called a Certificate Authority (CA).

Although using SSL provides secure data transmission across the Internet or on your intranet, there are three issues you may want to consider before using SSL:

- ► First, you do need to obtain a certificate through a CA. This can add costs to your Internet or intranet deployment.

- ► Second, after you have enabled SSL for your FastTrack Server, the entire FastTrack Web Server is secure. You cannot provide non-SSL connections to your FastTrack Server. (This restriction is for the FastTrack Server itself, and not necessarily for the Admin Server. Conversely, you can set up the Admin Server to use SSL, but not the FastTrack Server. The two servers are independent of each other, and therefore one can use SSL without the other being affected.)

▶ Finally, before using SSL on your FastTrack Server, you should consult the security manager for your company, because creating a secure environment requires significant planning. Before configuring the Keys and Certificates sections of the administration server, read the online documentation included with the FastTrack Server and create a careful plan for implementing a secure environment.

Using the Cluster Management Page

In the Netscape world, a cluster is a group of similar Netscape servers that can be administered from a single Netscape Admin Server. This feature enables you to manage multiple FastTrack Servers from a single location.

To set up a cluster, first make sure all participating FastTrack Servers are installed. These servers must have the same administrator user name and password. Then choose the server that will be the master administration server, which will handle administration for all servers in the cluster. When using cluster management on the NetWare platform, you need to use a valid host name. Cluster management will not work if you only specify an IP address. The host name of the clustered server must also be entered in your server's hosts file. Even with a valid DNS and host name, you are still required to enter the appropriate information in the hosts file.

When implementing cluster management on the NetWare platform, you cannot share configuration files between servers.

Click the Cluster Management button to set up your cluster management. To add remote servers to the cluster database, click the Add Server button to display the Add Remote Servers to Cluster Database screen, as shown in Figure 11.5. Enter the Admin Server host name and the port number of the FastTrack Server that you are adding to your cluster. Then click OK, and then click Save and Apply.

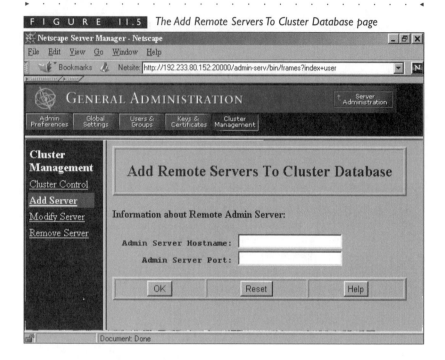

F I G U R E   11.5   *The Add Remote Servers To Cluster Database page*

Servers Supporting General Administration Options

Every Netscape server has individual configuration options that affect only that specific server. In the previous section, you learned about General Administration, which controls all Netscape servers on a single machine. On the main Administration Server page there is another section called Servers Supporting General Administration. Under that section, you see Netscape FastTrack Server, and beneath that is a button with the name of your NetWare server. Click this button to go to the pages that are specific to the FastTrack Server.

When the FastTrack Server Administration page appears, the Server Preferences button is selected by default, as shown in Figure 11.6.

On the left side of the screen you will see all of the options available under Server Preferences. Near the top right of the screen you will see two buttons: Apply and Admin.

F I G U R E   I I . 6   *The Server Preferences page*

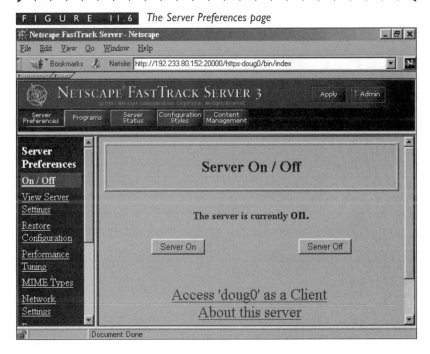

When you click the Apply button, it saves any changes you have made, and stops and restarts the server to make them take effect. Remember that if you are making many changes, you may not want to click apply after every change. Instead, wait to click Apply until after you have made all your changes.

The Admin button returns you to the main Server Administration page.

On the FastTrack Server Administration page, you will see five buttons near the top. These are links to the FastTrack configuration pages, which enable you to make modifications to the FastTrack Server configuration. The five available buttons are:

- ▶ Server Preferences
- ▶ Programs
- ▶ Server Status
- ▶ Configuration Styles
- ▶ Content Management

Each of these pages are described in the following sections. First, let's look at the options under Server Preferences.

Using the Server Preferences Page

The Server Preferences page enables you to manage a specific FastTrack Server's configuration. To open the options under Server Preferences, click the Server Preferences button. The options under Server Preferences are described in the following sections.

On/Off The First option you see when you select Server Preferences is On/Off. This page lets you start and stop the FastTrack Server. If you click the Off button, the Admin Server will unload all FastTrack files on the NetWare server. It will not, however, unload the Admin Server itself. The Admin Server stays up so you can click the On button to restart the server. This page also contains a link to the server's home page and an About This Server link. Remember that you can also start and stop the server from the Servers Supporting General Administration page by clicking the On/Off buttons located just left of the server's name.

View Server Settings Netscape server products use configuration files to store information about the servers. These files are virtually identical across all supported platforms. The main configuration files for the FastTrack Server are magnus.conf and obj.conf. These files are contained in the /novonyx/ suitespot/https-*servername*/config/ directory. (Replace *servername* with the name of your server.)

The View Server Settings page displays an abbreviated look at magnus.conf, showing information about your server. Just below the magnus.conf file is a partial listing of information contained in the obj.conf. Click any of the links to display a page that enables you to edit the information in these files. Make any necessary changes, click OK, and then click Save to apply the changes.

Because changes made to either of these files can have serious consequences, consult the online help before making changes. If you make a mistake and your server fails to load, you can edit either of these files by hand. You can open the files in a text editor, make any changes, and save the file. After you save the changes, attempt to reload the server. When the server has been restored, you will be notified that manual edits have taken place. You will want to click the Apply button at the top of the page to save those manual changes.

Restore Configuration If you have made changes to your server that have caused unwanted results, the Restore Configuration page can help you get back on track. Down the left side of the page, you will see a list of dates and times. These are backups of every configuration that your server has had.

FastTrack makes a backup copy of magnus.conf, obj.conf, and all other configuration files each time you make a change. These previous versions of your configuration files are stored in the sys:/novonyx/suitespot/https-*server-name*/conf_bk directory.

By clicking the button for a particular date and time, you can restore your server to the exact configuration it had at that specific time. Along with restoring a complete configuration, you can select specific configuration files you would like to restore. The View button enables you to look at a file before you restore it.

Performance Tuning The Performance Tuning page enables you to make some performance adjustments to the server. However, the changes made through this page are minor in comparison to the performance enhancements that can be made by editing the obj.conf by hand. Consult performance-tuning documents available through Netscape's and Novell's Web sites for complete performance-tuning information. Even though the default configuration is sufficient in most cases, significant performance improvements can be made in heavy load environments by making changes outlined in the performance-tuning documents.

MIME Types MIME (Multi-purpose Internet Mail Extensions) types control what file types the FastTrack server recognizes and supports. The configuration file mime.types (located in the sys:/novonyx/suitespot/ https-*servername*/conf/ directory) also specifies which applications support different file extensions.

For example, if you want to put MP3 files on your server, you must add the MP3 extension to your MIME types. If this is not added, the server transfers the file to the user as text, instead of as a sound file. The Global Mime Types page makes it easy to add new types. From this page, you can also delete or modify existing types.

Complete the following steps to add new MIME types to your server:

1. Click the type drop-down menu. You can keep the default or choose enc or lang. Enc is the encoding used for compression, and lang is used for language encoding.

2. In the Context_Type field, enter the context type that will be located in the HTTP header. This is the information the client uses to decide

what to do with the requested file. You can look at the included MIME types as examples to add an unsupported type or use the types that are officially assigned and listed by the IANA (Internet Assigned Numbers Authority). To see a list of the IANA's official context types, see the IANA Web site, at www.iana.org.

3. In the File Suffix field, enter the file extension.

4. Once you have entered the information, click the New Type button and your new MIME type will be added.

Network Settings The Network Settings page enables you to view or change configuration information contained in the magnus.conf file. (You are automatically brought to this Network Settings page when you click any of the magnus.conf change links in the View Server Settings page.) Any changes you make to magnus.conf should be made with care.

Error Responses The error messages sent to a client are fairly generic and do not give much information, so you can use the Error Responses page to create custom error messages.

When a server cannot complete a request, it can send one of the following four different error messages to the client:

▶ Unauthorized — Occurs when a user tries unsuccessfully to access a file in a secure area of the Web server.

▶ Forbidden — Occurs when the server does not have file system rights sufficient to read the requested data.

▶ Not Found — Occurs when a user tries to access data that does not exist.

▶ Server — Occurs when the server is improperly configured or when a fatal error occurs (such as the system running out of memory).

There are many situations in which you may want to use custom messages. For example, if users are denied access, instead of receiving a message that simply says "unauthorized," they could receive a custom error message that explains the reason they were denied access and points them to the help desk to have an account created.

To change the Error Response for your server, complete the following steps:

1. Select the error response you want to change (such as Unauthorized).

2. Enter the path to the file that you would like to replace the default error message (such as sys:\novonxy\custom\messages\unathorized.cgi).

3. If this response is a CGI script, click the CGI check box.

4. Repeat this process for each error message you would like to change.

5. When finished, click OK to confirm the changes.

6. If you would like to return to the default error messages, simply delete the file path and click OK to save the changes.

Restrict Access Restrict Access is one of the pages you will use most often when working with the FastTrack Server. This is where LDAP access control is configured. From this page and the accompanying Java applet, you can manage access rights to your server. There are many options for restricting access to the server. You can limit access by specific user or group. You can give access to every user in the authentication database. If you are using the LDAP Directory Server option on the Global Settings page, you can restrict access based on IP address or hostname. (This option is not available if you chose to use Native NDS for your directory type.)

Restricting access by IP address or hostname enables you to require users to be on a specific network (or even using a certain IP address) if they are going to access information on the Web server. Using the Restrict Access page also gives you the capability to assign different levels of security to the FastTrack Server. These levels include:

- ▶ Read access — Lets a user access data. Includes HTTP methods GET, HEAD, POST, and INDEX.

- ▶ Write access — Lets a user change or delete or modify data. Includes HTTP methods PUT, DELETE, MKDIR, RMDIR, and MOVE.

- ▶ Execute access — Applies to server-side applications (such as CGI programs, Java applets, and agents).

- ▶ Delete access — Allows a user to delete data.

- ▶ List access — Allows the user to access directory information (for example, the user can get a list of files in that specific directory).

- ▶ Info access — Allows the user access to header information. This access right includes the HTTP HEAD method.

Complete the following steps to set access levels:

I. Choose the resource you are going to edit. You can use the pull-down menu and choose the entire server, or you can click the browse button and choose one of the listed resources. You can also use wildcards to help select the correct resource.

2. After selecting a resource, click Edit Access Control. This will start up a Java applet for setting access control.

3. Click the Access Control Is On checkbox. Without this checked, your rules do not function. The default rule for this resource appears, as shown in Figure 11.7. Setting access control actions is the first thing you modify when creating a rule. Your options here are Allow or Deny. In most situations, you want to start with a rule that denies access to everyone. You then add new lines that create the access control model you are trying to achieve. Access control rules work from the top down. The server goes down the list and checks each rule until it finds a rule that doesn't match or that matches but is not set to continue. The last rule that matches is the one that is used to allow or deny access to a user. Click Submit to continue.

► . . . . ◄

FIGURE 11.7 *The Access Control Rules page*

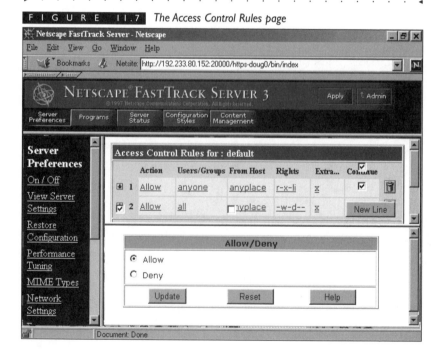

4. The Save and Apply Changes screen appears. You have three options:

- ▸ Save and Apply — Saves and commits the changes
- ▸ Save — Saves the changes but doesn't commit them (you will have to click the Apply button to commit the changes)
- ▸ Undo — Undoes the changes

5. When a JavaScript message appears, saying that the changes have been successfully saved and applied, click OK to continue.

6. Click the Users/Groups section of your rule. A screen similar to the one in Figure 11.8 appears, with the following options available for selecting users and setting rules:

- ▸ Anyone — Allows anyone to access your resource without logging in. This choice essentially removes all security.

- ▸ Authenticated people only — Must be selected if you are going to choose either of the following options:

  - • All in the authentication database — Allows any user who is located in the directory to access the resource. With this option selected, all users must supply a valid name and password for access.

  - • Only the following people — Allows you to grant access to specific users and groups. To grant access to a group of users, enter the LDAP name or click List to select the group from a list. To grant access to a user, enter the user ID. If you have more than one user, you can separate user IDs by commas. Clicking the List button enables you to search through the user database. This is only a listing; you are still required to enter each user ID into the user field.

- ▸ Prompt for authentication — Allows you to enter a message that you would like to appear when a user is asked to authenticate. This text can be purely informational but can also serve a purpose. Netscape browsers cache a user's name and password as long as the login text is the same. If you would like a user to re-authenticate with each resource accessed, simply change the text for every prompt for authentication.

- ▸ Authentication method — Provides four methods from which to choose:

  - • Default — Uses the method specified in the obj.conf file. Default can be helpful if you have many ACLs because it allows you to change the method for all ACLs by changing it one time in obj.conf.

- Basic — Use if no settings have been made in obj.conf. (Basic uses HTTP authentication.)

- SSL — Uses client certificates to authenticate the user. Server SSL must be turned on to use this method.

- Other — Allows you to create a custom method by using the access control API.

▶ Authentication Database — Allows you to select a database that the server uses to authenticate users.

7. Click Update to save your changes and return to the Access Control Rules page.

8. Click the From Host section of your rule.

9. Now that you have specified which users to grant access to, you can specify the IP address a user must have to access your server. The capability to specify an IP configuration for access to a resource is the

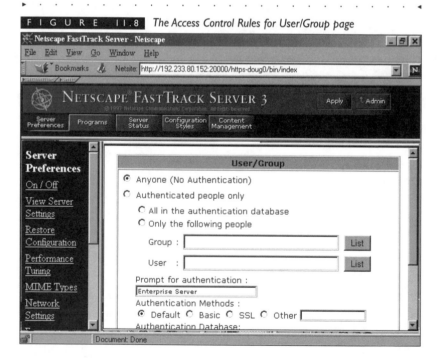

F I G U R E 11.8 *The Access Control Rules for User/Group page*

major difference between using LDAP or native NDS. This feature
gives you the capability to limit access only to people physically
located on a specific network or location. This access is controlled
regardless of what rights have been given to a specific user.

Decide how you want to implement control. There are different ways
to limit access based on IP information. The IP information you enter
in this section determines the IP access control. You can enter specific
IP addresses or groups of IP addresses. You can also use wildcards,
such as 100.100.100.*. Remember that the * has to replace an entire
byte in the IP address. The * must also be the right-most character.
You can add multiple IP addresses or wildcard addresses by separating
each entry with a comma. Entering hostnames is very similar to
entering IP addresses; you can add specific hostnames or use wildcards. When using wildcards for hostnames, the * must be the left-
most entry, as in *.NOVELL.COM or *.MARKETING.NOVELL.COM.

10. Click Update to save your changes and return to the Access Control
Rules page.

11. Click the Rights section of your rule.

12. Specify the file rights you want to grant. There are six different file
attributes that you can control:

- ▶ Read access — Allows users to view a file. It also allows GET, HEAD,
  POST, and INDEX.

- ▶ Write access — Allows PUT, DELETE, MKDIR, RMDIR, and MOVE.

- ▶ Execute access — Enables a user to execute an application, including
  CGI programs, Java applets, and Agents.

- ▶ Delete access — Allows a user to delete a complete directory or
  individual files.

- ▶ List access — Allows directory listings for all directories that do not
  contain an index.html file. List access is also used by the Web
  Publisher included in the Enterprise Server.

- ▶ Info access — Allows users to get file headers. (The HTTP header
  method is also used by the Web Publisher.)

13. Now that you have created your rule, you can customize the message
users see when they are denied access. By default, the Web server will
return an error 404. This tells the user that the file was not found or
the server will not allow the user to have it. If you would like to

forward the user to another page or give a clearer definition about the reason the user was denied, click the Response When Denied link. In the page, enter the location of your response file. This location works the same way as HTML links. If you would like the user to go to a different site, enter a complete URL.

14. Click Submit to save your access control rules.

15. An information page appears, listing all of the changes the system is about to save and commit. Review the information. Click Back if you want to make changes, or click Save and Apply to commit the changes.

16. You will receive a JavaScript message saying that the changes have been successfully saved and applied. Click OK to continue.

Encryption On/Off This page allows you to turn on and off encryption for the entire server.

Encryption Preferences This page allows you to set a number of system-wide preferences for SSL.

Using the Programs Page

FastTrack Server offers many options for Web application development, such as PERL, Java, JavaScript, CGI, and Netbasic. The Programs section of the Admin Server helps you manage the locations and configurations for your Web applications. To open the Programs section, click the Programs button at the top of the Admin Server screen. The available options under Programs are described in the following sections.

CGI Directory There are two ways to store Common Gateway Interface (CGI) programs on your FastTrack Server. The first way is to select a directory that contains only CGI programs. (The second way is described in the next section.) Every file located in this directory will be run as a program.

To specify a CGI directory in which to store CGI programs, complete the following steps:

1. Click the CGI Directory link.

2. In the URL prefix field, type the URL prefix you want to use. The text you type will be the URL path to the directory that you specify on the next line.

3. In the CGI Directory, type the complete path to your new CGI directory. (This path doesn't need to be located in your document root. It can be located anywhere on your server.)

4. Click OK to commit the changes. You should now see your new CGI directory in the list.

You can modify or remove any CGI directory using this page.

Server Side JavaScript JavaScript is one of the most widely used languages on the Internet today. Most JavaScript is client-based, meaning the JavaScript code is downloaded by the browser and executed on the workstation. Server-side JavaScript is different. Server-side JavaScript is code that has been compiled to form a Web file. This file is executed on a Web server. The information that is processed on the server is then passed to the client to be viewed.

A JavaScript compiler is included with the Netscape FastTrack Server. It is located in sys:/novonyx/suitespot/bin/https. You need two files in this directory: jsac.exe and libesnspr20.dll. It is important to note that you can write and compile your JavaScript applications on any platform, but they will only run on Windows NT or Windows NT Server.

The FastTrack Server includes sample applications that are simple examples of what can be written with server-side JavaScript. JavaScript applications can be written with a text editor, Visual Java Script from Netscape, or other development tools. See Netscape's developer Web site (developer.netscape.com) for more information on developing JavaScript applications.

NOTE The initial release of the FastTrack Server contained in NetWare 5 does not support ODBC. However, support for ODBC is expected to be included in an update to the FastTrack Server, which should be available for downloading from Novell's Web site (www.novell.com) by the time this book is published.

Because server-side JavaScript requires some server resources, it has been disabled by default. You should leave it disabled if it is not being used, so it doesn't use server resources unnecessarily. To turn on server-side JavaScript, complete the following steps:

1. Click Server Side JavaScript under the Programs button.

2. Under Activate the Server Side JavaScript Application Development, click Yes. Clicking Yes enables you to modify the obj.conf file.

3. By default, the option to require an administration server password for the JavaScript Application Manager is selected. This means you will be required to authenticate when you access the application manager. If you do not want to secure the JavaScript Application Manager, do not select this option.

4. Click OK.

5. Click OK to save your server-side JavaScript changes.

6. An information page appears, listing all the changes that the system is about to save and commit. Review the information. Click Back if you want to make changes, or click Save and Apply to commit the changes.

7. When you receive a JavaScript message saying that the changes have been successfully saved and applied, click OK to continue. JavaScript uses its own JavaScript application manager, which is described in the next section.

Application Manager Now that you have activated server-side JavaScript, you will see a link to the Application Manager located on the Server Side JavaScript page. When you click the link, it will launch a new browser window for the JavaScript Application Manager, as shown in Figure 11.9.

The JavaScript Application Manager looks similar to the Admin Server, but does not run on its own port. The Application Manager is a server-side JavaScript application that runs on the FastTrack server. You use it to manage all of the server-side JavaScript applications running on your server. You can also access it through the URL http://*server*.com/appmgr. (Replace *server* with the name of your server.)

On the Application Manager page, you will see a box listing all the applications currently running on the FastTrack Server. When you click one of the applications, an information page appears, showing information about that JavaScript application.

Below the applications box, you will see several links:

▶ Start — Allows you to start an application that has been stopped. Note that when you enabled Server Side JavaScript, all of the JavaScript applications on the server were started automatically.

▶ Stop — Unloads an individual application.

▶ Restart — Restarts an application. If an active application is not running correctly, you can click this button to stop and start the application automatically.

▶ Run — Brings up the application in a new browser window.

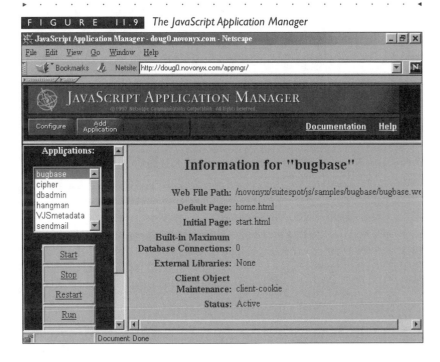

FIGURE 11.9 *The JavaScript Application Manager*

- ▶ Debug — Shows you what the application is doing. It can be displayed down the left side of the screen or in a separate window. (The debugging capabilities of this button are somewhat limited.)
- ▶ Modify — Allows you to change information located in the configuration fields.

Click the Add Application button at the top of the JavaScript Application Manager screen to see all the possible fields that are needed to add a new JavaScript application:

- ▶ Name — This is the name of your application. This name will also be the URL pointing to your application If you name your application "account," the URL will be http://*server*.com/account. (Replace *server* with the name of your server.)
- ▶ Web File Path — This is the location of your Web file (application). Web files can be located anywhere on the NetWare server. Be aware that all of the information for JavaScript applications is case sensitive.

▶ Default Page — This is the HTML page that is accessed when you run the JavaScript application.

▶ Initial Page — For database applications, this file contains information about the database objects you have used to create your application.

▶ Built-in Maximum Database Connections — This number specifies the number of users who can be connected to a database application at any one time. (If the number of connections is specified in your JavaScript code, this number will be ignored.)

▶ External Libraries — This is the location of any external libraries that may be used with your application.

▶ Client Object Maintenance — This allows you to select the client object maintenance mode. Your options are client-cookie, client-url, server-ip, server-cookie, and server-url.

If you click the Configure button at the top of the JavaScript Application Manager screen, you will see a page that enables you to enter default values that will be inserted each time you add a new application. This can be helpful if you are adding many applications that share the same files. There is also a list of preference changes you can make.

Using the Server Status Page

The FastTrack Server gives you two ways to monitor your server's activity. The first method enables you to monitor the server's status in real time (showing what is happening at the current moment compared to past performance). The second method is to monitor your server by recording, archiving, and viewing log files.

To open the Server Status page, click the Server Status button at the top of the Admin Server screen.

FastTrack also offers a log analyzer that lets you generate statistical reports such as a summary of activity, the most accessed URLs, highest utilization time frames, and which hosts are frequently accessing your server. The log analyzer can be run from the Server Manager or command line.

Using the Configuration Styles Page

Configuration styles give you an easy way to apply logging options to specific files or directories that you want monitor. To set configuration styles, click the Configuration Styles button at the top of the Admin Server screen.

Using the Content Management Page

The Netscape FastTrack server supports a variety of methods for organizing the information on your server. This information is managed through the content management page of the Admin Server. To open the content management page, click the Content Management button at the top of the Admin Server screen.

Document directories are the most common way to manage your content. These directories enable you to keep all Web documents in a single location. This allows for easier management and provides a better structure for implementing access control.

The content management section of the Admin Server also manages the use of hardware virtual servers, software virtual servers, forwarding URLs, default pages, and other document preferences. All of these options available allow flexibility and structure to the organization of Web documents. The following sections describe the options available in the Content Management page.

Primary Document Directory The primary document directory is the default location for all Web files. This document directory by default is /novonyx/suitespot/docs. You may change this to any location on your NetWare server by opening the Primary Document Directory screen, and then entering the complete path to the new directory.

Additional Document Directories In addition to your primary document directory, you can create additional document directories. This can be helpful if you would like to separately manage a group of documents. Using additional document directories enables you to use an additional URL prefix for your documents. When you specify a new URL prefix, any client that requests that URL will be served a file from your additional document directory. Figure 11.10 shows the Additional Document Directories screen.

To create an additional document directory, complete the following steps:

1. Be sure you have already created the directory in the file system on the NetWare 5 server.

2. Click Additional Document Directories.

3. In the URL Prefix field, enter the prefix you want to represent your document directory. For example, if you want to use the URL www.server.com/marketing, enter marketing/ as your prefix.

4. In the Map To Directory field, type the path of the directory you want mapped (such as vol1:\marketing\newdocs\).

5. (Optional) If you desire, select a configuration style for your directory.

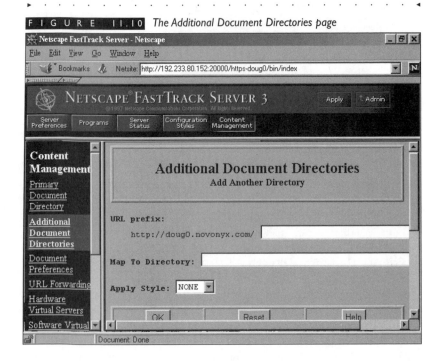

6. Click OK, and then click Save and Apply to commit your changes.

Document Preferences The Document Preferences section of Content Management enables you to set default values for your Web site. Figure 11.11 shows the Document Preferences screen.

You can configure the following document preferences from this screen:

- ▶ Index Filenames — When a user connects to a URL and does not specify a document name, the server automatically displays the index file for that directory. By default, the FastTrack Server first displays index.html. If that file cannot be found, it then displays home.html. Through the Document Preferences link, you can change the default index files or add to the current list.

- ▶ Directory Indexing — You will most likely have subdirectories off the root of your main document directory. You may want to access this directory structure through a browser interface. If you access a URL without specifying a file, the server first looks for your index files.

FIGURE 11.11
The Document Preferences Configuration page

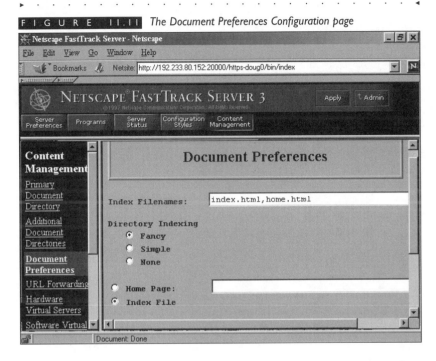

If there is no index file present, the server then generates an index file that lists all files located in that directory. This listing is similar to looking at a directory in File Manager or Windows Explorer. It lists filenames, sizes, and other information. From this option, you can choose one of the following ways to show directory listings:

• Fancy — Shows a graphic representation of the file including file type, the date the file was last modified, and the file size.

• Simple — Shows only the filename. The information is more limited but takes less time to load.

▶ No directory listing — Use this option if you want the contents of your directory to be hidden.

▶ Server Homepage — To access your Web server, most users probably type www.server.com. By default, the server displays the index file for that directory. With the Server Homepage option, you can specify another file to be the server's homepage.

► Default MIME Type — MIME types give information to the client about each file that is requested. This information helps the client know in what format the file should be displayed. With file types that are not currently located in the mime.types file, the server does not know how the file should be displayed. By setting a default MIME type, any file that has not been defined is sent as the default type. In most situations, this is set to a text format, but any file type can be used.

URL Forwarding Forwarding URLs is a common task on the Internet, because Web sites move to new locations for various reasons. URL forwarding enables you to specify a forwarding address for any URL on your server. That way, if you move your Web site, a user can still type the old URL, but his or her browser automatically connects to the new location. To forward a URL, complete the following steps:

1. Open the URL Forwarding option under Content Management.

2. In the URL prefix field, type the URL prefix you want to forward.

3. Select whether you want to forward requests to a URL prefix, or to a fixed URL. If you want to forward requests to another location on the same server, select a URL prefix. To forward requests to another site on a different server, choose a fixed URL.

4. Click OK, and then click Save and Apply to commit your changes.

Hardware Virtual Servers Hardware virtual servers have become an important feature for all Web servers that host multiple domains or have high traffic volumes. Hardware virtual servers allow a single Web server to serve pages on multiple IP addresses by mapping a document directory to each of these IP addresses. With NetWare 5, these additional addresses can all be bound to a single network board in your server, or you can add more network boards to handle the extra IP addresses. Using multiple network boards and hardware virtual servers will enable you to achieve the highest performance from your Web server.

The FastTrack Server enables you to map a document directory to each virtual server you are using. You can map a different document directory to each virtual server to host multiple sites, increase security, or more easily manage your Web site. Hardware virtual servers also enable you to map the same document directory to each virtual server for increased performance.

To set up a hardware virtual server on your FastTrack Server, complete the following steps:

1. Open the Hardware Virtual Servers page from the Content Management screen.

2. In the IP Address field, enter an IP address that has been configured on your server, as shown in Figure 11.12. The address must be configured before you can add the virtual server.

3. Enter the document directory that you want mapped to this virtual server.

4. Click OK, and then click Save and Apply to commit your changes.

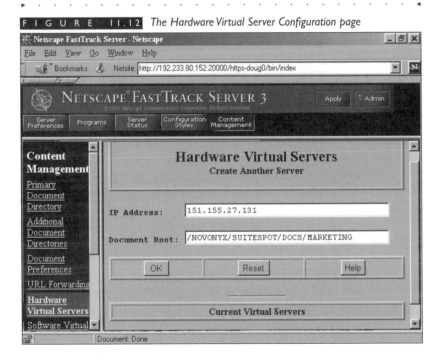

F I G U R E   11.12 *The Hardware Virtual Server Configuration page*

Software Virtual Servers Software virtual servers enable you to use the same IP address to host multiple Web sites. This is accomplished by first assigning multiple DNS names to the IP address on your server. After these names have been assigned, both names will resolve to the same IP address. For example, suppose www.server1.com and www.server2.com both resolve to the address 100.100.100.112. After you set the software virtual server, a client requesting www.server1.com will receive a different page than one requesting www.server2.com. Be aware that some older browsers will not support software virtual servers and will receive the page from the original DNS entry. Remember, for software virtual servers to work correctly, DNS information must be configured correctly for your IP address.

To set up a software virtual server, complete the following steps:

1. Open the Software Virtual option from the Content Management page.

2. In the URL Host field, enter the hostname for your new software virtual server.

3. In the Homepage field, enter the page that you want to use for this software virtual server. You can enter a complete path or a location that is subordinate to the primary document directory.

4. Click OK, and then click Save and Apply to commit your changes.

International Characters The FastTrack Server follows the character set specified in RFC 1700 (a document that defines Internet character set standards). You can override a browser's default character set setting for a document, a set of documents, or a directory by selecting a resource and entering a character set for that resource.

Document Footer The document footer allows you to include the last-modified time in the footer of all the documents in a specific area on the server without using server-parsed HTML.

This footer works for all files except CGI scripts or parsed HTML files. To make a footer appear on CGI scripts or parsed HTML files, you must enter your footer text into a separate file and add the code to the script so that the file's contents are appended to the page's output. The default footer displays the modification date.

Parse HTML When a client requests HTML data, the server normally reads the data and sends it "as is." However, with this option set, it is possible for the server to search the HTML files for special commands, modify the data (according to specific instructions), and then send it off to the requesting client. HTML parsing is disabled by default.

Cache-Control Directives Cache-control directives are a way for the FastTrack Server to control what type of information is cached by proxy servers and how it is cached. Cache-control directives allow you to override the default caching of the proxy to protect sensitive files or directories from being cached and retrieved.

CHAPTER 12

Disaster Planning and Recovery

Planning for Disasters

▶ Write an emergency plan, including emergency contacts and procedures.

▶ Keep good records of your network, including hardware settings, inventory, and so on.

▶ When troubleshooting a problem, isolate the problem and try solutions one at a time.

Why Plan for Disasters?

Disasters come in many guises. A disaster that affects your network could be anything from a crashed hard disk on your server, to a security breach, to a fire that destroys your building. When it comes to computers, a malfunctioning water sprinkler system can cause as much damage as a hurricane.

The best way to recover from a disaster, regardless of the type of disaster, is to have planned for one ahead of time. Armed with a disaster plan, good backups, and accurate records of your network, the task of reestablishing your network will not seem nearly as daunting.

Planning Ahead

If you haven't already created a disaster plan, do it today. It doesn't need to be a difficult task, and it could save a tremendous amount of wasted time, frustrated users, lost revenue, and sleepless nights. An earthquake or electrical fire isn't going to wait for a convenient time in your schedule to occur, so the sooner you plan for it, the better.

Be sure to document the plan. Write it down, get it approved by your organization's upper management, and then make copies and store them in several locations so you'll be able to find at least one copy if disaster strikes.

It's important to have a documented plan, because having the plan in your head only works if you happen to be around, of course. More important, if you've gotten the CEO to approve your plan to restore the production department's network before the administration department's, you won't have to deal with politics and egos while you're trying to restring cables.

What should be included in a disaster plan? Everyone's disaster plan will be different, but there are a few key points to consider when planning yours:

- ▶ Decide where you will store your emergency plan. It needs to be in a location where you or others can get to it easily. Ideally, there should be multiple copies of the plan, perhaps assigned to different individuals. Just storing the emergency plan in your office will not be adequate if the building burns down, so you may consider storing a copy off-site, such as in a safety deposit box or even at your home.

- ▶ List people to call in case of an emergency and include their names, home phone numbers, pager numbers, and cellular phone numbers in your emergency plan. Include key network personnel, such as any network administrators for various branches of the NDS tree, personnel who perform the weekly and daily backups, and so on. You may want to include names of security personnel who should be notified in case of a potential security breach.

▶ Plan the order in which you will restore service to your company. Who needs to be back online first? Is there a critical department that should be restored before any other? Are there key individuals who need to be reconnected first?

▶ Once you've identified the key people who need to be reconnected, determine whether there is an order to the files or services they'll need. Which servers need to be restored first? Which applications must those users have immediately? Which files will they need to access?

▶ Document the location of your network records. Where do you keep your hardware inventory, purchase requisitions, backup logs, and so forth?

▶ Document the location of your network backup tapes or disks. Don't forget to document instructions for restoring files (or indicate the location of the backup system's documentation), in case the backup operator is unavailable. Record your backup rotation schedule so other people can figure out how to restore files efficiently.

▶ Include a drawing of the network layout, showing the exact location of cables, servers, workstations, and other computers. Highlight the critical components, so anyone else reading your plan will know at a glance where to find the priority servers.

In addition to writing a disaster plan, there are other ways you can plan ahead to avert — or at least diminish — disaster. Some of these preparatory measures include:

▶ Keeping a faithful schedule of backups, and practicing restores so that files can be restored quickly.

▶ Implementing disk mirroring (or duplexing), so that a simple hard disk failure in the server won't cause users to lose working time and files because the server is down and they can't do their work.

▶ Using NetWare's TTS (Transaction Tracking System) if you use database applications. TTS ensures that any transactions that are in progress when the server dies or the power goes out are backed out completely, so the database isn't corrupted.

▶ Periodically reviewing your network's security, so you can make sure there are no potential security leaks. Investigate security measures such as NCP Packet Signature, access rights, and password security to make sure that your network is as secure as you need it to be.

Keeping Good Records of Your Network

Another line in your defense against disaster is to maintain up-to-date records about your network. When something goes wrong with your network, it is much easier to spot the problem if you have accurate documentation.

Good network documentation isn't just helpful in an emergency. Doing paperwork is always a distasteful task, but you'll be thankful you did it the next time you have to add new hardware to the network, resolve an interrupt conflict, justify your hardware budget to management, get a workstation repaired under warranty, call for technical support, or train a new assistant.

How you track your network information is up to you. You may want to keep a three-ring binder with printed information about the network, or you may prefer to keep the information online in databases or spreadsheets.

However you document your network, be sure you keep the information in more than one location. If a disaster occurs, you don't want to lose your only copy of the information that can help you restore the network quickly. Try to keep copies of your network information in separate buildings, if possible, so you won't lose everything if you can't access one building.

What types of network information should you record? Again, networks vary, so your documentation needs will vary, too. The worksheets in Appendix D can help you get started. You can photocopy and use those worksheets, or you can design your own worksheets or databases to keep track of the information you need.

Although you may need additional types of network documentation depending on your situation, most experts recommend that you maintain at least the following types of information:

▶ An inventory of hardware and software purchases. Record the product's version number, serial number, vendor, purchase date, length of warranty, and so on. This can help you when management asks for current capital assets or budget-planning information. It can also help you with insurance reports and replacements if a loss occurs.

► A record of configuration settings for servers, workstations, printers, and other hardware. This information can save you hours that you would otherwise spend locating and resolving interrupt conflicts.

► A history of hardware repairs. You may want to file all paperwork associated with repairs along with the worksheet that documents your original purchase of the item.

► A drawing of the network layout. If you store this with your disaster plan, you (and others) will be able to locate critical components quickly. On the drawing, show how all the workstations, servers, printers, and other equipment are connected. The drawing doesn't have to be to scale, but it should show each machine in its approximate location. Label each workstation with its make and model, its location, and its user. Show the cables that connect the hardware, and indicate what types of cable they are.

► Batch files and workstation boot files. Use a text editor or other program to print out these files and keep them with the worksheets that document the workstation. You may also want to store copies of the files on diskette. If you need to reinstall the workstation, you can re-create the user's environment quickly if you have archived these files.

► Backup information. It is very important to record your backup rotation schedule, the location of backup tapes or disks, the names of any backup operators, the labeling system you use on your backup tapes or disks, and any other information someone may need if you're not around to restore the system.

Troubleshooting Tips

Unfortunately, despite the best possible planning, something may still go wrong with your network. The majority of network problems are related to hardware issues — interrupt conflicts, faulty components, incompatible hardware, and so on. However, software creates its own set of problems, such as application incompatibility, OS bugs and incompatibility, and installation errors.

There are endless combinations of servers, workstations, cabling, networking hardware, operating systems, and applications. This makes it impossible to predict and document every possible problem. The best anyone can do is use a methodical system for isolating the problem, and then fixing it.

The following troubleshooting guidelines can help you isolate the problem and find solutions.

Narrow Down the List of Suspects

First, of course, you need to try to narrow your search to suspicious areas by answering the following types of questions:

- ▶ Were there any error messages? If so, look up their explanations in the online documentation that came with your NetWare 5 package.

- ▶ How many machines did the problem affect? If multiple machines were affected, the problem is affecting the network and could be related to the network cabling or network software. If the problem is isolated to one workstation, then the problem is most likely contained within the workstation's own hardware or software configuration.

- ▶ Can you identify a particular cabling segment that has the problem? If so, it could be a problem with the cable connections, the cabling itself, a hub or concentrator, a network address conflict, or the like.

- ▶ Is the problem isolated to a particular branch of the Directory tree?

- ▶ Does the problem occur only when a user accesses a particular application, or does it occur only when the user executes applications in a particular order? This could indicate an application problem that has nothing to do with the network. It could be related to the workstation's memory, to a conflict between two applications or devices that both expect to use the same port or address, or the like.

- ▶ If the problem occurred when you installed new workstations or servers on the network, have you checked their network addresses, IP addresses (if used), and hardware settings for conflicts with other boards or with machines that already exist on the network? Also, double-check the installation documentation to make sure you didn't misspell a command or accidentally skip a step.

- ▶ Are the servers and workstations using the same frame type to communicate? If a server is using Ethernet 802.2 and a workstation is using Ethernet 802.3, for example, they won't see each other. See Chapter 1 for more information about frame types.

- Are the servers and workstations using compatible NCP Packet Signature levels to communicate? See Chapter 7 for more information about NCP Packet Signatures.

- If a user is having trouble working with files or applications, have you checked the security features? Does the user have appropriate rights in the necessary directories? Are the files already opened by someone else? Have the files or directories been assigned attributes that restrict the user from some actions? See Chapter 7 for more information about file security.

- Is a user missing some of his or her DOS path commands? Look in the login scripts for search drive mappings that were mapped without using the INS keyword (which inserts the mapping into the DOS path instead of overwriting existing paths). See Chapter 6 for more information about login scripts.

- For printing problems with queue-based printing, have you checked that the printer, print server, and print queue are all correctly assigned to each other? You can use the NetWare Administrator utility to check your printing setup. Select the print server from the Browser, choose Details from the object menu, and then open the Print Layout page to see whether the print server, printer, and queue are all assigned together correctly. See Chapter 9 for more information about printing.

- If a user can't see an NDPS printer, did you configure the printer so that its drivers will be installed automatically on users' workstations? See Chapter 9 for more information about NDPS printing.

- If NDPS printers aren't available, make sure NDPSM.NLM is loaded on the server. See Chapter 9 for more information about NDPS printing.

- Do you have a volume that won't mount? If it is an NSS volume, you may need to run the REBUILD utility to fix it. If it is a traditional NetWare volume, you may need to run VREPAIR.NLM to fix it. (However, VREPAIR will usually run automatically if NetWare detects a problem with a traditional volume.) REBUILD and VREPAIR are explained in Chapter 8.

- Have you verified that applications are using the correct print drivers for your printers?

- Are all of the servers in the Directory tree running the same version of DS.NLM? If all servers are not running the same version, some conflicts could occur. See Chapter 5 for more information about NDS and DS.NLM.

Check the Hardware

Hardware problems can be relatively common in networks. Network cables are notorious for developing problems, partly because of the abuse they get from being coiled up, walked on, bent around corners, and so on. A network analyzer, such as NetWare LANalyzer, can be a useful tool for diagnosing cable problems. As you diagnose hardware problems, keep the following tips in mind:

▸ Cables have an annoying tendency to work loose from their connectors, so check all connections between cables and boards first.

▸ Test suspicious cables by replacing them with cables you know are working, and then see if the problem persists.

▸ Make sure cables are terminated correctly and that they don't exceed length limits. In addition, ensure that the cables are not connected into endless loops (unless you're using a topology that permits loops).

▸ If the problem is with a computer or printer, try disconnecting the problematic machine from the network and running it in standalone mode. If the problem still shows up in standalone mode, it's probably not a problem with the network connection. You can then eliminate the network components and concentrate on the configuration of the machine itself.

▸ Isolate sections of the network segment until the problem disappears. Add each section back to the network until you have identified the problem cable, board, connector, terminator, or other component.

▸ If the problem occurred when you installed a new workstation or server, or added a board to an existing computer, check hardware settings for conflicts with other boards or with machines that already exist on the network.

Refer to the Documentation

Forget the jokes about only reading the manual as a last resort. The NetWare online documentation contains explanations of error messages that may occur. In addition, the documentation includes troubleshooting tips, configuration instructions, and so on.

Be sure to check the manufacturer's documentation for any network hardware or applications you're using. Some applications have special instructions for installing on a network.

Look for Patches, Updates, or Workarounds

When Novell engineers find a problem with NetWare, they usually solve the problem with a patch (a piece of software that loads as an NLM on your server and repairs the problem), an updated version of a file, or a recommended workaround.

Novell distributes these patches, updates, and workarounds on its Internet Web site (www.novell.com) and in the *Novell Support Connection* (a set of update CD-ROMs available by subscription). See Appendix C for more information about these resources.

Try Each Solution by Itself

After you've isolated the problem, try implementing the solutions you've found one at a time. Start with the easiest, cheapest solution, and work up from there.

Most of us give in to the tendency to try several possible fixes simultaneously to save time. However, trying solutions simultaneously may save time in the short run, but it could cost you extra money for unnecessary repairs or replacements. For example, if you change the cable, the network board, and reinstall the NetWare client software all at the same time, you will have no way of knowing which one was the real solution. You may have just wasted money unnecessarily on a new network board.

In addition, you won't know for sure what fixed the problem, so you'll have to start from scratch again if the problem reappears on another machine or at another time.

Call for Technical Support

A wide variety of places exist where you can get help, advice, tips, and fixes for your NetWare problems or issues. Appendix C lists several of the resources you should know about. These resources range from Internet user groups, to classes, to publications that deal with NetWare support issues. If you're looking for more formal technical support, try these ideas:

▶ You can often find the technical help you need online, through the Internet user groups and mailing lists that focus on NetWare or through Novell's Internet Web site (www.novell.com).

▶ Try calling your reseller or consultant for help.

▶ Novell's technical support is available by calling 1-800-NETWARE. However, Novell's technical support is not free. You'll be charged a fee for each incident, so have your credit card handy. (An incident may involve more than one phone call, if necessary.)

▶ Before you call technical support, be sure you've tried your other resources first — especially the documentation. It's embarrassing and expensive to have technical support tell you that the answer to your question is on page 25 of the manual.

Document the Solution

When you find a solution, write it down and store it with your network documentation. This may prevent you or someone else from going through the same troubleshooting process to fix a similar problem later.

NET.CFG Parameters

NET.CFG is the main configuration file used by the Novell Client for DOS and Windows 3.1*x*. (NET.CFG is not used by the Novell Client for Windows 95/98 or Windows NT.) It can contain dozens of commands to configure various aspects of your client software, such as 16-bit ODI LAN driver settings, network management settings, and general items for the client software itself. It is created by the NetWare client installation. It is located in the NOVELL\CLIENT32 directory on the workstation and can be edited with a text editor.

Every workstation's NET.CFG file may be different because of the different hardware or software installed on the workstation. Using a text editor, open your workstation's NET.CFG file. Notice that the file is divided by headings. Each heading must be flush with the left margin; commands beneath that heading are indented once. (The only exception to these formatting conventions is NETBIOS commands. They are all flush with the left margin.) It doesn't matter if you use uppercase or lowercase in the commands in NET.CFG. (The examples in this chapter use mixed case for readability.)

The Link Driver heading contains indented lines that specify the information for your workstation's LAN driver. If you have two network boards installed in the workstation, the NET.CFG file will have two Link Driver headings.

The NetWare DOS Requester heading contains indented lines that specify general items for the Novell client software. There may also be headings for protocols, network management software, and so on. All of the parameters you can set in NET.CFG are explained in this appendix. They are also explained in the NET.CFG online help.

NET.CFG's help file is named NWCFGDW.HLP, and it is located in the NOVELL\CLIENT32 directory on the workstation. Locate that file from the Windows File Manager, and double-click it to open it. The help file explains all the parameters you can use, divided by categories (which correspond to the headings in the file).

The following is a sample NET.CFG file. Notice that the file is divided by headings:

▸ The Link Driver heading contains indented lines that specify the information for those LAN drivers.

▸ The Link Support heading contains indented lines that configure support for the Link Support Layer (LSL.COM) of the Novell client software. These commands set the number and size of configuration buffers, the size of the memory pool, and the maximum number of logical boards and protocol stacks that the workstation's LSL.COM file can handle.

▶ The NetWare DOS Requester heading contains indented lines that specify general items for the Novell client software. It specifies the first network drive letter, establishes the order in which NetWare protocols should be used (NDS first, bindery second), sets a preferred tree and name context to use when the user logs in, and indicates that the short machine type is IBM (this information can be used by other internal processes and commands in the workstation).

▶ The Protocol TCPIP heading contains indented lines that configure the TCP/IP protocol on this workstation.

Each heading is preceded by a blank line, which makes it easier to read the file. The NET.CFG file that will be created when you first install the Novell client software will vary from this sample, depending on your configuration.

```
Link Driver NCOMX
     INT 3
     PORT 2F8


Link Support
     Buffers 8 1500
     MemPool 8192
     Max Boards 4
     Max Stacks 4


Netware DOS Requester
     First Network Drive = F
     NETWARE PROTOCOL = NDS,BIND
     Preferred Tree BlueTree
     Name Context "blueco"
     SHORT MACHINE TYPE = IBM
```

```
Protocol TCPIP
    PATH TCP_CFG C:\NOVELL\CLIENT32\TCP
    TCP_SOCKETS 15
    UDP_SOCKETS 15
    TCP_WINDOW 10240

Link Driver ETHER
    FRAME Ethernet_802.2
    FRAME Ethernet_II
    PORT 300
```

There are 14 categories of NET.CFG parameters:

- ► Desktop SNMP
- ► Host MIB
- ► Link Driver
- ► Link Support
- ► Named Pipes
- ► NetBIOS
- ► NetWare DOS Requester
- ► NetWare DOS TSA
- ► NIOS
- ► NWIP
- ► Protocol IPX
- ► Protocol TCPIP
- ► SNMP Transport Provider IPX
- ► SNMP Transport Provider UDP

The following sections explain the available parameters for each of these categories.

Desktop SNMP Parameters

Desktop SNMP parameters configure the desktop SNMP option. SNMP (Simple Network Management Protocol) allows network management utilities to receive and manage information about network computers and about specified events that occur on the network. To use these parameters, add the Desktop SNMP heading to the NET.CFG file, and then place each parameter command beneath the heading, indented as shown here:

```
DESKTOP SNMP
        parameter
```

The following parameters can be used with this heading:

▶ **Control Community** = *name*   Specifies the control community, which is the read-write community that is allowed to do SET operations. Default: None. Values: Public, Private, or other name.

▶ **Enable Control Community** = *status*   Specifies which control communities can be used to gain access to and control the SNMP agent on the computer. Default: Off. Values: Specified, Any, or Off.

  • **Specified**   Only the community in the Control Community command is allowed.

  • **Any**   Any community is allowed.

  • **Off**   Access for this community type is disabled.

▶ **Enable Monitor Community** = *status*   Specifies which monitor communities can be used to gain access to and request information from the computer. Default: Any. Values: Specified, Any, or Off.

  • **Specified**   Only the community in the Monitor Community command is allowed.

  • **Any**   Any community is allowed.

  • **Off**   Access for this community type is disabled.

▶ **Enable Trap Community** = *status*   Specifies which trap communities can be used to gain access to alerts sent by the computer. Default: Specified. Values: Specified or Off. ("Any" is not a possible value for this parameter.)

  • **Specified**   Only the community in the Trap Community command is allowed.

  • **Off**   Access for this community type is disabled.

▶ **Monitor Community** = *name*   Specifies the monitor community, which is the read-only community that is allowed to do GET and GET NEXT operations. Default: Public. Values: Public, Private, or other name.

▶ **SNMPEnable-AuthenTrap** = *on/off* When set to On, tells the Desktop SNMP to send a trap message if an unauthorized user tries to use SNMP to get or change data that SNMP manages. Default: Off.

▶ **sysContact** = *name* Specifies the name of the person who should be notified if the workstation needs maintenance. You can enter a name and phone number, or other information, such as "Ray Snow ext. 3354."

▶ **sysLocation** = *location* Specifies the physical location of the workstation. Enter any location, such as "West wing 2nd floor."

▶ **sysName** = *name* Specifies the user's login name or TCP/IP host name, if available, such as lksmith.

▶ **Trap Community** = *name* Specifies the trap community that receives the computer's alert messages. Default: Public. Values: Public, Private, or other name.

Host MIB Parameters

Host MIB parameters configure information about hardware and software for the Host Resources MIB, which is used by an SNMP network management console. To use these parameters, add the Host MIB heading to the NET.CFG file, and then place each parameter command beneath the heading, indented as shown here:

```
HOST MIB

    parameter
```

The following parameters can be used with this heading:

▶ **Modem** = *"information"* Identifies a modem installed in the workstation. You can enter any descriptive information about the modem inside the quotation marks, such as "Hayes 56K." Default: None.

▶ **Printer** = *"information"* Identifies a printer attached to the workstation. You can enter any descriptive information about the printer inside the quotation marks, such as "Sales - Canon Color Laser." Default: None.

▸ **SWDirectory-Search** = *path*   Indicates the specific directories that the SNMP agent can search when scanning for software inventory. To tell the agent to search a directory and all its subdirectories, add an asterisk after the directory's name, as in C:\WINDOWS*. Default: None.

▸ **SWDirectorySearch-Depth** = *number*   Tells the SNMP agent how many subdirectories deep it can search when scanning for software inventory. Default: 1. Values: 0 to 4,294,967,295.

▸ **TapeDrive** = "*information*"   Identifies a tape drive attached to the workstation. You can enter any descriptive information about the drive inside the quotation marks, such as "Seagate Scorpion." Default: None.

Link Driver Parameters

Link Driver parameters configure hardware and software options for the workstation's 16-bit ODI LAN drivers. They also enable you to specify frame types and protocols for the LAN driver. (32-bit ODI LAN drivers do not use Link Driver parameters.)

To use these parameters, add the Link Driver heading to the NET.CFG file, and then place each parameter command beneath the heading, indented as shown here. Substitute the name of your LAN driver, such as 3C523, for *driver* in the heading.

```
LINK DRIVER driver
     parameter
```

The following parameters can be used with this heading:

▸ **Frame** *frametype* [*mode*]   Sets the frame type the LAN driver will use. Can also set the address mode to either LSB (canonical addressing mode) or MSB (noncanonical addressing mode) for LAN drivers that support this. Default frame types are:

  • For Ethernet drivers: Ethernet_802.2

  • For Token Ring drivers: Token-Ring

  • For TCP/IP ODI SLIP_PPP drivers: SLIP

▸ **Irq** [#1 or #2] *number*   Sets the interrupt (IRQ) that the network board will use. Use #1 or #2 to specify the network board you're configuring, and then replace *number* with the interrupt number you want to assign. Recommended values: 3, 5, or 7 for most network boards, to avoid conflicting with other hardware. See the manufacturer's documentation for more information.

► **Port [#1 or #2]** *address* **[number]**   Sets the hex address for the starting I/O port and, if necessary, the number of ports in the range. Use #1 or #2 to specify the appropriate network board.

► • ◄

Link Support Parameters

Link Support parameters configure options for the Link Support Layer (LSL.COM), such as the size of packet receive buffers, the size of memory pool buffers, and so on.

To use these parameters, add the Link Support heading to the NET.CFG file, and then place each parameter command beneath the heading, indented as shown here:

```
LINK SUPPORT
     parameter
```

The following parameters can be used with this heading:

► **Buffers** *number* **[size]**   Sets the number of communication buffers (if applicable) and the size (in bytes) of receive buffers that LSL.COM can handle. Used with 16-bit ODI drivers. The buffer size should be the same size as the largest packet size that your workstation receives over the network.

   • **For IPX**   Default *number*: 0 (IPX uses its own buffers and does not need the LSL to provide buffers for it.) Default *size*: 1500.

   • **For TCP/IP**   Default *number*: 8. Default *size*: 1500.

► **Max Boards** *number*   Sets the maximum number of logical boards LSL.COM can maintain. Used with 16-bit ODI drivers. Default: 4. Values: 1 to 16.

► **Max Buffer Size** *size*   Sets the maximum size packets that can be supported. Used with 32-bit ODI drivers. Used primarily on Token Ring networks, which can use larger packets than the default size. Default: 4736. Values: 100 to 24682.

► **Max Stacks** *number*   Sets the maximum number of logical protocol stack IDs that LSL.COM can support. Used with 16-bit ODI drivers. Default: 4. Values: 1 to 16.

▶ **Mempool** *number* [K]   Configures the size of the memory pool
buffers (in bytes) for some protocols (not used with IPXODI). Used
with 16-bit ODI drivers. Include the K option to indicate the value is
in kilobytes. Default: 0.

Named Pipes Parameters

Named Pipes parameters regulate how a workstation interacts with a
Named Pipes server.

To use these parameters, add the Named Pipes heading to the NET.CFG
file, and then place each parameter command beneath the heading, indented
as shown here:

```
NAMED PIPES
     parameter
```

The following parameters can be used with this heading:

▶ **NP Max Comm Buffers** *number*   Indicates the maximum number of
communication buffers that the extender can use when communicating
with the Named Pipes server. Default: 6. Values: 4 to 40.

▶ **NP Max Machine Names** *number*   Sets the DOSNP software for peer
mode and specifies how many Named Pipes servers the extender can
communicate with. Sets the maximum number of Named Pipes servers
that the DOSNP software can maintain in a local name table. Default:
10. Values: 4 to 50.

▶ **NP Max Open Named Pipes** *number*   Sets the maximum number of
Named Pipes that the workstation can have open simultaneously.
Default: 4. Values: 4 to 128.

▶ **NP Max Sessions** *number*   Sets the maximum number of Named
Pipes servers that the extender can communicate with in default mode.
Not used in peer mode. Default: 10. Values: 4 to 50.

▶ . . . . ◀

NetBIOS Parameters

NetBIOS parameters let you configure NetBIOS sessions, buffers, and broadcasts.

To use these parameters, you don't need to add a NetBIOS heading to the NET.CFG file. Each NetBIOS command can be entered flush with the left margin, as in this example:

```
NETBIOS parameter
NETBIOS parameter
```

The following NetBIOS parameters can be used:

▶ **NetBIOS Abort Timeout** *number*   Sets the time, in ticks, that NetBIOS waits for a response before ending a session. Default: 540 (approximately 30 seconds).

▶ **NetBIOS Broadcast Count** *number*   Sets how many queries or claims NetBIOS broadcasts for the name being used by the application. When multiplied by NetBIOS Broadcast Delay number, sets the time required to broadcast a name resolution packet across the network. With NetBIOS Internet On, default: 4. With NetBIOS Internet Off, default: 2. Values: 2 to 65535.

▶ **NetBIOS Broadcast Delay** *number*   Sets how many ticks NetBIOS waits between query or claim broadcasts. When multiplied by NetBIOS Broadcast Count number, sets the time required to broadcast a name resolution packet across the network. With NetBIOS Internet On, default: 36. With NetBIOS Internet Off, default: 18. Values: 18 to 65535.

▶ **NetBIOS Commands** *number*   Specifies the number of NetBIOS commands that can be buffered in the NetBIOS driver at a time. Default: 12. Values: 4 to 250.

▶ **NetBIOS Internet** *on/off*   Speeds up packets when set to Off if you are using NetBIOS applications on a single network. If using multiple networks through bridges, leave On. Default: On.

▶ **NetBIOS Listen Timeout** *number*   Sets the time, in ticks, that NetBIOS waits before requesting another packet to make sure the connection is still valid. Default: 108 (approximately 6 seconds). Values: 1 to 65535.

▶ **NetBIOS Receive Buffers** *number*   Sets the number of IPX receive buffers that NetBIOS uses. Default: 6. Values: 4 to 20.

▶ **NetBIOS Retry Count** *number*   Specifies how many times NetBIOS resends a packet to establish a NetBIOS session with a remote partner. With NetBIOS Internet On, default: 20. With NetBIOS Internet Off, default: 10. Values: 4 to 20.

▶ **NetBIOS Retry Delay** *number*   Specifies how long, in ticks, NetBIOS waits between sending packets to establish a session. Default: 10 (approximately 0.5 seconds). Values: 10 to 65535.

▶ **NetBIOS Send Buffers** *number*   Sets the number of IPX send buffers that NetBIOS uses. Default: 6. Values: 4 to 20.

▶ **NetBIOS Session** *number*   Specifies the maximum number of simultaneous NetBIOS sessions. Default: 32. Values: 4 to 250.

▶ **NetBIOS Verify Timeout** *number*   Sets the interval, in ticks, between packets sent to keep a connection open. Default: 54 (approximately 3 seconds). Values: 4 to 65535.

NetWare DOS Requester Parameters

NetWare DOS Requester parameters configure various settings for the workstation's environment and settings for CLIENT32.NLM.

To use these parameters, add the NetWare DOS Requester heading to the NET.CFG file, and then place each parameter command beneath the heading, indented as shown here:

```
NETWARE DOS REQUESTER
        parameter
```

The following parameters can be used with this heading:

▶ **Auto Reconnect Level=***on/off*   Specifies how the Novell client software performs when restoring the workstation's connection to the network. Default: 3. Values: 0 = does not reconnect; 1 = reconnects devices only (connections, drives, printers, etc.); 2 = reconnects devices and read-only files; 3 = reconnects devices and all files and file locks; 4 = reconnects devices, files, and file locks, and guarantees recovery.

▶ **Cache Writes=***on/off*   Specifies whether writes are cached. Default: On.

▶ **Checksum=***number*   Sets level at which NCP packets are validated. Default: 1. Values: 0 = disabled; 1 = enabled but not preferred; 2 = enabled and preferred; 3 = required.

▶ **Close Behind Ticks *number***   Specifies the amount of time, in ticks, that the client software waits before closing a file after receiving a close request. If set to 0, then the Delay Writes parameter is disabled. Default: 0. Values: 0 to 65535.

▶ **Delay Writes *on/off***   When set to On, allows writes to be delayed until after an application is closed. Default: Off.

▶ **Dos Name=***"name"*   Specifies the name of DOS on the workstation. Supplies this name for the %OS variable in login scripts. Enclose the *name* in quotation marks. Default: MSDOS.

▶ **End Of Job *on/off***   Sends an End of Job notice to each connected server when a process ends. Default: Off.

▶ **Environment Pad = *bytes***   Adds the specified number of bytes to the workstation's DOS environment. This enables DOS-based applications to increase the environment after Windows is loaded. Default: 17. Values: 17 to 512.

▶ **File Cache Level *number***   Specifies the type of file caching the workstation uses. Default: 2. Values: 0 = no caching; 1 = read-ahead and write behind caching only; 2 = short-lived caching; 3 = long-lived caching.

▶ **First Network Drive=***letter*   Specifies which drive letter will be the first network drive. Default: First available. Values: A to Z.

▶ **Force First Network Drive *on/off***   If set to On, ensures that, after the user logs out, the SYS:LOGIN directory is mapped to the same drive letter specified in the First Network Drive command. If set to Off, this command maps SYS:LOGIN to the drive letter from which the user logged out. Default: Off.

▶ **Handle Net Errors=***on/off*   Sets how network errors are handled. Default: On. Values: On = the Novell client software handles errors; Off = the Novell client software calls INT 24, allowing other applications to handle the error.

▶ **Large Internet Packets=***on/off*   Allows maximum packet size to be used instead of the default size of 576 bytes. (See Lip Start Size parameter.) Default: On.

▶ **Lip Start Size** *number*   Sets the starting LIP (Large Internet Packet) size, in bytes, used when negotiating LIP size. Default: 65535. Values: 512 to 655535.

▶ **Lock Delay=***number*   Specifies how long, in ticks, the Novell client software waits after receiving a SHARE failure, before trying to lock a file. Default: 1. Value: 1 to 65535.

▶ **Lock Retries=***number*   Specifies how many times the Novell client software tries to lock a file after receiving a SHARE failure. Default: 2.

▶ **Long Machine Type=***"name"*   Specifies the type of computer being used. Enclose the *name* in quotation marks. Used by the %MACHINE variable in login script drive mappings. The *name* can be one to six characters long. Default: IBM_PC.

▶ **Max Cache Size=***number*   Specifies the maximum amount of memory (in KB) that the Novell client software can use for caching. Default: 0. Values: 0 to 9999999.

▶ **Max Cur Dir Length=***number*   Specifies how many characters can be displayed at the DOS prompt when the prompt is set to show the current directory path. Default: 64. Values: 64 to 255.

▶ **Message Level=***number*   Specifies which messages are displayed during load. Default: 1. Values: 0 = copyright and critical errors; 1 = warning messages; 2 = load information for programs; 3 = configuration information; 4 = diagnostic information. (Each message level also displays the previous level's messages.)

▶ **Message Timeout=***number*   Specifies the length of time (in ticks) that the Novell client software will display a broadcast message before clearing it from the workstation's screen. Default: 0. Values: 0 (disables the timeout, so that the message remains on the screen until the user manually clears it) to 10000.

▶ **Minimum Time to Net=***milliseconds*   Overrides the time-to-net value defined by the local router during connections. Used on bridged WAN or satellite links with time-to-net values set too low for workstations to make a connection. Default: 0. Values: 1 to 65535.

▶ **Name Context=***"context"*   Sets the user's current location, or context, in the NDS tree. Enclose the *context* in quotation marks. Default: The root of the NDS tree.

▶ **NCP Max Timeout=*seconds*** Specifies how long (in seconds) the Novell client software waits for a network connection before displaying an error message. Default: 30. Values: 0 to 65535.

▶ **Net Status Busy Timeout=*seconds*** Specifies how long (in seconds) the Novell client software waits after before trying to automatically reconnect, after it has received a busy signal from the network. Default: 20. Values: 0 to 600.

▶ **Net Status Timeout=*seconds*** Specifies how long (in seconds) the Novell client software waits for a response before attempting to automatically reconnect to the network. Default: 30. Values: 0 to 600.

▶ **NetWare Protocol=*list*** Sets the order in which NetWare name service protocols (NDS and BIND) are used. Lets you prioritize the protocols for login or load order. Separate protocols by a comma or space. Default order: NDS BIND.

▶ **Network Printers=*number*** Specifies how many LPT ports can be captured by the Novell client software. Default: 3. Values: 0 to 9.

▶ **PB Buffers=*number*** When set to 0, turns Packet Burst off. When set to any number between 1 and 10, turns Packet Burst on. (The Novell Client for DOS and Windows 3.1*x* only recognizes that Packet Burst is turned on or off. Previous versions of the client allowed numbers between 1 and 10, so those numbers are still supported, but they all mean "On.") Default: 3. Values: 0 to 10.

▶ **Pburst Read Window Size=*number*** Specifies the maximum number of packets that Packet Burst can use for read bursts. Default: 24 (or 255 if Packet Burst detects a low bandwidth network connection). Values: 3 to 255.

▶ **Pburst Write Window Size=*number*** Specifies the maximum number of packets that Packet Burst can use for write bursts. Default: 10 (or 255 if Packet Burst detects a low bandwidth network connection). Values: 3 to 255.

▶ **Preferred Server=*server*** Specifies which server to attach to first. Default: none.

▶ **Preferred Tree=*tree*** Specifies which Directory tree to attach to first. Default: none.

▶ **Print Header=*bytes*** Specifies the size, in bytes, of the buffer to hold initialization information for each print job. Default: 64. Values: 0 to 1024.

▶ **Print Tail=***bytes*   Specifies the size, in bytes, of the buffer to hold reset information after a print job. Default: 16. Values: 0 to 1024.

▶ **Read Only Compatibility=***on/off*   If set to On, allows a read-only file to be opened with a read-write access call. Default: Off.

▶ **Resolve Name Using Primary=***on/off*   When set to On, uses the primary connection to do name resolves. When set to Off, the client software uses all connections when attempting to resolve names. Default: On.

▶ **Search Dirs First=***on/off*   When set to On, specifies that directories are displayed before files, when the DIR command is executed. When set to Off, displays files first. Default: Off.

▶ **Search Mode=***number*   Sets the search mode for finding files in directories. Default: 1. Values: 1 = searches the path specified in the file. If no path is found, searches the default directory, and then all search drives. 2 = Searches the path specified in the file. If no path is found, searches only the default directory. 3 = Searches the path specified in the file. If no path is found, searches the default directory. Then, if the open request is read-only, searches the search drives. 4 = Not used. 5 = Searches the path specified, and then searches all search drives. If no path is found, searches the default directory, and then all search drives. 6 = Not used. 7 = Searches the path specified. If the open request is read-only, searches the search drives. If no path is found, searches the default directory, and then all search drives.

▶ **Set Station Time=***on/off*   If set to On, the workstation's time is synchronized to the time of the server to which it first attaches. Default: On.

▶ **Short Machine Type=***"name"*   Sets the computer name to determine which overlay files to use. Used by the %SMACHINE variable in login scripts. Enclose the *name* in quotation marks. The *name* can be one to four characters long. Default: IBM.

▶ **Show Dots=***on/off*   If set to On, displays dots (. and ..) for parent directories in Windows 3.*x*. Default: On.

▶ **Signature Level=***number*   Sets the level of NCP Packet Signature security. Default: 1. Values: 0 = no signing; 1 = signs if server requests; 2 = signs if server can sign; 3 = required.

▶ **True Commit=***on/off*   When set to On, file data is stored in the workstation's memory until the Novell client software receives confirmation that the data was successfully written to the server's hard disk. Default: Off.

NetWare DOS TSA Parameters

NetWare DOS TSA parameters let you configure the DOS TSA (Target Service Agent) software. The DOS TSA lets you back up a DOS-based workstation using Enhanced SBACKUP.

To use these parameters, add the NetWare DOS TSA heading to the NET.CFG file, and then place each parameter command beneath the heading, indented as shown here:

```
NETWARE DOS TSA

      parameter
```

The following parameters can be used with this heading:

▶ **Disk Buffers=***size*   Specifies the size, in KB, of disk buffers. Default: 1. Values: 1 to 30.

▶ **Drives=***letter*   Specifies which hard disk drives are being managed by the TSA (Target Service Agent). Separate multiple drive letters with a space. Default: C.

▶ **Password=***name*   Sets a unique password for the workstation, which the backup administrator must supply before backing up the workstation's local drives. Default: none.

▶ **Stack Size=***bytes*   Sets the stack size, in bytes, for the TSA. Use only if the available RAM on the workstation is extremely limited. Default: 2048. Values: 512 to 4096.

▶ **TSA Server Name=***server*   Specifies the network server to which this workstation's TSA registers itself for backups. Default: none.

▶ **Workstation Name=***name*   Identifies this workstation's unique name for backups. Default: none.

NIOS Parameters

NIOS parameters configure NIOS.EXE. To use these parameters, add the NIOS heading to the NET.CFG file, and then place each parameter command beneath the heading, indented as shown here:

```
NIOS
        parameter
```

The following parameters can be used with this heading:

- **Alert Beep** *on/off*   When set to On, specifies that an alert beep sounds on the workstation each time the Novell client software displays a status message in text mode. Default: On.

- **Ignore Below 16meg Memory Allocate Flag=***on/off*   When set to On, allows NIOS.EXE to try to allocate memory below the 16MB boundary if it is specifically requested to do so. Default: Off.

- **Log File** *path/file*   Specifies the path and name of the Novell client log file. Default: NOVELL\CLIENT32\NIOS.LOG.

- **Log File Size** *bytes*   Specifies the maximum size (in bytes) that the NIOS log file can become. Default: 65535. Values: 1 to 1048576.

- **Mem Pool Size=***size*   Specifies the amount of memory (in KB) that the Novell client software can allocate for client components when no more extended memory is available, or if a client component is loaded from Windows. Default: 128. Values: 0 to 4,294,967,295. (If the size is set to 31KB or less, no memory pool is allocated.)

- **Use Video Bios** *on/off*   When set to On, NIOS.EXE will use BIOS calls to access video memory. (Set this parameter to On when messages in character mode do not display well.) When set to Off, NIOS.EXE uses direct video memory access, which is faster than using BIOS calls. Default: Off.

NWIP Parameters

NWIP parameters configure NetWare/IP, a Novell product in IntranetWare and NetWare 4.11. NetWare/IP is not included in NetWare 5, but this section is included because you may have NetWare/IP servers already installed on your network. To use these parameters, add the NWIP heading to the NET.CFG file, and then place each parameter command beneath the heading, indented as shown here:

```
NWIP
        parameter
```

The following parameters can be used with this heading:

▸ **Autoretries** *number*   Specifies how many times NetWare/IP will retry a DSS request before receiving a response. Default: 1. Values: 0 to 10.

▸ **Autoretry Secs** *seconds*   Specifies how long (in seconds) NetWare/IP will wait before retrying an unanswered DSS request. Default: 10. Values: 5 to 60.

▸ **Nearest NWIP Server** *name*   Specifies a list of the nearest NetWare/IP servers that this workstation can contact. Replace *name* with a server name, address, or address mask. You can indicate up to five servers in this command. Separate each server *name* with a space. Default: none.

▸ **NSQ Broadcast** *on/off*   When set to On, tells the client to use NSQ broadcasts to determine the nearest NetWare/IP server. Default: On.

▸ **NWIP Domain Name** *name*   Specifies the NetWare/IP domain name that has been configured for the workstation's area. Default: none.

▸ **NWIP1_1 Compatibility** *on/off*   When set to On, allows this client to communicate with servers running the first version (unpatched) of NetWare/IP and DSS. This parameter should be set as a temporary measure only. All NetWare/IP servers running version 1.1 should be patched or upgraded to 2.1 or later, as soon as possible. Default: Off.

▸ **Preferred DSS** *name*   Specifies a list of preferred domain SAP/RIP servers that this workstation can contact. Replace *name* with a server name, address, or address mask. You can indicate up to five servers in this command. Separate each server *name* with a space. Default: none.

Protocol IPX Parameters

Protocol IPX parameters configure the IPX protocol.

To use these parameters, add the Protocol IPX heading to the NET.CFG file, and then place each parameter command beneath the heading, indented as shown here:

```
PROTOCOL IPX
        parameter
```

The following parameters can be used with this heading:

- **Int64** *on/off*   If set to On, allows a DOS-based application to use interrupt 64h to access IPX services. When set to Off, allows applications to use this interrupt for other purposes. Default: On.

- **Int7a** *on/off*   If set to On, allows a DOS-based application to use interrupt 7ah to access IPX services. When set to Off, allows applications to use this interrupt for other purposes. Default: On.

- **IPX Diagnostics** *on/off*   When set to On, enables the IPX diagnostics function. When set to Off, prevents the network administrator from querying for IPX and SPX statistics on the workstation. Default: On.

- **IPX Retry Count** *number*   Specifies the number of times a workstation tries to find a valid route to a destination. Default: 20. Values: 0 to 65535.

- **Net Bind** *frame MlidShortName AdapterInstance*   Specifies the logical boards to which IPX is bound. Default: IPX binds automatically to all logical boards.

- **Pre-allocate Vgnma Memory** *on/off*   When set to on, allows 16-bit GNMA Responder applications to allocate conventional memory. Default: Off.

- **Primary** *frame MlidShortName AdapterInstance*   Specifies the network board that you want IPX to use as the primary board. Default: IPX selects the primary board.

- **Protocol** *name id frame*   Specifies a Protocol ID for IPX to use over the specified frame type. Default: none.

- **SPX Abort Timeout** *number*   Sets the time, in ticks, that SPX waits for a response before terminating a connection. Default: 540 (approximately 30 seconds). Values: 1 to 65535.

▶ **SPX Connections** *number*   Indicates the number that is given to applications when they ask for the number of available SPX connections. Does not set the maximum number of simultaneous SPX connections a workstation can have. Default: 15. Values: 1 to 255.

▶ **SPX Listen Timeout** *number*   Sets the time, in ticks, that SPX waits for a packet before requesting a confirmation packet to make sure the connection is still valid. Default: 108 (approximately 6 seconds). Values: 1 to 65535.

▶ **SPX Verify Timeout** *number*   Sets the interval, in ticks, between packets that SPX sends to verify a connection is working. Default: 54 (approximately 3 seconds). Values: 1 to 65535.

▶ **SPX Watchdogs** *on/off*   When set to On, tells SPX to respond to requests for connection watchdogging. Default: On.

Protocol TCPIP Parameters

Protocol TCPIP parameters configure the TCP/IP protocol.

To use these parameters, add the Protocol TCPIP heading to the NET.CFG file, and then place each parameter command beneath the heading, indented as shown here:

```
PROTOCOL TCPIP
        parameter
```

The following parameters can be used with this heading:

▶ **Arp_Aging_Timeout** *seconds*   Specifies how long (in seconds) an entry is kept in the ARP cache. Default: 300. Values: 1 to 7200.

▶ **Arp_Cache_Max** *number*   Specifies the maximum number of ARP cache entries. Default: 64. Values: 8 to 256.

▶ **Arp_Timeout** *seconds*   Specifies how long (in seconds) the Novell client software waits to receive a response from ARP requests before timing out. Default: 5. Values: 1 to 120.

▸ **Bind** *driver* [*number frametype network*] Binds the TCP/IP protocol to a LAN driver. Used only for compatibility with the LAN Workplace product. *Driver* is the LAN driver name. *Number* is the board number when you have two boards with the same name. *Frametype* is the frame type for your network connection. *Network* is a descriptive name for this network connection. Default: none.

▸ **If_Configuration** *method* Specifies the method used to obtain the configuration for a particular network board. Default: Static. Values: Static (configuration is defined by keywords, such as IP_ADDRESS); Bootp (configuration is obtained from a BOOTP server); DHCP (configuration is obtained from a DHCP server); Rarp (configuration is defined by additional keywords except for the IP address, which is obtained from a RARP server).

▸ **IP_Address** *address* [*name*] Specifies this workstation's IP address. *Name* is a descriptive name for this network connection. Default: none.

▸ **IP_Broadcast** *address* [*name*] Specifies this workstation's broadcast IP address. Default: 0.0.0.0

▸ **IP_Netmask** *address* [*name*] Specifies this workstation's default subnetwork mask if subnetworks are being used. *Name* is a descriptive name for this network connection. Default: none.

▸ **IP_Reassembly_Timeout** *seconds* Specifies how long, in seconds, the TCP/IP stack waits for all pieces of a fragmented IP packet to arrive. Default: 15. Values: 1 to 120.

▸ **IP_RIP** *yes/no* When set to Yes, allows IP to monitor RIP traffic for routing information. Default: No.

▸ **IP_Router** *address* [*name*] Specifies the default router's IP address for all packets being sent to remote networks. *Name* is a descriptive name for this network connection. Default: none.

▸ **IP_Trsw_Trigger** *number* Specifies the number of TCP retransmissions that cause the TCP/IP stack to identify a router as "dead," causing it to switch to another router. Default: 3. Values: 1 to the limit set by the Tcp_rxmit_limit plus 1.

▸ **IP_Ttl** *hops* Specifies the TTL (time to live) value (in hops) of an IP packet. Default: 128. Values: 1 to 255.

▸ **Net Bind** *frame MlidShortName AdapterInstance* Specifies the logical boards to which TCP/IP is bound. Default: none.

▶ **Path Tcp_cfg** *path*   Indicates the directory that contains the database configuration files such as HOSTS, NETWORKS, SERVICES, and RESOLV.CFG. This command works with the same syntax as the DOS PATH command. Default path: none.

▶ **Route** *host address mask*   Specifies a static route to a network or a host. Replace *host* with the name or IP address of the destination — either a host or a network. Replace *address* with the IP address of a router. You can also specify a subnet *mask* for the router. Default: none.

▶ **TCP_Connect_Retry** *number*   Specifies how many times TCP/IP will attempt to send a connection request packet to open a TCP/IP connection. Default: 5. Values: 1 to 256.

▶ **TCP_Keepalive** *yes/no*   When set to Yes, causes the Novell client software to send TCP "keepalive" packets. Default: Yes.

▶ **TCP_Keepalive_Interval** *seconds*   Specifies how long, in seconds, the Novell client software should wait before sending another "keepalive" packet. Default: 7200. Values: 1 to 14400.

▶ **TCP_Rcv_Windowsz** *number*   Specifies the maximum size, in bytes, of TCP receive windows. Default: 16384. Values 1 to 65535.

▶ **TCP_Release_Wait_Time** *seconds*   Specifies how long, in seconds, the Novell client software will wait for the release of a TCP socket. Default: 120. Values: 1 to 600.

▶ **TCP_Rxmit_Limit** *number*   Specifies the maximum number of times that TCP/IP will retransmit the same TCP packet before terminating the connection. Default: 12. Values: 1 to 24.

▶ **TCP_Rxmit_Maxtime** *milliseconds*   Specifies the maximum time, in milliseconds, the Novell client software will wait before resending a TCP packet. Default: 120000. Values: The number of milliseconds set by the Tcp_rxmit_mintime parameter plus 1, to 240000.

▶ **TCP_Rxmit_Mintime** *milliseconds*   Specifies the minimum time, in milliseconds, the Novell client software will wait before resending a TCP packet. Default: 110. Values: 2 to the number of milliseconds set by the Tcp_rxmit_maxtime parameter minus 1.

▶ **UDP_Checksum** *yes/no*   When set to Yes, causes the Novell client software to use UDP checksums. Default: Yes.

SNMP Transport Provider IPX Parameter

The SNMP Transport Provider parameter enables you to specify the trap target address for SNMP desktops. The Desktop SNMP transport provider STPIPX.COM reads the configuration file to find trap targets on the network.

To use this parameter, add the SNMP Transport Provider IPX heading to the NET.CFG file, and then place the parameter command beneath the heading, indented as shown here:

```
SNMP TRANSPORT PROVIDER IPX
        parameter
```

The following parameter can be used with this heading:

▸ **Trap Target** *address*   Specifies the management workstation address so the workstation can receive traps sent by Desktop SNMP. Replace *address* with the IPX address of the management workstation.

SNMP Transport Provider UDP Parameter

The SNMP Transport Provider parameter lets you specify the trap target address for SNMP desktops. The Desktop SNMP transport provider STPIPX.COM reads the configuration file to find trap targets on the network.

To use this parameter, add the SNMP Transport Provider UDP heading to the NET.CFG file, and then place the parameter command beneath the heading, indented as shown here:

```
SNMP TRANSPORT PROVIDER UDP
        parameter
```

The following parameter can be used with this heading:

▸ **Trap Target** *address*   Specifies the management workstation address so the workstation can receive traps sent by Desktop SNMP. Replace *address* with the IP address of the management workstation.

SET Parameters

When you first install NetWare 5, the operating system is tuned by default so that its performance is optimized for most systems. Over time, the server optimizes itself according to the network usage it encounters. Occasionally, however, you may find that you want to make manual changes to your system in some aspect of the server's operation.

For this reason, there are numerous server parameters you can set to change the way the server handles things such as memory or file locks. These server parameters, also called SET parameters, can be set in two different ways:

- ▶ At the server console, using the SET console command.

- ▶ In MONITOR.NLM, which enables you to select the parameters you want from menus instead of typing in complete SET commands at the console.

NOTE

When you make changes to server parameters, they are stored in a server configuration database, so that the changes will remain in effect even after the server is rebooted. Previous versions of NetWare required that you add SET commands to the STARTUP.NCF or AUTOEXEC.NCF files to make changes to server parameters permanent. This is no longer necessary in NetWare 5.

In most cases, you may not need to change any server parameters. However, if you need to change them, each server parameter is explained in this appendix.

The 16 categories of SET parameters are:

- ▶ Communication
- ▶ Directory Caching
- ▶ Directory Services
- ▶ Disk
- ▶ Error Handling
- ▶ File Caching
- ▶ File System
- ▶ Licensing Services
- ▶ Locks
- ▶ Memory
- ▶ Miscellaneous
- ▶ Multiprocessor

- NCP
- Service Location Protocol
- Time
- Transaction Tracking

The following sections explain the available server parameters for each of these categories.

Communication Parameters

Communication parameters configure the way the operating system handles communication buffers. The following communication parameters are available:

- **SPX Maximum Window Size=*number*** Sets the maximum SPXS window size. Default: 0 (which means to use the default size). Values: 0 to 16.

- **Load Balance Local LAN=*on/off*** Turns load balancing on or off. Default: Off.

- **TCP Defend Land Attacks=*on/off*** Sets whether or not TCP defends against land attacks. Default: On.

- **TCP Defend SYN Attacks=*on/off*** Sets whether or not TCP defends against SYN attacks. Default: Off.

- **IP Wan Client Validation=*on/off*** Sets whether or not IP WAN clients are validated when they dial in to the network remotely via NetWare Connect. Default: Off.

- **Allow IP Address Duplicates=*on/off*** When turned On, allows you to bind an IP address to a node even if it conflicts with another node's address on the network. Default: Off.

- **IPX Router Broadcast Delay=*number*** Sets how long the IPX router waits between SAP/RIP broadcast packets. Default: 0. Values: 0 = adjust the delay to the size of SAP/RIP tables; 1 = delay 1 tick; 2= delay 2 ticks.

- **Reply to get nearest server=*on/off*** When set to On, this server will respond to workstations that request a connection to their nearest server. Default: On.

- **IPX netbios replication option=*number*** Sets how replicated NetBIOS broadcasts are handled by the IPX router. Default: 2. Values: 0 = no replication of broadcasts; 1 = replicate broadcasts (causes duplicate broadcasts when there are redundant routes); 2 = replicate broadcasts, but suppress duplicate broadcasts; 3 = same as 2, but do not replicate to WAN links.

- **Use old watchdog packet type=*on/off*** Sets server to use type 0 instead of type 4 watchdog packets. Use this option if you use older router hardware that filters out type 4 IPX packets. Default: Off.

- **Number of watchdog packets=*number*** Sets the number of watchdog packets the server sends to an unresponsive workstation before clearing the workstation's connection. Default: 10. Values: 5 to 100.

- **Delay between watchdog packets=*time*** Sets the time the server waits before sending each watchdog packet. Default: 59.3 sec. Values: 9.9 sec to 10 min 26.2 sec.

- **Delay before first watchdog packet=*time*** Sets the time the server waits before sending the first watchdog packet to an unresponsive workstation. Default: 4 min 56.6 sec. Values: 15.7 sec to 14 days.

- **Console display watchdog logouts=*on/off*** When set to On, a console message is displayed when a workstation's connection is cleared by the watchdog. Default: Off.

- **Maximum packet receive buffers=*number*** Sets the maximum number of packet receive buffers the server can allocate. Default: 500. Values: 50 to 4294967295.

- **Minimum packet receive buffers=*number*** Sets the minimum number of packet receive buffers that the server can allocate. This number is allocated automatically when the server is booted. Default: 128. Values: 10 to 4294967295.

- **Maximum physical receive packet size=*number*** Sets the largest size of packets that can be received by an MLIB. Default size is acceptable for Ethernet and Token Ring boards. If some boards on the network can transmit more than 512 bytes of data per packet, use the largest packet size. Default: 4224 bytes. Values: 618 to 24682 bytes.

▶ **New packet receive buffer wait time=***seconds*   Sets the time the operating system waits after allocating the minimum number of buffers before granting the next packet receive buffer. Default: 0.1 sec. Values: 0.1 to 20 sec.

▶ **Maximum interrupt events=***number*   Sets the maximum number of interrupt time events (such as IPX routing) that occurs before a thread switch is guaranteed to have occurred. Default: 10. Values: 1 to 1000000.

▶ **IPX CMD Mode Routing=***on/off*   When set to On, turns on IPX Compatibility Mode routing. Default: Off.

Directory Caching Parameters

Directory Caching parameters enable you to configure how directory cache buffers are used to optimize access to frequently used directories. A *directory cache buffer* is a portion of server memory that holds a directory entry that is accessed frequently. A directory entry held in memory is accessed faster than a directory entry stored on the hard disk. The following Directory Caching parameters are available:

▶ **Dirty directory cache delay time=***seconds*   Specifies how long a directory table write request is kept in memory before it is written to disk. Default: 0.5 sec. Values: 0 to 10 sec.

▶ **Maximum concurrent directory cache writes=***number*   Sets the maximum number of write requests that can be stored before the disk head begins a sweep across the disk. Default: 75. Values: 5 to 500.

▶ **Directory cache allocation wait time=***time*   Specifies how long the server waits after allocating one directory cache buffer before allocating another one. Default: 2.2 sec. Values: 0.5 sec to 2 min.

▶ **Directory cache buffer nonreferenced delay=***time*   Sets how long a directory entry is held in cache before it is overwritten. Default: 5.5 sec. Values: 1 sec to 1 hour.

▶ **Maximum directory cache buffers=***number*   Sets the maximum number of directory cache buffers that the server can allocate. Prevents the server from allocating so many directory cache buffers that other server processes run out. Default: 500. Values: 20 to 200000.

▸ **Minimum directory cache buffers=*number*** Sets the minimum number of directory cache buffers to be allocated by the server before the server uses the Directory Cache Allocation Wait Time to determine if another directory cache buffer should be allocated. Allocating buffers too quickly will cause the server to eat up memory resources during peak loads. Waiting too long may cause a delay in file searches. This wait time creates a leveling factor between peak and low access times. Default: 150. Values: 10 to 100000.

▸ **Maximum number of internal directory handles=*number*** Sets the maximum number of directory handles that are available to internal NLMs that use connection 0. A directory handle is allocated each time an NLM accesses a file or directory. Allocating directory handles decreases the time required to gain access rights. Default: 100. Values: 40 to 1000.

▸ **Maximum number of directory handles=*number*** Sets the maximum number of directory handles that each connection can obtain. Default: 20. Values: 20 to 1000.

Directory Services Parameters

Directory Services parameters enable you to configure NDS maintenance characteristics. The following NDS parameters are available:

▸ **NDS external reference life span=*hours*** Sets the number of hours that unused external references (local IDs assigned to users when they access other servers) can exist before they are removed. Default: 192. Values: 1 to 384.

▸ **NDS inactivity synchronization interval=*minutes*** Sets how many minutes can elapse between exhaustive synchronization checks. Set high (up to 240 minutes) if replicas have to synchronize across WAN connections to reduce network traffic. Default: 60. Values: 2 to 1440.

▸ **NDS synchronization restrictions=*on/off, versions*** When set to Off, the server synchronizes with all versions of NDS that are available on the network. When this parameter is turned On, the server synchronizes only with the versions of NDS specified (such as "On, 489, 492, 599"). Default: Off.

- **NDS servers status=*up/down*** Sets the status of all Server objects in the local NDS database as either up or down, so you can force the network to recognize that a particular server is up when the network thinks it is down. Default: none.

- **NDS janitor interval=*minutes*** Specifies how often, in minutes, the janitor process runs. The janitor process cleans up unused records, reclaims disk space, and purges deleted objects. Default: 60. Values: 1 to 10080.

- **NDS Distributed reference link interval=*minutes*** Specifies how often, in minutes, the NDS distributed reference link consistency check is performed. Default: 780. Values: 2 to 10080.

- **NDS backlink interval=*minutes*** Specifies how often, in minutes, backlink consistency is checked. Backlinks indicate that an object in a replica has an ID on a server where the replica does not exist. Default: 780. Values: 2 to 10080.

- **NDS trace file length to zero=*on/off*** When set to On, the server deletes the contents of the NDS trace file (but does not delete the trace file itself). To delete the file contents, also set the NDS Trace to File parameter to On, so that the file will be open for the deletion process. Default: Off.

- **NDS bootstrap address=*address*** Specifies the address of a remote server with which this server can perform tree connectivity operations. Only set if this server does not hold a replica. Default: none.

- **Bindery context=*context;context;...*** Specifies which containers and their objects will be used as the server's "bindery" when the server provides bindery services. You can include up to 16 containers as part of this server's bindery context. Separate each context with a semicolon. Default: The bindery context set for this server during installation, if one was set.

- **NDS trace filename=*path\filename*** Specifies a different path name or file name for the NDS trace file. Default: SYSTEM/DSTRACE.DBG.

- **NDS trace to file=*on/off*** When set to On, the NDS trace information is sent to a file in the SYS:SYSTEM directory, named DSTRACE.DBG by default. Default: Off.

- **NDS trace to screen=*on/off*** When set to On, the NDS trace screen, which displays information about NDS events, is turned on. Default: Off.

Disk Parameters

Disk parameters allow you to control Hot Fix redirection, which helps protect data on the server from hard disk failures. The following Disk parameters are available:

▸ **Sequential elevator depth=***number*   Sets the maximum number of sequential requests that the Media Manager will send to the same device. If another device in the mirror group is idle when the first device contains this number of requests, Media Manager will begin sending requests to the idle device. Default: 8. Values: 0 to 4294967295.

▸ **Enable IO handicap attribute=***on/off*   When set to On, allows drivers and applications to set and use an attribute to inhibit (or handicap) read requests from one or more devices. When turned off, NetWare is able to treat the device like any other device. Do not turn this parameter on unless instructed to by the manufacturer. Default: Off.

▸ **Mirrored devices are out of sync message frequency=***minutes* Specifies how often devices are checked for out-of-sync status. Default: 28. Values: 5 to 9999.

▸ **Remirror block size=***number*   Specifies the remirror block size in multiples of 4K. Default: 1 (4K). Values: 1 to 8 (1 = 4K, 2 = 8K, 3 = 12K, and so on).

▸ **Concurrent remirror requests=***number*   Specifies how many simultaneous remirror requests can occur per logical disk partition. Default: 32. Values: 2 to 32.

▸ **Ignore disk geometry=***on/off*   When set to On, allows the creation of nonstandard and unsupported partitions on the server's hard disk. Default: Off.

▸ **Enable Hardware Write Back=***on/off*   Enables storage drivers to use the hardware write-back feature if they support it. This allows I/O write requests to be cached and processed before the data is actually written to the disk, which can increase performance. Default: Off.

▸ **Enable disk read after write verify=***on/off*   Specifies whether data written to disk is compared with the data in memory to verify its accuracy. If set to On, this parameter tells the driver to perform the highest level of read-after-write verification that it can. If set to Off, this parameter turns off any form of read-after-write verification that the driver may do. The disk controller may have a built-in function that performs read-after-write verification. If so, leave this parameter set to Off. Default: Off.

Error Handling Parameters

Error Handling parameters let you manage the server, volume, and TTS error log files. The server log file is named SYS$LOG.ERR. The volume log file is named VOL$LOG.ERR. The TTS log file is named TTS$LOG.ERR. The boot error log is named BOOT$LOG.ERR. The following parameters are available:

- **Volume log file state=*number*** Specifies what action to take when the log file reaches its maximum size. Default: 1. Values: 0 = take no action; 1 = delete the log file; 2 = rename the log file.

- **Volume TTS log file state=*number*** Specifies what action to take when the log file reaches its maximum size. Default: 1. Values: 0 = take no action; 1 = delete the log file; 2 = rename the log file.

- **Volume log file overflow size=*number*** Specifies the maximum size (in bytes) of the log file. Default: 4194304. Values: 65536 to 4294967295.

- **Volume TTS log file overflow size=*number*** Specifies the maximum size (in bytes) of the log file. Default: 4194304. Values: 65536 to 4294967295.

- **Server log file state=*number*** Specifies what action to take when the log file reaches its maximum size. Default: 1. Values: 0 = take no action; 1 = delete the log file; 2 = rename the log file.

- **Server log file overflow size=*number*** Specifies the maximum size (in bytes) of the log file. Default: 4194304. Values: 65536 to 4294967295.

- **Boot error log file state=*number*** Specifies what action to take when the log file reaches its maximum size. Default: 3. Values: 0 = take no action; 1 = delete the log file; 2 = rename the log file; 3 = start a new log file each time the server reboots.

- **Boot error log file overflow size=*number*** Specifies the maximum size (in bytes) of the log file. Default: 4194304. Values: 65536 to 4294967295.

► **Boot error log=***on/off*   When turned On, specifies that all console error messages are saved in the BOOT$LOG.ERR file. When turned Off, only error messages that occur during the boot procedure are saved in this file. Default: On.

► **Hung unload wait delay=***number*   Specifies how long the system will wait for a hung NLM to unload before asking the user whether to shut down the NLM's address space. Used only for NLMs loaded in protected memory spaces. Default: 30 sec. Values: 0 sec to 1 min 58.3 sec.

► **Auto restart after abend delay time=***minutes*   Sets the time, in minutes, that the server will wait before automatically shutting down and restarting after an abend occurs. Default: 2. Values: 2 to 60.

► **Auto restart after abend=***number*   Determines whether the server automatically shuts down and restarts itself if an abend occurs. Default: 1. Values: 0 = the server does not restart itself; 1 = the server determines the abend's cause, and then either keeps the computer running or shuts it down and restarts; 2 = the server attempts to recover, and then shuts down and restarts the server in the configured amount of time; 3 = the server immediately shuts down and restarts.

► . . . . ◄

File Caching Parameters

File Caching parameters enable you to configure how file cache buffers are used to optimize access to frequently used files. A *file cache buffer* is a portion of server memory that holds a file or portion of a file that is accessed frequently. A file in memory is accessed faster than a file on the hard disk. The following File Caching parameters are available:

► **Read ahead enabled=***on/off*   When set to On, background reads can be done during sequential file access so that blocks are placed into the cache before they are requested. Default: On.

► **Read ahead LRU sitting time threshold=***time*   Sets the time the server will wait before doing a read ahead. (LRU means Least Recently Used.) Default: 10 sec. Values: 0 sec to 1 hour.

► **Minimum file cache buffers=***number*   Sets the minimum number of cache buffers that must be reserved for file caching. Default: 20. Values: 20 to 2000.

▸ **Maximum concurrent disk cache writes=*number*** Sets the maximum number of write requests that can be stored before the disk head begins a sweep across the disk. Default: 750. Values: 10 to 4000.

▸ **Dirty disk cache delay time=*seconds*** Sets how long the server will keep a write request in memory before writing it to the disk. Default: 3.3 sec. Values: 0.1 sec to 10 sec.

▸ **Minimum file cache report threshold=*number*** Sets how close to the minimum number of allowed buffers the system can drop before a warning message is sent. Default: 20. Values: 0 to 2000.

File System Parameters

File System parameters enable you to configure aspects of the file system, such as volume disk space warnings, file purging, and file compression. The following parameters are available:

▸ **Minimum file delete wait time=*time*** Specifies how long a deleted file must be stored before it can be purged. Default: 1 min 5.9 sec. Values: 0 sec to 7 days.

▸ **File delete wait time=*time*** Sets the maximum amount of time a deleted file must be stored in a salvageable state. After this time has elapsed, the file can be purged if the space is needed. Default: 5 min 29.6 sec. Values: 0 sec to 7 days.

▸ **Automatically repair bad volumes=*on/off*** When set to On, automatically runs VREPAIR.NLM when a volume fails to mount. Default: On.

▸ **Allow deletion of active directories=*on/off*** When set to On, a directory can be deleted even if a user has a drive mapped to it. Default: On.

▸ **Maximum percent of volume space allowed for extended attributes=*number*** Limits the percentage of disk space that can be used to store extended attributes. Default: 10. Values: 5 to 50.

▸ **Maximum extended attributes per file or path=*number*** Specifies the maximum number of extended attributes that can be assigned to a file or a subdirectory (path) on any of the server's volumes. Default: 16. Values: 4 to 512.

▶ **Fast volume mounts=*on/off*** When set to On, allows the server to mount volumes more quickly by not checking certain less-important fields. This parameter should be on only if the volume was dismounted normally the last time. Default: On.

▶ **Maximum percent of volume used by directory=*number*** Limits the percentage of disk space that can be used as directory space. Default: 13. Values: 5 to 85.

▶ **Immediate purge of deleted files=*on/off*** Specifies whether files are purged immediately when they are deleted or stored in a salvageable state. If turned On, this parameter purges deleted files immediately, and they cannot be salvaged. Default: Off.

▶ **Maximum subdirectory tree depth=*number*** Sets the maximum level of subdirectories the server can support. Default: 25. Values: 10 to 100.

▶ **Volume low warn all users=*on/off*** When set to On, all users are notified when the free space on a volume reaches a minimum level. Default: On.

▶ **Volume low warning reset threshold=*number*** Specifies the number of disk blocks above the Volume Low Warning Threshold value that must be freed up to reset the low volume warning. This parameter controls how often you receive the low volume warning if your free space is fluctuating around the threshold. Default: 256. Values: 0 to 100000.

▶ **Volume low warning threshold=*number*** Sets the minimum amount of free space (in blocks) that a volume can have before it issues a warning that it is low on space. Default: 256. Values: 0 to 1000000.

▶ **Turbo FAT re-use wait time=*time*** Sets how long a turbo FAT (File Allocation Table) buffer stays in memory after an indexed file is closed. Default: 5 min 29.6 sec. Values: 0.3 sec to 1 hour 5 min 54.6 sec.

▶ **Compression daily check stop hour=*hour*** Specifies the hour when the file compressor stops searching volumes for files that need to be compressed. If this value is the same as the Compression Daily Check Starting Hour value, then the search starts at the specified starting hour and goes until all compressible files have been found. Default: 6 (6:00 a.m.). Values: 0 (midnight) to 23 (11:00 p.m.).

▶ **Compression daily check starting hour=***hour*   Specifies the hour when the file compressor begins searching volumes for files that need to be compressed. Default: 0 (midnight). Values: 0 to 23 (11:00 p.m.).

▶ **Minimum compression percentage gain=***number*   Specifies the minimum percentage that a file must be able to be compressed in order to remain compressed. Default: 20. Values: 0 to 50.

▶ **Enable file compression=***on/off*   When set to On, file compression is allowed to occur on volumes that were previously enabled for compression (during installation). (Just because a volume is enabled for compression doesn't mean compression will actually occur. This parameter must be turned on for compression to occur. For more information about file compression, see Chapter 8.) Default: On.

▶ **Maximum concurrent compressions=***number*   Specifies how many volumes can compress files at the same time. Increasing this value may slow down server performance during compression times. Default: 2. Values: 1 to 8.

▶ **Convert compressed to uncompressed option=***number*   Specifies how a compressed file is stored after it has been accessed. Default: 1. Values: 0 = always leave the file compressed; 1 = leave the file compressed after the first access within the time frame defined by the Days Untouched Before Compression parameter; then leave the file uncompressed after the second access; 2 = change the file to uncompressed after the first access.

▶ **Decompress percent disk space free to allow commit=***number*   Specifies the percentage of free disk space that is required on a volume before committing an uncompressed file to disk. This helps you avoid running out of disk space by uncompressing files. Default: 10. Values: 0 to 75.

▶ **Decompress free space warning interval=***time*   Specifies the interval between warnings when the volume doesn't have enough disk space for uncompressed files. Default: 31 min 18.5 sec. Values: 0 sec (which turns off warnings) to 29 days 15 hours, 50 min 3.8 sec.

▶ **Deleted files compression option=***number*   Specifies how the server handles deleted files. Default: 1. Values: 0 = don't compress deleted files; 1 = compress deleted files during the next day's search; 2 = compress deleted files immediately.

▸ **Days untouched before compression=***days*   Specifies how many days a file or directory must remain untouched before being compressed. Default: 14. Values: 0 to 100000.

▸ **Allow unowned files to be extended=***on/off*   When set to On, files can be changed even if their owner has been deleted. Default: On.

Licensing Services Parameters

Licensing Services parameters enable you to configure Novell Licensing Services. The following parameters are available:

▸ **Dirty certificate cache delay time=***time*   Specifies the minimum amount of time that licensing services will store certificate data in cache before writing it to NDS. Default: 1 min. Values: 1 min to 1 hour.

▸ **NLS search type=***number*   Specifies how far up the tree NLS should search when looking for a license certificate. Default: 0. Values: 0 = stop searching when it reaches the root of the tree; 1 = stop searching when it reaches the root of the partition.

Locks Parameters

Locks parameters enable you to configure how workstations and the server work with file and record locks. The following parameters are available:

▸ **Maximum record locks per connection=***number*   Sets the number of record locks a workstation can use simultaneously. Default: 500. Values: 10 to 100000.

▸ **Maximum file locks per connection=***number*   Sets the number of opened and locked files a workstation can use simultaneously. Default: 250. Values: 10 to 1000.

▸ **Maximum record locks=***number*   Sets the number of record locks the server can support simultaneously. Default: 20000. Values: 100 to 400000.

▸ **Maximum file locks=***number*   Sets how many opened and locked files the server can support simultaneously. Default: 10000. Values: 100 to 100000.

Memory Parameters

Memory parameters enable you to configure how the server's memory is managed. The following parameters are available:

- **Average page in alert threshold=***number*   If the average page "in" level in the virtual memory system reaches the specified number, an alert is sent to the console. Default: 2000. Values: 1 to 4294967295.

- **Memory protection no restart interval=***minutes*   If a protected address space is experiencing more than one fault during the specified number of minutes, the address space is not restarted. Default: 1. Values: 0 = 60. (0 = turns off this parameter, allowing the address space to restart regardless of faults.)

- **Memory protection fault cleanup=***on/off*   When set to On, specifies that an address space is removed and its NLMs unloaded if an NLM in the space attempts to violate memory protection. When set to Off, the address space isn't cleaned up, and the problem is left to be handled by the normal abend recovery process. Default: On.

- **Garbage collection interval=***time*   Sets the maximum time between garbage collections. Default: 5 min. Values: 1 min to 1 hour.

- **Alloc memory check flag=***on/off*   When set to On, the server is set to do corruption checking in the alloc memory nodes. Default: Off.

- **Reserved buffers below 16 meg=***number*   Sets a number of cache buffers in lower memory for device drivers that cannot access memory above 16MB. Default: 300. Values: 8 to 2000.

Miscellaneous Parameters

The Miscellaneous parameters set a variety of server options. The following parameters are available:

- **Display incomplete IPX packet alerts=***on/off*   When set to On, alert messages are displayed when IPX receives incomplete packets. Default: On.

- **Enable SECURE.NCF=***on/off*   When set to On, causes the SECURE.NCF file to be executed when the server boots. This file is used to set configuration parameters necessary for a C2 security-compliant system. See the NetWare security documentation for more information. Default: Off.

- **Allow audit passwords=*on/off*** When set to On, allows audit password requests to be used. Default: Off

- **Command line prompt default choice=*on/off*** Sets the default input for the "?" (conditional execution) console command. Default: On. Values: On (for Y) and Off (for N).

- **Command line prompt time out=*seconds*** Sets the number of seconds the command line ? command prompt will wait before using the default answer. If set to 0, the prompt will not time out. Default: 10. Values: 0 to 4294967295.

- **Sound bell for alerts=*on/off*** When set to On, a sound emits whenever an alert message appears on the server's console screen. Default: On.

- **Replace console prompt with server name=*on/off*** When set to On, the server's name is displayed as the console prompt on the server's screen. Default: On.

- **Alert message nodes=*number*** Determines how many alert message nodes are preallocated. Default: 20. Values: 10 to 256.

- **Worker thread execute in a row count=*number*** Determines how many times in a row the scheduler dispatches new work before allowing other threads to execute. Default: 10. Values: 1 to 20.

- **Halt system on invalid parameters=*on/off*** When set to On, the system stops whenever invalid parameters or conditions are detected. When this parameter is set to Off, the system displays an alert message but continues running if an invalid parameter is detected. Default: Off.

- **Display relinquish control alerts=*on/off*** When set to On, messages are displayed when an NLM uses the server's processor for more than 0.4 seconds without giving up control to other processes. This command is useful if you are writing your own NLMs and want to see if your NLM is using the CPU correctly. Default: Off.

- **Display old API names=*on/off*** When set to On, messages are displayed when API calls from older versions of NetWare are used by an NLM. If you receive these messages, you may want to contact the NLM's manufacturer for an upgrade that uses the faster, newer APIs. Default: Off.

- **CPU hog timeout amount=*time*** Sets the amount of time the system waits before terminating a process that has not relinquished control of the CPU. If set to zero, this option is disabled. Default: 1 min. Values: 0 sec to 1 hour.

- **Developer option=*on/off*** When set to On, options that are associated with a developer environment are enabled. Default: Off.

- **Display spurious interrupt alerts threshold=*number*** Specifies how many spurious interrupts per second must occur before a spurious interrupt alert is sent to the console. Default: 200. Values: 1 to 1000000.

- **Display lost interrupt alerts threshold=*number*** Specifies how many lost interrupts per second must occur before a lost interrupt alert is sent to the console. Default: 10. Values: 1 to 1000000.

- **Display spurious interrupt alerts=*on/off*** When set to On, error messages are displayed when the server hardware creates an interrupt that has been reserved for another device's interface board. If you receive this error, remove all add-on boards and run SERVER.EXE (the NetWare operating system). If the message doesn't appear after you remove everything, add the boards one at a time until you locate the board that is generating the message. Then contact the board's vendor or manufacturer for assistance. Default: Off.

- **Display lost interrupt alerts=*on/off*** When set to On, error messages are displayed when a driver or board makes an interrupt call but drops the request before it's filled. To identify the problem driver, unload all drivers, and then reload them one at a time. When you locate the driver that is generating the message, contact the driver's manufacturer. Default: Off.

- **Pseudo preemption count=*number*** Sets how many times threads can make file read or write system calls before they are forced to relinquish control. Default: 40. Values: 1 to 4294967295.

- **Global pseudo preemption=*on/off*** When set to On, all threads are forced to use pseudo preemption. Default: On.

- **Minimum service processes=*number*** Sets the minimum number of service processes the server can allocate without waiting for the amount of time specified in the New Service Process Wait Time parameter. Default: 100. Values: 10 to 500.

- **Maximum service processes=*number*** Sets the maximum number of service processes the server can create. Increase this parameter if the number of service processes (as shown in MONITOR.NLM) is at the maximum. Default: 500. Values: 5 to 1000.

- ▸ **New service process wait time=***seconds*   Determines how long the server waits to allocate another service process after receiving an NCP request. If a service process is freed up during this time, a new one will not be allocated. Default: 2.2 sec. Values: 0.3 sec to 20 sec.

- ▸ **Allow unencrypted passwords=***on/off*   When set to On, the server will accept unencrypted passwords. Only turn on this parameter if your network includes servers running NetWare 2.11 or earlier. If you have servers running NetWare 2.12 or 2.2, copy the NetWare 3.1*x* utilities to those servers and leave this parameter off, so that passwords will be encrypted. Default: Off.

Multiprocessor Parameters

Multiprocessor parameters enable you to configure settings for servers that use muliple processors. The following parameters are available:

- ▸ **System Threshold=***number*   Specifies the threshold for calculating thread shedding for load balancing. Default: 1536. Values: 0 to 102400.

- ▸ **Auto clear interrupt statistics=***on/off*   When set to On, the detailed statistics for an offline processor or removed interrupt handles are removed from memory. When set to Off, the statistics are retained in memory. Must be set in STARTUP.NCF. Changes will only take effect when server is rebooted. Default: On.

- ▸ **Auto start processors=***on/off*   When set to On, secondary processors are automatically started when the PSM (Platform Support Module) is loaded. When set to Off, you must use the console command START PROCESSORS to start secondary processors. Default: On.

NCP Parameters

NCP (NetWare Core Protocol) parameters enable you to configure NCP packets, control boundary checking, and change NCP Packet Signature security levels on the server. The following parameters are available:

- ▸ **NCP TCP keep alive interval=***time*   Specifies how long before "TCP keep alive" closes idle NCP connections. Default: 9 min 53.2 sec. Values: 0 sec to 15 hours 59 min 53.6 sec. (0 = idle connections are never closed.)

▸ **NCP packet signature option=***number* Sets the server's NCP Packet Signature security level. See Chapter 7 for more information about NCP Packet Signature levels. Default: 1. Values: 0 to 3.

▸ **Enable IPX checksums=***number* Sets the IPX checksum level. Default: 1. Values: 0 = no checksums; 1 = checksums performed if enabled on the client; 2 = checksums required.

▸ **Minimum NCP TCP receive window to advertise=***number* Sets the minimum receive window to advertise on NCP connections. Default: 4096. Values: 256 to 16384.

▸ **NCP TCP receive window=***number* Sets the advertised receive window on NCP connections. Default: 23360. Values: 1400 to 65535.

▸ **Enable UDP checksums on NCP packets=***number* Specifies how checksumming of NCP UDP packets is handled. Default: 1. Values: 0 = no checksumming; 1 = checksumming performed if enabled at the client; 2 = checksumming required.

▸ **NCP protocol preferences=***transports* Specifies the preferred protocol order of the loaded transports. List each transport separated by a space. Default: none. Values: IPX, TCP, UDP.

▸ **NCP file commit=***on/off* When set to On, an application is allowed to issue a File Commit NCP and flush the file immediately from cache to disk. Default: On.

▸ **Display NCP bad component warnings=***on/off* When set to On, NCP bad component alert messages are displayed. Default: Off.

▸ **Reject NCP packets with bad components=***on/off* When set to On, the server rejects NCP packets that fail component checking. Default: Off.

▸ **Display NCP bad length warnings=***on/off* When set to On, NCP bad-length alert messages are displayed. Default: Off.

▸ **Reject NCP packets with bad lengths=***on/off* When set to On, the server rejects NCP packets that fail boundary checking. Default: Off.

▸ **Maximum outstanding NCP searches=***number* Determines the maximum number of NCP directory searches that can be performed at the same time. Default: 51. Values: 10 to 1000.

► **Allow change to client rights=***on/off*   When set to On, a job server is allowed to assume a client's rights for NCP Packet Signature. If you are concerned that a job or print server may forge packets, turn off this parameter. Default: On.

► **Allow LIP=***on/off*   When set to On, support for Large Internet Packets is enabled. Default: On.

Service Location Protocol Parameters

Service Location Protocol (SLP) parameters enable you to configure SLP values. The following parameters are available:

► **SLP close idle TCP connections time=***seconds*   Specifies how many seconds the system must wait before closing idle TCP connections. Default: 300. Values: 0 to 86400.

► **SLP DA heart beat time=***seconds*   Specifies how many seconds the system must wait before sending the next DA heart beat packet. Default: 10800. Values: 0 to 65535.

► **SLP DA event timeout=***seconds*   Specifies how many seconds the system must wait before timing out a DA packet request. Default: 15. Values: 0 to 120.

► **SLP event timeout=***seconds*   Specifies how many seconds the system must wait before timing out a multicast packet request. Default: 3. Values: 0 to 120.

► **SLP SA default lifetime=***number*   Specifies the default lifetime for service registers. Default: 3600. Values: 0 to 65535.

► **SLP retry count=***number*   Specifies the maximum number of retry attempts. Default: 3. Values: 0 to 128.

► **SLP debug=***number*   When set to 0, turns off debug mode. When set to a number, turns on debug mode. Bit 0x01=COMM; 0x02=TRAN; 0x04=API; 0x08=ERR; 0x20=SA. Default: 0. Values: 0 to 65535.

► **SLP rediscover inactive directory agents=***seconds*   Specifies how many seconds the system must wait before issuing service requests to rediscover inactive DAs. Default: 60. Values: 0 to 86400.

► **SLP multicast radius=***number*   Specifies the multicast radius. Default: 32. Values: 0 to 32.

- **SLP DA discovery options=*number*** Sets the DA discovery options. Bit 0x01 = use multicast DA advertisements; 0x02 = use DHCP discovery; 0x04 = use static file SYS:ETC\SLP.CFG; 0x08 = scopes required. Default: 7. Values: 0 to 8.

- **SLP MTU size=*number*** Specifies the maximum transfer unit size. Default: 1450. Values: 0 to 24682.

- **SLP broadcast=*on/off*** When set to On, tells SLP to use broadcast packets instead of multicast packets. When set to Off, tells SLP to use multicast packets. Default: Off.

- **SLP TCP=*on/off*** When set to On, tells SLP to use TCP packets instead of UDP packets when possible. When set to Off, tells SLP to use UDP packets. Default: Off.

- **SLP scope list=*policy*** Specifies a scope policy list. Use a string delimited by commas. Default: none.

Time Parameters

Initially, you set up time services on the server during installation. Time services are controlled by TIMESYNC.NLM, which is loaded automatically when the server is started up. To modify time synchronization after installation, you can use the Time and Time Synchronization server parameters.

Although you can change all of the TimeSync parameters from within MONITOR.NLM, all parameters that start with the word "Timesync" must be added to the TIMESYNC.CFG file if you want them to remain in effect after the server is rebooted. Otherwise, the changes will only be temporary. Parameters that don't start with the word "Timesync" can be changed permanently from within MONITOR.NLM. Use EDIT.NLM to edit the TIME-SYNC.CFG file.

The following parameters are available:

- **Timesync configured sources=*on/off*** When set to On, the server ignores SAP (Service Advertising Protocol) time sources and instead accepts time sources configured with the TIMESYNC Time Source parameter. When this parameter is turned Off, it causes the server to listen to any advertising time source. Default: Off.

▶ **Timesync directory tree mode=*on/off*** When set to On, time synchronization ignores SAP (Service Advertising Protocol) packets that don't originate from within the server's Directory tree. When this parameter is set to Off, the server accepts SAP packets from any time source on the network, regardless of the tree from which it originates. If SAP is turned on, this parameter should also be set to On. Default: On.

▶ **Timesync hardware clock=*on/off*** When set to On, Primary and Secondary time servers set the hardware clock, and Single Reference and Reference servers set their time from the hardware clock at the start of each polling interval. Only set this parameter to Off if this server uses an external time source such as a radio clock. Default: On.

▶ **Timesync polling count=*number*** Determines the number of time packets to exchange while polling. Increasing this number may increase unnecessary traffic on the network. Default: 3. Values: 1 to 1000.

▶ **Timesync polling interval=*seconds*** Determines the polling interval, in seconds. All servers in the tree must use the same polling interval. Default: 600. Values: 10 to 2678400 (31 days).

▶ **Timesync reset=*on/off*** When set to On, all servers are removed from the time source list, and time synchronization is reset. The parameter automatically resets itself to Off. Default: Off.

▶ **Timesync restart flag=*on/off*** When set to On, you can reload TIMESYNC.NLM without rebooting the server. Default: Off.

▶ **Timesync service advertising=*on/off*** When set to On, SAP (Service Advertising Protocol) is turned on, meaning Single Reference, Reference, and Primary time sources advertise using SAP. Only set this parameter to Off if you are configuring a custom list of time sources. Default: On.

▶ **Timesync synchronization radius=*milliseconds*** Determines the maximum time (in milliseconds) that a server is allowed to vary from the synchronized time while still being considered synchronized. Do not set this parameter for under 2 seconds (2000 milliseconds) unless you have an application that uses synchronized time stamps that will not tolerate a 2-second deviation between time sources. Default: 2000. Values: 0 to 2147483647.

▶ **Timesync time adjustment=+*or-* hour:minute:second [at** **month/day/year hour:minute:second]**   Determines when a time adjustment will take place. This parameter does not apply to Secondary time servers. Use sparingly to correct network-wide time errors. Overuse can corrupt time synchronization. The default date and time is six polling intervals or one hour (whichever is longer) from the current time. Default: None scheduled.

▶ **Timesync time sources=*servers***   Specifies a server as a time source. If used at the console, and no server name is entered, the parameter displays the list of configured servers. To specify multiple servers, separate each one by a semicolon (;). The list of servers must contain at least one semicolon, even if only one server is listed. A semicolon alone clears the list of servers. Default: ;

▶ **Timesync type=*type***   Specifies the type (Single, Reference, Primary, or Secondary) of the default time source. Default: Single (for Single Reference) when this is the first server in the tree, or Secondary for all other servers. Values: Single, Reference, Primary, or Secondary.

▶ **New time with daylight savings time status=*on/off***   When set to On, the local time on the server is adjusted by adding or subtracting the time indicated in the Daylight Saving Time Offset parameter. Default: On.

▶ **Daylight savings time status=*on/off***   When set to On, this parameter indicates that Daylight Saving Time is currently in effect. If this parameter is set to On, also set the Daylight Savings Time Offset parameter. Changing this parameter does not change the local time on the server.

▶ **Daylight savings time offset=+*or-* hour:minute:second**   Specifies the offset applied to time calculations when Daylight Saving Time is in effect, causing UTC time to be recalculated from local time. Default: +1:00:00.

▶ **End of daylight savings time=*date time***   Indicates the day that Daylight Saving Time ends locally. (You must also set the starting date with the Start of Daylight Saving Time parameter.) To specify the end of Daylight Saving Time so it recurs every year, enclose the date and time in parentheses, and use the following format: (October Sunday Last 2:00:00 a.m.). If you do not enclose the date in parentheses, the change will occur only in the current year. "October Sunday Last" indicates that the change occurs on the last Sunday in October. Default: (October Sunday Last 2:00:00 a.m.).

▶ **Start of daylight savings time=***date time*   Indicates the day that Daylight Saving Time begins locally. (You must also set the ending date with the End of Daylight Saving Time parameter.) To specify the beginning of Daylight Saving Time so it recurs every year, enclose the date and time in parentheses, and use the following format: (April Sunday First 2:00:00 a.m.). If you do not enclose the date in parentheses, the change will occur only in the current year. "April Sunday First" indicates that the change occurs on the first Sunday in April. Default: (April Sunday First 2:00:00 a.m.).

▶ **Default time server type=***type*   Specifies the type of time server for this server. Default: Secondary. Values: Single (for Single Reference), Reference, Primary, or Secondary.

▶ **Time zone=***zone*   Specifies the abbreviation for this server's time zone, its offset from UTC (Universal Coordinated Time, which used to be called Greenwich Mean Time), and the abbreviation for this server's time zone that is used when Daylight Saving Time is in effect. Example: *zone* is MST7MDT for Mountain Standard Time in the U.S.A. Mountain Standard Time is offset 7 hours from UTC, and the abbreviation used when Daylight Saving Time is in effect is MDT.

▶ **Timesync configuration file=***path\filename*   Specifies the directory and filename of the time synchronization configuration file, if it is not SYS:SYSTEM\TIMESYNC.CFG.

Transaction Tracking Parameters

Transaction Tracking parameters enable you to configure NetWare's Transaction Tracking System. The following parameters are available:

▶ **Auto TTS backout flag=***on/off*   When set to On, incomplete transactions can be backed out automatically when a downed server is rebooted. Default: On.

▶ **TTS abort dump flag=***on/off*   When set to On, the TTS$LOG.ERR file is created to record backout data in the event of a failure. Default: Off.

▶ **Maximum transactions=***number*   Specifies how many transactions can occur simultaneously across all connections. Default: 10000. Values: 100 to 10000.

- ▶ **TTS unwritten cache wait time=*time*** Sets the time that a block of transactional data can be held in memory. Default: 1 min 5.9 sec. Values: 11 sec to 10 min 59.1 sec.

- ▶ **TTS backout file truncation wait time=*time*** Sets the minimum amount of time that allocated blocks remain available for the TTS backout file. Default 59 min 19.2 sec. Values: 1 min 5.9 sec to 1 day 2 hours 21 min 51.3 sec.

Sources of More Information and Help

Whenever a product becomes as popular and as widely used as NetWare, an entire support industry crops up around it. If you are looking for more information about NetWare, you're in luck. You can go to a variety of places for help.

NetWare information is as local as your bookstore or local user group, and as international as the Internet forums that focus on NetWare. It can be as informal as an article in a magazine, or as structured as a college course. This appendix describes the ways you can get more information or technical support for NetWare:

- ► General Novell product information
- ► Novell on the Internet
- ► Novell technical support
- ► Novell Consulting Services
- ► DeveloperNet, Novell's developer support
- ► *Novell AppNotes*
- ► Novell Education classes and CNE certification
- ► NetWare Users International (NUI)
- ► Network Professional Association (NPA)

General Novell Product Information

The main Novell information number, 1-800-NETWARE, is your inroad to all types of pre-sales information about Novell or its products.

By calling this number, you can obtain information about Novell products, the locations of your nearest resellers, pricing information, and phone numbers for other Novell programs.

For information on Novell's upgrade programs, call 1-800-304-7533.

To order the printed manuals for NetWare 5, you can use the order form that came in your NetWare 5 box, or call 800-336-3892 (in the United States) or 510-780-1250.

Novell on the Internet

There is a tremendous amount of information about Novell and NetWare products, both official and unofficial, on the Internet. Officially, you can obtain the latest information about Novell from Novell's Web site (www.novell.com). Unofficially, there are several active user forums that deal specifically with NetWare or generally with networking and computers.

The Novell sites offer users access to a wide variety of information and files dealing with NetWare and other Novell products, such as GroupWise. You can receive information such as technical advice from sysops (system operators) and other users, updated files and drivers, and the latest patches and workarounds for known problems in Novell products.

The Novell sites also provide a database of technical information from the Novell Technical Support division, as well as information about programs such as Novell Education classes and NetWare Users International (NUI). You can also find marketing and sales information about the various products that Novell produces.

The Novell sites are managed by Novell employees and by sysops who have extensive knowledge about NetWare. Public forums can be quite active, with many experienced users offering advice to those with problems.

Novell Technical Support

If you encounter a problem with your network that you can't solve on your own, there are several places you can go for help:

▶ Try calling your reseller or consultant.

▶ Go online, and see if anyone in the online forums or Usenet forums knows about the problem or can offer a solution. The knowledge of the people in those forums is broad and deep. Don't hesitate to take advantage of it, and don't forget to return the favor if you know some tidbit that might help others.

▶ Call Novell technical support. You may want to reserve this as a last resort, simply because Novell technical support charges a fee for each incident (an incident may involve more than one phone call, if necessary). The fee depends on the product for which you're requesting support.

When you call technical support, make sure you have all the necessary information ready, such as the versions of NetWare and any utility or application you're using, the type of hardware you're using, network or node addresses and hardware settings for any workstations or other machines being affected, and so on. You'll also need a major credit card.

Novell's technical support department also offers online information, technical bulletins, downloadable patches and drivers, and so on. In addition, they offer a subscription to the *Novell Support Connection*, a collection of CD-ROMs that is updated regularly. The *Novell Support Connection* CD-ROMs contain technical information such as:

- ► Novell Technical Information Documents
- ► Novell Labs hardware and software test bulletins
- ► Online product documentation
- ► *Novell AppNotes*
- ► All available NetWare patches, updates, fixes, and drivers

To get in touch with Novell's technical support, or to find out more about the *Technical Support Connection* CD-ROMs and other programs, visit their Web site at www.support.novell.com. To open a technical support incident call, call 1-800-858-4000.

Novell Consulting Services

Novell offers specialized, fee-based consulting services for customers needing system planning and design services. Novell Consulting Services can provide these design services, plus utilities and solutions that help customers take advantage of Novell products in their networking environment.

For more information about Novell Consulting Services, see the Novell Web site at www.novell.com. You can also call them at 801-861-7633, fax them at 801-861-2629, or send them e-mail at novell_consulting@ novell.com.

DeveloperNet: Novell's Developer Support

Developers who create applications designed to run on NetWare may qualify to join Novell's program for professional developers, called DeveloperNet. Subscription fees for joining DeveloperNet vary, depending on the subscription level and options you choose. If you are a developer, some of the benefits you can receive by joining DeveloperNet are:

- ▶ Novell development CD-ROMs, which contain development tools you can use to create and test your applications in NetWare environments
- ▶ Special pre-releases and early access releases of upcoming Novell products
- ▶ Special technical support geared specifically toward developers
- ▶ *Novell Research Developer Notes*, a monthly publication from the Novell Research department that covers software development topics for NetWare products
- ▶ Discounts on various events, products, and Novell Press books

For more information, to apply for membership, or to order an SDK, call 800-REDWORD or 801-861-5281, or contact the program administrator via e-mail at devprog@novell.com. More information is available online on the World Wide Web at http://developer.novell.com.

Novell AppNotes

Novell's Research Department produces a monthly publication called *Novell AppNotes*. Each issue of *Novell AppNotes* contains research reports and articles on a wide range of topics. The articles delve into topics such as network design, implementation, administration, and integration.

To order a subscription, call 800-377-4136 or 303-297-2725.

Novell Education Classes and CNE Certification

Are you looking for a way to learn about NetWare in a classroom setting, with hands-on labs and knowledgeable instructors? Novell offers a variety of classes on various aspects of running NetWare networks.

NetWare classes are taught at over 1,000 Novell Authorized Education Centers (NAECs) throughout the world. They are also taught at more than 100 NAEPs (Novell Authorized Education Partners), which are universities and colleges that teach these courses.

These classes often offer the best way to get some direct, hands-on training in just a few days. Some of the classes are also available in Computer-Based Training (CBT) form, in case you'd rather work through the material at your own pace, on your own workstation, than attend a class.

These classes also help prepare you if you want to become certified as a CNE, signifying that you are a Novell NetWare professional.

The Novell CNE program provides a way to ensure that networking professionals meet the necessary criteria to adequately install and manage NetWare networks. To achieve CNE status, you take a series of exams on different aspects of NetWare. In many cases, you may want to take the classes Novell offers through its NAECs to prepare for the exams, but the classes aren't required.

The classes and exams you take depend somewhat on the level of certification you want to achieve. Although certain core exams are required for all levels, you may also take additional "electives" to achieve the certification and specialization you want.

The following levels of certification are available:

▶ *CNA (Certified Novell Administrator)*. This certification is the most basic level. It prepares you to manage your own NetWare network. It does not delve into the more complex and technical aspects of NetWare. If you are relatively new to NetWare, the class offered for this certification is highly recommended.

▶ *CNE*. This certification level ensures that you can adequately install, manage, and support NetWare networks. While pursuing your CNE certification, you "declare a major," meaning that you choose to specialize in a particular Novell product family. For example, you may become a NetWare 5 CNE or a GroupWise CNE. There are several exams (and corresponding classes) involved in achieving this level of certification.

▶ *Master CNE*. This certification level allows you to go beyond CNE certification. To get a Master CNE, you declare a "graduate major." These areas of specialization delve deeper into the integration- and solution-oriented aspects of running a network than does the CNE level.

▶ *CNI (Certified Novell Instructor)*. CNIs are authorized to teach NetWare classes through NAECs. The tests and classes specific to this level ensure that the individual taking them will be able to adequately teach others how to install and manage NetWare.

CNEs and Master CNEs qualify for membership in the Network Professional Association (NPA), which is explained later in this Appendix.

For more information about Novell Education classes or to find the nearest NAEC near you, call 1-800-233-3382 in the United States or 1-801-222-7800. You can also visit Novell Education's Web site at www. education.novell.com.

To purchase a CBT version of a class, contact your nearest NAEC.

Numerous organizations also provide classes and seminars on NetWare products. Some of these unauthorized classes are quite good. Others are probably of lower quality, because Novell does not have any control over their course content or instructor qualifications. If you choose an unauthorized provider for your NetWare classes, try to talk to others who have taken a class from the provider before, so you'll have a better idea of how good the class is.

NetWare Users International (NUI)

NetWare Users International (NUI) is a nonprofit association for networking professionals. With more than 250 affiliated groups worldwide, NUI provides a forum for networking professionals to meet face to face, to learn from each other, to trade recommendations, or just to share war stories.

By joining the NetWare user group in your area, you can take advantage of the following benefits:

- Local user groups that hold regularly scheduled meetings

- A discount on Novell Press books through *NetWare Connection* magazine and also at NUI meetings and conferences

- *NetWare Connection,* a monthly magazine that provides feature articles on new technologies, network management tips, product reviews, NUI news, and other helpful information

- Regional NUI conferences, held in different major cities throughout the year (with a discount for members)

The best news is, there's usually no fee or only a very low fee for joining an NUI user group.

For more information or to join an NUI user group, call 800-228-4NUI or send a fax to 801-228-4577, or visit their Web site at www.novell. com/nui.

For a free subscription to *NetWare Connection,* go to the subscription Web site at www.novell.com/nwc/sub.html.

Network Professional Association (NPA)

If you've achieved, or are working toward, your CNE certification, you may want to join the Network Professional Association (NPA). The NPA is an organization for network computing professionals, including those who have certified as networking professionals in Novell, Microsoft, Banyan, and other manufacturers' products as well. Its goal is to keep its members current with the latest technology and information in the industry.

If you're a certified CNE, you can join the NPA as a full member. If you've started the certification process, but aren't finished yet, or if you are a CNA, you can join as an associate member (which gives you all the benefits of a full member except for the right to vote in the NPA's elections).

When you join the NPA, you can enjoy the following benefits:

- ▸ Local NPA chapters (more than 100 worldwide) that hold regularly scheduled meetings that include presentations and hands-on demonstrations of the latest technology

- ▸ A subscription to *Network Professional Journal*

- ▸ Access to NPA Labs that contain up-to-date technology and software for hands-on experience

- ▸ Job postings

- ▸ NPA's own professional certification programs

- ▸ Discounts or free admission to major trade shows and conferences, including NPA's own conferences

For more information or to join NPA, see their Web site at www.npa.org, or call 630-369-2488. For general information, you can send them e-mail at info@inpnet.org.

Worksheets

Keeping accurate and up-to-date documentation about the various aspects of your network can save you a tremendous amount of time and energy if something goes wrong. You can photocopy and use the worksheets in this section to begin documenting your network. If you prefer, you can design your own forms or databases for tracking important information such as hardware and software inventory, NDS information, and your backup schedules.

Worksheet A: Server Installation and Configuration

Server name: _____

Make and model:_____

Current location: _____

Serial number: _____

CPU speed: _____

Number of processors: _____

Memory: _____

Storage adapter name:_____

    Attached storage device: _____

    Attached storage device: _____

Storage adapter name:_____

    Attached storage device: _____

    Attached storage device: _____

Hard disk size:_____

DOS partition size: _____

Disks mirrored?   Yes __   No __

Disks duplexed?   Yes __   No __

Network board name: _____

    LAN driver: _____

    Protocol bound:_____ Frame type: _____

    Protocol bound:_____ Frame type: _____

    Settings: _____

    Node address: _____

    IP address (for TCP/IP only): _____

    Subnet mask (for TCP/IP only): _____

Network board name: _____

    LAN driver: _____

    Protocol bound: _____ Frame type:_____

    Protocol bound: _____ Frame type:_____

    Settings: _____

    Node address: _____

IP address (for TCP/IP only): _____

Subnet mask (for TCP/IP only): _____

Protocols loaded on server:

IPX: Yes ___ No ___

      Server's internal IPX network number: _____

IP: Yes ___ No ___

      Compatibility Mode On?   Yes ___ No ___

      Migration Agent installed?   Yes ___ No ___

      Server's IP address: _____

      Server's subnet mask: _____

      Router (gateway) address: _____

      DNS domain name: _____

AppleTalk: Yes ___ No ___

NDPS Broker installed? _____

Server's time zone: _____

Directory tree name: _____

Server's name context in the Directory tree: _____

Admin's name and context: _____

Type of TimeSync server: _____

Other boards or devices installed in server:

      Name: _____

      Settings: _____

      Name: _____

      Settings: _____

      Name: _____

      Settings: _____

      Name: _____

      Settings: _____

Comments: _____

_____

_____

_____

_____

Worksheet B: Volumes

Server name: _____

SYS Volume

    Size: _____

    Name spaces: _____

    File compression on?   Yes __   No __

    Block suballocation on?   Yes __   No __

Other volume (name): _____

    Size: _____

    Name spaces: _____

    NSS or Traditional? _____

    File compression on?   Yes __   No __

    Block suballocation on?   Yes __   No __

Other volume (name): _____

    Size: _____

    Name spaces: _____

    NSS or Traditional? _____

    File compression on?   Yes __   No __

    Block suballocation on?   Yes __   No __

Other volume (name): _____

    Size: _____

    Name spaces: _____

    NSS or Traditional? _____

    File compression on?   Yes __   No __

    Block suballocation on?   Yes __   No __

Comments: _____

_____

_____

_____

_____

_____

Worksheet C: Hardware and Software Purchases

Product: _____

Serial number: _____

Version number: _____

Vendor name: _____

    Address: _____

    _____

    Phone: _____

    Fax: _____

    E-mail or Web site: _____

Manufacturer name: _____

    Address: _____

    _____

    Phone: _____

    Fax: _____

    E-mail or Web site: _____

Purchase date: _____

Purchase order number: _____

Purchase price: _____

Warranty card sent in?   Yes __   No __   Not applicable __

Length of warranty: _____

Current location of product: _____

Comments: _____

_____

_____

_____

_____

_____

Worksheet D: Hardware Maintenance

Product: _____

Serial number: _____

Repair date: _____

Purchase order number: _____

Repair vendor name: _____

    Address: _____

    _____

    Phone:_____

    Fax:_____

    E-mail or Web site:_____

Repair cost:_____

    Repaired under warranty?   Yes __   No __

    New warranty granted?   Yes __   No __

    Warranty expiration date: _____

Comments:_____

_____

_____

_____

_____

_____

Worksheet E: Time Synchronization Servers

NDS Directory tree: _____

Single Reference server: _____

Reference server: _____

Primary servers: _____

_____

_____

_____

_____

_____

_____

_____

Comments: _____

_____

_____

_____

_____

_____

Worksheet F: Hot Fix Bad Block Tracking

Server:_____

Disk: _____

Total redirection area: _____

Date:_____	Hot Fix blocks used: _____
Date:_____	Hot Fix blocks used: _____
Date:_____	Hot Fix blocks used: _____
Date:_____	Hot Fix blocks used: _____
Date:_____	Hot Fix blocks used: _____
Date:_____	Hot Fix blocks used: _____
Date:_____	Hot Fix blocks used: _____
Date:_____	Hot Fix blocks used: _____
Date:_____	Hot Fix blocks used: _____
Date:_____	Hot Fix blocks used: _____
Date:_____	Hot Fix blocks used: _____
Date:_____	Hot Fix blocks used: _____
Date:_____	Hot Fix blocks used: _____
Date:_____	Hot Fix blocks used: _____
Date:_____	Hot Fix blocks used: _____
Date:_____	Hot Fix blocks used: _____
Date:_____	Hot Fix blocks used: _____

Comments: _____

_____

_____

_____

_____

_____

Worksheet G: Workstation Installation and Configuration

Workstation's user and/or location: _____

Make and model: _____

Serial number: _____

OS and version number: _____

Memory: _____

Size of hard disk: C:_____ D:_____

CD-ROM drive? Yes __ No __

Novell client software version: _____

Protocols installed: _____

Network Board

    Type: _____ Node address: _____

    LAN driver: _____ Frame type: _____

    Settings: _____

Network Board

    Type: _____ Node address: _____

    LAN driver: _____ Frame type: _____

    Settings: _____

Other Boards

    Name: _____

    Settings: _____

    Name: _____

    Settings: _____

    Name: _____

    Settings: _____

    Name: _____

    Settings: _____

Comments: _____

_____

_____

_____

_____

Worksheet H: Backup Schedule

Server name (of server backed up): _____

Server location: _____

Backup system used (hardware and software): _____

_____

_____

Type of backup media used: _____

Location of backup media: _____

_____

_____

Backup schedule: _____

    Full backup: _____

    Incremental backup: _____

    Differential backup: _____

If custom backups are done, describe: _____

_____

_____

_____

Media rotation schedule: _____

_____

Media labeling instructions: _____

_____

Location of session and error log files: _____

Primary backup administrator name: _____

    Phone numbers: _____

_____

_____

Secondary backup administrator name: _____

    Phone numbers: _____

_____

Comments: _____

_____

_____

_____

Worksheet I: Printer Installation and Configuration

Printer object's full name: _____

Make and model: _____

Current location: _____

Serial number: _____

Directory tree name: _____

How is the printer attached: To server __ To workstation __ Direct __

Printer type (parallel, serial, AppleTalk, etc.):_____

Interrupt mode (polled or specific IRQ): _____

Parallel printer configuration

    Port (LPT1, LPT2, or LPT3): _____

    Poll: _____

    Interrupt (LPT1=7, LPT2=8):_____

Serial Printer Configuration

    Port (COM1 or COM2):_____

    Baud rate: _____

    Word size:_____

    Stop bits: _____

    Parity:_____

    XON/XOFF: _____

    Poll: _____

    Interrupt (COM1=4, COM2=3): _____

Queue-Based:

    Printer number: _____

    Print queues assigned: _____

    _____

    Print server assigned: _____

    Print queue operators: _____

    Print server operators: _____

NDPS:

    Printer agent: _____

    Gateway used: _____

    NDPS Manager object: _____

    Public access or controlled access? _____

    Printer Managers: _____

    Printer Operators:_____

Comments:_____

_____

_____

NetWare Utilities and NLMs

Instant Access

Using Utilities

▶ NetWare workstation utilities are applications or commands you run from a network workstation. There are different utilities for the different tasks you can perform on the network, and different utilities for each workstation platform (DOS, Windows 3.1, Windows 95/98, and so on).

▶ NetWare console utilities are commands you execute from the server's console (or from a Remote Console session running on a workstation). These utilities are generally used to affect the server's operation.

▶ NLMs (NetWare Loadable Modules) are software modules that you load into the server's operating system to add or change functionality in the server.

▶ Java applications and applets are applications that can run on the server when it is running the Java Virtual Machine. Some Java applications and applets can also run on workstations.

Using NetWare Utilities

The four main types of NetWare utilities that you can use when working on the network are:

▸ *Workstation utilities* — applications or commands you run from a network workstation

▸ *Console utilities* — commands you execute from the server's console (or from a Remote Console session running on a workstation)

▸ *NLMs (NetWare Loadable Modules)* — software modules that you load into the server's operating system to add or change functionality in the server

▸ *Java applications and applets* — programs that run on the Java Virtual Machine on the server, or on a workstation with access to a Java engine

This appendix lists all of the available NetWare utilities in alphabetical order, regardless of type. Some are common utilities you will use often. Others are used less frequently or rarely, and may be associated with some of the more advanced or obscure features of NetWare.

Each type of utility (workstation, console, or NLM) is executed differently, as explained in the following sections.

NOTE
In many cases, to execute the utility, you simply type the name of the utility at the DOS prompt (for workstation utilities) or at the server prompt (for console utilities and NLMs). Where there are parameters or options you must enter along with the utility name, the command format to use is indicated.

Using Workstation Utilities

How you execute a workstation utility depends on the type of utility it is, and the workstation operating system you're using. Workstation utilities are generally used to work with network services (such as the NDS tree), printing services, and so on.

To execute a NetWare utility that runs in DOS (such as NCOPY), you type the utility's name, plus any additional parameters that may be necessary, at a DOS prompt on the workstation. (These are often called *command-line utilities*, because you execute them by typing a command.) Some NetWare utilities that run in DOS may display menus, from which you choose the tasks or options you want. (These are called *menu utilities*.)

TIP

If you're using Windows 95/98 or Windows NT, you may also be able to run a DOS-based NetWare utility from the MS-DOS Prompt feature inside Windows. (Accessing the MS-DOS Prompt from Windows is sometimes called *opening a DOS box*.) However, occasionally Windows 95/98 and Windows NT exhibit some incompatibilities with DOS-based programs, so not all NetWare utilities may work from within a DOS box.

To execute a NetWare utility that runs in Windows 95/98 or Windows NT (such as NetWare Administrator), you have to add the utility to your workstation's desktop first. To do this, you use the normal Windows method for adding a new application's icon. (Most NetWare utilities are located in SYS:PUBLIC or SYS:PUBLIC\WIN32 on the server.) Most NetWare workstation utilities have online help.

- To read help for a NetWare command-line utility that runs in DOS, type the name of the utility, followed by /?. For example, to read help for the CAPTURE command, type **CAPTURE /?**.

- To read help for a NetWare menu utility that runs in DOS, press the F1 key while you're in the menu.

- To read help for NetWare utilities running in Windows 95/98 or Windows NT, click the Help button that appears on the utility's screen.

The following workstation utilities are described in this appendix:

Application Explorer	NDIR
Application Launcher	NDS Manager
ATOTAL	NetWare Administrator
AUDITCON	NetWare User Tools
CAPTURE	NLIST
CX	NLS Manager
FILER	Novell Printer Manager
FLAG	Novell Upgrade Wizard
LOGIN	NPRINT
LOGOUT	NPRINTER.EXE
MAP	NPTWIN95.EXE
NCOPY	NVER

NWBACK32

PURGE

RCONSOLE

RIGHTS

Schema Manager

SETPASS

TSA for Windows 95/98 or Windows NT

UIMPORT

Using Console Utilities

Console utilities, such as MOUNT, are commands that you execute by typing a command at the server's console.

TIP

You can also execute console utilities from a Remote Console session running on a workstation. See Chapter 3 for instructions on setting up a Remote Console session on your workstation.

In general, you use console commands to change some aspect of the server or view information about it. Console utilities are built into the operating system, just as internal DOS commands are built into DOS. For convenience, a small number of executable files are also included in this category, although they aren't technically internal console commands. For example, SERVER.EXE, the executable file that starts the NetWare operating system, is included in this category. In addition, .NCF files such as STARTX.NCF are also included in this category, because you execute them at the server console and they launch a program or utility on the server.

To read online help for console utilities, use the HELP console utility. Use the following command format, substituting the name of the utility (such as SCAN FOR NEW DEVICES) for *utility*:

```
HELP utility
```

The following console utilities are described in this appendix:

ABORT REMIRROR

ADD NAME SPACE

ALERT

ALIAS

APPLET

BIND

BINDERY

BROADCAST

C1START.NCF

CLEAR STATION

CLS

CONFIG

CPUCHECK

CSET

DISABLE LOGIN

DISABLE TTS

DISMOUNT

DISPLAY ENVIRONMENT

DISPLAY INTERRUPTS

DISPLAY MODIFIED ENVIRONMENT

DISPLAY NETWORKS

DISPLAY PROCESSORS

DISPLAY SERVERS

DOWN

ENABLE LOGIN

ENABLE TTS

ENVSET

FILE SERVER NAME

HELP

IPX INTERNAL NET

JAR

JAVA

JAVAC

JAVADOC

JAVAH

JAVAKEY

JAVAP

LANGUAGE

LIST DEVICES

LIST STORAGE ADAPTERS

LIST STORAGE DEVICE BINDINGS

LOAD

LOADSTAGE

MAGAZINE

MEDIA

MEMORY

MEMORY MAP

MIRROR STATUS

MODULES

MOUNT

NAME

NATIVE2ASCII

NCP ADDRESSES

NCP DUMP

NCP STATS

NCP TRACE

OFF

PROTECT

PROTECTED

PROTECTION

PROTOCOL

REBUILD

REGISTER MEMORY

REMIRROR PARTITION

REMOVE NETWORK ADAPTER

REMOVE NETWORK INTERFACE

REMOVE STORAGE ADAPTER

RESET ENVIRONMENT

RESET NETWORK ADAPTER

RESET NETWORK INTERFACE

RESET ROUTER

RESET SERVER

RESTART SERVER

RMIC

RMIREGISTRY

SCAN ALL

SCAN FOR NEW DEVICES

SEARCH   START PROCESSORS

SECURE CONSOLE   STARTX.NCF

SEND   STOP PROCESSORS

SERIALVER   SWAP

SERVER.EXE   TIME

SET   TRACK OFF

SET TIME   TRACK ON

SET TIME ZONE   UNBIND

SHUTDOWN NETWORK   UNLOAD
INTERFACE
                                         VERIFY
SPEED
                                         VERSION
SPOOL
                                         VOLUME

Using NLMs

NetWare Loadable Modules (NLMs), such as NWCONFIG and MONITOR, are software modules that can add functionality to a server. They can enable the server to support Mac OS files, provide backup services, support different protocols, install new features, and so on.

Many NLMs are installed automatically with the NetWare operating system. Others are optional; you can load them if your particular situation requires them. You can load and unload NLMs while the server is running. You don't have to reboot the server to make the new NLMs take effect — they are immediately effective.

NOTE Many NLMs that can be used on a NetWare server are also available from third-party companies. Third-party NLM products may include backup software, UPS management software, and the like. See the documentation that comes with these products for more information about their NLMs.

There are four types of NLMs that you can use to add different types of functionality to your server: NLMs, name space modules, LAN drivers, and disk drivers. These types of NLMs are described in Chapter 3.

Once loaded, many NLMs have their own status screen that displays continuously on the server. Because you can have multiple NLMs running simultaneously, you may have multiple active NLM screens, but you can only see one at a time. To move between active NLM screens on the server's console, press Alt+Esc to cycle through the available NLM screens. You can also press Ctrl+Esc to bring up a list of all available screens, from which you can select one.

To load NLMs, type the name of the NLM (you do not need to type the .NLM or other filename extension).

For example, to load MONITOR.NLM, type:

```
MONITOR
```

To unload an NLM, use the UNLOAD command. For example, to unload MONITOR.NLM, type:

```
UNLOAD MONITOR
```

NOTE   In previous versions of NetWare, you must use the LOAD command to load an NLM. For example, to load MONITOR.NLM in NetWare 4.11, you must type LOAD MONITOR. In NetWare 5, it is no longer necessary to use the LOAD command to load NLMs.

This appendix describes the core NLMs. Many NLMs have related NLMs that automatically load when necessary. These "autoloaded" NLMs are not listed here, because you should never need to load them manually. The following NLMs are described in this appendix:

AIOCOMX.NLM	DSREPAIR.NLM
APPLETLK.NLM	EDIT.NLM
ATCON.NLM	FILTCFG.NLM
ATFLT.NLM	INETCFG.NLM
ATMCON.NLM	INSTALL.NLM
AURP.NLM	IPFLT.NLM
BROKER.NLM	IPXCON.NLM
CD9660.NSS	IPXFLT.NLM
CDHFS.NSS	IPXPING.NLM
CDROM.NLM	JAVA.NLM
CHARSET.NLM	KEYB.NLM
CONLOG.NLM	LONG.NAM
DS.NLM	MAC.NAM
DSDIAG.NLM	MONITOR.NLM
DSMERGE.NLM	NCMCON.NLM

NDPSM.NLM

NFS.NAM

NIASCFG.NLM

NPRINTER.NLM

NSS.NLM

NWCONFIG.NLM

ORBCMD.NLM

OSAGENT.NLM

PING.NLM

PSERVER.NLM

PSM.NLM

QMAN.NLM

RCONAG6.NLM

RCONPRXY.NLM

REMOTE.NLM

ROUTE.NLM

RS232.NLM

RSPX.NLM

SBACKUP.NLM

SBCON.NLM

SBSC.NLM

SCRSAVER.NLM

SERVMAN.NLM

SMDR.NLM

SMSDI.NLM

SPXCONFG.NLM

TCPCON.NLM

TCPIP.NLM

TECHWALK.NLM

TIMESYNC.NLM

TPING.NLM

TSA410.NLM

TSA500.NLM

TSADOSP.NLM

TSANDS.NLM

TSAPROXY.NLM

UNICON.NLM

UPS_AIO.NLM

V_LONG.NLM

V_MAC.NLM

V_NFS.NLM

VIEW.NLM

VREPAIR.NLM

WTM.NLM

Using Java Applications and Applets

NetWare 5 includes a Java Virtual Machine (JVM), which is software that enables Java-based applications and applets to run on the server. NetWare 5 also includes a handful of Java applications and applets.

The applications and applets that are included in NetWare 5 can be run from the server's graphical desktop. From the server desktop, click the Novell button and choose ConsoleOne. RConsoleJ and Console Manager are located under the Tools icon in ConsoleOne. Some demonstration applets are located under the Shortcuts icon. The following Java applications and applets are described in this appendix:

Console Manager

ConsoleOne

DNS/DHCP Management Console

JEditor

RConsoleJ

The Utilities and NLMs

The core NetWare utilities and NLMs are explained in the following sections.

ABORT REMIRROR (Console Utility)

Use this utility at the server to stop disk partitions from remirroring. Use the following command format, replacing *number* with the number of the logical disk partition you want to stop from remirroring:

```
ABORT REMIRROR number
```

See Chapter 3 for more information about disk mirroring.

ADD NAME SPACE (Console Utility)

Use this utility at the server console to add support for a name space (LONG.NAM for OS/2, Windows 95/98, and Windows NT files; MAC.NAM for Macintosh files; and NFS.NAM for UNIX files). See Chapter 3 for more information about name space modules.

Use the following command format, replacing *name* with the name of the name space module (such as MAC), and *volume* with the volume's name:

```
ADD NAME SPACE name TO volume
```

To display the name spaces currently loaded, simply type:

```
ADD NAME SPACE
```

AIOCOMX (NLM)

Load this NLM, which is a communications port driver, on the server to use with utilities such as Remote Console, if you are using asynchronous communications. (For example, use this module if you're using Remote Console to access a server across a modem.) See Chapter 3 for more information about using Remote Console.

ALERT (Console Utility)

Use this utility at the server to control how alerts are handled by the server, if you are using SNMP network management tools. You can use this utility to turn on and off specified types of alerts, control where they are displayed or recorded, and so on. Use the following command format, substituting the number of the alert for *nmID* (optional) and one of the options listed in Table E.1 for *option*. Then choose either On or Off to turn on or off the alert and option you chose. You can only specify one option at a time, unless you use the ALL option, which sets the Log, Console, Everyone, and Bell options simultaneously. To specify more than one option, repeat the ALERT command multiple times, using a different option in each command.

```
ALERT nmID option ON/OFF
```

TABLE E.1 *ALERT Commands*

OPTION	DESCRIPTION
Event	When set to On, generates an event when the alert occurs. When set to Off, an event is not generated.
Log	When set to On, records the alert message in a log file.
Everyone	When set to On, sends the alert to all network users who are logged in.
Console	When set to On, displays the alert message on the server's console.
Bell	When set to On, sounds a warning noise when the alert occurs.
ID	When set to On, displays ID information. (Used only in older alert messages.)
Locus	When set to On, displays locus information. (Used only in older alert messages.)
Alert	When set to On, generates the alert.
Nmid	When set to On, causes the alert nmID to appear in the alert message.
All	When set to On, turns on the Log, Console, Everyone, and Bell commands at the same time.

ALIAS (Console Utility)

Use this utility at the server to create an alias for a particular console utility or command, so you can type the alias, rather than the regular utility name, to execute the utility. Use the following command format, replacing *alias* with the new command you want to be able to type, and replacing *command* with the original utility name or command you want to execute when you type the alias:

ALIAS *alias command*

APPLET (Console Utility)

Use this utility at the server to execute a Java-based applet. Type the following command at the server prompt, substituting the applet's file name for *html_file*:

APPLET *html_file*

To execute a Java application, see the JAVA console utility.

APPLETLK (NLM)

Use this NLM to load the AppleTalk protocol stack on the server. Use it to create an AppleTalk router on the server to support AppleTalk networks connected to the NetWare network.

Application Explorer (Workstation Utility)

Use this utility on a Windows 95/98 or Windows NT workstation to allow users to find and launch network applications easily. This utility is a part of Z.E.N.works, which must be installed on a workstation from the client CD-ROM.

This utility is similar to the Application Launcher utility, but allows application objects to be added to Windows Explorer, the desktop, or the system tray. When the Application Explorer is set up on users' workstations, you can use NetWare Administrator to make an application become an object in the NDS tree. Then, the icon for the Application object will appear automatically on the desktops of the users you assign to that application.

The users don't need to know where the application is located; they don't need to map drives or enter launch parameters; and you don't need to update login scripts. When you update the application, the icons in all of the desktops will continue to point to the new application.

For more information, and for instructions on setting up Z.E.N.works and the Application Launcher, see Chapter 5.

Application Launcher (Workstation Utility)

Use this utility on a Windows 3.1, Windows 95/98, or Windows NT workstation to enable users to find and launch network applications easily. This utility is a part of Z.E.N.works, which must be installed on a workstation from the client CD-ROM.

Once you have the Application Launcher set up on each user's workstation, you can use NetWare Administrator to make an application become an object in the NDS tree. Then, the icon for the Application object will appear automatically on the desktop of each user you assign to that application.

The users don't need to know where the application is located; they don't need to map drives or enter launch parameters; and you don't need to update login scripts. When you update the application, the icons in all of the desktops will continue to point to the new application.

For more information, and for instructions on setting up Z.E.N.works and the Application Launcher, see Chapter 5.

ATCON (NLM)

Load this NLM on the server to monitor and configure the AppleTalk protocol stack and AppleTalk router on the server.

ATCON lets you see the status of the AppleTalk Update-based Router protocol, which lets AppleTalk be tunneled through IP. ATCON also enables you to see information about network interfaces, manage the error log files, do a Name Binding Protocol (NBP) look-up of network entities, see statistics about AppleTalk packets, display the configuration of the AppleTalk router, and so on.

When using ATCON, press the F1 key to read help for each option.

ATFLT (NLM)

Load this AppleTalk filter NLM on the server to restrict how routers see and communicate with other AppleTalk routers.

ATMCON (NLM)

Load this NLM to monitor and troubleshoot ATM traffic and ATM/Link interfaces on your network.

ATOTAL (Workstation Utility)

Use this utility at a workstation's DOS prompt to create a report totaling the usage statistics tracked by the accounting feature on a server. See Chapter 3 for more information about accounting.

To display the totals on a workstation screen, type:

```
ATOTAL
```

To redirect the output of ATOTAL's report to a text file, use the following command format, substituting a filename for *filename*:

```
ATOTAL > filename
```

AUDITCON (Workstation Utility)

Use this menu utility from a workstation's DOS prompt to configure and view audit trails from a server's volume and container object. This utility lets an auditor see auditing information about NDS and file system or volume events. Auditors cannot, however, open or modify files without appropriate NDS or file system rights.

NOTE NetWare's auditing feature tracks how your network is being used. An independent auditor can then access the information and evaluate it, much like a financial auditor might audit your financial books. With auditing, only the auditor has rights to read the auditing information — even the Admin user cannot access this information. See the Novell documentation for more information about setting up auditing on your network.

AURP (NLM)

Load this NLM on the server to allow AppleTalk to be tunneled through IP, which lets AppleTalk networks connect to each other through an IP internetwork. (AURP stands for AppleTalk Update-based Routing Protocol.) See the Novell documentation for more information about the AppleTalk and IP protocols.

BIND (Console Utility)

Use this utility to assign a protocol such as IPX or AppleTalk to a LAN driver or network board, so the LAN driver or board knows which protocol to use. Any configuration parameters you specify when you load the LAN driver must also be added to the BIND command so the protocol is bound to the correct board. You can place BIND commands in AUTOEXEC.NCF so they are permanent. (You may find it easier to load LAN drivers and bind protocols to them by using NWCONFIG.NLM instead of using BIND.)

Use the following command format, replacing *protocol* with the name of the protocol (such as IPX or APPLETLK), *driver* with the name of the LAN driver or network board, and *parameters* with any necessary driver or protocol parameters:

BIND *protocol driver parameters*

The most common protocol parameter for the IPX protocol is:

NET=*number*

Replace *number* with the unique network number for the network on which this board is running. (Each network board in a server will have a different network number.)

The most common driver parameters are described in Table E.2.

TABLE E.2	Common Driver Parameters
DRIVER PARAMETER	**DESCRIPTION**
DMA=*number*	Indicates the DMA channel the board should use.
FRAME=*type*	Indicates the frame type (Ethernet or Token Ring) this board should use. The available frames types are:
	Ethernet_802.2 (default)
	Ethernet_802.3
	Ethernet_II
	Ethernet_SNAP
	Token-Ring (default)
	Token-Ring_SNAP
INT=*number*	Indicates the interrupt (in hex) that the board should use.
MEM=*number*	Indicates the memory address the board should use.
NODE=*number*	Indicates the board's node address.
PORT=*number*	Indicates the I/O port the board should use.
SLOT=*number*	Indicates the slot in which the board is installed.

BINDERY (Console Command)

Use this utility at the server to add or delete a bindery context in the list of bindery contexts this server uses. To add a bindery context to a server, use the following command format, substituting a valid context for *context*:

BINDERY ADD CONTEXT = context

To delete a bindery context from a server, type:

BINDERY DELETE CONTEXT = context

You can also use the SET BINDERY CONTEXT server parameter to set a bindery context, as explained in Chapter 5.

BROADCAST (Console Utility)

Use this utility at the server to send a short message from the server console to users on the network. To send a message to a user, use the following command format, replacing *message* with the message you want displayed (no more than 55 characters long) and *user* with either the name of the user or that workstation's connection number (as seen in MONITOR.NLM):

BROADCAST "message" user

To send the message to multiple users, separate each user name or connection number with a comma or space. To send the message to all users, don't specify any user name at all. (You can also use the SEND console utility to accomplish the same thing.)

BROKER (NLM)

This NLM is automatically loaded on the server. It manages centralized printing services for all NDPS printers on the network. It provides three services:

- ▶ Resource Management Service
- ▶ Event Notification Service
- ▶ Service Registry Service

NDPS Brokers are created automatically by the regular NetWare server installation. By default, all three of the Broker's services are enabled when the Broker is installed. If you want to disable (or reenable) a service, you can disable it from BROKER.NLM's console screen on the server. For more information about NDPS printing, see Chapter 9.

C1START (.NCF)

Use this utility at the server's console prompt to start the graphical server desktop and load ConsoleOne at the same time. Java-based applications, such as ConsoleOne, can execute from the graphical server desktop.

CAPTURE (Workstation Utility)

Use this utility at a workstation's DOS prompt to redirect the workstation's LPT port to a network print queue. Many network applications can redirect print jobs to a network print queue automatically, but others don't, so it's a good idea to put a CAPTURE command in the login script just in case. (See Chapter 9 for more information about printing.)

In general, you can use the following command format, replacing *port* with the number of the LPT port and *queue* with the name of the print queue (you may need to specify the complete Directory name of the queue, if it isn't in your own context). Replace *options* with one of the additional options listed in Table E.3.

```
CAPTURE L=port Q=queue options
```

TABLE E.3   *CAPTURE Options*

OPTION	DESCRIPTION
AU	End capture Automatically — Sends a print job to the printer when you exit the application.
B=text	Banner — Specifies that a banner page (displaying the *text* you specify) is printed before the print job. The default text is the print job file name.
C=number	Copies — Specifies how many copies are printed (1 to 999; the default is 1).
CR=path	Create — Redirects the print job to a file instead of to a printer. Replace *path* with the directory path and name of the file you want to create.
D	Details — Displays details of printing parameters for a capture, and shows whether a print job configuration was used.

(continued)

	TABLE E.3	*CAPTURE Options (continued)*

OPTION	DESCRIPTION
EC	End Capture—Stops capturing data to the LPT1 port, and if the data was being captured to a file, closes the file.
	To end a capture to another port, use EC L=*n* and replace *n* with the LPT number.
	To end a capture and delete the data that was being captured, use ECCA.
	To end the capture of all LPT ports, use EC ALL.
F=*form*	Form—Specifies the number or name of the form (paper type) on which this job should be printed.
FF	Form Feed—Causes a form feed at the end of a print job so that the next job prints on the next page. This option is only necessary if the application doesn't cause a form feed automatically.
HOLD	Hold—Sends a print job to a queue, but doesn't print it. To release the Hold, use the NetWare Administrator utility.
J=*name*	Job configuration—Specifies the name of a print job configuration to use. This option is necessary only if you don't want to use the default print job configuration.
K	Keep—Instructs your workstation to keep all captured data in case your workstation loses power while capturing data. The network server will send the captured data to the printer if it detects that your workstation is down.
L=*number*	LPT port—Specifies which LPT port should be captured (1, 2, or 3).
NA	No Auto Endcap—Prevents the workstation from sending captured data to the printer when you exit an application.
NAM=*name*	Name—Specifies the name that should appear on the banner page (the default is your login name).
NB	No Banner—Eliminates the banner page.
NFF	No Form Feed—Eliminates the form feed.

OPTION	DESCRIPTION
NNOTI	No Notification — Prevents a message from appearing on your workstation telling you that the print job is finished. This option is necessary only if the print job configuration requests notification and you don't want it.
NOTI	Notify — Specifies that your workstation receives notification when a print job is finished. This option is disabled by default.
NT	No Tabs — This option is necessary only if your application has a print formatter, but has problems printing graphics or creates unexpected formats. It enables an application's print formatter to determine how many spaces are in a tab stop.
P=*printer*	Printer — Specifies a network printer.
Q=*name*	Queue — Specifies a network print queue.
S=*name*	Server — Specifies to which network server a print job should be sent.
SH	Show — Displays a list of your workstation's captured ports and the print queues to which they are redirected.
T=*number*	Tabs — Specifies how many spaces are in a tab stop. This is necessary only if your application has no print formatter.
TI=*number*	Timeout — Specifies the *timeout* (the number of seconds to wait before printing) instead of waiting for the user to exit the application. The default is 0, meaning that timeout is disabled.
/VER	Version — Displays the version number of this utility and any files it requires.
/?	Help — Displays help for CAPTURE.

CD9660.NSS (NLM)

Load this NLM on the server to allow the server to mount an ISO 9660-format CD-ROM as an NSS volume. (This module is automatically loaded when CDROM.NLM is loaded.)

CDHFS.NSS (NLM)

Load this NLM on the server to enable the server to mount a Macintosh HPFS-formatted (High Performance File System) CD-ROM as an NSS volume. (This module is automatically loaded when CDROM.NLM is loaded.)

CDROM (NLM)

Load this NLM on the server to mount a CD-ROM as an NSS volume that can then be accessed by users like any other network volume. This NLM supports the ISO 9660 format and the HFS (Apple) format. (This means you can access Macintosh files on the CD from a Mac OS workstation.)

CHARSET (NLM)

Load this module on the server to change the code page that the server uses. A code page is a table that defines the characters used by a language. Different languages use different code pages. To change the code page used by the server, type the following command, substituting the number of the code page you want to use for *nnn*. (You can use any of the following code page numbers on a NetWare 5 server: 437, 737, 850, 852, 855, 857, 860, 861, 863, 865, 866, or 869.)

```
CHARSET CPnnn
```

After changing the code page, CHARSET unloads itself from memory. If you want the CHARSET code to remain in memory, use the following command:

```
CHARSET CPnnn stay
```

CLEAR STATION (Console Utility)

Use this command at the server to close a workstation's open files and remove the workstation's connection from the server. This is necessary only if the workstation has crashed and left files open and the user can't log out normally.

Use the following command format, replacing *number* with the workstation's connection number (as seen in MONITOR.NLM) or the word ALL to clear all connections:

```
CLEAR STATION number
```

CLS (Console Utility)

Use this utility at the server to clear the server's console screen (just as the CLS command works on DOS workstations).

CONFIG (Console Utility)

Use this utility at the server to see configuration information about the server. This utility displays information such as:

- The server's name
- The server's internal network number
- The LAN drivers that are loaded on the server
- The server's hardware settings
- The protocols the server is currently supporting
- The node address of each network board installed in the server
- The server's tree name
- The server's bindery context

CONLOG (NLM)

Load this NLM on the server to capture the console messages that occur during system initialization.

You can use this NLM if you want to see which error messages may be displayed when the server initializes. The messages are captured and sent to a file called CONSOLE.LOG in the SYS:ETC directory by default. This file is overwritten each time CONLOG is executed, unless you specify that you want to save backups of this file. You can use any text editor to open and read this file.

To stop capturing messages in this file, type UNLOAD CONLOG.

To use CONLOG, use the following command format, substituting *options* with one or more of the options listed in Table E.4:

```
CONLOG options
```

TABLE E.4	CONLOG Options
OPTION	**DESCRIPTION**
ARCHIVE=YES	Saves up to 1,000 backups of old CONLOG log files. Each time CONLOG is executed, the existing CONLOG log file is renamed to CONSOLE.*xxx* (beginning with 000), up to CONSOLE.999.
ENTIRE=YES	Adds any existing console messages that already appear on the screen to the CONSOLE.LOG file. By default, CONLOG will only record messages that occur after CONLOG is executed.

(continued)

TABLE E.4	CONLOG Options (continued)
OPTION	**DESCRIPTION**
FILE=path\filename	Lets you specify a different path or filename for the CONLOG log file.
MAXIMUM=size	Lets you specify the maximum size to which the CONLOG log file can grow before it is overwritten by a new version of the file (or renamed if you use the SAVE option). By default, there is no size limit for the CONLOG log file.
NEXT=hh:mm:ss	Lets you specify the exact time that you want the existing CONLOG log file to be saved and renamed, so that a new version can be opened. Use this option with the SAVE or ARCHIVE options.
SAVE=filename	Lets you specify that if a CONLOG log file already exists, it is saved and renamed to the filename you specify, rather than being overwritten by a new version of the file. This option will only save one previous version of the log file. If you want to save multiple previous versions of the log file, use the ARCHIVE option.
HELP	Use this option to see help for the CONLOG options.

CONSOLE MANAGER (Java Applet)

Use this Java applet on the server's graphical desktop or from a workstation to view other server console screens. To use this applet, make sure RCONAG6.NLM is loaded on the server whose console screens you want to view. Then, run Console Manager by using one of the following methods:

- From ConsoleOne, open My Server, then open Tools, and click Console Manager.

- From the server's console prompt, type **CONMAN.NCF.**

- From a Windows 95/98 or Windows NT workstation, run CONMAN.EXE from the SYS:PUBLIC\MGMT folder.

Because of the memory requirements and slowness of this applet, you may find it easier to switch between console screens on the server using Alt+Esc instead of using this applet. In addition, you may find it easier to use Remote Console from a workstation.

CONSOLEONE (Java Application)

The ConsoleOne management utility is a Java-based utility that runs either on the server or on a workstation, provided the server or workstation is running a Java engine. The ConsoleOne utility combines many of the management tasks available in other console utilities or NLMs, so you can execute server management tasks from a single utility. ConsoleOne gives the server a graphical interface, much like using an application in Windows instead of in DOS.

To load ConsoleOne from the server's graphical desktop, click the Novell button and select ConsoleOne from the menu that appears. When ConsoleOne loads, you must log in to NDS by typing in the tree name, your context, your user name, and your password.

The first release of ConsoleOne contained in NetWare 5 is a relatively limited administrative application, encompassing some of the features of other familiar NetWare utilities, such as MONITOR and NetWare Administrator. ConsoleOne is built in a modular fashion so that future modules, called *snapins*, can be added to it as they are developed. For more information about ConsoleOne, see the Novell online documentation or the online help inside ConsoleOne itself.

CPUCHECK (Console Utility)

Use this utility at the server to display information about the server's processor, such as the CPU speed, model, and cache. If the server has more than one processor, typing **CPUCHECK** will display information about all the server's processors. To see information about only one of the processors, use the following command format, substituting the processor number for *number*:

```
CPUCHECK number
```

CSET (Console Utility)

Use this utility at the server to display and set server (SET) parameters by category. Use the following command format, substituting the parameter category for *category*:

```
CSET category
```

For example, to see each server parameter in the Memory category, and to be given the opportunity to change each one as it is displayed, type:

```
CSET MEMORY
```

It is often easier to use MONITOR.NLM to view and change server parameters than to use CSET from the console.

CX (Workstation Utility)

Use this utility at a workstation's DOS prompt to change your current context in the Directory tree. With CX, you can move up and down through containers in the Directory tree. This utility is similar to DOS's CD utility, which lets you move around in the file system's subdirectory structure. (See Chapter 5 for more information about name contexts.)

Use the following command format, replacing *context* with the NDS context you want to move to (such as .MKTG.RESEARCH.BIGTIME), or replacing *option* with one of the options listed in Table E.5:

```
CX context /option
```

TABLE E.5 *CX Options*

OPTION	DESCRIPTION
/A	Includes all objects in the context (use with /T or /CONT).
/C	Causes the display to scroll continuously down the screen.
/CONT	Displays a list of containers in your current context, or in the context you specify in the command.
/R	Displays a list of the containers at the root level, or changes the context in relation to the root.
/T	Displays a list of the containers below your current context or the context you specify in the command.
/?	Displays help for CX.

DISABLE LOGIN (Console Utility)

Use this utility at the server to prevent users from logging in to the server (such as when you want to perform maintenance on the server). Users who are already logged in won't be affected, but additional users cannot log in. To allow users to log in again, use ENABLE LOGIN.

DISABLE TTS (Console Utility)

Use this utility at the server to disable TTS (NetWare's Transaction Tracking System). You should not need to disable TTS using this utility, unless you are an application developer and have a specific need to do so. If you disable TTS, you can turn it back on using ENABLE TTS.

DISMOUNT (Console Utility)

Use this utility at the server to dismount a volume (usually in preparation for repairing or deleting a volume). Use the following command format, replacing *volume* with the name of the volume you want to dismount:

```
DISMOUNT volume
```

DISPLAY ENVIRONMENT (Console Utility)

Use this utility at the server to display the current values of all server parameters.

DISPLAY INTERRUPTS (Console Utility)

Use this utility at the server to display information about the interrupt handler and interrupt statistics on the server. To display information for the interrupts currently in use, type the following command:

```
DISPLAY INTERRUPTS
```

To see more detailed information, use the following command format, substituting one of the options listed in Table E.6 for *option*:

```
DISPLAY INTERRUPTS option
```

TABLE E.6   *DISPLAY INTERRUPTS Options*

OPTION	DESCRIPTION
n	Displays information for the specific interrupt number (replace *n* with the interrupt number). To display information for more than one interrupt, separate each interrupt number with a space.
ALL	Displays information about all interrupts.
ALLOC	Displays information for allocated interrupts.
PROC	Displays interrupt information by processor.
REAL	Displays the interrupts that occurred while the operating system was in real mode, and that were sent to protected mode for servicing.

DISPLAY MODIFIED ENVIRONMENT (Console Utility)

Use this utility at the server to display the server parameters that have been changed from their default values. This utility displays both the current value and the original default value.

DISPLAY NETWORKS (Console Utility)

Use this utility at the server to display a list of all the networks (shown by their network numbers) that this server recognizes. It also displays how many hops (cable segments between servers or routers) away these networks are, and the time (in ticks — approximately $\frac{1}{18}$ of a second) it takes for a packet to reach these networks.

DISPLAY PROCESSORS (Console Utility)

Use this utility on the server to display the status of all processors in the server. To display information about all processors, type:

```
DISPLAY PROCESSORS
```

To see information about specific processors, type the following command, substituting the number of the processor for *n*. If you want to list more than one processor, separate each processor number with a space.

```
DISPLAY PROCESSORS n
```

DISPLAY SERVERS (Console Utility)

Use this command to display a list of all the servers that this server recognizes and records in its router table. It also displays how many hops (cable segments between servers or routers) away those servers are.

The command DISPLAY SERVERS lists all servers on the network. To see information about a single server or set of servers that start with the same letters, use the following command format, replacing *server* with a server's name (or use the wildcard character * to display multiple servers that begin with the same letters, such as B*):

```
DISPLAY SERVERS server
```

DNS/DHCP Management Console (Java Application)

Use this Java application on a Windows NT workstation to create, configure, and manage NDS objects for use with DNS and DHCP. To install this application on the workstation, run the file SETUP.EXE from the SYS:PUBLIC\DNSDHCP folder. This utility requires a minimum of 32MB of memory on the workstation (although 64MB is recommended).

After you've installed the application, you can run it by double-clicking the icon on the desktop, or by choosing it from the Tools menu in NetWare Administrator.

See the Novell documentation for more information about using the DNS/DHCP Management Console.

DOWN (Console Utility)

Use this utility at the server to shut down the server cleanly. This command closes any open files, writes any data left in the cache buffers to the disk, and so on, so that the server files will not be damaged when you shut down the server.

After you've brought down the server with the DOWN command, you can safely turn off the computer.

DS (NLM)

This NLM (along with several related NLMs) loads Novell Directory Services on the server. Networks will generally work more efficiently and have fewer conflicts if all servers in the tree are using the same version of DS.NLM. This NLM is loaded on the server automatically when the server starts up.

See Chapter 5 for more information about managing NDS.

DSDIAG (NLM)

Load this module on the server to create diagnostic reports that show the status of your NDS replica rings, Directory partitions, NDS versions installed in the tree, and so on. When you load this module, choose Generate Report from the main menu. The utility offers you several different types of reports to generate. Select a report type (such as "Check NDS Versions").

You can specify where information is retrieved (such as NDS), the search context, and so on. You can also specify whether the report is sent to a file, or just displayed on the screen. By default, the "Report File" option is disabled, meaning that the report will only display on the screen. To send the report to a file, select Report File, and then press Enter and indicate a filename to use. When ready to generate the report, press F10.

DSMERGE (NLM)

Load this NLM on the server to merge two or more NDS trees into a single tree. (Do not use this utility to merge Directory partitions. This utility should only be used for merging two Directory trees.) You can also use this utility to rename a tree.

See Chapter 5 for more information about merging Directory trees.

DSREPAIR (NLM)

Load this NLM on the server to repair possible problems with the NDS database on individual servers. You have to run it on each server that has a problem. DSREPAIR can also perform replica synchronization operations and enable you to see the current status of this server's view of the network or Directory.

To run DSREPAIR, type the following command:

```
DSREPAIR
```

To run DSREPAIR and have it automatically exit and unload itself when it is finished running, without user intervention, type:

```
DSREPAIR -U
```

See Chapter 5 for more information about using DSREPAIR.NLM.

EDIT (NLM)

Load this NLM on the server to edit text files (such as AUTOEXEC.NCF or STARTUP.NCF) on the server. When you load EDIT, you will be prompted for the path and name of the file to edit. This NLM works like any other simple text editor.

ENABLE LOGIN (Console Utility)

Use this utility at the server to allow users to log in to the network. This is necessary only if you've used DISABLE LOGIN to prevent users from logging in.

ENABLE TTS (Console Utility)

Use this utility at the server to restart TTS (Transaction Tracking System) after the server has disabled TTS. The server will disable TTS if the SYS volume gets too full or if the server doesn't have enough memory to run TTS. (You can also disable TTS manually by using the DISABLE TTS console utility.)

ENVSET (Console Utility)

Use this utility at the server to display and modify global environment variables for the server. To display all environment variables, type:

```
ENVSET
```

To set or modify a variable, type the following command, substituting the variable you want for *variable*, and substituting a string or value for *value*:

```
ENVSET variable = value
```

If you leave *value* blank after the equal sign, the variable is removed from the environment.

FILE SERVER NAME (Console Utility)

Use this utility at the server to set the server's name. Use the following command format, substituting the new server name for *name*:

```
FILE SERVER NAME name
```

FILER (Workstation Utility)

Use this menu utility from a workstation's DOS prompt to work with files, directories, and volumes on the network. With FILER, you can see and work with the following types of file and directory information:

- ▶ List of subdirectories and files within a directory
- ▶ Trustees
- ▶ File system rights
- ▶ File owners
- ▶ Creation dates and times
- ▶ Available disk space and directory entries for a volume
- ▶ File and directory attributes
- ▶ Salvageable files

FILTCFG (NLM)

Load this NLM on the server to set up and configure filters for IPX, TCP/IP, and AppleTalk protocols. Filters provide additional network security by limiting what type of information is broadcast across the network by routers.

See the Novell documentation for more information about protocol filters.

FLAG (Workstation Utility)

Use this utility at a workstation's DOS prompt to view and assign file and directory attributes. To use FLAG to set file and directory attributes, use the following command format:

FLAG *path attributes /options*

For *path*, indicate the path to the directory or file whose attributes you're changing. For *attributes*, insert the list of abbreviations for the attributes you want to assign. See Table E.7 for a description of these file and directory attributes.

You can also use FLAG to assign search modes for executable files. (Search modes are instructions that tell the workstation where to look for a particular file.) To specify a search mode, use the following command format:

FLAG *path /M=number*

For *path*, specify the path to the file or directory whose search mode you want to change. For *number*, insert the number of the search mode you want to be used for the executable files in this path. The search modes are explained in Table E.8.

T A B L E E.7	*File and Directory Attributes*			
ATTRIBUTE	**ABBREVIATION**	**FILE**	**DIRECTORY**	**DESCRIPTION**
Delete Inhibit	Di	X	X	Prevents users from deleting the file or directory.
Hidden	H	X	X	Hides the file or directory so it isn't listed by the DOS DIR command or in the Windows File Manager or Explorer, and can't be copied or deleted.

ATTRIBUTE	ABBREVIATION	FILE	DIRECTORY	DESCRIPTION
Purge (Also called Purge Immediate)	P	X	X	Purges the file or directory immediately upon deletion. Purged files can't be salvaged.
Rename Inhibit	Ri	X	X	Prevents users from renaming the file or directory.
System	Sy	X	X	Indicates a system directory that may contain system files (such as DOS files). Prevents users from seeing, copying, or deleting the directory. (However, does not assign the System attribute to the files in the directory.)
Don't Migrate	Dm	X	X	Prevents a file or directory from being migrated to another storage device.
Immediate Compress	Ic	X	X	Compresses the file or directory immediately.

(continued)

T A B L E E.7   *File and Directory Attributes (continued)*

ATTRIBUTE	ABBREVIATION	FILE	DIRECTORY	DESCRIPTION
Don't Compress	Dc	X	X	Prevents the file or directory from being compressed.
Archive Needed	A	X		Indicates that the file has been changed since the last time it was backed up.
Execute Only	X	X		Prevents an executable file from being copied, modified, or deleted. Use with caution! Once assigned, it cannot be removed, so assign it only if you have a backup copy of the file. You may prefer to assign the Read-Only attribute instead of the Executable Only attribute.
Read-Write	Rw	X		Allows the file to be opened and modified. Most files are set to Read-Write by default.

ATTRIBUTE	ABBREVIATION	FILE	DIRECTORY	DESCRIPTION
Read-Only	Ro	X		Allows the file to be opened and read, but not modified. All NetWare files in SYS:SYSTEM, SYS:PUBLIC, and SYS:LOGIN are Read-Only. Assigning the Read-Only attribute automatically assigns Delete Inhibit and Rename Inhibit.
Shareable	Sh	X		Allows the file to be used by more than one user simultaneously. Useful for utilities, commands, applications, and some database files. All NetWare files in SYS:SYSTEM,SYS: PUBLIC, and SYS:LOGIN are Shareable. Most data and work files should not be Shareable, so that users' changes do not conflict.

(continued)

T A B L E E.7	*File and Directory Attributes (continued)*			
ATTRIBUTE	**ABBREVIATION**	**FILE**	**DIRECTORY**	**DESCRIPTION**
Transactional	T	X		When used on database files, allows NetWare's Transactional Tracking System (TTS) to protect the files from being corrupted if the transaction is interrupted.
Copy Inhibit	Ci	X		Prevents Macintosh files from being copied. (Does not apply to DOS files.)
Don't Suballocate	Ds	X		Prevents a file from being suballocated. Use on files, such as some database files, that may need to be enlarged or appended to frequently. (See Chapter 8 for information on block suballocation.)

SEARCH MODE NUMBER	DESCRIPTION
0	Looks for search instructions in the NET.CFG file. (Default mode.)
1	Searches the path specified in the file. If no path is found, searches the default directory, and then all search drives.
2	Searches the path specified in the file. If no path is found, searches only the default directory.
3	Searches the path specified in the file. If no path is found, searches the default directory. Then, if the open request is read-only, searches the search drives.
4	Not used.
5	Searches the path specified, and then searches all search drives. If no path is found, searches the default directory, and then all search drives.
6	Not used.
7	Searches the path specified. If the open request is read-only, searches the search drives. If no path is found, searches the default directory, and then all search drives.

TABLE E.8   *FLAG Search Modes*

HELP (Console Utility)

Use this utility at the server to display help for console utilities. To see a list of available console utilities, type **HELP** at the server console. To display help for a specific console utility, use the following format, replacing *utility* with the name of the console utility whose help file you want to read:

```
HELP utility
```

INETCFG (NLM)

Load this NLM on the server to configure both data link and network protocols. INETCFG is a menu-driven NLM that makes it relatively easy to configure the protocols. If you install Novell Internet Access Server (NIAS), you will use NIASCFG.NLM instead of this utility.

See the Novell documentation for more information about using INETCFG and NIASCFG.

INSTALL (NLM)
This NLM has been replaced by NWCONFIG.NLM.

IPFLT (NLM)
Load this IP filter NLM on the server to restrict how routers see and communicate with other IP routers.

See the Novell documentation for more information about using the IP protocol and IP routers.

IPX INTERNAL NET (Console Utility)
Use this utility at the server to set the server's internal IPX network address.

IPXCON (NLM)
Load this module on the server to monitor information about IPX. With this utility, you can configure SNMP parameters; display IPX statistics and error counts; display information about NLSP, RIP, and SAP on the network; and list information such as known services and destination networks. When using IPXCON, press the F1 key to read help for each option.

IPXFLT (NLM)
Load this IPX filter NLM on the server to restrict how routers see and communicate with other IPX routers.

See the Novell documentation for more information about IPX routers.

IPXPING (NLM)
Load this NLM on the server to send test messages (pings) to another node on the network to see if it is communicating with this server via IPX. You will need to specify the target node's IPX internal network number and its node number.

See the Novell documentation for more information about IPX.

JAR (Console Utility)

This utility is the Java Archive Tool. See the Novell documentation for more information.

JAVA (Console Utility)

Use this command at the server to execute a Java-based application. The version of the command you type depends on how you want the application to run. If the application doesn't require user input, or if it runs in a graphical user interface, type the following command, substituting the application's name for *class*:

```
JAVA class
```

If you want to use options with this command, use the following command format, substituting one of the options in Table E.9 for *options*. Remember to precede each option with a minus sign (–).

TABLE E.9	JAVA Options
OPTION	DESCRIPTION
–HELP	Displays help for the JAVA command.
–NWHELP	Displays help for NetWare-specific options for the JAVA command.
–CLASSPATH *dir;dir;...*	Specifies the directories in which to search for classes.
–D*property=value*	Redefines a property's value.
–DEBUG	Enables remote Java debugging.
–ENV*variable*	Sets an environment variable for the Java application.
–EXIT	Exits all currently running Java applications and unloads Java from the server.
–KILL*id*	Kills a running Java application. (To see the *id* of a particular Java application, use the -SHOW option.)
–MS*number*	Sets the initial Java heap size.
–MX*number*	Sets the maximum Java heap size.
–NOASYNCGC	Prevents asynchronous garbage collection.

(continued)

TABLE E.9	JAVA Options (continued)
OPTION	**DESCRIPTION**
–NOCLASSGC	Prevents class garbage collection.
–NOVERIFY	Prevents verification of any class.
–NS	Brings up a separate console screen for the application. Use if the application is text-based and requires user input.
–OSSnumber	Sets the Java stack size for a process.
–PROF	Sends profiling data to ./java.prof.
–SHOW	Displays all currently running Java applications.
–SSnumber	Sets the C stack size of a process.
–VERBOSE	Turns on verbose mode (which displays informational messages).
–VERBOSEGC	Displays a message whenever garbage collection occurs.
–VERIFY	Verifies all classes when they are read in.
–VERIFYREMOTE	Verifies classes that are read in over the network (this is the default setting).
–VERSION	Displays the build version number of Java.
–VMsize	Specifies a specific amount of virtual memory for the Java application to use. Substitute the amount of memory (in megabytes) for size. The default size is 32MB.

JAVA (NLM)

Load this module on the server to load the Java Virtual Machine (JVM). After the JVM is loaded, you can execute Java applications and applets on the server. See Chapter 3 for more information about running Java applications on the server.

JAVAC (Console Utility)

This is the Java compiler utility. See the Novell documentation for more information.

JAVADOC (Console Utility)

This utility is the Java Documentation Generator. See the Novell documentation for more information.

JAVAH (Console Utility)

This utility is the Java C Header and Stub File Generator. See the Novell documentation for more information.

JAVAKEY (Console Utility)

This utility is the Java Digital Signing Tool. See the Novell documentation for more information.

JAVAP (Console Utility)

This utility is the Java Class File Disassembler. See the Novell documentation for more information.

JEDITOR (Java Applet)

Use this Java applet on the server to edit text files. Use JEditor like any other text editor. To run JEditor, use one of the following methods:

- ► From ConsoleOne, right-click a file you want to edit, and choose Edit from the menu that appears.
- ► From the server console, type **JEDITOR**.

KEYB (NLM)

Load this NLM on the server to indicate the type of keyboard that is attached to your server. The default type of keyboard supported by NetWare is the type used in the United States with the English language. Different countries and languages may require different types of keyboards. You only need to use this NLM if you're not using a United States/English keyboard on the server.

If you aren't using a United States keyboard with English, use the following command format to specify a different keyboard type, replacing *country* with the name of the country you want to choose:

```
KEYB country
```

To see a list of the countries from which you can choose, type **KEYB** without specifying any country.

LANGUAGE (Console Utility)

Use this utility at the server to change the language that displays when NLMs are loaded at the server console. This will not change the language of the operating system or of NLMs that are already loaded. It only affects the NLMs that are loaded after this utility is executed.

To display the current language being used by NLMs, type:

LANGUAGE

To display a list of all available languages, type:

LANGUAGE LIST

To change the language to be used by subsequently loaded NLMs, use the following command format, replacing *name* with either the name or number of the language:

LANGUAGE *name*

LIST DEVICES (Console Utility)

Use this utility at the server to display a list of all the storage devices you have installed on the server, such as CD-ROM drives, disk drives, and tape drives.

LIST STORAGE ADAPTERS (Console Utility)

Use this utility at the server to list all the server's storage adapters and HAMs (host adapter modules), and their associated storage devices.

LIST STORAGE DEVICE BINDINGS (Console Utility)

Use this utility at the server to list all the HAMs (host adapter modules) that are bound to a storage device, such as a disk drive. Use the following command format, substituting the storage device's number for *number*:

LIST STORAGE DEVICE BINDINGS *number*

To see the device number for a storage device, use the LIST DEVICES console utility.

LOAD (Console Utility)

Use this utility at the server to load NLMs on the server. However, in NetWare 5, using the LOAD command is optional; you can load NLMs simply by typing their name. If you want to use LOAD, use the following command format, replacing *module* with the name of the NLM you're loading (you don't need to include the .NLM extension in the module name):

```
LOAD module
```

To unload an NLM, use the UNLOAD console utility.

LOADSTAGE (Console Utility)

Use this utility at the server to load a stage. Use the following command format, substituting the name of the stage or the word ALL for *name*:

```
LOADSTAGE name
```

LOGIN (Workstation Utility)

Use this utility at a workstation to log in to the network. LOGIN authenticates you to the network and it can also execute login scripts to set up your work environment. There are two versions of this utility. The DOS-based version is a command you execute at the DOS prompt of your workstation. For DOS, use the following command format, replacing *tree* with either a Directory tree name or a server name (this is not necessary if you want to log in to the default tree or server), and replacing *username* with your login name. You can also add one or more *options* to the command if you want. These options are listed in Table E.10.

```
LOGIN tree/username option
```

If you are using Windows 3.1, Windows 95/98, or Windows NT on your workstation, you can log in to the network using the graphical version of LOGIN. The Login program for Windows 3.1, Windows 95/98, and Windows NT is installed as part of the NetWare client software. To log in using the graphical Login program, use one of the following methods (depending on your workstation's OS):

► To log in to the network from Windows 3.1, double-click the Login Program icon, and specify a login name and a password.

► From Windows 95/98 or NT, open the Network Neighborhood, right-click the desired server or tree, click either Authenticate or Login to NDS Tree, and then enter a login name and password. (To open the

Network Neighborhood, either double-click the Network Neighborhood icon or double-click the N logo in the system tray.) You can also log in by opening the Windows Start menu, and then selecting Programs, then Novell, and then NetWare Login.

For more information about logging in to the network and about login scripts, see Chapter 6.

T A B L E E . I 0	*DOS-based LOGIN Options*
OPTION	**DESCRIPTION**
/B	Specifies a bindery-based login instead of an NDS-based login.
/NB	Prevents the Novell banner screen from displaying during login.
/NOSWAP	Prevents LOGIN from swapping into extended memory, expanded memory, or to disk.
/NS	Prevents a login script from being executed, and prevents LOGIN from logging the user out of other servers.
/PR=*object*	Specifies a Profile object whose profile login script you want to execute for this user. Replace *object* with the name of the Profile object.
/S *path*	Displays a login script. Replace *path* with either the path and file name of a login script file or with the object name of an NDS object whose script you want to execute for this user.
/SWAP	Tells LOGIN to swap to the specified path when executing external commands.
/VER	Displays the version number of LOGIN.EXE.
/?	Displays help for LOGIN.

LOGOUT (Workstation Utility)

Use this utility at a workstation to log out of the network. How you log out depends on the operating system you're using on your workstation:

▶ If you're using a DOS workstation, simply type the following command at the DOS prompt:

```
LOGOUT
```

▶ If you're using a Windows 3.1 workstation, you can either go to DOS and type LOGOUT at the DOS prompt, or you can use the NetWare User Tools utility to log out. Double-click NetWare User Tools, select NetWare Connections, choose the server or tree from which you want to log out, and choose Logout.

▶ If you're using a Windows 95/98 or NT workstation, double-click the Network Neighborhood icon, right-click the NDS tree or server from which you want to log out, and choose Logout.

See Chapter 6 for more information about logging out.

LONG.NAM (NLM)

Load this NLM on the server to make the server support OS/2, Windows NT, and Windows 95/98 long filenames. After you've loaded this NLM, use the ADD NAME SPACE console command to assign the name space to a particular volume. (This name space is loaded on all NetWare 5 servers by default.)

See Chapter 3 for more information about loading name spaces.

MAC.NAM (NLM)

Load this NLM on the server to make the server support Mac OS long filenames and file formats on the server. After you've loaded this NLM, use the ADD NAME SPACE console command to assign the name space to a particular volume.

See Chapter 3 for more information about loading name spaces.

MAGAZINE (Console Utility)

If the server prompts you to insert a new media magazine during some task, use this utility to indicate to the server that you've inserted or removed a media magazine. Use the following command format, replacing *option* with one of the options listed in Table E.11:

```
MAGAZINE option
```

T A B L E E.II	*MAGAZINE Options*
OPTION	**DESCRIPTION**
Inserted	Tells the server you've inserted the media magazine.
Not Inserted	Tells the server that you have not inserted the media magazine.
Removed	Tells the server that you have removed the media magazine.
Not Removed	Tells the server that you have not removed the media magazine.

MAP (Workstation Utility)

Use this utility at a workstation to map drive letters on the workstation to network directories. You can execute MAP commands at the workstation's DOS prompt, or you can put MAP commands in a login script, so that the same drives are mapped every time the user logs in.

The MAP utility and drive mappings are explained in Chapter 6, under the "Login Script Commands" section.

MEDIA (Console Utility)

If the server prompts you to insert a specified storage medium during some task, use this utility to indicate to the server that you've inserted or removed the medium. Use the following command format, replacing *option* with one of the options listed in Table E.12:

```
MEDIA option
```

T A B L E E.I2	*MEDIA Options*
OPTION	**DESCRIPTION**
Inserted	Tells the server you've inserted the medium.
Not Inserted	Tells the server that you have not inserted the medium.
Removed	Tells the server that you have removed the medium.
Not Removed	Tells the server that you have not removed the medium.

MEMORY (Console Utility)

Use this utility at the server to see the total amount of memory currently installed in the server.

MEMORY MAP (Console Utility)

Use this utility at the server to see how much of the server's memory is allocated to DOS and to the server.

MIRROR STATUS (Console Utility)

Use this utility at a server to list all the disk partitions on the server and display their mirror status. The following five states are possible:

- ► Being Remirrored — This means the disk partition is being synchronized with another and will soon be mirrored.

- ► Fully Synchronized — This means the disk partitions are mirrored and working correctly, so that both partitions contain identical data.

- ► Not Mirrored — This means the disk partition isn't mirrored with any other partition.

- ► Orphaned State — This means the disk partition used to be mirrored with another, but isn't now. The integrity of this partition's data may not be ensured anymore.

- ► Out of Synchronization — This means the two disk partitions that are mirrored do not have identical data and, therefore, need to be remirrored.

MODULES (Console Utility)

Use this utility at a server to display a list of all the NLMs currently loaded on the server. If you want to see information about a single NLM, use the following command format, replacing *module* with an NLM's name:

```
MODULES module
```

You can use the wildcard character "*" to display multiple NLMs that begin with the same letter or letters. For example, to see all the loaded NLMs that start with the letter DS, type

```
MODULES DS*
```

MONITOR (NLM)

Load this NLM on the server to monitor the server's performance. This is one of the most frequently used management utilities for NetWare servers. It enables you to track and modify your server's performance characteristics. For more information about MONITOR.NLM, see Chapter 3.

MOUNT (Console Utility)

Use this utility at a server to mount a volume on a server so network users can access it. Use the following command format, replacing *volume* with the volume's name (or with ALL to mount all volumes):

```
MOUNT volume
```

NAME (Console Utility)

Use this utility at the server to display the server's name.

NATIVE2ASCII (Console Utility)

Use this utility at the server to convert a native-language file to ASCII format. Use the following command format, substituting the file's name for *filename*:

```
NATIVE2ASCII filename
```

NCMCON (NLM)

Load this module on the server to monitor, install, and remove PCI Hot Plug adapters. When it is loaded on the server, it constantly monitors the status of PCI slots and the adapters in them, and displays any change of status. For more information about using PCI Hot Plug technology, see Chapter 3.

NCOPY (Workstation Utility)

Use this utility at a workstation's DOS prompt to copy files and directories from one drive or disk to another. To use NCOPY, use the following command format:

```
NCOPY source/filename destination/filename /options
```

The options that can be used with the NCOPY utility are listed in Table E.13.

T A B L E   E.13   *NCOPY Options*

OPTION	DESCRIPTION
/A	Archive Bit Only — Copies only those files that have the Archive Needed attribute (also called the archive bit). NCOPY does not, however, remove the attribute from the source file, so the file will still have the Archive Needed attribute.

OPTION	DESCRIPTION
/C	Copy — Copies files, but does not preserve extended attributes or name space information.
/F	Force Sparse Files — Forces the operating system to copy sparse files, which aren't normally copied.
/I	Inform — Notifies the user when extended attributes or name space information can't be copied because the destination volume doesn't support those features.
/M	Archive Bit Set — Copies files that have the Archive Needed attribute, and removes the attribute from the source file. This allows NCOPY to be used as a backup tool.
/R	Retain Compression — Keeps compressed files compressed, rather than decompressing them during the copy process.
/R/U	Retain Unsupported Compression — Keeps compressed files compressed even if they are copied to a destination volume that doesn't support compression.
/S	Subdirectories — Copies all of the subdirectories (except empty subdirectories) as well as the files in the specified path.
/S/E	Subdirectories, Empty — Copies all the subdirectories, including empty subdirectories, as well as files in the specified path.
/V	Verify — Verifies that the original and the new files are identical. This option is useful for copies made on local DOS drives only.

For example, to copy all the files from drive G to drive L, use the following command:

```
NCOPY G:*.* L:
```

To copy all of the files plus the subdirectories (including empty ones) from drive G to drive L, use the following command:

```
NCOPY G:*.* L: /S/E
```

NCP ADDRESSES (Console Utility)

Use this utility at the server to display a list of all known NCP network service addresses.

NCP DUMP (Console Utility)

Use this utility at the server to record all NCP standard deviation statistics in a specified file. Use the following command format, substituting the file's name for *filename*:

```
NCP DUMP filename
```

NCP STATS (Console Utility)

Use this utility on the server to display all NCP statistics on incoming NCP requests. To display the statistics, type the following command:

```
NCP STATS
```

To reset the counter for these statistics, type the following command:

```
NCP STATS RESET
```

NCP TRACE (Console Utility)

Use this utility to decode incoming NCP packets and display them on an active server screen. You can also send the data to a file. Use the following command format to display the information on the screen:

```
NCP TRACE ON
```

Use the following command to send the information to a file, substituting the name of the file for *filename*:

```
NCP TRACE ON filename
```

Use the following command to turn off the NCP Trace screen:

```
NCP TRACE OFF
```

NDIR (Workstation Utility)

Use this utility at a workstation's DOS prompt to list a directory's files, sub-directories, and related information. With it, you can see the following types of information about files and directories:

- ▶ List of subdirectories and files within a directory
- ▶ Inherited Rights Filters
- ▶ Effective file system rights
- ▶ File owners
- ▶ Creation dates and times

- ▶ File sizes
- ▶ File and directory attributes
- ▶ Archive information
- ▶ File version (for Novell files)
- ▶ Volume information

With NDIR, you can sort the display of files so they appear in different orders, such as from largest to smallest, newest to oldest, all those owned by a particular owner, and so on.

To use NDIR, use the following command format. Replace *path* with the path, directory, or file whose information you want to see. If you desire, you can replace *option* with one of the options listed in Table E.14.

NDIR *path* /option

For example, to list all the files in the directory that is mapped to drive G, use the following command:

NDIR G:

To display the NDIR help screens, use the following command:

NDIR /?

TABLE E.14 *NDIR Options*

OPTION	DESCRIPTION
/attributes	Displays directories or files that have been assigned the specified attributes. See the FLAG utility for a list of the attribute abbreviations you can use.
/C	Continuously scrolls the NDIR information down the screen.
/COMP	Displays information about compressed files.
/D	Displays detailed file and directory information.
/DA	Displays file and directory date information.
/DO	Displays directories only.
/FI	Displays the location where a file is found within a search directory.
/FO	Displays files only.

(continued)

TABLE E.14	NDIR Options (continued)
OPTION	DESCRIPTION
/L	Displays long filenames.
/MAC	Displays information about Macintosh files.
/NOT *attributes*	Displays directories or files that do not have the specified attributes. See the FLAG utility for a list of the attribute abbreviations you can use.
/R	Displays rights, filters, and attributes for the files and directories.
/REV SORT *option qualifier value*	Displays files and directories in the reverse order. (See the /SORT option.)
/S	Displays not only the files in the specified path, but also all files in the path's subdirectories.
/SORT *option qualifier value*	Displays files and directories according to the *option* you specify. Replace *option* with one of the following: AC (last accessed date), AR (last archived date), CR (creation date), OW (owner), SI (size), UP (last updated date), UN (unsorted — files are displayed in no particular order). If you want, you can further narrow the display by adding a qualifier and value to the option. The following qualifiers can be used: LE (less than), GR (greater than), EQ (equal to), BEF (before), or AFT (after). For *value*, insert the value you want the option to have, such as an owner name or a date.
/SPA	Displays information about directory space.
/VER	Displays the version number for NDIR.
/VOL	Displays information about volumes.
/? ALL	Displays help screens for NDIR.

NDPSM (NLM)

Load this NLM on the server to manage NDPS printer agents and the NDPS Manager. (You can also manage the NDPS Manager from the NetWare Administrator utility, which is often easier to use.) You can load NDPSM.NLM and select the NDPS Manager you want to use from a menu, or you can specify the NDPS Manager in the load command, by typing:

```
NDPSM manager
```

Replace *manager* with the name of the NDPSM Manager object (you may need to specify the object's full name context). See Chapter 9 for more information about NDPS printing and about using this utility.

NDS Manager (Workstation Utility)

Use this utility on a Windows 95/98 or Windows NT workstation to analyze and repair (if necessary) Directory partitions and replicas. This utility can be executed by itself, or as a feature of the NetWare Administrator utility under the Tools option.

NDS Manager automatically executes DSREPAIR.NLM for repair options, so you may prefer to use NDS Manager from a workstation instead of using DSREPAIR from the console.

By default, NDS Manager is not part of NetWare Administrator, but you can add it easily. If you don't want to add it to NetWare Administrator, you must add NDS Manager to your workstation desktop as its own icon before you can use it.

To add the NDS Manager utility to the NetWare Administrator utility on a Windows 95/98 or Windows NT workstation, simply copy the file NMSNAP32.DLL from the SYS:PUBLIC/WIN32 folder to SYS:PUBLIC/WIN32/SNAPINS. The next time you start the NetWare Administrator utility, NDS Manager will appear as an option under the Tools menu.

To set up NDS Manager as a standalone utility on your Windows 95/98 or Windows NT desktop, create a Shortcut or icon on your desktop that points to the file NDSMGR32.EXE, located in the SYS:PUBLIC/WIN32 folder.

For more information about NDS Manager, see Chapter 5.

NetWare Administrator (Workstation Utility)

Use this utility on a Windows 95/98 or Windows NT workstation to manage your network. NetWare Administrator enables you to do tasks such as:

- ▶ Create, delete, or modify NDS objects
- ▶ Set up print services
- ▶ Assign NDS rights
- ▶ Modify login scripts

Before you can use NetWare Administrator, you need to install it on your workstation. To do this, create a Shortcut or icon on your desktop that points to the file NWADMN32.EXE, located in the SYS:PUBLIC\WIN32 folder.

For more information about using NetWare Administrator, see Chapter 5.

NetWare User Tools (Workstation Utility)

Use this utility from a Windows 3.1-based workstation to perform common network tasks, such as selecting print queues, sending messages to other users, changing passwords, mapping drive letters to directories, and logging in and out of the network. (Most Windows 95/98 users will use the Windows Explorer and Network Neighborhood instead of NetWare User Tools to complete network tasks.)

For more information about the NetWare User Tools utility, see Chapter 5.

NFS.NAM (NLM)

Use this NLM to load support for UNIX long filenames on the server. After you've loaded this NLM, use the ADD NAME SPACE console command to assign the name space to a particular volume.

See Chapter 3 for more information about using name spaces.

NIASCFG (NLM)

Use this NLM to manage Novell Internet Access Server (NIAS) features, such as remote access, protocols, and routing. After you've loaded this NLM, additional NIAS console utilities become available. For more information about using NIASCFG, see the Novell documentation.

NLIST (Workstation Utility)

Use this utility at a workstation's DOS prompt to display a variety of information about NDS objects, such as users, groups, servers, and volumes. Use the following command format, replacing *class* with the type of object you want to display (such as SERVER, USER, or GROUP) and *option* with one of the options listed in Table E.15:

```
NLIST class option
```

You can also specify a specific object name (or use wildcards to list those that begin with the same letters) by using the following command format:

```
NLIST class=name option
```

You can use options and variations of this command to display many kinds of information. To read help screens and see examples of NLIST commands, type:

NLIST /? ALL

For more information about NDS object classes, see Chapter 5.

T A B L E E.15 *NLIST Options*

OPTION	DESCRIPTION
/A	Displays active users or servers.
/B	Displays bindery information.
/C	Continuously scrolls information down the screen.
/CO *context*	Displays objects in the specified context. (Enclose the context in quotation marks if it includes any spaces.)
/D	Displays detailed information.
/N	Displays only the object's name.
/R	Displays objects at the Root context.
/S	Lists objects in subordinate contexts as well as the current or specified context.
SHOW *property*	Displays each object's specific value for the NDS property you specify. Replace *property* with a valid NDS property name, such as "Given Name" or "Title." To list multiple properties, separate each one by a comma, and if the property name includes spaces, enclose the name in quotation marks.
/TREE	Displays all available NDS trees.
/VER	Displays the version number of NLIST.
WHERE *property qualifier value*	Displays objects whose NDS property values match the qualifier and value you specify. Replace *property* with a valid NDS property name. Replace *qualifier* with one of the following: EQ (equal to), NE (not equal to), GT (greater than), GE (greater than or equal to), LT (less than), LE (less than or equal to), EXISTS (property exists), or NEXISTS (property does not exist). Replace *value* with the value you want to specify for the property, such as a name or number.
/? ALL	Displays all help screens for NLIST.

NLS Manager (Workstation Utility)

Use this utility at a Windows 95/98 or Windows NT workstation to manage NetWare Licensing Services (NLS). Before you can use NLS Manager, you need to install it on your workstation. To do this, create a Shortcut or icon on your desktop that points to the file NLSMAN32.EXE, located in the SYS: PUBLIC\WIN32 folder.

You can use NLS Manager to install license certificates, create metering certificates, display licensing information, and so on. This lets you track and limit the number of users who are allowed to use a particular product. See the Novell documentation for more information about NLS.

Novell Printer Manager (Workstation Utility)

Use the Novell Printer Manager utility to manually install NDPS printer support on a workstation. To use the Printer Manager utility, create a Shortcut or icon on the workstation's desktop that points to the utility:

- ► For a Windows 3.1 workstation, create an icon for the file called NWPMW16.EXE, located in the SYS:PUBLIC folder.

- ► For Windows 95/98 and Windows NT workstations, create a Shortcut to the file called NWPMW32.EXE, located in the SYS:PUBLIC\WIN32 folder.

The main Printer Manager window displays all the NDPS printers currently installed on the workstation. From here, users can add more printers to their workstation, if necessary.

In addition, the Printer Manager utility displays information about the printer, such as its status, its attributes (such as whether it prints in color), any problems with the printer (such as a paper jam or low toner), and so on. Users can also use the Printer Manager utility to see and change the status of their print jobs. For more information about using NDPS printing, see Chapter 9.

Novell Upgrade Wizard (Workstation Utility)

Use this utility on a Windows 95/98 or Windows NT workstation to upgrade the bindery and file system of a NetWare 3.1x server to NDS, while simultaneously moving the data to a NetWare 5 server. See Chapter 2 for more information about using this utility to upgrade NetWare 3.1x networks.

NPRINT (Workstation Utility)

Use this utility at a workstation's DOS prompt to print a job from outside an application (such as printing an ASCII file or a workstation screen). Use the following command format, replacing *options* with options from Table E.16:

NPRINT *options*

T A B L E E . 1 6 *NPRINT Options*

OPTION	DESCRIPTION
B=*text*	Banner — Specifies that a banner page (displaying the *text* you specify) is printed before the print job. The default text is the print job filename.
C=*number*	Copies — Specifies how many copies are printed (1 to 65,000; the default is 1).
D	Details — Displays the printing parameters for the print job, and shows whether a print job configuration was used.
DEL	Delete — Specifies that the file is deleted after it's printed.
F=*form*	Form — Specifies the number or name of the form (paper type) on which this job should be printed.
FF	Form Feed — Causes a form feed at the end of a print job, so that the next job prints on the next page. This option is necessary only if the application doesn't already cause a form feed.
HOLD	Hold — Sends a print job to a queue, but doesn't print it. To release the Hold, use the NetWare Administrator utility.
J=*name*	Job configuration — Specifies the name of a print job configuration to use. This option is necessary only if you don't want to use the default print job configuration.
NAM=*name*	Name — Specifies the name that should appear on the banner page (the default is your login name).
NB	No Banner — Eliminates the banner page.
NFF	No Form Feed — Eliminates the form feed.

(continued)

TABLE E.16	NPRINT Options (continued)
OPTION	DESCRIPTION
NNOTI	No Notification — Prevents a message from appearing on your workstation telling you that the print job is finished. (This is only necessary if the print job configuration requests notification and you don't want it.)
NOTI	Notify — Specifies that your workstation receives notification when a print job is finished. Disabled by default.
NT	No Tabs — Allows an application's print formatter to determine how many spaces are in a tab stop. This option is necessary only if your application has a print formatter, but has problems printing graphics or creates unexpected formats.
P=name	Printer — Specifies a printer.
Q=name	Queue — Specifies a network print queue.
S=name	Server — Specifies which network server to send a print job to.
T=number	Tabs — Specifies how many spaces are in a tab stop. This option is necessary only if your application doesn't have a print formatter.
/?	Help — Displays help for NPRINT.

NPRINTER.EXE (Workstation Utility)

Use this utility on a DOS or Windows 3.1 workstation to load a port driver on the workstation. The port driver is software that routes jobs out of the print queue, through the proper port on the workstation, and to the printer. This utility is used with queue-based printing only. See Chapter 9 for more information about queue-based printing.

To load the NPRINTER port driver on a workstation, type:

```
NPRINTER
```

To load the NPRINTER port driver on a workstation and specify options, such as indicating a particular printer, use the following command format. Replace *printer* with either a printer object name or with the name of the print server plus the printer number. Replace *option* with one or more of the options in Table E.17.

```
NPRINTER printer option
```

TABLE E.17	NPRINTER Options
OPTION	**DESCRIPTION**
B=n	Specifies the buffer size in KB. Default: 3. Values: 3 to 60.
/S	Displays the current status of all port drivers loaded on the workstation.
T=n	Specifies the duration of the strobe signal. Increasing the number gives more priority to foreground tasks, improving workstation performance but decreasing printing speed. Default: 1. Values: 1 to 9.
/U	Unloads the NPRINTER port driver. (If more than one is loaded, unloads the most recently loaded port driver.)
/VER	Displays the version number of NPRINTER.
/?	Displays help for NPRINTER.

NPRINTER (NLM)

Load this NLM on the server to load a port driver on the server. The port driver is software that routes jobs out of the print queue, through the proper port on the server, and to the printer. This utility is used with queue-based printing only.

To load the NPRINTER port driver on a server, type:

```
NPRINTER
```

To load the NPRINTER port driver on a server and specify a particular printer, use the following command format. Replace *printer* with either a printer object name or with the name of the print server plus the printer number.

```
NPRINTER printer
```

See Chapter 9 for more information about printing.

NPTWIN95.EXE (Workstation Utility)

Use this utility on a Windows 95/98 workstation to load a port driver on the workstation. The port driver is software that routes jobs out of the print queue, through the proper port on the workstation, and to the printer. This utility is used with queue-based printing only.

See Chapter 9 for more information about printing.

NSS (NLM)

Type **NSS** at the server console to load NSS support on the server. (You can also add the NSS command to the AUTOEXEC.NCF file to ensure that NSS support is loaded each time the server is rebooted.) Loading NSS will load necessary NLMs. In addition, it will make available the NSS administration console utility, which you can use to create and manage NSS volumes. See Chapter 8 for more information about NSS.

To see all the NSS console commands that are available after you've loaded NSS support, type the following command at the server console:

NSS HELP

To bring up the main NSS administration utility, type:

NSS MENU

You can use the NSS administration console utility to create and modify NSS volumes at any time after the server installation. The NSS administration utility also provides two additional utilities that let you rebuild and verify NSS volumes that have become corrupted: REBUILD and VERIFY.

NVER (Workstation Utility)

Use this utility at a workstation's DOS prompt to display the version number of the following types of programs running on the workstation or server:

- ▸ NetBIOS
- ▸ IPX and SPX
- ▸ LAN drivers
- ▸ NetWare client software
- ▸ The workstation's operating system
- ▸ The version of NetWare running on the server

NWBACK32 (Workstation Utility)

Use this utility on a Windows 95/98 or Windows NT workstation if you want to use Enhanced SBACKUP to back up network files. This is the workstation-based version of Enhanced SBACKUP. (The server-based version of this utility is called SBCON.NLM.) To use this utility, create a Shortcut to NWBACK32.EXE, which is located in the SYS:PUBLIC folder.

NWBACK32 enables you to back up and restore files from target servers or workstations onto a variety of backup media. This module replaces the older SBACKUP.NLM, available in previous versions of NetWare. For more information about using NWBACK32.NLM, see Chapter 8.

NWCONFIG (NLM)

Load this module on a server to modify the server, create or modify volumes, install additional products such as Novell's PKI Services, replace hard disks, modify disk partitions, and other types of server management tasks. This utility replaced INSTALL.NLM from previous versions of NetWare.

OFF (Console Utility)

Use this utility at the server to clear the server's console screen. You can also use the CLS utility to accomplish the same thing.

ORBCMD (NLM)

Load this module on the server to enable the Novell Object Request Broker (ORB). If you are using CORBA-compliant applications, they will require an ORB to be running on the server. When you load ORBCMD.NLM on the server, the Novell Java Virtual Machine (JVM) and other related NLMs will also load. In addition, ORBCMD activates VisiBroker CORBA commands, which you can then use from the server. See the Novell documentation for more information.

After loading ORBCMD, you must also load OSAGENT.NLM (Novell's Smart Agent).

OSAGENT (NLM)

Load this module on the server to start Novell's Smart Agent, which provides directory services and failure detection for the Novell ORB (ORBCMD.NLM). See the Novell documentation for more information.

PING (NLM)

Load this NLM on the server to test if the server can communicate with an IP node on the network. PING sends an ICMP (Internet Control Message Protocol) echo request packet to an IP node.

PROTECT (Console Utility)

Use this utility at the server to specify that all NLMs loaded from within an .NCF file should be loaded in a protected address space. For more information about protected address spaces, see Chapter 3. Use the following command format, substituting the name of the .NCF file for *filename*:

```
PROTECT filename
```

PROTECTED (Console Utility)

Use this utility at the server to load an NLM into a protected address space. Type the following command when you load the NLM, substituting the module's name for *module*:

```
PROTECTED module
```

This will create a new protected address space, called ADDRESS_SPACE*n*, and load the NLM into it. For more information about protected address spaces, see Chapter 3.

PROTECTION (Console Utility)

Use this utility at the server to list and see information about the protected address spaces currently being used on the server. For more information about protected address spaces, see Chapter 3.

PROTOCOL (Console Utility)

Use this utility at the server to register a new protocol or frame type with the server so the server will support it. You don't need to use this utility to register IPX, IP, or AppleTalk because they are registered automatically during installation or configuration, but you may need to use this if you use a different protocol. See the protocol's manufacturer for more details.

To list all the protocols that are currently registered on the server, simply type:

```
PROTOCOL
```

To use this utility to register a new protocol, use the following command format, replacing *protocol* with the name of the protocol, *frame* with the frame type, and *id* with the Protocol ID (PID, also called Ethernet Type, E-Type, or SAP) number assigned to the protocol:

```
PROTOCOL REGISTER protocol frame id
```

PSERVER (NLM)

Use this NLM to load a print server on the server, so that the print server can regulate network print queues and printers. This utility is used with queue-based printing only.

Use the following command format, replacing *name* with the name of the print server you created by using the NetWare Administrator utility:

`LOAD PSERVER name`

See Chapter 9 for more information about using PSERVER.

PSM (Console Utility)

Use this utility at the server to execute a PSM (platform support module) console command. PSMs are used to support multiple processors in a server. To see all the PSM commands available, type:

`PSM ?`

PURGE (Workstation Utility)

Use this utility at a workstation's DOS prompt to permanently erase files from the server. Usually, when files are deleted, they are retained in a salvageable state until the server needs the disk space and automatically purges them. To completely remove these files without waiting for the server to run out of disk space, you can use either the PURGE utility or the NetWare Administrator utility.

To use PURGE, use the following command format, replacing *path* with the path to the files you want to purge, and *filename* with a filename for the specific file or files (wildcards are acceptable):

`PURGE path\filename /option`

If desired, you can replace *option* with one of the following:

/A   Purges all files in the current directory and all of its subdirectories.

/VER Displays the version number of PURGE.

/?   Displays help screens for PURGE.

For more information about purging and salvaging files, see Chapter 8.

QMAN (NLM)

Use this module with Enhanced SBACKUP. This module loads the SMS Queue Manager, which will create a job queue for the backup program to use.

The backup queue is an object named "*Server* Backup Queue" (with the server's name substituted for *Server*). To load the Queue Manager on the host server, type:

```
QMAN
```

If you want to create a new Queue object, type QMAN NEW at the console instead, and enter a new name and context for the job queue.

RCONAG6 (NLM)

Use this module to set up a target server for the Java-based version of Remote Console. (This module is the equivalent of RSPX.NLM, which is used with the DOS-based version of Remote Console.) When you load RCONAG6.NLM, you are asked for a password. Enter any password you choose. (You will have to supply this same password when you use Remote Console from the workstation.) RCONAG6 will also prompt you for a TCP port number and an SPX port number.

To load RCONAG6.NLM, type:

```
RCONAG6
```

If you want to encrypt the Remote Console password for storage in an NCF file (so that Remote Console can be activated during server startup), use the following command:

```
RCONAG6 ENCRYPT
```

See Chapter 3 for more information about the Java-based version of Remote Console (RConsoleJ).

RCONPRXY (NLM)

Use this module to set up a proxy server, when using the Java-based version of Remote Console to access an IPX server. This module will prompt you for the SPX port number you assigned to the target server when you loaded RCONAG6.NLM.

See Chapter 3 for more information about the Java-based version of Remote Console (RConsoleJ).

RCONSOLE (Workstation Utility)

Use this utility at a workstation's DOS prompt to start a Remote Console session from a workstation. For more information about Remote Console and using RCONSOLE, see Chapter 3.

RCONSOLEJ (Java Application)

Use this utility on a workstation or a server to start a Java-based Remote Console session. Use one of the following methods to launch the Remote Console software (called RConsoleJ) from the server:

- From the server console prompt, type **RCONJ**.

- From the server's ConsoleOne screen, open My Server, then open Tools, and then click RConsoleJ.

Use one of the following methods to launch the Remote Console software from the workstation:

- From the NetWare Administrator utility, open the Tools menu, and then choose Pure IP Remote Console.

- From the Windows Start or Run option, locate and execute the RCONJ.EXE file in the SYS:PUBLIC\MGMT folder.

For more information about using the Java-based Remote Console, see Chapter 3.

REBUILD (NSS Console Utility)

Use this utility to rebuild a corrupted NSS volume. To run the REBUILD utility, make sure NSS is loaded, and then launch the NSS administration utility by typing:

```
NSS MENU
```

Then, from the Utilities menu, select Rebuild NSS Volume.

Alternatively, you can execute REBUILD by typing the following NSS command:

```
NSS REBUILDVOLUME
```

The REBUILD utility will go through the volume, checking and repairing any errors it finds. REBUILD will keep an error log of any errors it finds and records. This file is located in the SYS volume, and is named with the volume's name, followed by the extension .RLF. For example, if your NSS volume is named NSSVOL, the error log will be named NSSVOL.RLF. See Chapter 8 for more information about NSS volumes.

REGISTER MEMORY (Console Utility)

Use this utility on ISA (AT bus) servers to register memory above 16MB so that NetWare can address it. This command is unnecessary for EISA or MCA computers because NetWare automatically registers memory above 16MB on EISA machines. On a PCI computer, NetWare recognizes up to 64MB. (Refer to your manufacturer's documentation to verify whether your computer uses ISA, EISA, MCA, or PCI technology.)

Use the following command format, replacing *start* with the hexadecimal address of where the memory above the limit begins (16MB starts at 1000000, 64MB starts at 4000000), and replacing *length* with the hexadecimal length of the memory above 16MB or 64MB. (See Table E.18 for some *length* numbers for different amounts of memory.)

REGISTER MEMORY *start length*

Hexadecimal numbers can use the numerals 0 through 9 and the letters A through F.

NOTE

T A B L E   E.18 *Length Values for Memory*

MEMORY ABOVE THE MINIMUM (16MB OR 64MB)	LENGTH
4	400000
8	800000
12	C00000
16	1000000
20	1400000
24	1800000
48	3000000
96	6000000
112	7000000
240	F000000
384	18000000
984	3D800000
2936	B7800000
2984	BA800000

REMIRROR PARTITION (Console Utility)

Use this utility at the server to restart the remirroring process if something halted the server's remirroring of its disk partitions. Use the following command format, replacing *number* with the number of the disk partition you want to remirror:

```
REMIRROR PARTITION number
```

REMOTE (NLM)

Load this NLM on the server to allow a NetWare server to support Remote Console sessions from a workstation. This NLM will ask you to specify a password that a Remote Console user will have to provide in order to start a Remote Console session from his or her workstation. To load REMOTE.NLM, type:

```
REMOTE
```

You can, if you prefer, indicate the Remote Console password in the command by typing the following command. However, the password will be displayed on the screen.

```
REMOTE password
```

If you want to encrypt the Remote Console password for storage in an NCF file (so that Remote Console can be activated during server startup), use the following command:

```
REMOTE ENCRYPT
```

See Chapter 3 for more information about using Remote Console and encrypting the password.

REMOVE NETWORK ADAPTER (Console Utility)

Use this utility at the server to unload one instance of a LAN driver, when the LAN driver has been loaded multiple times for use with more than one network board. This command unloads the driver from one board, but leaves the driver bound to the other boards. Use the following command, substituting the filename of the LAN driver for *driver* and, if necessary, the instance number of the board for *board* if there are multiple boards of the same type.

```
REMOTE NETWORK ADAPTER driver board
```

You can find the instance number of a board by using MONITOR.NLM, selecting LAN/WAN Drivers, and then highlighting the driver.

REMOVE NETWORK INTERFACE (Console Utility)

Use this utility at the server to unload a single frame type from a LAN driver, if that LAN driver has been loaded with multiple frame types. (Each time a driver is loaded with a frame type, it is called a logical board. Therefore, you can have several logical boards loaded, even though there is only one real, physical board in the server.)

This command unloads one frame type from the LAN driver, but leaves the LAN driver loaded with the other specified frame types. Use the following command, substituting the logical board number for *board*:

```
REMOVE NETWORK INTERFACE board
```

You can find the logical board number of a board by using MONITOR.NLM, selecting LAN/WAN Drivers, and then highlighting the driver.

REMOVE STORAGE ADAPTER (Console Utility)

Use this utility at the server to unload a single instance of a storage driver. If that storage driver has been loaded for use with more than one storage device, then only the instance you specify will be unloaded. The other devices will still remain intact, with the storage driver active. If this storage driver is bound to only one storage device, the entire driver is unloaded.

Use the following command, substituting the adapter number for *n*:

```
REMOVE STORAGE ADAPTER An
```

You can find the A*n* number of each instance of the storage driver by using the console utility LIST STORAGE ADAPTERS. The A*n* number is enclosed in square brackets at the beginning of the adapter's name.

RESET ENVIRONMENT (Console Utility)

Use this utility at the server to restore all server (SET) parameters to their original default values.

RESET NETWORK ADAPTER (Console Utility)

Use this utility at the server to stop whatever task a network board was doing, and reset it to a clean state. Use this utility if you suspect something is wrong with the board. Use the following command, substituting the filename of the board's LAN driver for *driver* and, if necessary, the instance number of the board for *board* if there are multiple boards of the same type.

```
RESET NETWORK ADAPTER driver board
```

You can find the instance number of a board by using MONITOR.NLM, selecting LAN/WAN Drivers, and then highlighting the driver.

RESET NETWORK INTERFACE (Console Utility)

Use this utility at the server to restart a logical board that was previously shut down using the SHUTDOWN NETWORK INTERFACE utility. This utility enables you to restart the logical board without having to reload and bind the LAN driver. (Each time a driver is loaded with a frame type, it is called a logical board. Therefore, you can have several logical boards loaded, even though there is only one real, physical board in the server.)

Use the following command, substituting the logical board number for *board*:

```
RESET NETWORK INTERFACE board
```

You can find the logical board number of a board by using MONITOR.NLM, selecting LAN/WAN Drivers, and then highlighting the driver.

RESET ROUTER (Console Utility)

Use this utility at the server to clear the router table and force a new table to be built on the server, updating any changes to servers or routers that have gone down or come back up. The table is rebuilt every two minutes automatically, so you only need to use this utility if you don't want to wait for the next automatic rebuild.

See the Novell documentation for more information about using routers.

RESET SERVER (Console Utility)

Use this utility to bring down the server and do a warm reboot of the computer. You can also use DOWN and RESTART SERVER to bring down and restart the server without booting the machine.

RESTART SERVER (Console Utility)

Use this utility at the server to restart the server after you have brought it down. See Chapter 3 for more information about bringing down and rebooting the server.

RIGHTS (Workstation Utility)

Use this utility at a workstation's DOS prompt to see or change your effective rights in a directory. To see your effective rights, use the following command format, replacing *path* with the path to the directory you want (you can omit the *path* if you want to see your rights in your current directory), and replacing *options* with any of the options shown in Table E.19:

RIGHTS *path* /*options*

To assign new rights that overwrite existing rights, use the following command format, replacing *rights* with the list of abbreviations for the rights you want to assign. The rights you can use are listed in Table E.20.

RIGHTS *path rights* /*options*

If you want to retain the existing rights assignment but want to add or delete rights to that assignment, use the following command format:

RIGHTS *path +rights-rights/options*

If you are adding rights, use the plus sign and list the added rights after it. If you are deleting rights, use the minus sign and list the deleted rights after it. You can add and delete rights in the same command, if you choose.

TABLE E.19   *RIGHTS Options*

OPTION	DESCRIPTION
C	Causes the display to scroll continuously down the screen.
F	Displays the Inherited Rights Filter (IRF).
I	Shows from where the inherited rights came.
NAME=*username*	Replace *username* with the name of a user or group whose rights you want to see or change.
S	Lets you see or change subdirectories below the current directory.
T	Displays trustee assignments for a directory.
/VER	Displays the version number of RIGHTS.
/?	Displays help for RIGHTS.

T A B L E E.20   *Trustee Rights*

RIGHT	DESCRIPTION
R	Read. Allows the trustee to open and read the file (or the files within the directory).
W	Write. Allows the trustee to open and write to (change) the file (or the files within the directory).
C	Create. Allows the trustee to salvage a deleted file (or to create new files and subdirectories within the directory).
E	Erase. Allows the trustee to delete the file (or directory and its files and subdirectories).
M	Modify. Allows the trustee to change the file's name or attributes (or the name and attributes of the directory and its contents).
F	File Scan. Allows the trustee to see the name of the file (or the name of the directory and all its contents).
A	Access Control. Allows the trustee to change the IRF and trustee assignments of the file (or of the directory and its contents).
S	Supervisor. Grants the trustee all rights to the file (or directory and its contents).
N	No rights. Removes all rights from the trustee.
REM	Remove. Removes the user or group as a trustee of the file (or directory).
ALL	Adds all rights except Supervisor.

See Chapter 7 for more information about rights, and for instructions on using NetWare Administrator to work with rights.

RMIC (Console Utility)

This utility is the Java RMI Stub Converter. See the Novell documentation for more information.

RMIREGISTRY (Console Utility)

This utility is the Java Remote Object Registry. See the Novell documentation for more information.

ROUTE (NLM)

Load this NLM on the server to allow NetWare to support an IBM bridge on a Token Ring network using Source Routing. Load this NLM once for every Token Ring network board you have installed in your server. Use the following command format, replacing *options* with one or more of the options shown in Table E.21:

ROUTE *options*

T A B L E E.21   *ROUTE.NLM Options*

OPTION	DESCRIPTION
BOARD=*number*	Indicates the network board's number, if the Token Ring LAN driver wasn't the first LAN driver loaded.
CLEAR	Clears all information from the Source Routing table so it can be rebuilt with updated information.
DEF	Causes frames (packets) with unknown destination addresses to be forwarded as All Routes Broadcast packets, which means they won't be sent across Single Route IBM bridges.
GBR	Causes General Broadcast frames to be sent as All Routes Broadcast frames, instead of being sent as Single Route Broadcast frames.
MBR	Causes Multicast Broadcast frames to be sent as All Routes Broadcast frames, instead of being sent as Single Route Broadcast frames.
NAME=*board*	Specifies the name of the network board.
REMOVE=*number*	If a bridge has gone down, use this option to remove a node address from the server's Source Routing table, forcing the server to find a new route.

OPTION	DESCRIPTION
RSP=*response*	Indicates how the server must respond to a broadcast request. Replace *response* with:
	NR (Not Required). Default: Respond to all requests directly.
	AR (All Routes). Respond with an All Routes Broadcast frame.
	SR (Single Route). Respond with a Single Route Broadcast frame.
TIME=*seconds*	Determines how often to update the server's Source Routing table. Default: 03. Range: 03 to 255.
UNLOAD	Removes Source Routing support from a network board. (Specify the board you want first by using the BOARD= option, and then use this UNLOAD option.)
XTX=*number*	Sets how many times to transmit on a timed-out route using the old route. Default: 02. Range: 00 to 255.

RS232 (NLM)

Load this NLM on the server to enable the server to support Remote Console sessions over an asynchronous connection (via a modem). Use the following command format, replacing *port* and *baud* with the appropriate communications port number (1 or 2) and baud rate being used by your modem:

RS232 *port baud*

If you want to use the Callback feature (where the server terminates the session and calls back the workstation if the workstation's modem number is authorized), use the following command:

RS232 *port baud* C

See Chapter 3 for more information about running Remote Console.

RSPX (NLM)

Load this NLM on the server to enable the server to support Remote Console sessions over a direct network connection (in other words, if the workstation is connected directly to the network and doesn't require a modem to access the server). Loading RSPX.NLM automatically loads REMOTE.NLM. When you load RSPX.NLM, you are asked for a password. Enter any password you choose. (You will have to supply this same password when you use Remote Console from the workstation.)

See Chapter 3 for more information about running Remote Console.

SBACKUP (NLM)

This utility has been replaced. See SBCON for the server-based version of Enhanced SBACKUP. See NWBACK32 for the workstation-based version of Enhanced SBACKUP.

SBCON (NLM)

Load this module on the host server if you want to use Enhanced SBACKUP to back up network files. This is the server-based version of Enhanced SBACKUP. (The workstation-based version of this utility is called NWBACK32.EXE.)

SBCON.NLM enables you to back up and restore files from target servers or workstations, onto a variety of backup media. This module replaces the older SBACKUP.NLM, available in previous versions of NetWare. For more information about using SBCON.NLM, see Chapter 8.

SBSC (NLM)

Use this module with Enhanced SBACKUP. This is the SBACKUP Communication module, which you load on the host server. For more information about Enhanced SBACKUP, see Chapter 8.

SCAN ALL (Console Utility)

Use this utility at the server to search for and display all logical unit numbers (LUNs) on SCSI adapters in the server. A LUN is used to designate individual devices that are attached to a single bus.

To display all LUNs on all SCSI adapters in the server, type:

```
SCAN ALL
```

To display all LUNs on a particular SCSI adapter, type the following command, substituting the number of the adapter for *n*:

```
SCAN ALL An
```

SCAN FOR NEW DEVICES (Console Utility)

Use this utility at the server to cause the server to look for and recognize any new storage devices (disk drives, CD-ROM drives, and so on) that may have been added since the server was booted.

Schema Manager (Workstation Utility)

Use this utility to see the object classes and properties that are allowed in your current schema, or to change or expand the schema. This utility is a tool within the NDS Manager utility. To open Schema Manager, first launch NDS Manager. Then select a Directory partition. From the Object menu, choose Schema Manager. See Chapter 5 for more information about the Schema Manager utility.

Schema Manager enables you to perform the following types of tasks:

▶ View the current schema. You can see all the object classes and properties that are currently allowed in your tree.

▶ Extend the schema. You can add an object class to the schema, or you can add a property to an existing object class.

▶ Compare the schemas on two different trees, and print the comparison.

▶ Delete an object class from the schema.

SCRSAVER (NLM)

Load this module on the server to load a screen saver on the server and to lock the server's console. By default, this module will lock the server's console when the screen saver activates (which occurs after 10 minutes of inactivity, unless you specify otherwise). To unlock the console while the screen saver is displayed, press any key, and then enter a user name and password. The user name must have valid access rights to the server, such as Admin. You can change the screen saver's activation time, and you can specify whether or not the screen saver locks the console.

To load SCRSAVER with its default values (activating after 10 minutes and locking the console), type:

SCRSAVER

To see help for SCRSAVER, type:

SCRSAVER HELP

To change SCRSAVER's options, type the following command, substituting the options in Table E.22 for *option*. You can use more than one option in the same command, separating each option with a semicolon (;).

SCRSAVER *option;option*

T A B L E E.22	SCRSAVER Options
OPTION	**DESCRIPTION**
Activate	Immediately activates the screen saver, without waiting for the normal period of inactivity.
Auto clear delay	Specifies how many seconds to wait for input before removing the "unlock screen" (which lets a user enter a password to unlock the console). Default: 60. Range: 1 to 300.
Delay	Specifies how many seconds of inactivity must occur before the screen saver activates. Default: 600. Range: 1 to 7200.
Disable	Disables the screen saver so it will not activate.
Disable auto clear	Prevents the "unlock screen" from being cleared. The "unlock screen" will remain on the screen until the user inputs an authorized password.
Disable lock	Disables the locking feature. The screen saver will activate as normal, but the console will not be locked. Pressing any key during the screen saver will return the server's console to the screen, without asking for a username and password.
Enable	Reenables the screen saver. (Use after the Disable option has been used.)
Enable auto clear	Reenables the clearing feature that removes the "unlock screen" after the specified number of seconds of inactivity. (Use after the Disable Auto Clear option has been used.)
Enable lock	Reenables the console locking feature. (Use after the Disable Lock option has been used.)
No password	If NDS is unavailable, unlocks the console without requesting a password.
Status	Shows the current screen saver features that have been set.

SEARCH (Console Utility)

Use this utility at the server to set the paths that the server should search through when looking for an .NCF (configuration) file or an NLM. The default search path is SYS:SYSTEM. If volume SYS isn't mounted, the default search path becomes the DOS boot directory on the server.

To display the server's current search paths, simply type **SEARCH**.

To add a search path, use the following command format, replacing *path* with the directory path you want the server to search:

SEARCH ADD *path*

To delete a search path, use the following command format, replacing *number* with the number of the search drive you want to remove (drive numbers are displayed when you type SEARCH):

SEARCH DEL *number*

SECURE CONSOLE (Console Utility)

Use this utility at the server to prevent anyone from loading NLMs from anywhere but SYS:SYSTEM. (This prevents unauthorized users from loading NLMs from an area where they may have more rights than in SYS:SYSTEM, such as from a diskette in the server's diskette drive.) This utility also prevents anyone from accessing the operating system's debugger from the server's keyboard, and allows only the administrator to change the server's date and time. To disable this feature, reboot the server.

SEND (Console Utility)

Use this utility at the server to send a short message from the server console to users on the network. To send a message to a user, use the following command format, replacing *message* with the message you want displayed (no more than 55 characters long) and *user* with either the name of the user or that workstation's connection number (as seen in MONITOR.NLM):

SEND *"message" user*

To send the message to multiple users, separate each user name or connection number with a comma or space. To send the message to all users, don't specify any user name at all. (You can also use the BROADCAST console utility to accomplish the same thing.)

SERIALVER (Console Utility)

This utility is the Java Serial Version Command. See the Novell documentation for more information.

SERVER (.EXE)

This is the command that loads the NetWare server from DOS. When the server computer first boots up, it is running DOS. From DOS, you change to the NWSERVER directory, and then type **SERVER** to execute SERVER.EXE, which loads the network operating system and turns the computer into a server.

You can add the command SERVER to the server's AUTOEXEC.BAT file so that the server loads automatically when the computer is booted.

Normally, you will just type the following command to execute the server:

SERVER

However, you can also specify how to execute the server's startup files by using the following command, replacing *option* with one of the options listed in Table E.23:

SERVER *option*

T A B L E E.23	SERVER.EXE Options
OPTION	**DESCRIPTION**
–NA	Prevents the AUOTEXEC.NCF file from executing.
–NL	Prevents the Novell logo screen from displaying while the server is starting up.
–NS	Prevents both the AUOTEXEC.NCF file and the STARTUP.NCF file from executing.
–S *filename.ncf*	Specifies a different .NCF file to execute instead of STARTUP.NCF.

SERVMAN (NLM)

This utility has been eliminated, and its functionality moved to MONITOR.NLM.

SET (Console Utility)

Use this utility at the server to change performance parameters on the server. You may prefer to use MONITOR.NLM to change server parameters, because MONITOR enables you to select the parameters from menus rather than having to type long commands.

See Appendix B for more information about server parameters.

SET TIME (Console Utility)

Use this utility at the server to change the server's date and time. Use the following command format:

`SET TIME month/day/year hour:minute:second`

SET TIMEZONE (Console Utility)

Use this utility at the server to change the server's time zone information. When using this utility's command format, replace the variables with the correct information:

- ▶ Replace *zone* with the three-letter abbreviation for your time zone (such as EST, CST, MST, or PST).

- ▶ Replace *hours* with the number of hours you are east or west of Greenwich Mean Time. Use a "−" (minus) sign before the number if you're east.

- ▶ Replace *daylight* with the three-letter abbreviation for your area's Daylight Saving Time (only if you are currently on Daylight Saving Time).

Use the following command format:

`SET TIMEZONE zone hours daylight`

For example, to set the time zone to Eastern Daylight Saving Time, type:

`SET TIMEZONE EST5EDT`

SETPASS (Workstation Utility)

Use this utility at a workstation's DOS prompt to change your network password. When you execute this utility, follow the prompts to type in your old and new passwords. See Chapter 7 for more information about using and changing passwords.

SHUTDOWN NETWORK INTERFACE (Console Utility)

Use this utility at the server to shut down a logical board, while leaving its resources intact on the server. This allows the logical board to be restarted (with the RESET NETWORK INTERFACE utility) without having to reload and bind the LAN driver. (Each time a driver is loaded with a frame type, it is called a logical board. Therefore, you can have several logical boards loaded, even though there is only one real, physical board in the server.)

Use the following command, substituting the logical board number for *board*:

```
SHUTDOWN NETWORK INTERFACE board
```

You can find the logical board number of a board by using MONITOR.NLM, selecting LAN/WAN Drivers, and then highlighting the driver.

SMDR (NLM)

Use this module with Enhanced SBACKUP. This module loads the SMS Data Requester on a host server, and automatically creates an SMS SMDR Group object in the server's context. This Group object will contain each server and workstation that will be backed up by this host server. Load SMDR.NLM by typing:

```
SMDR
```

If you want to create a new SMDR Group object, type **SMDR NEW** at the console instead, and enter a new name and context for the SMDR Group object. See Chapter 8 for more information about using Enhanced SBACKUP.

SMSDI (NLM)

Use this module with Enhanced SBACKUP. This is the SMS Device Interface module, which enables the SBACKUP program to communicate with the backup device. Load this module on the host server. See Chapter 8 for more information about using Enhanced SBACKUP.

SPEED (Console Utility)

Use this utility at the server to display the server's processor speed.

SPOOL (Console Utility)

Use this utility at the server to display or create spooler mappings so applications that print to printer numbers will direct their print jobs to print queues instead. Most current network applications do not require this utility to be executed. If used, this utility also specifies the default print queue for NPRINT and CAPTURE.

Use the following command format, replacing *number* with the printer number (which will also be the spooler number), and *queue* with the name of the print queue:

```
SPOOL number TO QUEUE queue
```

See Chapter 9 for more information about printing.

SPXCONFG (NLM)

Load this NLM on the server to configure SPX parameters. Use the following command, replacing *option* with one or more of the options listed in Table E.24:

```
SPXCONFG option
```

If you do not specify any options, SPXCONFG runs in interactive mode. See the Novell documentation for more information about protocols and SPX.

TABLE E.24 *SPXCONFG.NLM Options*

OPTION	DESCRIPTION
A=*ticks*	Sets the abort timeout, in ticks. Values: 540 to 5400.
I=*number*	Sets the maximum open IPX sockets. Values: 120 to 65520.
Q=1	Puts the utility in quiet mode, so that it doesn't pause when it terminates.
R=*number*	Sets the number of default retries. Values: 1 to 255.
S=*number*	Sets the maximum concurrent SPX sessions. Values: 100 to 2000.
V=*ticks*	Sets the verify timeout, in ticks. Values: 10 to 255.
W=*ticks*	Sets the ack wait timeout, in ticks. Values: 10 to 3240.
H	Displays help for SPXCONFG.

START PROCESSORS (Console Utility)

Use this utility at the server to start all secondary processors in a multi-processor server. Use the following command format, substituting the number of each processor you want to start for *number*. To specify more than one processor, separate each number with a space. To start all processors, leave *number* blank.

```
START PROCESSORS number
```

STARTX (.NCF)

Use this utility at the server's console prompt to start the graphical server desktop. Java-based applications, such as ConsoleOne, can execute from the graphical server desktop.

STOP PROCESSORS (Console Utility)

Use this utility at the server to stop all secondary processors in a multi-processor server. Use the following command format, substituting the number of each processor you want to stop for *number*. To specify more than one processor, separate each number with a space. To stop all secondary processors, leave *number* blank.

```
STOP PROCESSORS number
```

SWAP (Console Utility)

Use this utility at the server to view, create, and delete virtual memory swap files. For example, to see information about a server's swap files, type the following command at the server's console:

```
SWAP
```

To create a new swap file, type the following command. Substitute the name of the volume for *volume*:

```
SWAP ADD volume
```

By default, this command will create a swap file with a minimum size of 2MB, a maximum size of 5MB, and will leave a minimum of 5MB of free space on the volume. To change any of these parameters (all of which are optional), type the following command instead (substituting the number of megabytes for *size*). You can use any (or all) of these optional parameters.

```
SWAP ADD volume MIN=size MAX=size MIN FREE=size
```

To delete a swap file from a volume, type:

SWAP DEL *volume*

For more information about the SWAP console utility, type:

HELP SWAP

TCPCON (NLM)

Load this NLM on the server to monitor information about the TCP/IP protocol suite that is loaded on the server. You can view information about the protocols in the TCP/IP suite, SNMP configuration information, user statistics, and so on.

TCPIP (NLM)

Load this NLM on the server to load TCP/IP support on the network server.

TECHWALK (NLM)

Load this NLM on the server to record INETCFG settings in a file called TECHWALK.OUT in the SYS:ETC directory. It may take this utility anywhere from 5 to 60 minutes to record all your information. If you want to record configuration information for a specific NLM, use the following command format, replacing *module* with the name of the NLM:

LOAD TECHWALK *module*

See the Novell documentation for more information about using INETCFG.

TIME (Console Utility)

Use this utility to display the server's date, time, Daylight Saving Time status, and time synchronization information. (To change the date or time, use the SET TIME console utility. To change the server's time zone information, use the SET TIMEZONE console utility.)

TIMESYNC (NLM)

This NLM is automatically loaded when the server boots, and is used to control the server's time services. See Chapter 3 for more information about using TIMESYNC.NLM

TPING (NLM)

Load this NLM on the server to send ICMP packets to an IP node to see if the server can communicate with that node. Use the following command format, replacing *host* with the symbolic host name or IP address of a TCP/IP system, *size* with the size (in bytes) of the ICMP packets, and *retries* with the number of times the packet should be sent to the host if it doesn't reply the first time (default is 5):

```
LOAD TPING host size retries
```

TRACK OFF (Console Utility)

Use this utility at the server to turn off the display of routing information (which is displayed if you used the TRACK ON console utility).

See the Novell documentation for more information about routers.

TRACK ON (Console Utility)

Use this utility at the server to display the routing information that your server is broadcasting and receiving.

See the Novell documentation for more information about routers.

TSA for Windows 95/98 or Windows NT (Workstation Utility)

Use this utility to configure a Windows 95/98 or Windows NT workstation so it can be backed up using Enhanced SBACKUP. You must install the workstation TSA on the workstation using the Novell client installation program (check the Target Service Agent option to install the TSA support). After the TSA software is installed, you must configure it by adding information to its Properties page. For more information about configuring the TSA and using Enhanced SBACKUP, see Chapter 8.

TSA410 (NLM)

Load this module on a NetWare 4.1x server that you want to back up using Enhanced SBACKUP. This module is the Target Service Agent for NetWare 4.1x servers. When this module is loaded on a server, the server becomes a target server, capable of being backed up. See Chapter 8 for more information about using Enhanced SBACKUP.

TSA500 (NLM)

Load this module on a NetWare 5 server that you want to back up using Enhanced SBACKUP. This module is the Target Service Agent for NetWare 5. When this module is loaded on a server, the server becomes a target server, capable of being backed up. See Chapter 8 for more information about using Enhanced SBACKUP.

TSADOSP (NLM)

Load this module on a NetWare 5 server if you want to back up its DOS partition using Enhanced SBACKUP. This module is the Target Service Agent for a NetWare 5 server's DOS partition. See Chapter 8 for more information about using Enhanced SBACKUP.

TSANDS (NLM)

Load this module on a NetWare 5 server whose NDS database you want to back up using Enhanced SBACKUP. This module is the Target Service Agent for NDS. When this module is loaded on a server, the server becomes a target server, capable of being backed up. It's usually best to load this on a server that contains a replica of the tree's largest Directory partition. See Chapter 8 for more information about using Enhanced SBACKUP.

TSAPROXY (NLM)

Load this module on a host server if you are going to back up a Windows 95/98 or Windows NT workstation using Enhanced SBACKUP. See Chapter 8 for more information about using Enhanced SBACKUP.

UIMPORT (Workstation Utility)

Use this utility at a workstation's DOS prompt to create User objects in the Directory database by importing user information from another database. This can be a quick way to create multiple users if you've already defined all of their information in some other database.

Use the following command format, replacing *controlfile* with the name of the file that contains information on how to load user data into the directory, and replacing *datafile* with the name of the text file that contains the actual user data (property values):

```
UIMPORT controlfile datafile
```

See the Novell documentation for more information about using UIMPORT.

UNBIND (Console Utility)

Use this utility at the server to unbind a protocol, such as IPX or AppleTalk, from a network board. Use the following command format, replacing *protocol* with the name of the protocol, *driver* with the name of the LAN driver or network board from which you want the protocol unbound, and *parameters* with the same parameters you originally specified when you loaded the driver (so the UNBIND command knows exactly which LAN driver or network board you intend):

```
UNBIND protocol FROM driver parameters
```

See the explanation of the BIND console utility for more information about driver parameters.

UNICON (NLM)

Load this NLM on the server to manage the NetWare Domain Name System and the NetWare/IP Domain SAP/RIP Service, if you have installed NetWare/IP on your server.

UNLOAD (Console Utility)

Use this utility at the server to unload an NLM that's been previously loaded. Use the following command format, replacing *module* with the name of the NLM you want to unload (you can omit the .NLM extension of the NLM's filename):

```
UNLOAD module
```

UPS_AIO (NLM)

Load this NLM on the server if your UPS is attached to your server's serial port.

See Chapter 3 for more information about using a UPS with your server.

V_LONG (NLM)

This NLM is used on the server by VREPAIR.NLM to repair volumes that use the LONG.NAM name space module. LONG.NAM enables the server to support Windows NT, Windows 95/98, and OS/2 long filenames and formats, and it is loaded by default when you install NetWare. This support NLM and VREPAIR are located in the server's DOS boot partition so you can use them even if volume SYS is down.

See Chapter 3 for more information about repairing volumes.

V_MAC (NLM)

This NLM is used on the server by VREPAIR.NLM to repair volumes that use the MAC.NAM name space module. MAC.NAM enables the server to support Mac OS long filenames and formats. This support NLM and VREPAIR are located in the server's DOS boot partition so you can use them even if volume SYS is down.

See Chapter 3 for more information about repairing volumes.

V_NFS (NLM)

This NLM is used on the server by VREPAIR.NLM to repair volumes that use the NFS.NAM name space module. NFS.NAM enables the server to support UNIX long filenames and formats. This support NLM and VREPAIR are located in the server's DOS boot partition so you can use them even if volume SYS is down.

See Chapter 3 for more information about repairing volumes.

VERIFY (NSS Console Utility)

Use this utility to verify the integrity of an NSS volume. Use it when you suspect a volume may be corrupted, or to verify that a volume is intact after you've run the REBUILD utility. To run the VERIFY utility, make sure NSS is loaded, and then launch the NSS administration utility by typing:

```
NSS MENU
```

Then, from the Utilities menu, select Verify NSS Volume.

Alternatively, you can execute VERIFY by typing the following NSS command:

```
NSS VERIFYVOLUME
```

See Chapter 8 for more information about NSS volumes.

VERSION (Console Utility)

Use this utility at the server to see the version of NetWare that is running on the server.

VIEW (NLM)

Load this NLM on the server to display a file on the server console. You cannot edit or create a file with VIEW.NLM, however. You must use EDIT.NLM to edit or create a file. Use the following command format, replacing *filename* with the name of the file you want to see:

```
VIEW filename
```

VOLUME (Console Utility)

Use this utility at the server to display a list of all the volumes currently mounted on the server. The display also indicates which name spaces each volume supports.

See Chapter 3 for more information about name spaces, and see Chapter 8 for more information about volumes.

VREPAIR (NLM)

Load this NLM on the server to repair minor problems with a volume or to remove a name space from a volume. If the server detects a volume problem when it boots, it will run VREPAIR automatically. You can also run VREPAIR manually if you need to, but you can only run it on dismounted volumes. VREPAIR also requires the name space support modules (V_MAC.NLM, V_LONG.NLM, or V_NFS.NLM) if the volume supports any of those name spaces.

VREPAIR.NLM and the support NLMs are located in the server's DOS boot partition so you can use them even if volume SYS is down.

Use the following command format, replacing *volume* with the name of the volume you want to repair. If you choose, you can also specify the name of a log file, into which the VREPAIR data will be recorded, by substituting the name of a file for *filename.*

```
VREPAIR volume filename
```

See Chapter 3 for more information about repairing volumes.

WTM (NLM)

Load this module on the server to activate WAN Traffic Manager on the server. This module examines all NDS traffic on the network and determines whether it is affected by a WAN Traffic policy that has been set. Based on the policy instructions, this module then controls how and when the NDS traffic is transmitted. For more information about WAN Traffic Manager, see Chapter 5.

WE WROTE THE BOOK
ON NETWORKING

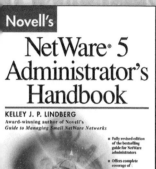
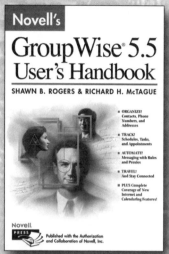

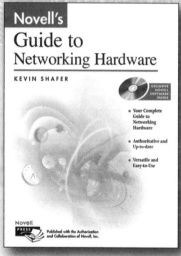

Index

Numbers

10Base2. *See* thin Ethernet cable (RG-58 coaxial)
10Base5. *See* thick Ethernet cable (RG-8 coaxial)
10BaseT. *See* twisted-pair cables
1-3AM Group policy, described, 157
16Mbps transmission speed, Token Ring architecture support, 14
411_UPG.TXT file, DS.NLM version 5.99 upgrade information, 32
4Mbps transmission speed, Token Ring architecture support, 14
7AM-6PM Group policy, described, 157
8mm backup media, advantages/disadvantages, 292

A

ABEND.LOG file
    described, 91
    error history, 64
abends (abnormal ends)
    ABEND.LOG file error tracking, 91
    described, 95
ABORT REMIRROR console utility, 65, 490
account restrictions
    login security, 226–227
    user controls, 175
accounting services charge
    ATOTAL utility, 65
    monitoring, 107–109
ACL (Access Control List), NDS security, 228
ACTON.NLM, 493
ACU (Automatic Client Upgrade)
    described, 128–130
    workstation upgrades, 114
adapter cards, server installation information, 33
ADD NAME SPACE console utility, 490
Additional Document Directories option, Content Management, 393–394
Address Range object, described, 138
Admin Preferences, General Administration, 371–372
Admin user, server installation information planning, 36–37
Administrator Group object, described, 138

Advanced Configuration, NSS volumes, 275–276
AFP Server object, described, 138
AIOCOMX.NLM, 490
Alert Beep parameter, NIOS, 427
ALERT console utility, 491
Alert message nodes, Miscellaneous parameter, 450
ALIAS console utility, 492
Alias object, described, 138
alloc memory check, Memory parameter, 449
Allow audit password, Miscellaneous parameter, 450
Allow change to client rights, NCP parameter, 454
Allow deletion of active directories, File System parameter, 445
Allow IP Address Duplicates, communication parameter, 437
Allow LIP, NCP parameter, 454
Allow unencrypted passwords, Miscellaneous parameter, 452
Allow unknown files to be extended, File System parameter, 448
APPLET console utility, 492
AppleTalk networks, 2, 4, 17, 25
APPLETLK.NLM, 492
applets, JIT (Just In Time) compiler, 64
application directories, described, 267–268
Application Explorer workstation utility, 492–493
Application Folder object, described, 139
Application Launcher workstation utility, 493
Application Manager, FastTrack server, 390–392
Application Object, Z.E.N.works Starter Pack, 188–190
ARCnet architecture, NetWare 5 non-support, 4
Arp_Aging_Timeout parameter, Protocol TCPIP, 430
Arp_Cache_Max parameter, Protocol TCPIP, 430
Arp_Timeout parameter, Protocol TCPIP, 430
at sign (@) command, login scripts, 195
ATFLT.NLM, 493
ATMCON.NLM, 493
ATOTAL workstation utility, 494
    accounting services charge, 65
    accounting services charge monitoring, 107–109
    described, 107

ATTACH command, login scripts, 195–196
attributes. *See also* properties
　file/directory security settings, 243–246
　FLAG utility, 510–515
　NDS object properties, 135
Audit File object, described, 139
AUDITCON workstation utility, 494
auditing, network security technique, 255
AURP.NLM, 494
Auto Reconnect Level parameter, NetWare DOS
　Requester, 421
Auto restart after abend delay time, Error
　Handling parameter, 444
Auto restart after abend, Error Handling
　parameter, 444
Auto TTS backout, Transaction Tracking
　parameter, 458
AUTOEXEC.BAT file
　CD NWSERVER command, 72
　SERVER command, 72
　SERVER.EXE file issues, 46
　Windows 3.1x/DOS client configuration, 125
AUTOEXEC.NCF file
　CONSOLE.LOG activation, 91
　DOS-based Remote Console activation, 77–78
　IP target server activation, 80–81
　PCI Hot Plug support, 103
　server startup process, 65, 105–106
Automatically repair bad volumes, File System
　parameter, 445
Autoretries parameter, NWIP, 428
Autoretry Secs parameter, NWIP, 428
Average page in alert threshold, Memory
　parameter, 449

B

Backup Schedule worksheet, 478
backups
　described, 290–291
　Enhanced Backup utility, 293–301
　Enhanced SBACKUP, 258
　incremental, 293
　media rotation planning, 294–295
　media storage concerns, 295
　media types, 292–293
　NWBACK32.EXE, 303–305
　restore process testing, 295
　restoring files from, 305–307
　SBCON.NLM utility, 301–303
　schedule planning, 293–294

strategies, 291–295
　workstation, 298
BIND console utility, 494–495
Bind driver parameter, Protocol TCPIP, 431
BINDERY console utility, 496
Bindery context, Directory Services parameter,
　441
Bindery Object, described, 139
Bindery Queue object, described, 139
bindery services
　described, 155–156
　SET BINDERY CONTEXT parameter, 132
　viewing content with SET command, 156
block size, described, 34
block suballocation, described, 34, 286–287
BNC barrel connectors, thin Ethernet cable, 10
BNC grounded terminators, when to use, 11
BNC T-connectors, when to use, 10
BNC terminators, when to use, 10
Boot error log file overflow size, Error Handling
　parameter, 443
Boot error log file state, Error Handling
　parameter, 443
Boot error log, Error Handling parameter, 444
BOOT$LOG.ERR file
　described, 91
　error history, 64
BorderManager, pure IPX network
　environment, 27
BREAK ON command, login scripts, 196
BROADCAST console utility, 496
Broker services, NDPS types, 37
BROKER.NLM, 496
Browser
　installing with documentation files, 356,
　　359–361
　setting up, 359–361
buffers
　directory cache, 88
　packet receive, 88–89
Buffers parameter, Link Support, 418
bus topology, diagrammed, 5

C

C1START command, ConsoleOne management
　utility loading, 71
C1START.NCF utility, 497
cables
　described, 7
　Ethernet architecture, 9–14
　fiber-optic, 2

MAUs (Multistation Access Units), 15
patch, 10
PVC-covered plenum space restrictions, 10
shielded twisted-pair, 13–14
thick Ethernet cable (RG-8 coaxial), 11–13
thin Ethernet cable (RG-58 coaxial), 10–11
Token Ring architecture, 14–16
trunk, 10
unshielded twisted-pair, 13–14
cache buffers, monitoring, 88
Cache Write parameter, NetWare DOS Requester, 421
Cache-Control Directives option, Content Management, 398
callback lists, DOS-based Remote Console, 75
CALLBACK.LST file, DOS-based Remote Console callback lists, 75
CAPTURE workstation utility, 497–499
case, in NET.CFG commands, 412
Catalog Services, 132, 159–161
CD NSWERVER command, removing from the AUTOEXEC.BAT file, 72
CD9660.NSS file, ISO 9660 format, 105
CD9660.NSS NLM, 499
CDHFS, HFS CD-ROM support, 105
CDHFS.NSS NLM, 500
CD-R (Compact Disk-Recordable), backup media, 293
CD-ROM drives
El Torito compatibility, 32
ISO 9660 compatibility requirements, 32
server management, 104–105
CDROM.NLM utility, 500
CD-ROM management, 104–105
mounting CD-ROMs as network volumes, 66
CD-ROMs
mounting as network volumes, 66
Novell Support Connection, 98
viewing online documentation, 362
Certificate Authority object, described, 139
CGI Directory option, FastTrack server, 388–389
CHARSET.NLM, 500
CheaperNet. See thin Ethernet cable (RG-58 coaxial)
Checksum parameter, NetWare DOS Requester, 422
child partitions, Directory tree, 148
classes, NDS object categories, 135–137
CLEAR STATION console utility, 500
client software
ACU (Automatic Client Upgrade) process, 128–130

AUTOEXEC.BAT file configuration, 125
CONFIG.SYS file configuration, 124
described, 19, 114
DOS computer installation/removal process, 122–128
installation methods, 115
NET.CFG file configuration, 126
removing from Windows 3.1x/DOS machines, 126–128
STARTNET.BAT file configuration, 125–126
Windows 3.1x installation/removal process, 120–128
Windows 95/98/NT installation/removal process, 116–120
clients, described, 114
Close Behind Ticks parameter, NetWare DOS Requester, 422
CLS command, login scripts, 196
CLS console utility, 500
Cluster Management, General Administration, 377–378
CN (common name), NDS objects, 147
CNE certification, resources, 465–467
Command line prompt default choice, Miscellaneous parameter, 450
Command line prompt time out, Miscellaneous parameter, 450
commands. See also console utilities; utilities and workstation utilities
C1START, 71
DOWN, 72
FDISK, DOS, 19
FLAG, 243–248
FORMAT, DOS, 19
HELP, 67
HELP SWAP, 90
LOAD, 69, 488
LOAD EDIT, 91
login scripts, 194–211
MAP, 172, 258
NAME CONTEXT, 172
NDS TRACE, 164–165
PROTECTED, 64, 96
PROTECTION, 96
PURGE, 258, 289
RESTART SERVER, 72
SECURE CONSOLE, 254
SERVER, 556
SET, 156
SETPASS, 172, 228
STARTX, 71

(continued)

commands (continued)
  SWAP, 90
  SWAP ADD, 90
  SWAP DEL, 90
  UNLOAD, 96
  UNLOAD CONLOG, 91
communication parameters, 437–439,
compatibility mode
  enabling on installation, 34–35
  pure IP environment, 26–27
Compression daily check starting hour, File
  System parameter, 447
Compression daily check stop hour, File System
  parameter, 446
Computer object, described, 139
COMSPEC command, login scripts, 196
Concurrent remirror request, Disk parameter, 442
CONFIG console utility, 501
  displaying bindery content, 132
  server hardware information display, 64
CONFIG.SYS file, Windows 3.1x/DOS client
  configuration, 124
Configuration Styles options, FastTrack server,
  392
CONLOG.NLM, 501–502
connections, workstation monitoring, 98
connectors
  BNC, 10
  described, 8
  DIX, 12
  RJ-45, 14
console commands, BINDERY, 496
Console display watchdog logouts, communica-
  tion parameter, 438
console utilities. See also commands and utilities
  ABORT REMIRROR, 65, 490
  ADD NAME SPACE, 490
  ALERT, 491
  ALIAS, 492
  APPLET, 492
  ATOTAL, 65
  BIND, 494–495
  BINDERY, 496
  BROADCAST, 496
  CLEAR STATION, 500
  CLS, 500
  CONFIG, 64, 132, 501
  CPUCHECK, 64, 503
  CSET, 503
  described, 67
  DISABLE LOGIN, 65, 504
  DISABLE TTS, 504

DISMOUNT, 270, 278–279, 505
DISPLAY ENVIRONMENT, 505
DISPLAY INTERRUPTS, 505
DISPLAY MODIFIED ENVIRONMENT, 506
DISPLAY NETWORKS, 66, 506
DISPLAY PROCESSORS, 506
DISPLAY SERVERS, 66, 506
DOWN, 65, 507
EDIT.NLM, 64
ENABLE LOGIN, 65, 508
ENABLE TTS, 508
ENVSET, 509
executing, 485–487
FILE, SERVER NAME, 509
HELP, 515
INETCFG.NLM, 66
INITIALIZE SYSTEM, 66
INSTALL, 47–55
IPX INTERNAL NET, 516
JAR, 517
JAVA, 517–518
JAVAC, 517
JAVADOC, 519
JAVAKEY, 519
JAVAP, 519
LANGUAGE, 520
LIST DEVICES, 64, 520
LIST STORAGE ADAPTERS, 520
LIST STORAGE DEVICE BINDINGS, 520
LOAD, 521
LOADSTAGE, 521
MAGAZINE, 523–524
MEDIA, 524
MEMORY, 64, 524
MEMORY MAP, 64, 535
MIRROR STATUS, 65, 525
MODULES, 31, 65, 525
MOUNT, 270, 526
NAME, 64, 526
NATIVE2BASCII, 526
NCP ADDRESSES, 527
NCP DUMP, 528
NCP STATS, 528
NCP TRACE, 528
OFF, 539
online help, 67
PROTECT, 540
PROTECTED, 540
PROTECTION, 540
PROTOCOL, 540
PSM, 541
REGISTER MEMORY, 64, 543–544

REINITIALIZE SYSTEM, 66
REMIRROR PARTITION, 65, 545
Remote Console, 65
REMOVE NETWORK ADAPTER, 545
REMOVE NETWORK INTERFACE, 546
REMOVE STORAGE ADAPTER, 546
RESET ENVIRONMENT, 546
RESET NETWORK ADAPTER, 546–547
RESET NETWORK INTERFACE, 547
RESET ROUTER, 547
RESET SERVER, 547
RESTART SERVER, 65, 547
RMIC, 549
RMIREGISTRY, 550
SCAN FOR NEW DEVICES, 553
SCANALL, 552
SEARCH, 555
SECURE CONSOLE, 225, 555
SEND, 555
SERIALVER, 556
server information display, 97
SET, 557
SET NDS TRACE, 133
SET TIME, 65, 557
SET TIMEZONE, 65, 557
SHUTDOWN NETWORK INTERFACE, 558
SPEED, 558
SPOOL, 559
START PROCESSORS, 560
STOP PROCESSORS, 560
SWAP, 64, 560–561
SYSTIME, 65
TIME, 65, 561
TRACK OFF, 66, 562
TRACK ON, 66, 562
UNBIND, 564
UNLOAD, 65, 564
VERSION, 65, 565
VOLUME, 65, 566
CONSOLE.LOG file
described, 91
maximum size limiting, 92
ConsoleOne management utility
described, 68
GUI server desktop, 70
Java based, 70
loading from the GUI server desktop, 71
login procedure, 71
memory requirements, 71
NDPS Broker setup, 322–324
NDS objects management, 150
supported task types, 70
consulting services, 464

container login scripts, described, 191–192
container objects, described, 135–136
Content Management, 393–398
CONTEXT command, login scripts, 197
Control Community parameter, Desktop SNMP
parameter, 415
Control Panel, Windows 95/98/NT client configu-
ration, 119
controlled access printers
creating, 328–330
described, 318
Convert compressed to uncompressed option,
File System parameter, 447
COSTL20 Group policy, described, 157
Counter object, described, 139
Country object, described, 136
CPU hog timeout amount, Miscellaneous
parameter, 450
CPUCHECK console utility, 503
CPUCHECK utility, server hardware information
display, 64
CSET console utility, 503
CX workstation utility, 147–148, 504

D

DAT (Digital Audio Tape), backup media, 292
data link protocols, described, 24–25
data packets, Ethernet architecture, 8
database structures, flat versus hierarchical, 134
database transactions, protection schemes, 259
databases
NDS directory tree, 134–135
TTS (Transaction Tracking System), 307–308
Daylight Saving Time, server time zone settings, 36
Daylight savings time offset, Time parameter, 457
Daylight savings time status, Time parameter, 457
Days untouched before compression, File System
parameter, 448
Decompress free space warning interval, File
System parameter, 447
Decompress percent disk space free to allow
commit, File System parameter, 447
default time server type, Time parameter, 458
Delay before first watchdog packets, communica-
tion parameter, 438
Delay between watchdog packets, communication
parameter, 438
Delay Writes parameter, NetWare DOS Requester,
422
Delete files compression option, File System para-
meter, 447

DELETED.SAV directory
  deleted file storage, 287–288
  described, 267
Desktop SNMP parameters, 415–416
DESREPAIR.NLM utility, calling from NDS
  Manager utility, 151
Developer option, Miscellaneous parameter, 451
DeveloperNet, developer support, 464–465
device drivers, described, 22
DHCP Server object, described, 139
differential backup, Enhanced Backup utility, 296
direct network connection, DOS-based Remote
  Console setup, 74
directories, 267–268, 287–288
directory attributes, file system security, 243–246
Directory cache allocation wait time, Directory
  caching parameter, 439
Directory cache buffer nonreferenced delay,
  Directory caching parameter, 439
directory cache buffers
  described, 439
  monitoring, 88
Directory Caching parameters, 439–440
Directory Map object, described, 140
Directory security, NetWare Administrator utility,
  224
Directory Services parameters, 440–441
Directory tree, 36, 137, 145–149, 162–164
dirty cache buffers, described, 88
Dirty directory cache delay time, Directory
  caching parameter, 439
Dirty disk cache delay time, File Caching
  parameter, 445
DISABLE LOGIN console utility, 65, 504
DISABLE TTS console utility, 504
disasters
  check documentation, 407
  check hardware, 407
  check patches, updates and workarounds,
    408
  document solution, 409
  keep good network records, 403–404
  locating the problem, 405–406
  plan, 401–404
  solutions one at a time, 408
  technical support, 406–409
disk (storage) drivers
  described, 68–69
  protected address space non-support, 96
Disk buffers parameter, NetWare DOS TSA, 426

disk drivers, described, 22
disk duplexing, described, 100
disk mirroring, described, 100
Disk parameters, 442
disk partitions, described, 19
disk redirection area, described, 99
DISMOUNT console utility, 505
  dismounting NSS volumes, 278–279
  dismounting traditional volumes, 270
DISPLAY command, login scripts, 197
DISPLAY ENVIRONMENT console utility, 505
Display incomplete IPX packet alerts,
  Miscellaneous parameter, 449
DISPLAY INTERRUPTS console utility, 505
Display lost interrupt alerts, Miscellaneous
  parameter, 451
DISPLAY MODIFIED ENVIRONMENT console
  utility, 506
Display NCP bad component warnings, NCP
  parameter, 453
Display NCP bad length warnings, NCP
  parameter, 453
DISPLAY NETWORKS console utility, 66, 506
Display old API names, Miscellaneous parameter,
  450
DISPLAY PROCESSORS console utility, 506
Display relinquish control alerts, Miscellaneous
  parameter, 450
DISPLAY SERVERS console utility, 66, 506
Display spurious interrupt alerts, Miscellaneous
  parameter, 451
Display spurious interrupt alerts threshold,
  Miscellaneous parameter, 451
Distribution List object, described, 140
DIX connectors, drop cables, 12
DLT (Digital Linear Tape), backup media, 292
DNS (Domain Name Services), IP server installa-
  tion requirements, 36
DNS Resource Record Set object, described, 140
DNS/DHCP Group object, described, 140
DNS/DHCP Locator object, described, 140
Document Footer option, Content Management,
  398
Document Preferences option, Content
  Management, 394–396

documentation
  online, 354–364
  ordering printed, 356
  refer to for problems, 407
DOS box, utilities, 484
DOS BREAK ON command, login scripts, 197
DOS computers
  client configuration files, 124–126
  hard disk partition requirements, 32
  log out process, 181–182
  LOGIN.EXE utility, 179–181
  removing client software from, 126–128
  user name context specifications, 180–181
  workstation installation, 122–124
Dos Name parameter, NetWare DOS Requester,
  422
DOS prompt, starting the server from the
  NWSERVER directory, 72
DOS VERIFY ON command, login scripts, 197
DOS-based Remote Console, 73–79. *See also*
  Remote Console
DOWN command, shutting down the server, 72
DOWN console utility, 65, 507
dredger, described, 159
DRIVE command, login scripts, 198
drivers, 2, 22
Drives parameter, NetWare DOS TSA, 426
drop cables (transceiver cables)
  described, 10
  DIX connectors, 12
  when to use, 12
DSDIAG.NLM, 507
DSMERGE.NLM utility, 508
  described, 162
  local source tree, 162
  merging multiple NDS trees, 162–164
  NDS tree merge, 132
  target tree, 162
DS.NLM file, 507
  determining version number, 31–32
  upgrading to version 5.99, 31
  update URL, 168
DSREPAIR.NLM utility, 508
  NDS tree repair, 133
  NDS troubleshooting, 166–167
dual stack network environment, described, 27
dump files, DSREPAIR.NLM, 166
DVD (Digital Video Disc), backup media, 293

E

EDIT.NLM utility, 64, 508
  server startup file editing, 65
  viewing error log files, 91
education classes, 465–467
effective file system rights, described, 238
effective NDS rights, NDS security, 232
El Torito specifications, CD-ROM drive compatibility, 32
electrical power, server protection schemes, 93
e-mail accounts, users, 175
e-mail addresses, InterNIC, 35
e-mail services, described, 2
Enable Control Community parameter, Desktop
  SNMP, 415
Enable disk read after write verify, Disk
  parameter, 442
Enable file compression, File System parameter,
  447
Enable Hardware Write Back, Disk parameter,
  442
Enable IO handicap attribute, Disk parameter,
  442
Enable IPX checksums, NCP parameter, 453
ENABLE LOGIN console utility, 508
ENABLE LOGIN utility, workstation connection
  management, 65
Enable Monitor Community parameter, Desktop
  SNMP, 415
Enable SECURE.NCF, Miscellaneous parameter,
  449
Enable Trap Community parameter, Desktop
  SNMP, 415
ENABLE TTS console utility, 508
Enable UDP checksums on NCP packets, NCP
  parameter, 453
Encryption On/Off option, Server Preferences,
  388
Encryption Preferences option, Server
  Preferences, 388
End of daylight savings time, Time parameter,
  457
End of Job parameter, NetWare DOS Requester,
  422
Enhanced Backup utility, 258, 293, 296–298
environment
  new server installation process, 41–45
  upgrade server process, 50–55
Environment Pad parameter, NetWare DOS
  Requester, 422
ENVSET console utility, 509

Error Handling parameters, 443–444
error history files, types, 64
error log files, 91–92
Error Responses option, Server Preferences, 382–383
ETC directory, described, 267
Ethernet 802.2 frame type, described, 9
Ethernet 802.3 frame type, described, 9
Ethernet architecture
  advantages, 2, 8
  BNC connectors/terminators, 10
  cable options, 9–14
  data packets, 8
  frame types, 8–9
  repeaters, 11
  thick Ethernet cable (RG-8 coaxial), 11–13
  thin Ethernet cable (RG-58 coaxial), 10–11
  twisted-pair cables, 13–14
Ethernet II frame type, described, 8
Ethernet SNAP frame type, described, 9
EtherTalk
  AppleTalk network architecture, 2, 4
  described, 17
Event Notification Service
  default installation, 37
  NDPS Broker, 317
executable files, virus protection schemes, 95
EXIT command, login scripts, 198
external concentrator, described, 13
External Entity object, described, 140

F

fake root, creating, 258
Fast Ethernet architecture
  described, 17
  high-speed, 4
Fast volume mounts, File System parameter, 446
FastTrack server
  Administration server connections, 369–398
  Application Manager, 390–392
  Configuration Styles options, 392
  Content Management options, 393–398
  described, 367
  General Administration options, 370–378
  installation, 366–369
  management techniques, 366
  ODBC non-support, 389
  server side JavaScript, 389–390
  Server Status options, 392

Servers Supporting General Administration, 378–398
  system requirements, 368
FDDITalk, described, 17
FDISK command, DOS, 19
FDISPLAY command, login scripts, 198–199
fiber-optic cables, high-speed architecture, 2, 17
file attributers, file system security, 243–246
File Cache Level parameter, NetWare DOS Requester, 422
File Caching parameters, 444–445
file compression
  described, 283
  enabling/disabling, 283–284
  NetWare Administrator utility, 284–286
  SET parameters, 284–286
  volume storage issues, 34
File delete wait time, File System parameter, 445
file management
  disk space conservation techniques, 282–289
  file system planning criteria, 265–268
  traditional versus NSS volumes, 260–264
file security, NetWare Administrator utility, 224
FILE SERVER NAME console utility, 509
file system
  application directories, 267–268
  block suballocation, 286–287
  compression techniques, 283–286
  creating automatic directories, 266–267
  DELETED.SAV directory, 267, 287–288
  disk space conservation techniques, 282–289
  ETC directory, 267
  file backup techniques, 290–305
  LOGIN directory, 266
  MAIL directory, 267
  name space volume addition, 289–290
  NSS (NetWare Storage Services), 33–34
  planning criteria, 265–268
  PUBLIC directory, 267
  purging files, 287–289
  restoring from backups, 305–307
  salvaging files, 287–289
  SYSTEM directory, 267
  traditional volume management, 269–273
  TTS (Transaction Tracking System), 307–308
  user disk space restriction techniques, 287
File System parameters, 445–448
file system security
  described, 234
  effective file system rights, 238
  equivalence, 237
  file/directory attributes, 243–246

inheriting rights, 237
trustee rights, 235–236
viewing/changing, 238–242
file system trustee rights, user access, 175
FILER workstation utility, 509
files
    ABEND.LOG, 64, 91
    AUTOEXEC.BAT, 125
    AUTOEXEC.NCF, 65, 77–81, 91, 103–106
    backing up, 258
    BOOT$LOG.ERR, 64, 91
    CALLBACK.LST, 75
    CD9660.NSS, 105
    CONFIG.SYS, 124
    CONSOLE.LOG, 91
    error history, 64
    error log, 91–92
    installing online documentation, 356–359
    LDREMOTE.NCF, 78
    NDSMGR32.EXE, 151
    NET.CFG, 114, 126
    NMSNAP32.EXE, 151
    NPRINTER.EXE, 336
    NPTWIN95.EXE, 336
    NTP.NCF, 111–112
    NWADMIN32.EXE, 150
    NWBACK32.EXE, 303–307
    purging, 258
    restoring from a backup, 258
    salvaging, 258
    SERVER.EXE, 72
    STARTNET.BAT, 125–126
    STARTUP.NCF, 65, 105–106
    swap, 90
    SYS$LOG.ERR, 64, 91
    TIMESYNC.CFG, 110–111
    TTS$LOG.ERR, 64, 91
    VOL$LOG.ERR, 64, 91
FILTCFG.NLM utility, RIP/SAP packet filter
    configuration, 66, 509
filters, RIP/SAP packets, 66
FIRE PHASERS command, login scripts, 199
First Network drive parameter, NetWare DOS
    Requester, 422
FLAG command, file/directory attributes,
    243–248
FLAG workstation utility, 510–515
flags. See attributes
flat database structure, described, 134
floptical disks, backup media, 293
Force First Network drive parameter, NetWare
    DOS Requester, 422

FORMAT command, DOS, 19
Frame parameter, Link Driver, 417
frame types
    described, 8
    Ethernet architecture, 8–9
full backup, Enhanced Backup utility, 296
full distinguished name, NDS objects, 147

G

Garbage collection interval, Memory parameter,
    449
gateways
    described, 3, 22–23, 316–317
    IP server installation requirement, 35
General Administration
    Admin Preferences, 371–372
    Cluster Management, 377–378
    Global Settings, 372–374
    Keys and Certificates, 376–377
    Netscape Server Administration, 369–378
    options, 370–378
    Users and Groups, 374–375
Gigabit Ethernet architecture, described, 4, 17
Global pseudo preemption, Miscellaneous para-
    meter, 451
Global Settings, General Administration, 372–374
GOTO command, login scripts, 199
group memberships, user rights, 174
Group object, described, 140
groups, creating, 172, 178
GUI (graphical user interface) server desktop
    described, 70
    loading/unloading, 71
    preference settings, 71
    switching between active screens (Alt+Esc), 71

H

Halt system on invalid parameters, Miscellaneous
    parameter, 450
Handle Net Errors parameter, NetWare DOS
    Requester, 422
hard disks
    disk duplexing, 100–101
    disk mirroring, 100–101
    disk redirection area, 99
    disk space conservation techniques, 282–289
    DOS partition requirements, 32

(continued)

hard disks *(continued)*
    failure protection schemes, 96
    Hot Fix management, 66, 99–100
    mirroring, 65
    NetWare 5 requirements, 32
    NWCONFIG.NLM utility, 65
    out-of-sync file recovery, 101
    partitioning, 19
    replacing existing, 102–103
    server addition/configuration, 102
    SYS volume storage requirements, 33
hardware
    checking for trouble, 407
    failure protection schemes, 96
    new server installation process, 38–41
    types, 2
    upgrade server process, 48–50
Hardware and Software Purchases worksheet, 473
Hardware Maintenance worksheet, 474
Hardware Virtual Servers option, Content
    Management, 396–397
HELP console utilities, 67, 515
HELP SWAP command, SWAP console utility
    help, 90
help, console utilities, 67
HFS (Apple) extensions, CDROM.NLM utility
    support, 105
hierarchical database structure, described, 134
High Sierra format, CDROM.NLM utility support,
    105
high-speed architecture
    described, 2, 4, 17
    Fast Ethernet, 4
    fiber-optic cables, 2, 17
home directory, users file storage, 174
hops, NDPS Broker, 317–318
Host MIB parameters
    Modem, 416
    Printer, 416
    SWDirectory-Search, 417
    SWDirectorySearch-Depth, 417
    TapeDrive, 417
host server, backup NLM storage, 296–298
Hot Fix Bad Block tracking worksheet, 476
Hot Fix utility
    described, 99
    disk redirection area, 99
    hard disk failure protection, 96
    hard disk management, 99–100
    hard disk repair, 66
    Used Hot Fix Block monitoring, 100
hubs
    described, 8

peer, 13
standalone, 13
twisted-pair cables limits and restrictions, 14
Hung unload wait delay, Error Handling
    parameter, 444

I

IBM, Token Ring architecture cable types, 15–16
identifier variables, 211–218
IF..THEN command, login scripts, 199–200
If_Configuration parameter, Protocol TCPIP, 431
Ignore Below 16meg Memory Allocate Flag para-
    meter, NIOS, 427
Ignore disk geometry, Disk parameter, 442
Immediate purge of deleted files, File System
    parameter, 446
INCLUDE command, login scripts, 200–201
incremental backups
    described, 293
    Enhanced Backup utility, 296
INETCFG.NLM, 66, 515–516
information
    general product, 462
    Novell/NetWare on the net, 462–463
inheritance rights
    file system security, 237
    NDS security, 230–231
INITIALIZE SYSTEM utility, executing protocol
    configuration commands, 66
INSTALL utility, upgrading previous NetWare
    version, 47–55
INSTALL.NLM, 516
installation
    existing server preparations, 31–32
    FastTrack server, 366–369
    INSTALL utility upgrade process, 47–55
    IP compatibility mode, 34–35
    JVM (Java Virtual Machine), 85
    NDPS, 321–322
    NDPS broker information planning, 37
    NDS information planning, 36–37
    new server, 38–46
    new server hard disk, 102
    Novell Upgrade Wizard process, 55–61
    online documentation files, 356–359
    patches, 97–98
    preparing for, 31–37
    protocol information planning, 34–36
    queue-based printing, 339–347
    updated modules, 97–98

upgrading from previous NetWare version, 46–61
UPS (uninterruptible power supply), 93–94
volume information planning, 33–34
WAN Traffic Manager utility, 156
Windows 3.1x workstations, 120–122
Windows 95/98/NT workstations, 116–120
workstation printers, 331–332
workstations, 113–130
Z.E.N.works Starter Pack, 184–186
Int64 parameter, Protocol IPX, 429
Int7a parameter, Protocol IPX, 429
International Characters option, Content Management, 398
Internet
    IPX/XPX versus TCP/IP protocol, 15–16
    NetWare 5 protocols, 25–26
    Novell/NetWare products, 462–463
InterNIC (Internet Network Information Center), IP address registration, 35
intruder detection
    described, 249–251
    NCP Packet Signature, 251–253
    NetWare Administrator utility, 224
    network security techniques, 224
IP address
    InterNIC registration, 35
    IP server installation requirement, 35
IP Address object, described, 141
IP protocol
    compatibility mode selection criteria, 26–27
    default NetWare 5 protocol, 26
    described, 3
    enabling compatibility mode on installation, 34–35
    NetWare 5 default protocol, 3
    NetWare 5 support, 25–26
IP servers, 35–36
IP target server
    activating from AUTOEXEC.NCF file, 80–81
    RConsoleJ setup, 80–82
IP Wan Client validation, communication parameter, 437
IP_Address parameter, Protocol TCPIP, 431
IP_Broadcast Address parameter, Protocol TCPIP, 431
IP_Netmask parameter, Protocol TCPIP, 431
IP_Reassembly parameter, Protocol TCPIP, 431
IP_RIP parameter, Protocol TCPIP, 431
IP_Router parameter, Protocol TCPIP, 431
IP_Trsw_Trigger parameter, Protocol TCPIP, 431
IP_Ttl parameter, Protocol TCPIP, 431

IPFLT.NLM, 516
IPX CMD Mode Routing, communication parameter, 439
IPX diagnosis parameter, Protocol IPX, 429
IPX Group policy, described, 157
IPX INTERNAL NET console utility, 516
IPX netbios replication option, communication parameter, 438
IPX packets, tunneling, 15
IPX protocol, enabling compatibility mode on installation, 34–35
IPX Retry Count parameter, Protocol IPX, 429
IPX Router Broadcast delay, communication parameter, 437
IPX servers, internal IPX network number installation requirement, 35
IPXCON.NLM, 516
IPXFLT.NLM, 516
IPXPING.NLM, 516
IPX/SPX protocol
    NetWare support, 3
    versus TCP/IP, 25–26
Irq number parameter, Link Driver 417
ISA bus, REGISTER MEMORY console utility memory registration, 90
ISO 9660 format
    CD-ROM drive compatibility requirements, 32
    CDROM.NLM utility support, 105
ISP (Internet Service Provider), IP address registration information, 35

J

JAR console utility, 517
Java, applications and applets, using, 489–490
Java applets
    CONSOLE MANAGER, 502
    JEDITOR, 519
Java applications
    CONSOLEONE, 503
    DNS/DHCP Management Console, 506–507
    JIT (Just In Time) compiler, 64
    RCONSOLEJ, 543
JAVA console utility, 517–518
Java Virtual Machine (JVM), 489
Java-based Remote Console. *See* RConsoleJ
JAVA.NLM utility, Java applets, 64, 518
JAVAC console utility, 517
JAVADOC console utility, 519
JAVAKEY console utility, 519

JAVAP console utility, 519
JavaScript Application Manager, described, 390–392
JavaScript compiler, accessing, 389
JIT (Just In Time) compiler, Java applications, 64
JVM (Java Virtual Machine)
  described, 84–85
  installation procedure, 85
  running Java applications from a server, 84–86
  shutting down properly, 86
  virtual memory support, 89–90

K

key indicators, performance monitoring, 86
Key Material object, described, 141
KEYB.NLM, 519–520
keyboards, DOS-based Remote Console navigation keystrokes, 79
Keys and Certificates, General Administration, 376–377

L

LAN Area object
  creating, 157
  described, 141
LAN drivers
  described, 22, 68–69
  protected address space non-support, 96
LANGUAGE console utility, 520
Large Internet Packets parameter, NetWare DOS Requester, 422
LASTLOGINTIME command, login scripts, 201
launching, Netscape Communicator, 361–362
LDAP (Lightweight Directory Access Protocol) Services for NDS
  described, 167–168
  LDAP client management, 132
LDAP clients, LDAP Services for NDS, 132
LDAP Group object, described, 141
LDREMOTE.NCF file, DOS-based Remote Console password encryption, 78
leaf objects, described, 136
License Catalog object, described, 141
License Certificate object, described, 141
License Container object, described, 136
License object, described, 141
Licensing Services parameters, 448

Link Driver parameters, 417–418
Link Support parameters, 418–419
Lip Start Size parameter, NetWare DOS Requester, 423
LIST DEVICES console utility, 64, 520
List object, described, 142
LIST STORAGE ADAPTERS console utility, 520
LIST STORAGE DEVICE BINDINGS console utility, 520
Load Balance Local LAN, communication parameter, 437
LOAD command
  NLM loading unrequired, 69
  NLMs, 488
LOAD console utility, 521
LOAD EDIT command, loading EDIT.NLM utility, 91
LOADSTAGE console utility, 521
local source tree, merging, 162–164
Locality object, described, 136, 142
LocalTalk, AppleTalk network architecture, 2, 17
Lock Delay parameter, NetWare DOS Requester, 423
Lock Retries parameter, NetWare DOS Requester, 423
Locks parameters, 448
Log File Size parameter, NIOS, 427
LOGIN directory, described, 266
login scripts
  command conventions, 193–194
  command listing, 194–211
  creating, 193–194
  described, 191
  example script, 218–222
  identifier variables, 211–218
  miscellaneous identifier variables, 218
  network identifier variables, 216–217
  percent sign (%) identifier variable, 212–214
  time identifier variables, 217
  types, 191–192
  user drive mapping, 174
  user identifier variables, 214–215
  user profile assignments, 194
  workstation identifier variables, 215–216
login security, 224–228
LOGIN workstation utility, 179–181, 521–522
LOGIN.EXE utility, DOS-based user log in, 179–181
LOGOUT command, login scripts, 201
LOGOUT workstation utility, 522–523
Long Machine type parameter, NetWare DOS Requester, 423

long term cache hits, tracking, 89–90
LONG.NAME.NLM, 523
LSP Server object, described, 142

M

MAC.NAM NLM, Mac OS files, 33, 523
MACHINE command, login scripts, 201–202
Macintosh
    AppleTalk architecture, 17
    AppleTalk peer-to-peer networking support, 2
    HFS (Apple) extensions support, 105
    name space module, 33
    name space volume addition, 289–290
MAGAZINE console utility, 523–524
magneto-optical disk, backup media, 293
MAIL directory, described, 267
managed object, NSS volume free space ownership, 263
MAP command
    fake root creation, 258
    login scripts, 202–205
    network drive mapping, 172
MAP workstation utility, 524
master catalog
    browse/read right settings, 161
    creating, 160–161
Master Catalog object, catalog services management, 132
Master replica
    deletion non-support, 152–153
    described, 148
    receiving updates from, 154
MAUs (Multistation Access Units), Token Ring architecture, 15–16
Max Boards parameter, Link Support, 418
Max Buffer Size parameter, Link Support, 418
Max Cache Size parameter, NetWare DOS Requester, 423
Max Current Directory Length parameter, NetWare DOS Requester, 423
Max Stacks parameter, Link Support, 418
Maximum concurrent compression, File System parameter, 447
Maximum concurrent directory cache writes, Directory caching parameter, 439
Maximum concurrent disk cache writes, File Caching parameter, 445
Maximum directory cache buffers, Directory Caching parameter, 439
Maximum extended attributes per file or path, File System parameter, 445

Maximum interrupt events, communication parameter, 439
Maximum number of directory handles, Directory Caching parameter, 440
Maximum number of internal directory handles, Directory Caching parameter, 440
Maximum outstanding NCP searches, NCP parameter, 453
Maximum packet receive buffers, communication parameter, 438
Maximum percent of volume used by directory, File System parameter, 446
Maximum percent volspace allowed extended attributes, File System parameter, 445
Maximum physical receive packet size, communication parameter, 438
Maximum service processes, Miscellaneous parameter, 451
Maximum subdirectory tree depth, File System parameter, 446
Maximum transactions, Transaction Tracking parameter, 458
MEDIA console utility, 524
Mem Pool Size parameter, NIOS, 427
memory
    ConsoleOne management utility requirements, 71
    protected address spaces, 95–96
    protection schemes, 95–96
    server requirements, 32
    usage monitoring, 89–90
MEMORY console utility, 524
MEMORY MAP console utility, 64, 535
Memory parameters, 449
Memory protection fault cleanup, Memory parameter, 449
Memory protection no restart interval, Memory parameter, 449
MEMORY utility, 64
Mempool parameter, Link Support, 419
Message Level parameter, NetWare DOS Requester, 423
Message Routing Group object, described, 142
Message Timeout parameter, NetWare DOS Requester, 423
Messaging Server object, described, 142
Metered Certificate object, described, 142
Migration agent
    IP server installation issues, 35–36
    IP/IPX protocol communications, 35
MIME Types option, Server Preferences, 381–382
Minimum compression percentage gain, File System parameter, 447

Minimum directory cache buffers, Directory caching parameter, 440
Minimum file cache buffers, File Caching parameter, 444
Minimum file cache report threshold, File Caching parameter, 445
Minimum file delete wait time, File System parameter, 445
Minimum NCP TCP receive window to advertise, NCP parameter, 453
Minimum packet receive buffers, communication parameter, 438
Minimum service process, Miscellaneous parameter, 451
Minimum Time to Net parameter, NetWare DOS Requester, 423
MIRROR STATUS console utility, 65, 525
Mirrored devices are out of sync message frequency, Disk parameter, 442
mirrored disks
    hard disk data protection, 100–101
    out-of-sync file recovery, 101
Miscellaneous parameters, 449–452
modem connection, DOS-based Remote Console setup, 75–77
Modem parameter, Host MIB, 416
modules, update installation procedures, 97–98
MODULES console utility, 525
    displaying DS.NLM version number, 31–32
    displaying currently loaded NLMs, 65
Monitor Community parameter, Desktop SNMP, 415
MONITOR.NLM utility, 64, 525
    bindery context parameter setting, 156
    bindery services parameters, 132
    cache buffer monitoring, 88
    disk redirection block allocation, 100
    error log file maximum size limiting, 92
    error log files, 91–92
    file compression, 258
    loading, 87–88
    long term cache hit monitoring, 89–90
    memory usage monitoring, 89–90
    NCP Packet Signature settings, 252–253
    NDS Trace parameter setting, 165
    packet receive buffer monitoring, 88–89
    performance monitoring, 64
    protected address space non-support, 96
    screen elements, 87
    server performance monitoring, 87–90
    workstation connection management, 65
MOUNT console utility, 270, 526

multiprocessor computer devices, PSMs (Platform Support Modules), 68
Multiprocessor parameters, 452

N

NAME console utility, 526
name context
    described, 146–147
    Directory tree, 146–148
NAME CONTEXT command, default name context, 172
Name Context parameter, NetWare DOS Requester, 423
name space, volume addition, 289–290
name space module
    described, 68–69
    Macintosh file support, 33
NAME utility, server name display, 64
Named Pipes parameters
    NP Max Comm Buffers, 419
    NP Max Machine Names, 419
    NP Max Sessions, 419
    NP MaxOpen Named Pipes, 419
NASA Ames Research Center, time synchronization, 112
NATIVE2BASCII console utility, 526
NCMCON.NLM utility, 65, 103–104, 526
NCOPY workstation utility, 526–527
NCP ADDRESSES console utility, 527
NCP DUMP console utility, 528
NCP file commit, NCP parameter, 453
NCP Max Timeout parameter, NetWare DOS Requester, 424
NCP Packet Signature
    intruder prevention, 251–253
    intruder security, 224
    NCP parameter, 453
NCP parameters, 452–454
NCP protocol preference, NCP parameter, 453
NCP STATS console utility, 528
NCP TCP keep alive interval, NCP parameter, 452
NCP TCP receive window, NCP parameter, 453
NCP TRACE console utility, 528
NDIR workstation utility, 528–530
NDPS (NetWare Distributed Print Services), 312–332
NDPS Broker
    adding printer drivers, 323–324
    described, 317

disabling, 324
hops, 317–318
server installation planning, 37
setup process, 322–324
NDPS Broker object, described, 142
NDPS Manager
  described, 317
  server creation, 324–326
NDPS Manager object, described, 142
NDPS Printer object, described, 142
NDPSM.NLM utility, server creation process,
  324–326, 530–531
NDS (Novell Directory Services)
  bindery service mimicking, 155–156
  Catalog Services, 159–162
  database directory tree, 134–135
  described, 2, 20, 134–135
  Directory tree planning, 145–149
  DSMERGE.NLM utility, 162–164
  DSREPAIR.NLM utility, 166–167
  hierarchical database structure, 134
  installation planning, 36–37
  LDAP Services for NDS, 167–168
  NDS Manager utility, 150–154
  NetWare Administrator, 149–150
  Novell DNS/DHCP Services, 168
  objects, 135–145
  partitions, 148–149
  replicas, 148–149
  tools, 149–164
  troubleshooting, 164–167
  update URL, 168
  WAN Traffic Manager utility, 156–159
NDS accounts, user information, 174
NDS backlink interval, Directory Services
  parameter, 441
NDS bootstrap address, Directory Services
  parameter, 441
NDS Distributed reference link interval, Directory
  Services parameter, 441
NDS external reference life span, Directory
  Services parameter, 440
NDS inactivity synchronization interval, Directory
  Services parameter, 440
NDS janitor interval, Directory Services
  parameter, 441
NDS Manager workstation utility, 531
  adding to NetWare Administrator, 151
  described, 150–152
  versus DSREPAIR.NLM, 166
  NDSMGR32.EXE file, 151
  NMSNAP32.DLL file, 151

partition management, 132
printing displayed information, 154
replica management, 132
Schema Manager, 154
task types, 151–154
NDS objects
  class categories, 135–137
  CN (common name), 147
  ConsoleOne utility management, 150
  containers, 135–136
  Country, 136
  creating/managing with NetWare
    Administrator utility, 132
  default object class listing, 138–145
  Directory tree name context, 146–148
  directory tree structure, 137
  full distinguished name, 147
  leafs, 136
  License Container, 136
  Locality, 136
  NDS schema, 137–138
  NetWare Administrator management utility,
    149–150
  Organization, 136
  Organizational Unit, 136
  partial name, 147
  properties, 135
  relative distinguished name, 147
  Root, 135
  security issues, 145
  X.500 naming specifications, 136–137
NDS schema
  described, 137–138
  managing with Schema Manager utility, 132
NDS security, 224, 228–234
NDS servers status, Directory Services parameter,
  441
NDS synchronization restrictions, Directory
  Services parameter, 440
NDS TRACE command, NDS troubleshooting,
  164–165
NDS trace file length to zero, Directory Services
  parameter, 441
NDS trace filename, Directory Services parameter,
  441
NDS trace to file, Directory Services parameter,
  441
NDS trace to screen, Directory Services
  parameter, 441
NDS tree merge, DSMERGE.NLM utility, 132
NDS trustee rights, user NDS object viewing, 175
NDSCat:Master Catalog object, described, 143

NDSCat:Slave Catalog object, described, 143
NDSMGR32.EXE file, NDS Manager utility, 152
NDSTTYPS Group policy, described, 157
Nearest NWIP Server parameter, NWIP, 428
Net Bind parameter
    Protocol IPX, 429
    Protocol TCPIP, 431
Net Status Busy Timeout parameter, NetWare
    DOS Requester, 424
Net Status Timeout parameter, NetWare DOS
    Requester, 424
NET.CFG file
    Desktop SNMP parameters, 414–416
    Host MIB parameters, 416–417
    Link Driver parameters, 417–418
    Link Support parameters, 418–419
    Named Pipes parameters, 419
    NetBIOS parameters, 420–421
    NetWare DOS Requester parameters,
      421–426
    NetWare DOS TSA parameters, 426
    NIOS parameters, 427
    NWIP parameters, 427–428
    Protocol IPX parameters, 429–430
    Protocol TCPIP parameters, 430–432
    SNMP Transport Provider IPX parameters,
      433
    SNMP Transport Provider UDP parameters,
      433
    Windows 3.1x/DOS client configuration, 126
    workstation configuration, 114
NetBIOS Abort Timeout parameter, NetBIOS, 420
NetBIOS Broadcast Count parameter, NetBIOS,
    420
NetBIOS Broadcast Delay parameter, NetBIOS,
    420
NetBIOS Commands parameter, NetBIOS, 420
NetBIOS Internet on/off parameter, NetBIOS, 420
NetBIOS Listen Timeout parameter, NetBIOS,
    420
NetBIOS parameters, 420–421
NetBIOS Receive buffers parameter, NetBIOS,
    421
NetBIOS Retry Count parameter, NetBIOS, 421
NetBIOS Retry Delay parameter, NetBIOS, 421
NetBIOS Send Buffers parameter, NetBIOS, 421
NetBIOS Session number parameter, NetBIOS,
    421
NetBIOS Verify Timeout parameter, NetBIOS, 421
Netscape Communicator, launching, 361–362
NetWare 3.1x
    Novell Upgrade Wizard preparations, 56–58

upgrade issues, 46–47
upgrading from, 30
NetWare 4.1x
    displaying DS.NLM version number, 31–32
    upgrade issues, 46
    upgrading from, 30
NetWare 5
    AppleTalk protocol support, 25
    ARCnet non-support, 4
    drivers, 22
    gateways, 22–23
    hard disk partition requirements, 32
    Internet protocols, 25–26
    IP protocol as default, 3, 26
    native operating system replacement, 2
    NDPS Broker services, 37
    NDS (Novell Directory Services), 20
    NDS schema extension message, 138
    network services, 21
    routers, 22–23
    server hardware configuration issues, 32
    server memory requirements, 32
    SET commands unnecessary, 87, 436
    software components, 18–23
    utilities, 21
    workstation (client) software, 19
    Z.E.N.works Starter Pack, 184–190
NetWare Administrator Browser
    intruder detection, 249–251
    user information editing, 177–178
NetWare Administrator workstation utility
    account restrictions, 226–227
    adding NDS Manager utility to, 151
    controlled access printer setup, 328–330
    creating users/groups, 162, 175–176
    described, 149–150, 531–532
    directory attribute assignment, 247–248
    directory management, 307–308
    Directory security, 224
    file attribute assignment, 247–248
    file compression management, 284–286
    file information display, 258
    file management, 307–308
    file security rights, 224
    intruder detection, 224, 249–251
    login passwords, 224
    login script creation, 193–194
    NDS object creation, 132
    NDS tree repair, 133
    NWADMIN32.EXE file, 150
    object tasks, 150

password restrictions, 227
    Performance Tuning option, 381
    printer setup, 312
    public access printer creation, 326–327
    public/controlled printer conversion, 330
    purging files, 288
    Query Catalog option, 132
    Quick Setup option, 339–343
    salvaging files, 288
    server usage charge monitoring, 107–109
    setup process, 150
    user disk space management, 258
    user disk space restrictions, 287
    user Template object creation, 177
    view/change file system rights, 238–242
    viewing/changing NDS security, 224
NetWare Application Launcher
    client upgrades, 129
    workstation upgrades, 114
NetWare client software, versus Microsoft
        client, 19
NetWare Connection, 467
NetWare DOS Requester parameters, 421–425
NetWare DOS TSA parameters, 426
NetWare printing, described, 314–315
NetWare Protocol parameter, NetWare DOS
        Requester, 424
NetWare Server object, described, 143
NetWare servers, described, 18–19
NetWare User Tools utility, Windows 3.1x tasks,
        182–183
NetWare User Tools workstation utility, 532
NetWare Users International (NUI), 467
NetWare utilities, using, 483–490
network boards
    configuration process, 98
    described, 7
    server installation information, 33
    thick Ethernet cable (RG-8 coaxial) require-
        ment, 12
    thin Ethernet cable (RG-58 coaxial) require-
        ment, 10
    Token Ring architecture requirement, 15
    twisted-pair cable requirements, 13
network cabling architecture, described, 4
network identifier variables, described, 216–217
Network Neighborhood, Windows 95/98/NT
        client configuration, 119
Network Printer parameter, NetWare DOS
        Requester, 424
network printers
    creating, 326
    user access, 175

Network Professional Association (NPA), 468
network protocols, described, 24–25
network services, described, 21
Network Settings option, Server Preferences, 382
network topologies
    bus, 5
    described, 4
    ring, 6
    star, 7
    types, 5–17
network-direct printers, described, 336
networks
    AppleTalk, 2, 4, 17
    Ethernet, 2, 4, 8–14
    high-speed, 2, 4, 17
    keep records in case of disasters, 403–404
    listing with DISPLAY NETWORKS utility, 66
    peer-to-peer, 2
    Token Ring, 2, 4, 14–16
New packet receive buffer wait time, communica-
        tion parameter, 439
New service process wait time, Miscellaneous
        parameter, 452
New time with daylight savings time status, Time
        parameter, 457
NFS.NAM NLM, 532
NIASCFG.NLM, 532
NIOS parameters, 427
NLIST workstation utility, 532–533
NLMs (NetWare Loadable Modules)
    ACTON, 493
    AIOCOMX, 490
    APPLETLK, 492
    ATFLT, 493
    ATMCON, 493
    AURP, 494
    BROKER, 496
    CD9660.NSS, 499
    CDHFS.NSS, 500
    CDROM, 500
    CHARSET, 500
    CONLOG, 501–502
    described, 68–69
    DS, 507
    DSDIAG, 507
    DSMERGE, 508
    DSREPAIR, 508
    EDIT, 508
    file cache buffers, 90
    FILTCFG, 509
    INETCFG, 515–516
    INSTALL, 516

(continued)

NLMs (continued)
 IPFLT, 516
 IPXCON, 516
 IPXFLT, 516
 IPXPING, 516
 JAVA, 518
 KEYB, 519–520
 LOAD command unnecessary, 488
 loading into protected address space, 96
 loading/unloading, 69–70
 LONG.NAME, 523
 MAC.NAME, 523
 memory protection schemes, 95–96
 MONITOR, 525
 moving between screens (Alt+Esc), 69
 NCMCON, 526
 NDPSM, 530–531
 NFS.NAM, 532
 NIASCFG, 532
 NPRINTER, 537
 NSS, 538
 NWCONFIG, 539
 ORBCMD, 539
 OSAGENT, 539
 PING, 539
 PSERVER, 541
 QMAN, 541–542
 RCONAG6, 542
 RCONPRXY, 542
 REMOTE, 545
 ROUTE, 550–551
 RS232, 551
 RSPX, 551–552
 SBACKUP, 552
 SBACON, 552
 screen listing (Ctrl+Esc), 69
 SCRSAVER, 553–554
 SERVMAN, 556
 SMDR, 558
 SMSDI, 558
 SNSC, 552
 SPXCONFG, 559
 TCPCON, 561
 TCPIP, 561
 TECHWALK, 561
 third-party providers, 487
 third-party support, 68
 TIMESYNC, 561
 TPING, 562
 TSA410, 562
 TSA500, 563
 TSADOSP, 563

 TSANDS, 563
 TSAPROXY, 563
 types, 68–70
 UNICON, 564
 UPS_AIO, 564
 using, 487–489
 V_LONG, 564–565
 V_MAC, 565
 V_NFS, 565
 VIEW, 566
 VREPAIR, 566
 WTM, 566
NLS Manager workstation utility, 534
NMSNAP32.DLL file, NDS Manager utility, 151
NO_DEFAULT command, login scripts, 206
nodes
 thick Ethernet cable limits and restrictions, 13
 thin Ethernet cable limits and restrictions, 11
 Token Ring architecture limits and restric-
  tions, 16
 twisted-pair cables limits and restrictions, 14
NOS (network operating system)
 described, 18–19
 versus OS (operating system), 18–19
NOSWAP command, login scripts, 206
Novell AppNotes, resources, 465
Novell Client Property, workstations configura-
  tion, 114
Novell DNS/DHCP Services
 described, 168
 DNS-DHCP address management/integration,
  133
Novell online documentation, viewing, 362–364
Novell Printer Manager workstation utility, 534
 print job management, 183
 workstation printer setup, 332
Novell product information, 462
Novell Upgrade Wizard
 NetWare 3.1x preparations, 56–58
 server upgrade process, 55–61
 transferring server data to a NetWare 5
  machine, 30
Novell Upgrade Wizard workstation utility, 534
NP Max Comm Buffers parameter, Named Pipes,
  419
NP Max Machine Names parameter, Named
  Pipes, 419
NP Max Sessions parameter, Named Pipes, 419
NP MaxOpen Named Pipes parameter, Named
  Pipes, 419
NPRINT workstation utility, 535–536

NPRINTER.EXE file, 336, 536–537
NPRINTER.NLM, 336, 537
NPTWIN95.EXE file, 336, 537
N-series barrel connectors, when to use, 12
N-series grounded terminators, when to use, 12
N-series T-connectors (vampire taps), when to use, 12
N-series terminators, when to use, 12
NSQ Broadcast parameter, NWIP, 428
NSS (NetWare Storage Services)
    described, 33–34, 262–264
    protected address space non-support, 96
    Hot Fix non-support, 99
NSS console utilities
    REBUILD, 543
    VERIFY, 565
NSS volumes, 260–264, 273–276, 280–282
NSS.NLM, 538
NTP.NCF file, time synchronization, 111–112
NTP.NLM utility, time synchronization, 111
Number of watchdog packets, communication parameter, 438
NVER workstation utility, 538
NWADMIN32.EXE file, NetWare Administrator utility setup, 150
NWBACK32.EXE file
    described, 538–539
    restoring backup files, 306–307
    workstation backups, 303–305
NWCONFIG.NLM utility
    adding/replacing hard disks, 65
    described, 539
    hard disk installation/replacement, 102–103
    monitoring hard disk bad blocks, 66
    network board configuration, 98
    NSS volume management, 273–282
    out-of-sync file recovery, 101
    traditional volume management, 269–273
    volume management, 258
NWIP Domain Name parameter, NWIP, 428
NWIP parameters, 428
NWIP1_1 Compatibility parameter, NWIP, 428
NWSERVER directory, starting the server from the DOS prompt, 72

O

object rights, described, 229
objects
    described, 134
    Master Catalog, 132

OFF console utility, 539
On/Off option, Server Preferences, 380
One-Step Configuration, NSS volumes, 274–275
online documentation
    described, 355–356
    installing files, 356–359
    viewing, 362–364
online help, console utilities, 67
ONOSPOOF Group policy, described, 157
operating systems
    NetWare servers, 18–19
    versus NOS (network operating system), 18–19
    replaced by NetWare 5, 2
OPNSPOOF Group policy, described, 157
optical disks, backup media, 293
ORBCMD.NLM, 539
Organization object, described, 136, 143
Organizational List object, described, 143
Organizational Role object, described, 143
Organizational Unit object, described, 136
OSAGENT.NLM, 539
out-of-sync disks, recovering files from, 101

P

packet receive buffers, monitoring, 88–89
packets, described, 24
parameters. See individual category or name
Parse HTML option, Content Management, 398
partial name, NDS objects, 147
partitions, 19, 32, 148–154
Password parameter, NetWare DOS TSA, 426
passwords
    DOS-based Remote Console encryption importance, 77–78
    login security, 224, 227–228
    naming conventions, 227
patch cable
    described, 10
    MAUs (Multistation Access Units), 15
patches
    disasters, 408
    installation procedures, 97–98
    Novell download URL, 65
Path Tcp_cfg parameter, Protocol TCPIP, 432
PAUSE command, login scripts, 206
PB Buffers parameter, NetWare DOS Requester, 424
Pburst Read Window Size parameter, NetWare DOS Requester, 424

Pburst Write Window Size parameter, NetWare DOS Requester, 424
PCCOMPATIBLE command, login scripts, 206
PCI bus, REGISTER MEMORY console utility memory registration, 90
PCI Hot Plug
    described, 103–104
    NCMON.NLM utility, 65, 103–104
peer hubs, described, 13
peer-to-peer networks, AppleTalk, 2
Pentium processors, NetWare 5 requirements, 31
percent sign (%) character, identifier variables, 212–214
performance monitoring
    key indicators, 86
    MONITOR.NLM utility, 64, 87–90
    need/usage pattern differences between servers, 86
Performance Tuning option, Server Preferences, 381
physical damage, server protection schemes, 93
PING.NLM, 539
PKI (Novell Public Key Infrastructure) services, 255
planning, disasters, 401–409
plenum cable, described, 10
plenum space, described, 10
policies, WAN Traffic Policy, 157
Policy Package object, described, 143
port address parameter, Link Driver, 418
pound (#) command, login scripts, 195
Pre-allocate Vgnma Memory parameter, Protocol IPX, 429
Preferred DSS parameter, NWIP, 428
Preferred Server parameter, NetWare DOS Requester, 424
Preferred Tree parameter, NetWare DOS Requester, 424
Primary Document Directory option, Content Management, 393
Primary parameter, Protocol IPX, 429
Primary server, time server designation, 110
Primary time servers, installation planning, 37
print device definitions, queue-based printing, 347–348
Print Header parameter, NetWare DOS Requester, 424
print jobs
    described, 313
    NDPS management, 333–334
    user management, 183
Print Queue object, described, 143
print queues, described, 335

Print Server (Non-NDPS) object, described, 143
print servers, described, 335
print services, described, 2
Print Tail parameter, NetWare DOS Requester, 425
printed documentation, ordering, 356
Printer (Non-NDPS) object, described, 143
printer agents, described, 316
printer drivers, NDPS Broker setup, 323–324
Printer Installation and Configuration worksheet, 479
Printer parameter, Host MIB, 416
printers
    attachment points, 336
    controlled access, 328–330
    creating on a network, 326
    defining print options, 312
    network-direct, 336
    public access, 326–327, 330–331
    public access versus controlled access, 318
    surge suppressors, 93
    user management tasks, 183
    workstation installation, 331–332
printing
    described, 314–315
    NDS Manager utility information display, 154
    queue-based, 312, 334–351
processors, NetWare 5 requirements, 31
PROFILE command, login scripts, 207
profile login scripts
    described, 191–192
    user assignments, 194
Profile object, described, 144
properties, NDS objects, 135
Property rights, described, 229–230
PROTECT console utility, 540
protected address spaces
    described, 95–96
    loading NLMs to, 96
PROTECTED console utility, 96, 540
PROTECTION console utility, 96, 540
PROTOCOL console utility console utility, 540
Protocol IPX parameters, 429–430
Protocol parameter, Protocol IPX, 429
Protocol TCPIP parameters, 430–432
protocols
    character associations, 24
    compatibility mode, 26–27
    data link, 24–25
    data link versus network, 24–25
    described, 24
    dual stack network environment, 27
    IP, 25–26, 34–35

IPX, 34–35
IPX/SPX versus TCP/IP, 15–16
network, 24–25
pure IPX network environment, 27
SAP (Service Advertising Protocol), 26
selection criteria, 26–27
server installation planning, 34–36
TCP/IP, 15–16
types, 3
proxy servers, described, 79
PSERVER.NLM utility, 541
print servers, 335
unloading, 350–351
Pseudo preemption count, Miscellaneous
parameter, 451
PSM (Platform Support Module) console utility,
68, 541
public access printers
converting to controlled access, 330–331
creating, 326–327
described, 318
PUBLIC directory, described, 267
publications
NetWare Connection, 467
Novell AppNotes, 465
punch-down blocks, twisted-pair cables, 14
pure IPX network environment, described, 27
PURGE workstation utility, 258, 289, 541
PVC-covered cable, plenum space restrictions, 10

Q

QIC (Quarter-Inch Cartridge), backup media,
292
QMAN.NLM, 541–542
Query Catalog option, catalog services management, 132
querying a catalog, described, 161–162
queue server mode, described, 336
queue-based printing
custom print services setup, 343–347
described, 312, 334–337
installation, 339–347
management techniques, 349–350
versus NDPS, 314–315
planning, 337–339
print device definitions, 347–348
printer attachment points, 336
printing process, 337
Quick Setup option setup, 339–343
remote printer mode, 336
restrictions, 337–339

setup verification, 348–349
unloading PSERVER.NLM, 350–351

R

RCONAG6.NLM, 542
RCONPRXY.NLM, 542
RCONSOLE workstation utility, 542
RConsoleJ. See also Java-based Remote Console
activating IP target server from
AUTOEXEC.NCF file, 80–81
IP connection support, 79
IP target server setup, 80–82
IPX server support, 79
proxy servers, 79
running from a server, 83–84
running from a workstation, 82–83
software types, 80
Read ahead enabled, File Caching parameter, 444
Read ahead LRU sitting time threshold, File
Caching parameter, 444
Read Only compatibility parameter, NetWare
DOS Requester, 425
read-only replica, described, 148
read-write replica, described, 148
REBUILD NSS console utility
described, 543
repairing NSS volumes, 282
Reference server, time server designation, 110
Reference time servers, installation planning, 37
REGISTER MEMORY console utility, 64, 543–544
REINITIALIZE SYSTEM utility, executing protocol
configuration commands, 66
Reject NCP packets with bad lengths, NCP para-
meter, 453
Reject packets with bad components, NCP para-
meter, 453
relative distinguished name, NDS objects, 147
REMARK command, login scripts, 207
Remirror block size, Disk parameter, 442
REMIRROR PARTITION console utility, 65, 545
Remote Console
controlling the server from a workstation, 65,
72–84
described, 72–73
DOS-based setup procedure, 73–79
Java-based setup procedure, 79–84
Java-based versus DOS-based versions, 73
Remote Printer Management, workstation printer
installation, 331
remote printer mode, described, 336

REMOTE.NLM utility, server security, 254, 545

REMOVE NETWORK ADAPTER console utility, 545

REMOVE NETWORK INTERFACE console utility, 546

REMOVE STORAGE ADAPTER console utility, 546

repeaters
  described, 11–12
  Ethernet architecture, 11
  when to use, 12, 15

Replace console prompts with server name, Miscellaneous parameter, 450

replicas
  creating, 151
  deleting, 151–152
  described, 148
  information viewing, 151
  managing with NDS Manager utility, 132
  NDS, 148–154
  repairing, 154
  sending updates between, 154
  synchronizing, 153
  type editing, 153
  types, 148–149

Reply to nearest server, communication parameter, 437

Reserved buffers below16 meg, Memory parameter, 449

RESET ENVIRONMENT console utility, 546

RESET NETWORK ADAPTER console utility, 546–547

RESET NETWORK INTERFACE console utility, 547

RESET ROUTER console utility, 547

RESET SERVER console utility, 547

Resolve Name Using Primary parameter, NetWare DOS Requester, 425

Resource Management Service, default installation, 37

Resource Management Service, NDPS Broker, 317

resources
  CNE certification, 465–467
  DeveloperNet, 464–465
  education classes, 465–467
  general product information, 462
  Internet, 462–463
  NetWare Users International (NUI), 467
  Network Professional Association (NPA), 468
  Novell AppNotes, 465
  Novell consulting services, 464
  Novell support connection, CDs, 98
  Novell technical support, 463–464

RESTART SERVER console utility, 65, 72, 547

Restore Configuration option, Server Preferences, 381

Restrict Access option, Server Preferences, 383–388

rights inheritance
  file system security, 237
  NDS security, 230–231

RIGHTS workstation utility, 548–549

Ring 3. *See* protected address spaces

ring topology, diagrammed, 6

RIP/SAP packet filtering, FILTCFG.NLM utility, 66

RJ-45 connectors, twisted-pair cables, 14

RMIC console utility, 549

RMIREGISTRY console utility, 550

Root object, described, 135, 144

Route parameter, Protocol TCPIP, 432

ROUTE.NLM, 550–551

routers
  described, 3, 22–23
  IP server installation requirement, 35
  TRACK ON/TRACK OFF utility information display, 66

RS232, 551

RSPX.NLM, 551–552

S

SAMEAREA Group policy, described, 157

SAP (Service Advertising Protocol), described, 26

SAP broadcasts, TimeSync synchronization, 111

SBACKUP.NLM, 552

SBCON.NLM utility
  described, 552
  file backups, 301–303
  restoring backup files, 305–306

SCAN FOR NEW DEVICES console utility, 553

SCANALL console utility, 552

schema, NDS objects, 137–138

Schema Manager workstation utility
  described, 154, 553
  NDS objects management, 138
  NDS schema management, 132

SCRIPT_SERVER command, login scripts, 207

SCRSAVER.NLM utility, server security, 224, 253–254, 553–554

SEARCH console utility, 555

Search Dirs First parameter, NetWare DOS Requester, 425

Search Mode parameter, NetWare DOS Requester, 425

searches, catalogs, 161–162
Secondary server, time server designation, 110
Secondary time servers, installation planning, 37
SECURE CONSOLE console utility, 225, 254, 555
security
    file systems, 234–249
    intruder detection, 249–251
    login, 224–228
    NCP Packet Signature, 251–253
    NDS, 224, 228–234
    NDS objects, 145
    PKI (Novell Public Key Infrastructure), 255
    SCRSAVER.NLM utility, 253–254
    server protection schemes, 253–255
    types, 225
security equivalence
    file system security, 237
    NDS security, 231
Security object, described, 144
security services, described, 2
SEND console utility, 555
Sequential elevator depth, Disk parameter, 442
serial ports, UPS installation, 93–94
SERIALVER console utility, 556
SERVER command
    removing from the AUTOEXEC.BAT file, 72
    starting the server from the NWSERVER directory, 72
Server Installation and Configuration worksheet, 470–471
Server log file overflow size, Error Handling parameter, 443
Server log file state, Error Handling parameter, 443
server management
    accounting services charge, 65
    CD-ROM drives, 104–105
    ConsoleOne management utility, 70–71
    displaying currently loaded NLMs, 65
    electrical power protection issues, 93
    hard disk addition/configuration, 102
    hard disk replacement, 102–103
    hard disks, 99–103
    hardware failure protection schemes, 96
    hardware information display, 64
    Java application support, 64
    maintenance tasks, 96–98
    MEMORY MAP utility, 64
    memory protection schemes, 95–96
    MEMORY utility, 64

MONITOR.NLM utility, 64
    name display, 64
    network board addition/configuration, 99
    Novell patches/update download URL, 65
    PCI Hot Plug technology, 103–104
    performance optimization/monitoring, 86–92
    physical damage protection issues, 93
    protected address spaces, 95–96
    PROTECTED load command, 64
    protection schemes, 93–96
    rebooting with RESTART SERVER utility, 65
    REGISTER MEMORY utility, 64
    Remote Console utility workstation server control, 65
    router management techniques, 66
    running Java applications from a server, 84–86
    server information display, 97
    server time synchronization, 109–112
    server usage charges, 107–109
    setting server time, 65
    shutting down with DOWN utility, 65
    starting/stopping the server, 72
    startup activity modifications, 105–106
    startup file activities, 65
    storage devices, 65–66
    task types, 67
    time synchronization, 65
    time/time zone settings, 65
    tools, 67–69
    unloading NLMs, 65
    UPS (uninterruptible power supply), 64
    version information display, 65
    virus protection, 64, 95
    volume information display, 65
    workstation connection monitoring, 98
    workstation connections, 65
Server Preferences, 381–388
Server Side JavaScript, FastTrack server options, 389–390
server startup files
    BOOT$LOG.ERR file, 91
    editing with EDIT.NLM utility, 65
Server Status options, FastTrack server, 392
server usage charges, monitoring, 107–109
SERVER.EXE file
    described, 556
    executing from AUTOEXEC.BAT file, 46
    protected address space non-support, 96
    starting the server from the NWSERVER directory, 72

servers
    automatic optimization, 87
    changing parameters, 436
    deleting, 153
    described, 21
    DOS partition requirements, 32
    electrical power protection schemes, 93
    FastTrack, 367–398
    hard disk addition/configuration, 102
    hard disk replacement, 102–103
    hardware configuration issues, 32
    hardware information display, 64
    hardware setup, 38–41
    hardware upgrade installation process, 48–50
    information display, 97
    installation information planning, 32–33
    installation preparations, 31–32
    IP target, 80
    listing with DISPLAY SERVERS utility, 66
    maintenance tasks, 96–98
    memory requirements, 32
    name display, 64
    naming conventions, 32
    NDPS Manager creation, 324–326
    NDS version display, 153
    NDS version update, 153
    NetWare, 18–19
    network board types, 33
    new installation process, 38–46
    new server environment settings, 41–45
    Novell Upgrade Wizard installation process, 55–61
    PCI Hot Plug technology, 103–104
    physical damage protection issues, 93
    print, 335
    protocol information planning, 34–36
    proxy, 79
    rebooting properly, 65
    running Java applications from, 84–86
    running RConsoleJ from, 83–84
    security schemes, 253–255
    shutting down properly, 65
    starting/stopping, 72
    storage device types, 33
    time synchronization types, 37
    time zone settings, 36
    upgrade server environment settings, 50–55
    upgrading from previous NetWare versions, 30–61
    version information display, 65
    volume installation planning, 33–34
    WAN policy assignment, 158–159
    Web, 21
    Z.E.N.works Starter Pack installation, 185–186
Servers Supporting General Administration
    Configuration Styles, 392
    Content Management, 393–398
    described, 378–380
    Programs options, 388–392
    Server Preferences, 380–388
    Server Status options, 392
Service Location Protocol parameters, 454–455
Service Registry Service
    default installation, 37
    NDPS Broker, 317
SERVMAN.NLM, 556
SET BINDERY CONTEXT parameter, bindery services, 132
SET console utility
    bindery context viewing, 156
    described, 557
    login scripts, 207–208
SET NDS TRACE console utility, NDS message monitoring, 133
SET parameters
    communication, 437–439
    described, 86
    Directory Caching, 439–440
    Directory Services, 440–441
    Disk, 442–443
    Error Handling, 443–444
    File Caching, 444–445
    file compression, 284–286
    File system, 445–448
    Licensing Service, 448
    Locks, 448
    Memory, 449
    Miscellaneous parameters, 449–452
    Multiprocessor, 452
    NCP, 452–454
    Service Location Protocol, 454–455
    Time parameters, 455–458
    Transaction Tracking, 458–459
Set Station Time parameter, NetWare DOS Requester, 425
SET TIME console utility, 65, 557
SET TIMEZONE console utility, 65, 557
SET_TIME OFF command, login scripts, 208
SETPASS workstation utility, 172, 228, 557
shielded twisted-pair cables
    advantages, 14
    described, 13–14
SHIFT command, login scripts, 208

Short Machine Type parameter, NetWare DOS Requester, 425
Show Dots parameter, NetWare DOS Requester, 425
SHUTDOWN NETWORK INTERFACE console utility, 558
Signature Level parameter, NetWare DOS Requester, 425
Single Reference server, time server designation, 109
Single Reference time servers, installation planning, 37
slave catalog, creating, 161
SLP close idle TCP connections time, Service Location parameter, 454
SLP DA discovery option, Service Location parameter, 455
SLP DA event timeout, Service Location parameter, 454
SLP DA heart beat time, Service Location parameter, 454
SLP debug, Service Location parameter, 454
SLP Directory Agent object, described, 144
SLP event timeout, Service Location parameter, 454
SLP MTU size, Service Location parameter, 455
SLP multicast radius, Service Location parameter, 454
SLP rediscover inactive directory agents, Service Location parameter, 454
SLP retry count, Service Location parameter, 454
SLP SA default lifetime, Service Location parameter, 454
SLP scope list, Service Location parameter, 455
SLP Scope Unit object, described, 144
SLP TCP, Service Location parameter, 455
SLPbroadcast, Service Location parameter, 455
SMDR.NLM, 558
SMSDI.NLM, 558
snAppShot, Z.E.N.works Starter Pack, 186–188
SNMP (Simple Network Management Protocol), 36, 414
SNMPEnable-Authen Trap parameter, Desktop SNMP, 416
SNSC.NLM, 552
Software Virtual Servers option, Content Management, 397–398
solutions, disasters, 408–409
Sound bell for alerts, Miscellaneous parameter, 450
SPEED console utility, 558
SPOOL console utility, 559

SPX Abort Timeout parameter, Protocol IPX, 429
SPX Connection parameter, Protocol IPX, 429
SPX Listen Timeout parameter, Protocol IPX, 430
SPX Maximum Window Size, communication parameter 437
SPX Verify Timeout parameter, Protocol IPX, 430
SPX Watchdogs parameter, Protocol IPX, 430
SPXCONFG.NLM, 559
Stack Size parameter, NetWare DOS TSA, 426
standalone hubs, described, 13
Standard Ethernet. See thick Ethernet cable (RG-8 coaxial)
star topology, diagrammed, 7
Start of daylight savings time, Time parameter, 458
START PROCESSORS console utility, 560
STARTNET.BAT file, Windows 3.1x/DOS client configuration, 125–126
startup process, server management techniques, 105–106
STARTUP.NCF file, server startup process, 65, 105–106
STARTX.NCF utility, 71, 560
STOP PROCESSORS console utility, 560
storage (disk) drivers
    described, 68–69
    protected address space non-support, 96
storage devices
    management utilities, 65–66
    server installation information, 33
storage groups, NSS volume free space, 262–263
storage provider, NSS volumes, 263
subnet mask, IP servers, 35
Subnet object, described, 144
Subnet Pool object, described, 144
subordinate reference replica, described, 149
surge suppressors, workstation power protection, 93
SWAP ADD command, swap file creation, 90
SWAP console utility, 64, 560–561
    accessing help, 90
    login scripts, 208–209
    swap file information display, 90
SWAP DEL command, swap file deletion, 90
swap files
    adding/deleting, 90
    ConsoleOne management utility requirements, 71
    described, 90
SWDirectory-Search parameter, Host MIB, 417
SWDirectorySearch-Depth parameter, Host MIB, 417

SYS volume
    hard disk storage requirements, 33
    new server installation process, 38–41
    swap file creation, 90
    upgrade server process, 48–50
SYS$LOG.ERR file
    described, 91
    error history, 64
sysContact parameter, Desktop SNMP, 416
sysLocation parameter, Desktop SNMP, 416
sysName parameter, Desktop SNMP, 416
SYSTEM directory, described, 267
SYSTIME utility, setting server time, 65

T

tape backup media, described, 292
TapeDrive parameter, Host MIB, 417
target server, described, 80, 298
target tree, merging, 162–164
TCP Defend Land Attacks, communication para-
    meter, 437
TCP Defend SYN Attacks, communication para-
    meter, 437
TCP/IP protocol, versus IPX/SPX, 25–26
TCP_Keepalive parameter, Protocol TCPIP, 432
TCP_Keepalive_Interval parameter, Protocol
    TCPIP, 432
TCP_Rcv_Windows parameter, Protocol TCPIP,
    432
TCP_Release_Wait_Time parameter, Protocol
    TCPIP, 432
TCP_Rxmit_Limit parameter, Protocol TCPIP, 432
TCP_Rxmit_Maxtime parameter, Protocol TCPIP,
    432
TCP_Rxmit_Mintime parameter, Protocol TCPIP,
    432
TCPCON.NLM, 561
TCPIP Group policy, described, 157
TCPIP.NLM, 561
technical support
    disasters, 408–409
    Novell, 98, 463–464
TECHWALK.NLM, 561
telephone numbers, general product information,
    462
Template object
    assigning identical properties to multiple
        users, 177
    described, 144
TERM command, login scripts, 209

terminators
    BNC, 10–11
    described, 8
    N-series, 12
    N-series grounded, 12
text editors, EDIT.NLM utility, 64
thick Ethernet cable (RG-8 coaxial), 11–13
ThickNet. *See* thick Ethernet cable (RG-8 coaxial)
thin Ethernet cable (RG-58 coaxial), 10–11
ThinNet. *See* thin Ethernet cable (RG-58 coaxial)
third party companies, NLMs, 487
TIME console utility, 561
time identifier variables, described, 217
Time parameters, 456–458
time servers, types, 37
time synchronization
    server installation planning, 37
    server management, 109–112
    TIMESYNC.NLM utility, 110–111
Time Synchronization Servers worksheet, 475
TIME utility, server time, 65
time zone
    server installation requirement, 36
    SET TIME ZONE utility, 65
    Time parameter, 458
TIMECOST Group policy, described, 157
TimeSync
    server designations, 109–110
    server time synchronization, 109–112
    TIMESYNC.NLM utility, 110–111
Timesync configuration, Time parameter, 458
Timesync configured source, Time parameter, 455
Timesync directory tree, Time parameter, 456
Timesync hardware clock, Time parameter, 456
Timesync polling count, Time parameter, 456
Timesync polling interval, Time parameter, 456
Timesync reset, Time parameter, 456
Timesync restart, Time parameter, 456
Timesync service advertising, Time parameter,
    456
Timesync synchronization radius, Time
    parameter, 456
Timesync time adjustment, Time parameter, 457
Timesync time sources, Time parameter, 457
Timesync type, Time parameter, 457
TIMESYNC.CFG file, time synchronization
    settings, 110–111
TIMESYNC.NLM utility
    described, 561
    server time synchronization, 65
    time synchronization, 110–111
Token Ring architecture, 2, 14–16

TokenTalk
    AppleTalk network architecture, 2, 4
    described, 17
tools
    NDS management, 149–164
    server management, 67–69
topologies, 4–17
TPING.NLM, 562
TRACK OFF console utility, 66, 562
TRACK ON console utility, 66, 562
traditional volumes
    creating, 269–270
    deleting, 270–271
    dismounting, 270–271
    mounting, 270
    versus NSS volumes, 260–264
    repairing with VREPAIR.NLM, 272–273
    sizing, 271–272
    Transaction Tracking parameters, 458–459
transceiver cables (drop cables), when to use, 12
transceivers, described, 12
transmission speed, Token Ring architecture
    types, 14
Trap Community parameter, Desktop SNMP, 416
Trap Target address parameter
    SNMP Transport Provider IPX, 433
    SNMP Transport Provider UDP, 433
TREE command, login scripts, 209
troubleshooting tips
    check hardware, 407
    check patches, updates and workarounds,
        408
    document solution, 409
    DSREPAIR.NLM utility, 166–167
    locating the problem, 405–406
    NDS, 164–167
    NDS TRACE, 164–165
    solutions tried individually, 408
    technical support, 408–409
True Commit parameter, NetWare DOS
    Requester, 425
trunk cable, described, 10
trunk segments
    thick Ethernet cable limits and restrictions, 12
    thin Ethernet cable limits and restrictions, 11
trustee rights
    ACL (Access Control List), 228
    file system security, 235–236
    NDS object security, 145
    NDS security, 228
    Object rights, 229
    Property rights, 229–230

TSA for Windows 95/98/NT workstation utility,
    562
TSA Server Name parameter, NetWare DOS TSA,
    426
TSA410.NLM, 562
TSA500.NLM, 563
TSADOSP.NLM, 563
TSANDS.NLM, 563
TSAPROXY.NLM, 563
TSAs (Target Service Agents)
    Enhanced Backup utility, 296–298
    Windows 95/98 configuration, 299–300
    Windows NT configuration, 300–301
TTS (NetWare Transaction Tracking System)
    database transactions, 259
    described, 307
    TTS$LOG.ERR file, 91
TTS abort dump flag, Transaction Tracking para-
    meter, 458
TTS backout file truncation wait time,
    Transaction Tracking parameter, 459
TTS unwritten cache wait time, Transaction
    Tracking parameter, 459
TTS$LOG.ERR file
    described, 91
    error history, 64
tunneling, described, 15
Turbo FAT re-use wait time, File System
    parameter, 446
twisted-pair cables, 13–14
Type 1 (shielded twisted-pair) cables, Token Ring
    architecture, 15
Type 2 (hybrid) cables, Token Ring architecture, 15
Type 3 (unshielded twisted-pair) cables, Token
    Ring architecture, 15
Type 4 cables, Token Ring architecture, 15
Type 5 cables (fiber-optic), Token Ring architec-
    ture, 15
Type 6 cable, Token Ring architecture, 15
Type 7 cable, Token Ring architecture, 15
Type 8 cable, Token Ring architecture, 16
Type 9 cable, Token Ring architecture, 16

U

UDP_checksum parameter, Protocol TCPIP, 432
UIMPORT workstation utility, 563
UNBIND console utility, 564
UNICON.NLM, 564
UNIX, name space volume addition, 290
Unknown object, described, 144

UNLOAD CONLOG command, stopping
  CONSOLE.LOG file error trapping, 91
UNLOAD console utility, 65, 69, 96, 564
unshielded twisted-pair cables, described, 13–14
updated modules
  installation procedures, 97–98
  Novell download URL, 65
updates, disasters, 408
upgrades
  DS.NLM version 5.99, 31
  preparing for, 31–37
  previous NetWare version installation process,
    46–61
UPS (uninterruptible power supply)
  power protection, 254
  serial port connections, 93–94
  server power protection, 93–94
UPS_AIO.NLM utility, UPS management, 64,
  93–94, 564
URL Forwarding option, Content Management,
  396
Use old watchdog packet type, communication
  parameter, 438
Use Video Bios parameter, NIOS, 427
user identifier variables, described, 214–215
user login scripts, described, 191–192
User object, described, 144
user tasks, 172
user Template object, creating, 177
users
  account restrictions, 175
  assigning identical properties to multiple
    users, 177
  creating, 172, 175–176
  disk space restriction techniques, 287
  editing information on several users at once,
    177–178
  e-mail accounts, 175
  file system trustee rights, 175
  group memberships, 174
  home directory, 174
  log in process, 179–181
  log out process, 181–182
  logging in without login script, 192
  login scripts, 174, 191–222
  name context specifications, 180–181
  NDS account setup information, 174
  NDS trustee rights, 175
  needs determinations, 174–175
  network activity types, 178–183
  network printer access rights, 175
  network tasks, 182–183

printer/print job management, 183
profile login script assignment, 194
Template object, 177
virus protection issues, 95
work environment management, 173
Z.E.N.works Starter Pack, 184–190
Users and Groups, General Administration,
  374–375
utilities. *See also* console utilities and workstation
  utilities
ATOTAL, 107–109
C1START.NCF, 497
CDROM.NLM, 66, 104–105
ConsoleOne, 68, 322–324
CX, 147–148
described, 21
DESREPAIR.NLM, 151
DSMERGE.NLM, 132, 162–164
DSREPAIR.NLM, 133, 166–167
EDIT.NLM, 65, 91
Enhanced SBACKUP, 293–301
executing, 483
FILTCFG.NLM, 66
Hot Fix, 66
JAVA.NLM, 64
LOGIN, 179–181
LOGIN.EXE, 179–181
mirrored disks, 101
MONITOR.NLM, 64–65, 87–90, 100, 132,
  156, 165, 252–253, 258
NCMON.NLM, 65, 103–104
NDPSM.NLM, 324–326
NDS Manager, 150–154, 166
NetWare Administrator, 107–109, 132–133,
  149–150, 162, 175–176, 224–228,
  238–242, 247–248, 288, 339–343
NetWare User Tools, 182–183
Novell Printer Manager, 183, 332
NPRINTER.NLM, 336
NTP.NLM, 111
NWCONFIG.NLM, 66, 98, 101–103, 258,
  269–282
PSERVER.NLM, 335
REBUILD, 282
REMOTE.NLM, 254
SBCON.NLM, 301–303, 305–306
Schema Manager, 154, 138
SCRSAVER.NLM, 253–254
server startup file editing, 106
SERVER.EXE
STARTX.NCF, 560
time services, 112

TIMESYNC.NLM, 65, 110–111
UPS_AIO.NLM, 64, 93–94
VREPAIR.NLM, 258, 272–273
WAN Traffic Manager, 156–159
workstation, 483–485
workstation connection monitoring, 98
UTP Ethernet. *See* twisted-pair cables

V

vampire taps (N-series T-connectors), when to
    use, 12
variables, login script identifiers, 211–218
VERIFY NSS console utility, 565
VERSION console utility, 65, 565
View Server Settings option, Server Preferences,
    380
VIEW.NLM, 566
virtual memory
    ConsoleOne management utility require-
        ments, 71
    described, 89–90
    swap files, 90
viruses, server protection schemes, 64, 95
V_LONG.NLM, 564–565
V_MAC.NLM, 565
V_NFS.NLM, 565
VOL$LOG.ERR file
    described, 91
    error history, 64
VOLUME console utility, 566
Volume log file state, Error Handling parameter,
    443
Volume low warn all users, File System
    parameter, 446
Volume low warning reset threshold, File System
    parameter, 446
Volume low warning threshold, File System
    parameter, 446
Volume object, described, 144
Volume TTS log file state, Error Handling
    parameter, 443
volumes
    adding name space support, 259
    block size, 34
    block suballocation, 34
    described, 261
    file compression support, 34
    file management, 260–264
    information display, 65
    Macintosh name space module, 33

management utilities, 258–259
name space addition, 289–290
NSS (NetWare Storage Services), 33–34
NSS (Novell Storage Systems), 262–264
server installation planning, 33–34
supported types, 33
SYS, 33, 38–41, 48–50
traditional management techniques, 269–273
traditional versus NSS, 260–264
VOL$LOG.ERR file, 91
VOLUMES utility, volume information display, 65
Volumes worksheet, 472
VREPAIR.NLM utility, 566
    repairing traditional volumes, 272–273
    volume repairs, 258–259

W

WAN Traffic Manager utility
    described, 156
    installation, 156
    LAN Area object creation, 158
    preventing open WAN links, 132
    WAN policy server assignment, 158–159
    WAN Traffic Policy, 157
Web servers, described, 21
Web sites
    DeveloperNet, 465
    Microsoft Service Pack 1, 116
    NDS updates, 168
    NetWare Connection, 467
    Novell, 65
    Novell client software updates, 114–115
    Novell patches/update modules, 98
Windows 3.1x, 120-122, 124–128, 180–183
Windows 95/98/NT
    Add Printer feature, 332
    client configuration, 119
    client installation requirements, 116
    client software removal, 119–120
    log out process, 181–182
    name context specifications, 181
    TSA (Target Service Agent) configuration,
        299–301
    user log in process, 180
    user network tasks, 183
    workstation configuration, 116–120
workarounds, disasters, 408
Worker thread execute in a row count,
    Miscellaneous parameter, 450
worksheets, 470–478

Workstation Group object, described, 145
workstation identifier variables, described,
    215–216
Workstation Installation and Configuration work-
    sheet, 477
Workstation Name parameter, NetWare DOS
    TSA, 426
Workstation object, described, 145
workstation utilities. *See also* utilities
    Application Explorer, 492–493
    Application Launcher, 493
    ATOTAL, 494
    AUDITCON, 494
    CAPTURE, 497–499
    CX, 504
    FILER, 509
    FLAG, 510–515
    LOGIN, 521–522
    LOGOUT, 522–523
    MAP, 524
    NCOPY, 526–527
    NDIR, 528–530
    NDS Manager, 531
    NetWare Administrator, 531–532
    NetWare User Tools, 532
    NLIST, 532–533
    NLS Manager, 534
    Novell Printer Manager, 534
    Novell Upgrade Wizard, 534
    NPRINT, 535–536
    NPRINTER.EXE, 536–537
    NPTWIN95.EXE, 537
    NVER, 538
    NWBACK32, 538–539
    PURGE, 541
    RCONSOLE, 542
    RIGHTS, 548–549
    Schema Manager, 553
    SETPASS, 557
    TSA for Windows 95/98/NT, 562
    UIMPORT, 563
    using, 483–485
workstations
    ACU (Automatic Client Upgrade), 114,
        128–130
    AUTOEXEC.BAT file configuration, 125
    backups, 298
    client software installation methods, 115
    CONFIG.SYS file configuration, 124
    connection monitoring, 98
    ConsoleOne management utility issues, 70

controlling server with Remote Console util-
        ity, 65
    controlling the server from, 72–84
    DOS computer configuration files, 124–126
    DOS computer installation, 122–124
    MONITOR.NLM utility connection manage-
        ment, 65
    NET.CFG file configuration, 114, 126
    NetWare 5 software requirements, 2, 19
    NetWare Application Launcher, 114, 129
    Novell Client Property configuration, 114
    NPRINTER.EXE file, 336
    NPTWIN95.EXE file, 336
    NWBACK32.EXE file, 303–305
    printer support installation, 331–332
    removing client software from Windows
        3.1x/DOS, 126–128
    running RConsoleJ from, 82–83
    setting up Browser, 359–361
    surge suppressors, 93
    SYSTIME utility, 65
    UPS power protection, 93
    Windows 3.1x configuration files, 124–126
    Windows 3.1x installation, 120–122
    Windows 95/98/NT configuration, 116–120
WRITE command, login scripts, 209–210
WTM.NLM, 566

X

X.500 naming specifications, NDS objects,
    136–137

Z

Z.E.N.works Starter Pack
    Application Object creation, 188–190
    described, 184–185
    installation process, 184–186
    snAppShot, 186–188
    user application launching, 173
Zone object, described, 145